AFRICAN FOLKLORE

The editor, Richard M. Dorson, is Distinguished Professor of History and Folklore and the Director of the Folklore Institute at Indiana University. Author of numerous books and articles, his latest book is AMERICAN FOLKLORE AND THE HISTORIAN. He is also the General Editor of the Folktales of the World Series, published by the University of Chicago Press.

African Folklore

RICHARD M. DORSON

ANCHOR BOOKS
Doubleday & Company, Inc.
Garden City, New York
1972

The Anchor Books edition is the first
publication of AFRICAN FOLKLORE.

Anchor Books edition: 1972
Library of Congress Catalog Card Number 77–186052
Copyright © 1972 by Richard M. Dorson
All Rights Reserved
Printed in the United States of America
First Edition

Also available in hardbound from
Indiana University Press

CONTENTS

PREFACE

This volume had its genesis in a Conference on African Folklore, the first of its kind, held July 16–18, 1970, on the campus of Indiana University. Africans and non-Africans trained in folklore, linguistics, anthropology, and oral literature met to discuss folkloristic concepts in African studies and to offer papers on their research areas. Sixteen of these papers constitute Part II of the book. To introduce them I have in Part I attempted a general essay on "Africa and the Folklorist" seeking to distinguish between the concepts of the folklore scholar and those of the anthropologist, the literary critic, and the oral historian. In Part III, samples of African folklore are presented from hitherto unpublished texts collected in the field by various of the conference participants. They are faithful examples of African oral narrative and oral poetry, unlike the polished and pretty versions often given to the public. I have provided brief comparative headnotes for the texts in Part III. The three sections thus closely complement each other.

For a travel grant assisting me in visiting six countries of Africa in March 1970 and for support of the African Folklore Conference, I am grateful to the Research Committee of Indiana University. The critical reading of my introductory essay by Ayodele Ogundipe and Dan Ben-Amos has aided me, although they are not responsible for my heresies. Dr. Ben-Amos has been generous also with bibliographical clues. My research assistant, Inta Carpenter, has given graciously of her talents. It was a pleasure to work with the conference participants in our new fraternity of Africa-minded folklorists.

Richard M. Dorson
Bloomington, Indiana, August 18, 1971

PART I

Africa and the Folklorist

AFRICA AND THE FOLKLORIST

Richard M. Dorson

Folklorists are just beginning to look at Africa. A great quantity of folklore materials have been gathered from African countries in the past century and published by missionaries, travelers, administrators, linguists, and anthropologists incidentally to their main pursuits. No fieldworker has devoted himself exclusively or even largely to the recording and analysis of folklore materials, according to a committee of the African Studies Association reporting in 1966 on the state of research in the African arts.[1] Yet Africa is the continent supreme for traditional cultures that nurture folklore. Why this neglect?

The answer may be given in terms of the sociology of knowledge. Folklore as a study—in the nineteenth century it was called a science—has emerged in those nations where Western civilization created a chasm between the learned and the tradition-oriented classes. The term *folklore* was coined in England in 1846, when members of the educated gentry discovered with astonishment that an alien culture of the "lower orders" surrounded them and was expressed in collections of local tales, customs, and beliefs. On the continent the study flourished in every European country, following the stimulation given by the Grimm brothers in Ger-

[1] A.R.C. Conference on the African Arts, Indiana University, March 25–26, 1966, "Report of Folklore Group," typescript.

many, who collected peasant folktales as supportive evidence for their researches in Germanic philology and religious and legal antiquities. The same impulse of romantic nationalism directed attention to peasant folklore in Russia and Greece, Finland and Norway, France and Ireland, Poland and Serbia, and resulted in university chairs and research institutes of folklore. In the United States, where the folk could not be identified with a peasantry, but rather with multiple ethnic, regional, and racial groups, folklore studies came of age in the 1960s, when folklore departments at Indiana University and the University of Pennsylvania began turning out Ph.D.s in numbers. Latin America and Asia now possess a scattering of professional folklorists.

Two main conditions for the study of folklore are just being realized in Africa: the appearance of an intellectual class with a culture partly different from that of the mass of the people, and the emergence of national states. In the tribal culture all the members share the values, participate in the rituals, and belong fully to the culture, even if some hold privileged positions as chiefs and diviners. In the national culture a schism divides the society. The intellectuals in the professions, on the university faculties, and in the government seem sometimes to have more in common with intellectuals in other countries than with their tribal countrymen. This point was forcefully dramatized for me at an East African Writers Workshop I attended at Makerere University, in Kampala, the capital of Uganda, in March 1970, directed by James Ngugi, the Kenyan novelist. The recurrent theme and leitmotif of the conference proved to be the divided cultural allegiance of the young writers. They debated passionately whether they should write in English and French or in the vernaculars; whether they should deal with life in Kampala and Nairobi or in the bush; whether they should build upon traditional literature or follow Western forms. Their emotional loyalty to pan-African cultures and their desire to serve as spokesmen for Africa in lieu of patronizing colonialists were clear enough (although one gifted young Ugandan discomfited the conference with the question, can the Indian resident in Africa write the African novel?). What was at issue were the pragmatic questions of the language, medium, and audience for their communication. The very first conference of African writers in English had also been held at Makerere University, in 1962, and had wrestled with the same problems.[2] At a congress in Ghana in 1962 Bernard B. Dadie, speaking on "Folklore and Literature" to fellow Africans, had deplored the embarrassment felt by some educated Africans at their own inheritance and values, scoffed at by Europeans as "folklore" in its derided sense. Dadie spoke out emotionally for our "rich, luxuriant folklore" as a source for the new African literature.[3]

At this historical stage the concept of *folk* becomes useful. Tribal culture, as it fragments under the impact of modern ways, turns into the submerged folk culture in the new nation. African folklorists are now beginning to study this African folklore which also attracts their American and European colleagues. African students came to Indiana University from Nigeria, Uganda, and the Sudan in the late 1960s for the doctorate in folklore; a young woman from Egypt, Mona Fikry-Atallah (a contributor to this book), completed her doctorate in 1969 with a dissertation based upon fifteen months of field-work among the Wala, of Wa, in Ghana; a Nigerian, E. Ojo Arewa, prepared a type index of folktales from northeast Africa in 1966 as a Berkeley dissertation; American students seeking the Ph.D. in folklore, or already holding it (such as Dan Ben-Amos, another contributor), have lately done field research in Africa; specialists in oral literature are being appointed to the faculties of African universities. The French have organized a Research Group in African Oral Literature at the Centre d'Études Africaines in Paris to investigate folkloric problems.

Part of this impulse to study folklore is intellectualistic, part is nationalistic, and the two impulses often work at cross purposes. The new nations of Europe looked to their peasant traditions for sources of a common heritage in the nineteenth

[2] Ezekiel Mphahlee, "African Literature," in *The Proceedings of the First International Congress of Africanists,* ed. Lalage Bown and Michael Crowder (n.p.: Longmans, 1964), p. 220.

[3] Bernard B. Dadie, ibid., 207.

century, and the new nations of Africa look to their tribal cultures for similar unifying symbols today. The intellectual turns to his own tribal inheritance of oral poetry, drama, and ritual when he becomes research-minded. Joel Adedeji, one of the present contributors, composed his doctoral dissertation at the University of Ibadan, in 1969, on "The Alaringo Theatre," from the folk-theater history of his own Yoruba people. A major modern work in African folklore, *The Content and Form of Yoruba Ijala* (1966), dealing with a genre of traditional chants, was originally written as a doctoral dissertation at Oxford University by S. A. Babalọla, also a Yoruba and himself a leader in the Yoruba studies movement in Nigeria. His student Wande Abimbọla similarly completed his doctor's degree, in 1970, by writing on the Yoruba oral poetry of his own culture. In reaction against this Yoruba dominance, John Pepper Clark, chairman of the English Department at the University of Lagos, betook himself to his own Ijaw people to record their staged epic of Ozidi, which he adapted into a verse drama and is publishing in the original Ijaw text with English translation, as well as producing a documentary film on the performance. In East Africa, John S. Mbiti, professor of religious studies at Makerere University, followed his urge to collect the folktales told in Kikamba among the million Akamba people in his native Kenya, and published them under the title *Akamba Stories* (1966). In these instances university-trained African scholars are recording and studying parts of the oral tribal culture into which they were born. They do not study the folklore of other tribal peoples. But university institutes of African studies are developing a broad comparative view.

For the new African nation-states are multitribal, and forces are at work to bridge and fuse the tribal traditions. Two examples of this tendency came to my attention while I was in Liberia in March 1970. At the National Culture Center, a few miles outside the capital, Monrovia, in a spacious area by the ocean, huts built according to tribal design house young dancers from sixteen Liberian tribes. At the Center they both rehearse their traditional dances and perform them before metropolitan audiences. The choreographer, Roger Dorsinville, a Haitian, who directed a rehearsal for me, explained that he was maintaining the authentic character of the dances, save for the necessity of shortening them and requiring the dancers to face the grandstand rather than dance to an encircling audience as in the village. But of course the presentation of these multitribal dances before outside spectators constitutes a novel phenomenon, appealing to national sentiment and transcending regional allegiances. These kinds of national dance troupes from African countries have become internationally known. As the ethnomusicologist Alan Merriam said to me, "Now they're show biz."

My other illustration involves a radio program, "Liberian Songs and Legends," that was broadcast for four years from Monrovia. Its directors, Bai T. Moore and Jangaba Johnson, who were Vai, presented storytellers, singers, and musicians from the tribal groups among whom they had themselves assiduously collected folklore over many years.[4] They played me one tape of a program on which they introduced a Gio performer, and much laughter ensued from the studio audience at the ignorance of the Vais about Gio names and terms. Soon the Gio is playing, singing, and telling tales. Here one could recognize the exchange of tribal traditions taking place before a national radio audience of Libero-Americans and tribal peoples. The end product will represent not so much an intertribal blend as a synthetic—and I use the word with double sense—folklore shaped by the mass media and Western concepts of public relations and stereotypes for tourist consumption. The hotel's brochure of weekly goings-on in Dakar featured, the day I arrived in Senegal, a

[4] See e.g. S. Jangaba M. Johnson, *Traditional History and Folklore of the Vai Tribe* (Monrovia, Liberia: The Bureau of Folklore, Department of Interior, n.d.), 119 pp.; Bai T. Moore and S. Jangaba M. Johnson, "Crime Does Not Pay" [typescript of Liberian folktales], 78 pp.; S. Jangaba M. Johnson, "The Traditions, History and Folklore of the Belle Tribe," *Liberian Studies Journal* I (1969): 45–73; Bai T. Moore, "Categories of Traditional Liberian Songs," *Liberian Studies Journal* 2 (1970): 117–37; Bai T. Moore, *Proverbs of Liberia: Vai, Gola, Grebo* (Monrovia: Liberian Information Service, 1963), 34 pp.

cover emblazoned FOLKLORE with a picture of a briefly clad African female dancer in a sinuously contorted stance.

Nationalism and regionalism have formed two sides of the folklore coin ever since the concept of folklore emerged in the nineteenth century. Substitute tribalism for regionalism, and the African situation is well described. Folklore can be a unifying and nationalizing factor when utilized by a repressed people seeking to establish their political and cultural identity against an alien ruler, as did the Irish against the English, the Finns against the Russians and Swedes, and the Norwegians against the Danes. These pent-up peoples engaged in a national quest for an independent language, a separate history, a representative literature, along with a special folklore. But folklore can also be divisive, if regional and ethnic traditions are stressed. When the Federal Writers Project launched its nationwide folklore-collecting activities throughout the United States in the early 1930s, its sponsors hoped to procure evidence of an American body of national traditions. But much of what they unearthed through thousands of interviews turned out to represent the lore of Chinese, or Italians, or occupational workers, and so was never published, since it was not homogenized American folkstuff.

If folklorists as such are only now entering African studies, we may ask how the materials of African folklore have been dealt with heretofore by the practitioners of other disciplines. The anthropologists and linguists have, in the first place, shied away from the term *folklore*. Dealing with unified societies where all is oral and almost all is traditional, the distinction between folk and sophisticated layers of culture makes no sense to them. To distinguish artistic styles in Benin sculptures, William Fagg has spoken of the admired bronze antiquities as Benin court style and the recent woodcarvings as Benin tribal style.[5] Discussing the concepts of peasants, tribesmen, and the folk as applied to African societies, Lloyd A. Fallers concludes that the elite-folk differentiation of Eu-

[5] William Fagg, *Nigerian Images* (New York and London, 1930), p. 30.

ropean communities seems absent in the African kingdoms, largely due to the lack of literary religious systems. The African might be considered a peasant economically and politically, but not culturally.[6] African tribesmen possess a much fuller view of their society than do European peasants, agrees Daniel McCall.[7] When it comes to the materials of folklore, Melville Herskovits has proposed drawing a boundary between traditional literature as the province of the folklorist and traditional custom as the domain of the ethnologist, and calling the first *oral art*.[8] His premise is followed by other scholars. Jack Berry titled his inaugural lecture as Professor of West African Languages at the University of London in 1960 "Spoken Art in West Africa."[9] Herskovits' student and colleague William Bascom has advocated the phrase *verbal art* to avoid the ambiguity in *folklore*. Melville and Frances Herskovits even eschew the label *folktale* in the collection of oral prose traditions they titled *Dahomean Narrative*. The only full-bodied description to date of African folklore genres is called by its author, Ruth Finnegan, *Oral Literature in Africa*. Comparably, Jan Vansina named his treatise on an African historical methodology employing verbal sources *Oral Tradition*. The notable group of French Africanists, including Calame Griaule and Denise Paulme, refer to their work as studies in oral literature (*littérature orale*), like Finnegan but with a different rationale, as the French have always found ways to circumvent the term *folklore*, the coinage of an Englishman.

To identify *folklore* with *oral literature* or *verbal art* or some other euphemism misleads and misinforms the student of African life. Both in its content and in its method the study of folklore departs considerably from the disciplines with which it is often loosely coupled. I will examine the

[6] L. A. Fallers, "Are African Cultivators to Be Called 'Peasants'?" *Current Anthropology* 2 (April 1961): 108–10.

[7] Daniel F. McCall, *Africa in Time-Perspective* (Boston and Legon, 1964), p. 47.

[8] "The Study of African Oral Art," *Journal of American Folklore* 74 (1961): 451–56.

[9] (London: School of Oriental and African Studies, University of London, 1961), 24 pp.

relationship of folklore to three disciplines in the African field with which it does indeed overlap but with which it should not be confused: oral literature, anthropology, and oral history.

ORAL LITERATURE AND FOLKLORE

The oral-literature approach to African folk traditions gains increasing support as the interest in these traditions develops. A valuable series of books from Oxford University Press presenting original and translated texts of African oral prose and poetry carries the title Oxford Library of African Literature. A new Department of African Languages and Literature at the University of Wisconsin has on its faculty such specialists in oral literature as Daniel Kunene, Philip Noss, and Harold Scheub, all contributors to the present volume. The one comprehensive work appraising the verbal side of African folklore is Ruth Finnegan's *Oral Literature in Africa* (1970), and the author named it deliberately.

Many of the materials she discusses are folklore by anyone's definition: tales and songs, proverbs and riddles, that travel by word of mouth in variant forms. When she does grudgingly use the terms "folklore" and "folktales," she encases them in quotation marks to indicate their dubious status. And in her England, that is indeed their status since the decline of the golden amateurs of Victorian folklore studies. At Oxford, where she took her doctorate, Finnegan could pursue anthropology and literature, but not folklore—and the same applies to Cambridge. Her heart is really in folklore, and in a shrewd article in *Man* she ticked off British social anthropologists for embracing kinship systems to the neglect of oral literature.[10] She contributed to the Oxford Library of African Literature an earlier volume, *Limba Stories and Story-Telling*, based on her own fieldwork in Sierra Leone, a

[10] "Attitudes to the Study of Oral Literature in British Social Anthropology," *Man* 4 (March 1969): 59–69.

meaty collection providing a lavish background of the setting and the society, but flawed by inadequate comparative notes. Lacking direct access to folklore methodology, she develops in her new book a thesis of oral literature as a branch of literature proper. Distinctions between oral and written literature are, she claims, artificially made—a line of reasoning pursued by the Soviet folklorists, with different ends, as they seek to demonstrate that the common people possess in their oral forms equal or greater creative power than the aristocracy with their belles-lettres. Throughout her long treatise, richly packed with illustrative examples and astute commentary on African oral genres, she argues that this subject matter should be appraised with the same principles and standards as are applied to written literature. The student of African oral forms should be a literary critic, concerned with stylistics, characterization, symbolism, the creative imagination. Yet all the evidence and stress of her initial chapters, in which she discusses with admirable detail the performance aspects of African oral prose and poetry, belie her contention. As Finnegan and the authorities she cites demonstrate, and as Ben-Amos, Noss, and Scheub in the present work emphasize, the text of tale or song written down from an oral performance falls far short of conveying the ambiance of the event. The bard and narrator facing their live audience employ gestures, eye contact, intonation, pantomime, histrionics, acrobatics, and sometimes costumes and props, as the author of written words never does. Novelist, essayist, biographer, and poet cater to private readers—except on occasions when a poet reads his pieces aloud, but even so he renders a fixed text, while the reciter, singer, or chanter continually varies his words. An author rewrites, edits, and polishes his composition before he sends it out to his readers. An oral performer does not worry about grammatical perfection, for his audience follows his message with a variety of signals. Pampered readers accustomed to fluency on the page are aghast to see how crooked and snarled are the sentences they have been listening to when congealed in type—whether delivered by an American president or a folk narrator. African audiences, from families listening to taletellers in their hints to chiefs and their retinues hearing bards deliver praise poems, enter into the performances with laughter, group singing at choral parts, corrections, interjections, and other interactions. Recognizing these basic facts of the oral forms, Finnegan nevertheless shunts aside folklore methods for her thesis of oral literature.

The cold-shouldering of the folklore approach is most evident in the priorities Finnegan assigns to oral poetry and oral prose. She devotes eight chapters to songs and poems of many kinds: praise poems, dirges, hymns, divining songs, hunters' songs, war songs, political songs, children's game songs, and other poetic forms. Following this section she relegates prose narratives to two chapters, of which one deals unsympathetically with folklore theories, in a curious deviation from the descriptive thread of her work. The reason for these priorities is soon clear: Finnegan associates the sins of folklorists with their emphasis on folktales. Tale collections are easier to assemble and publish than collections of oral verses, and so African folklore has come to be associated in the mind of the public with tales of the spider and the rabbit. Finnegan is right in her criticism of the improper collecting, translating, and presenting of many editions of African folktales, but professional folklorists advance the same criticisms, and they will further criticize the Limba stories of Finnegan, the Akamba stories of Mbiti, and the pan-African ragbag of stories put together by Whiteley, all in the Oxford Library of African Literature series, for completely unsatisfactory comparative notes.[11] The oral-literature scholars, like the anthropologists, have no idea how to identify and annotate a traditional tale. They lack the expertise of the folklorists in assigning type and motif numbers to variant texts.

In his comparative references the folklorist will profit from earlier valid collections, themselves sometimes well annotated. Familiarity with the history of folkloristics, a tortuous but treasure-laden history, will further divide the folk-

[11] Ruth Finnegan, *Limba Stories and Story-Telling* (Oxford, 1967); John S. Mbiti, *Akamba Stories* (Oxford, 1966); *A Selection of African Prose: I, Traditional Oral Texts*, compiled by W. H. Whiteley (Oxford, 1964).

lorist from the non-folklorist, who too often fails to invoke his predecessors. In chronicling the history of folklore studies in England, I devoted a chapter to painstaking nineteenth-century collectors in Africa, from the missionary Sigismund W. Koelle, who in 1854 published in London *African Native Literature, Proverbs, Tales, Fables, and Historical Fragments in the Kanuri or Bornu Language,* through Wilhelm Bleek, Canon Callaway, Richard Burton, Mary Kingsley, and other intrepid missionaries and travelers. Their works, while dated in some respects, often contain valuable early texts and bold comparisons. Writing in 1868, Callaway, a medical missionary, likened elements in his Zulu narratives to Irish, Scottish, Italian, Polynesian, Scandinavian, biblical, and Hottentot traditions, all without benefit of indexes![12] The American Folklore Society published as its first memoir, in 1894, the well-documented *Folk-Tales of Angola,* by Heli Chatelain, a business agent who actually mentioned his informants; and for its twentieth, in 1927, the *Lamba Folk-Lore,* collected by Clement M. Doke in northern Rhodesia and the Belgian Congo, containing 159 folktales, 1695 aphorisms, 95 songs, and 144 riddles. A superior earlier collection from the Akamba, in Kenya, made in 1911 and 1912 but not published until 1928, is the *Kamba Folklore* of Gerhard Lindblom, who could say even then, "The enormous amount of material connected with folklore that has been collected in Africa will certainly by and by be subjected to extensive comparative examination."[13] Lindblom estimated there were well over seven thousand African folktales in print, and he drew upon them for his meaty sections of "Comparative Notes." In the genre of the proverb, a now-classic work is George Herzog's *Jabo Proverbs from Liberia* (1936), strong in its ethnographic glosses and linkages of sayings with anecdotes, although it offers comparisons only to the Kru. Older works of this caliber can readily fatten the notes of modern collectors such as Finnegan and Mbiti.

[12] Richard M. Dorson, *The British Folklorists, a History* (London, 1968), p. 354.
[13] Gerhard Lindblom, *Kamba Folklore,* 3 parts (Uppsala, 1928–34), I, xi.

In discussing folklore theories, Finnegan is consistently negative. She remarks on the obsolescence of the nineteenth-century evolutionists, but this is old history. She scores the structural-functional school for inattention to aesthetics, not realizing that younger American folklorists such as Roger Abrahams and Dan Ben-Amos are much concerned with aesthetics. She chides the practitioners of the historical-geographical method for concentrating on the dull business of typologizing tale plots when there is more important work to be done, she feels, in examining the latent meanings in oral literature. To underline her point that the traditional core of the tale counts for less than the creative style of the individual narrator, she juxtaposes what she considers two variants of the same skeletal story (pages 338–41), one from the Kikuyu of East Africa, the other from the Limba of Sierra Leone, which exhibit widely differing cultural and personal styles. But Finnegan does not recognize that the two tales belong to different basic types. In the first, "The Vulture and the Hen," the hen borrows a razor from the vulture to shave her chickens. She loses the razor, and so today the vulture swoops down and carries off chickens in compensation, and the hen scratches in the ground looking for the razor. In the other story, "The Finch, the Eagle, and the Hen," the finch borrows money from the eagle's grand-father and never returns the money. The eagle searches for the finch and through the help of the hen finds the finch watching people pound rice. Accosted by the eagle, the sly finch discovers that the hen tattled on him, and in reprisal promises to deliver the hen to the eagle. Since the eagle is skeptical, the finch takes the large bird to the finch family home to see the pile of hen feathers lining the nest, as proof that the hens are slaves to the finches. Satisfied, the eagle begins to carry off hens, and still does so.

Clearly some common motifs link the two tales, notably the aetiological ending, which explains the predatory nature of vulture and eagle toward hens, and the initial episode, in which the hen or finch fails to return an object or money to the large bird. But motifs are narrative elements and types are narrative units, and Finnegan, like other non-folklorists, has confused them. The core of the second tale deals with the deception employed by the finch on the eagle; the finch is the trickster and the eagle the dupe in two classic roles of folk narrative the world over. Trickster and dupe may be god, man, or beast, but always the one makes a fool of the other. The finch never does return the money to the eagle, and through a ruse shifts onto a third party, the luckless hen who has tattled on her, the burden of compensation. In the first tale there is no trickster and no dupe, just a straightforward loss of the borrowed object by the hen and an equally straightforward retribution by the vulture: a simpler and quite different tale type.[14]

What should astonish all dealers in folklore is not the divergences of core plots on the lips of individual raconteurs in far-removed cultures, or even in the same culture, but the close similarities that persist in oral texts dispersed over the five continents. One evening in Monrovia I sat with two Vai friends, Bai T. Moore, undersecretary for cultural affairs, novelist, poet, and folklorist, and his cousin, the venerable Jangaba Johnson, also an active collector of Liberian tribal traditions. They began telling folktales, and to my amazement came forth with one about how Turtle made Leopard his Riding Horse. I say to my amazement for, although it had some nice local African touches, such as Leopard being ill with malaria, it belonged to the same type well known in the United States, and which I had myself collected from American Negroes, as Rabbit Makes Fox His Riding Horse. Since I had strongly espoused the thesis of European rather than African origins of American Negro folktales, this parallelism gave me a jolt—although of course a folklorist is always prepared to find such examples of diffusion. But which way did the riding-horse story diffuse— from Europe to West Africa and then to North America, or from Europe directly to the United States and thence back to West Africa with ex-slaves returning to Liberia? or did it originate in Africa? or India, where the tar-baby story is supposed to have gotten started? How can Finnegan say

---

[14] The motifs of the "Gullible Fool" (J2300) and "Deception in payment of debt" (K200) are lacking in the first tale.

such questions are not of much interest? They are among the most fascinating questions in the history of man and his cultures. (See Part III for the text.)

There is also the vexing matter of folk-narrative categories and those slippery terms *myth, legend,* and *folktale.* Here Finnegan relies on the statements about those terms offered by William Bascom, an anthropologist oriented to Africa and sympathetic to folklore, like his mentor Melville Herskovits.[15] But Bascom (one of the contributors to this volume) relies chiefly on examples from non-literate societies, where these labels do not fit well, and are in any case inadequate. He fails to consider the category of memorat,[16] or personal-experience narrative, now in common usage among European and American folklorists. Folklorists may prefer terms within the given culture, where available, to denote the nuances of traditional narrative, rather than the old-fashioned terminology of the nineteenth century. The late A. C. Jordan, among others, made this point in discussing South African folktales, which the Xhosa divided into *ntsomi,* a fiction, and *siganeko* or *mbali,* for a historical event that could verge on the *buntsomi,* or fabulous. But most African languages, he pointed out, had no word for myth.[17] As the Finnish folklorist Lauri Honko illustrates, the scholar of oral narratives must slide back and forth between a nominalist and a realist nomenclature, and he himself uses such terms as memorate, fabulate, local belief legend, entertainment legend, folktale, and fict.[18] The 1969 Conference on American Folk Legend, at Los Angeles, and preceding European conferences on legend catalogues have amply shown how subtle and complex is the concept of legend. In the light of contemporary

[15] "The Forms of Folklore: Prose Narratives," *Journal of American Folklore* 78 (1965): 3–20.

[16] Spelled memorate by European scholars.

[17] A. C. Jordan, "Tale, Teller and Audience," *Proceedings of a Conference on African Languages and Literatures, Held at Northwestern University, April 28–30, 1966,* ed. Jack Berry et al. (Evanston, Ill., n.d.), pp. 33–44.

[18] Lauri Honko, "Genre Analysis in Folkloristics and Comparative Religion," *Tenemos* 3 (1968): 60. See also his "Memorates and Folk Beliefs," *Journal of the Folklore Institute* I (1963): 5–19.

scholarship, *myth, legend,* and *folktale* have little utility as conceptual categories. They do not, for instance, make a place for jokes, the most pervasive form of folk narrative in modern society, about which Finnegan says nary a word. The fact is, anthropologists do not know what folklore is; the Herskovits school calls tales and proverbs "folklore" and beliefs in unnatural beings "pagan supernaturalism."[19]

These criticisms of *Oral Literature in Africa* are not volunteered because it is a bad book but because it is a good one, good enough indeed to crystallize misconceptions about the relationship of oral literature to folklore. A large part of Finnegan's treatise opens doors for folklorists to investigate further the unconventional forms she brings within range, such as drum messages, personal names, funeral dirges, panegyric poetry, oratory, and puppet playlets. She appreciates the influence of Islamic writings and teachings on African oral traditions, a point any comparative folklorist will underscore. And she recognizes the contemporaneity and topicality of a good deal of oral poetry and prose. Here a dividing line can be drawn between the domains of oral literature and folklore. Composed topical songs, connected, say, with internal politics, as in the examples she gives (pages 290–93) of the bickering in Guinea between the French administration party of Barry Diawadou and the R.D.A. (Rassemblement Démocratique Africain) party of Sekou Touré, hinge on passing personalities and do not sink into tradition. Hence they fall outside the province of folklore, although we must be careful since the forms of these songs of praise and abuse follow traditional patterns. The great bulk of oral literature is traditional, but a mass of folklore falls outside oral tradition: the realm of belief, ritual, festival; the field of folk art; the topic of folk medicine; and other subjects, such as folk costume, folk cuisine, folk crafts. As yet, most of these matters belong to tribal custom rather than to folklore, but they are in the process of transition, as detribalization and fermenting nationalism divide society into elite and folk classes.

[19] See the review of John Messenger's *Inis Beag, Isle of Ireland,* by Ellen Ettlinger, in *Folklore* 81 (1970): 150.

Folklore studies further diverge from oral-literature studies in considering the crossing of genres and crossing of media. The folklorist works with variants, but his variant texts slip outside the bounds of one or another genre. A core plot may take the shape of a historical tradition, a jocular tradition, a fictional tradition, or a poetic tradition in different times and places. A belief may exist as an independent entity, or be incorporated in a memorat, or wear proverbial dress. Riddles and proverbs, in Africa particularly, may merge.[20] The legendary theme finds expression in sculpture as well as in oral prose and verse. Many genres converge in the nightlong and week-long festivals that combine music, dance, drama, narrative, song, and ritual. The oral and the written words mutually influence each other and affect the course of tradition. One of the main inquiries of folklorists is the influence of folklore sources of inspiration on the creative writer, but Finnegan rules this question outside her scope, and since she identifies oral with written literature, she cannot very well distinguish them, although African writers themselves are very conscious of the distinction. Printed sources close to the grass roots, such as tabloid newspapers, mass magazines, and lurid best sellers, may contribute to folk tradition, and the folklorist must pursue these tangled trails.

While full-scale studies of African folklore as it traverses genres and media have yet to appear, there are some admirable limited investigations or sections of larger monographs that point the way. I will mention a few.

A praiseworthy exploration of one genre of African oral poetry by an African scholar is S. Adeboye Babalọla's *The Content and Form of Yoruba Ijala*. The Yoruba of western Nigeria chant *ijala* on special occasions in honor of Ogun, a major deity especially revered by hunters. *Ijala* are poetic compositions of varying lengths, from a dozen to several hundred lines, conforming to specific rules in the use of themes, metrics, and language. They make a nice example of the overlap between oral literature and folklore. Their

---

[20] John C. Messenger, "Anang Proverb-Riddles," *Journal of American Folklore* 73 (1960): 225–35, and the exchange between Messenger and Donald C. Simmons, *idem* 74 (1961): 245–46.

form is traditional and conventional, but so is the form of a sonnet. Unlike written sonnets read on the page, *ijala* live on the lips of *ijala* artists, who are composers and improvisers as well as chanters of standard pieces. In recording *ijala*, Babalọla was struck by the similar and near-identical texts known to performers in scattered Yoruba towns. There thus exists a corpus of *ijala* chants that meet the criteria of the folklorist: they are known traditionally and circulate in variant versions, like the English and Scottish popular ballads canonized by Francis James Child into three hundred and five basic types. A Yoruba scholar may one day typologize *ijala* in such a manner. He will not be able to include all known *ijala* in his scheme, since bards are continually creating new pieces, which cannot be considered folk poems until they pass into general oral currency. There will always be a threefold division of *ijala:* anonymous and long-lived chants in folk circulation; recent compositions beginning to diffuse; and new compositions not yet borrowed by other performers. If this last class does not attract attention and repetition, it will not qualify as folk poetry. In the Yoruba mind, there are no individual composers, but only bards inspired by Ogun.

While many *ijala* are folk songs, they touch folklore in other ways too. *Ijala* are closely connected with a body of legendary traditions accounting for the fabulous exploits of Ogun and explaining the origin of *ijala* chanting in his honor. These legends vary widely. Ogun, ill through the magic of his enemies, consulted a diviner, who ordered him to chant *ijala* from town to town to entrance his enemies; before his death he commanded his children to chant to him as a divinity to receive his favors. In another tradition, Ogun descended to earth and came to a river, where a boatman refused to punt him across because of his warlike mien; thereupon Ogun struck his sword into the bank and chanted these enigmatic verses to the punter:

The *lanmirin* grass is the cult colleague of the
palm-frond arrow.

The *langanran* grass is the cult colleague of the
  labèlabe grass.
A root which grows from a tree on one bank of a river
And appears on the other bank does not pass through
  the river's water.
This is the clue for me, Ogun Mọja, wearing aggression's
  palm-fronds round my waist,
Wearing a straw hat and standing at a distance.
Brandishing a two-edged cutlass dazzlingly.
I, Ogun Mọja, will unfailingly perform my
  entertainment till nightfall.
I, Ogun Mọja.

So chanting, Ogun vanished, only to reappear a moment
later on the other side of the river. The astonished boatman
spread abroad the account of Ogun's feat and his mysterious
chant. Followers flocked to Ogun to enjoy and imitate his
chants, which they called "Ogun's entertainment," or *ijala*.[21]

This legend, told to Babalọla by a cult chief, contains an
illustrative chant, in which the god foretells his miracle,
likening himself to the root that mysteriously traverses the
river. Prose and verse, legend and chant, serious belief
and merrymaking commingle here and overflow any rigid
category of oral genres. That Ogun regards his chanting
as a *performance* is striking in view of the consensus among
folklorists today to describe the singing of a song or telling
of a tale with just that term.

Besides the legends dealing specifically with Ogun, many
ijala salute lineages of the Yoruba and commemorate marvelous and legendary incidents in the traditional histories of
those lineages. On a coarser level, some *ijala* incorporate
off-color jokes, and it is regrettable that Babalọla chose to
exclude them.[22] Still another way in which the *ijala* relate
to folklore is on the plane of magic. By praising Ogun, *ijala*
help assure success to the hunters. Sick persons may be
cured by hearing *ijala*. Performers of *ijala* employ medicinal

---

[21] S. A. Babalọla, *The Content and Form of Yoruba Ijala* (Oxford, 1966), pp. 6–7.
[22] Ibid., 39.

charms to strengthen their memories.[23] Again, the ritual and festival occasions on which *ijala* are chanted are themselves folkloric events. The folkloric ramifications of *ijala* seem to pervade the whole Yoruba culture.

Other collections of praise poems in the Oxford Library of African Literature do not explore so well these ramifications. Besides Babaḷọla's volume the series includes collections for the Bahima, Tswana, and Zulu.[24] As with Finnegan, the editors value panegyric poetry above folk narrative. Cope writes in his introduction to the Zulu praise poetry:

> Within the body of traditional Zulu literature a distinction may be made between the prose of legends and folk-tales on the one hand and the poetry of songs and praises on the other. The Zulu folk-tales . . . have neither the seriousness of purpose nor the concentration and emotional effect of the praise-poems, which represent without doubt the highest development of literary art among the Zulus.[25]

Yet soon Cope blurs the distinction he has made between oral prose and oral poetry to stress links between praises and proverbs and the function of praise poems in recording talked-about events. When Cope speaks of the "natural simplicity" of Zulu folktales and folk songs as the most attractive feature of this "primitive art," we are hearing the language of nineteenth-century colonialists.[26] These vivid praise poems, heroic recitations, panegyrics, or whatever term one uses, are based upon verbal traditions of the great deeds of chiefs, which could be recorded today by the new methods of African oral historians. Heroic legend and heroic epic flourish

[23] Ibid., 43.
[24] H. F. Morris, *The Heroic Recitations of the Bahima of Ankole*, with a Foreword by A. T. Hatto (Oxford, 1964); I. Schapera, *Praise Poems of Tswana Chiefs* (Oxford, 1965); *Izibongo, Zulu Praise Poems*, collected by James Stuart, trans. Daniel Malcolm, ed. Trevor Cope (Oxford, 1968).
[25] *Izibongo*, p. 24.
[26] Ibid., 25.

side by side around the world, as the Chadwicks make clear in their majestic studies of the Heroic Age, and A. T. Hatto, in his Foreword to the Bahima boast-verses, appropriately observes that Professor Hector Chadwick would have been delighted with Morris' study of Bahima heroic poetry.

The whole conception of African praise poets held by British social anthropologists and linguists is challenged by Archie Mafeje in a provocative essay that uses the comparative method of folklore.[27] He singles out I. Schapera, who in his *Praise Poems of Tswana Chiefs* states the orthodox position that the poet functions primarily to praise his chief. Rather, Mafeje contends, the poet mediates between the people and the political authorities, and he will express strong and bitter criticism against what he considers an unjust political system. For a case in point Mafeje presents a number of protest poems, translated from the Xhosa, that were orally delivered between 1959 and 1963 by Melikhaya Mbutuma, a South African from the Transkei. The Xhosa chiefs were divided over the question whether or not to support the South African government's policies. Mbutuma spoke strongly against the pro-government chiefs and in behalf of Sabata, a chief who resisted the government.

> These things are to be expected from
>   a coercive Government.
> They come as no surprise from a partial administration.
> From a dictatorship, I expect anything.
> It's just as well that the chiefs have
>   discredited themselves;
> Otherwise we would never have known the
>   potential of the black nation.
> Angels and heavenly spirits, come and
>   be protectors to Sabata.
> Our heavenly Father, stretch your arms
>   and protect us;
> Jehovah! your mercy is everlasting.[28]

[27] "The Role of the Bard in a Contemporary African Community," *Journal of African Languages* 6 (1967): 193–223.
[28] Ibid., 203.

This scarcely sounds like praise! Mbutuma is appealing to the people to carry on their struggle without their wavering chiefs. He can cleverly shift gears from straightforward political criticism to a satirical use of folklore characters:

> At the top of the Mdlunkulu River is a miracle;
> There, I found a pole-cat and a leguan
>   having a conversation.
> The leguan says, "It is nice and cool in
>   the water below."
> The pole-cat replies, "It is nice and warm in
>   the sun above."
> They continued, challenging and daring each other.
> The leguan came out and basked in the sun
>   to its satisfaction.
> Behold! the pole-cat jumped into the
>   depth of the lake.
> That was the end of it, for it came out
>   rotten and stinking.
> Our heavenly Father, stretch your arms
>   and protect us;
> Jehovah! your mercy is everlasting.[29]

In the polecat, the poet caricatures Chief Matanzima, a government supporter, who imagines that he can have the best of the two worlds, black and white, like the leguan, who enjoys both water and land. But what the white South African (the leguan) can do at the present, the Xhosa cannot, and in betraying his trust and his traditions Matanzima loses the faith of his people.

If the Xhosa word *mbongi* is not to be translated as praise poet, what term, then, should be used? Mafeje opts for bard, on the basis of analogies with the Celtic bards of Wales, Ireland, and Scotland, who voiced national and religious attitudes of the common people. In modern South Africa, the

[29] Ibid.

scope of the *mbongi*'s poetry has expanded from intertribal to national issues, and he has become spokesman for a nation. Celtic and South African bards alike celebrate national victories and individual achievements, chant the national laws and customs, recite royal genealogies, and, on the other side, criticize the chiefs if they disregard the laws and customs, abuse their power, and neglect the people. Unlike the Celtic bard, his South African counterpart does not attain his position hereditarily and is not organized into a guild. Still the resemblances justify Mafeje's revision of the English term and the underlying concept from praise poet to bard. To arrive at this revision he considered comparable practices of oral poetic composition in other cultures, and this is an essential folkloric method. Bardic poems express folk sentiments, and to the extent that they circulate orally they become folk poetry.

The relation of folklore to literature is a problem that can properly be studied only by a critic trained in folklore as well as in literary studies. Without such training, critics cannot properly identify the folkloristic elements in fiction, poetry, and drama, a ticklish business even for one steeped in folklore. Oral-literature scholars such as Finnegan eschew the task, but the folklorist finds it one of his most intriguing concerns. For the creative writer has often found nourishment and inspiration in folk sources, and recognized kindred spirits in folk narrators and folk bards. Elsewhere I have suggested that the folk-literary scholar could apply three tests to a piece of creative writing to determine its folklore content: the biographical, to see if the author had direct contact with folk traditions; the internal, to uncover in the piece itself evidence of familiarity with the texts and contexts of folklore; and the corroborative, to document the internal folk matter with known traditions recorded in standard indexes and field collections.[30] This scheme can apply as well to African as to American literature, better in fact on the

---

[30] "The Identification of Folklore in American Literature," *Journal of American Folklore* 70 (1957), reprinted in Richard M. Dorson, *American Folklore and the Historian* (Chicago, 1971), pp. 186–203.

biographical side, because African authors are alive and accessible and very aware of their traditional inheritance.

On a short trip to Africa I was able to meet such celebrated writers as Camara Laye, Birago Diop, Bai T. Moore, John Pepper Clark, and James Ngugi, and to learn of their debts to folk themes. After Camara Laye had shown me in Dakar the Hungarian edition of his *L'Enfant Noir,* saying it had been translated into twenty-seven languages, he announced matter-of-factly that he was leaving in the morning for the bush to record a *griot:* "Une légende, un roman!" Also in Dakar resided Birago Diop, the ex-diplomat turned veterinarian, whom I interviewed among ailing cats and dogs; his *Contes d'Amadou Koumba* explicitly acknowledged, in title and preface, his dependence upon a silver-tongued *griot* for the traditional tales he had rewritten. In Lagos, versatile young John Pepper Clark let me examine the typescript of the Ijaw festival to the hero Ozidi he had recorded and filmed from three narrators; he had already fashioned a heroic drama, *Ozidi,* in stirring blank verse, and now he was publishing his field texts in the Oxford Library of African Literature series. Such evidence of his folklore sources furnished by the author may be unique in literary history. In Monrovia, Bai T. Moore talked folklore with me, gave me copies of his field collections of Liberian folk songs and folk narratives, issued in mimeographed form through the Liberian Bureau of Folkways, and incidentally mentioned his novel *Murder in the Cassava Patch* and his volume of poems *Ebony Dust.* At Makerere University I heard James Ngugi lead a spirited East African Writers Workshop through an agonized debate on whether African writers should link with oral literature and vernacular languages or aim for Western audiences. One participant, John Ruganda, read aloud his play for television "My Father the Glutton," based on a well-known Baganda folktale, with the folkloric character of the stupid ogre evoking merriment from the audience. These empirical evidences of the intimacy between African writer and folklore sources represent only the beginning of the quest of the folk-literary scholar, for an author may draw his folklore from literary sources and will adapt folklore, oral or literary, in a variety of ways for his imaginative purposes. Although the case of Birago Diop's debt to folk narrative seems so clear-cut, his *contes* belong with the literary short story rather than the oral folktale.

Literary critics responding to the new African belleslettres have floundered over the question of how these novels, stories, plays, and poems relate to folklore and oral literature. In his essay in this book Bernth Lindfors has discussed some of these uninformed reviews, and in an earlier article on Amos Tutuola he provides a model study of an African writer's involvement with folklore.[31] The various English and American critics who heralded Tutuola's *The Palm-Wine Drinkard* and *My Life in the Bush of Ghosts* were aware of some vague relationship between the author and Yoruba oral traditions, but none could spell it out very clearly. Lindfors uses all three methods, of biographical, internal, and corroborative evidence, and a fourth that should be added to my criteria, literary sources, to define the relationship. On the biographical side, Tutuola has stated that he grew up in his village listening to and telling folklore stories, and that he heard the yarn of his first book from an old man on a Yoruba palm plantation sitting by the bank of a big river under the shade of palm trees drinking bamboo tumblers of wine. "When he believed that I could enjoy what he wanted to tell me, then he told me the story of the Palm-Wine Drinkard."[32] On the internal side, Lindfors points out characteristics of oral narrative art in Tutuola's fiction, and persuasively argues that the novels represent a sequence of separate, individual folktales—marked by beginning and ending formulas—rather than any consecutive plot. On the corroborative side, Lindfors calls attention to variant tale texts in Yoruba and other West African folklore collections that closely match the ones used by Tutuola. He also cites wellknown folk motifs employed by Tutuola—"the quarrel between heaven and earth, the carrying of a sacrifice to heaven, the tiny creature that makes newly-cleared fields sprout

---

[31] "Amos Tutuola: Debts and Assets," *Cahiers d'Études Africaines* 10 (1970): 306–34.
[32] Ibid., 310.

weeds, the *enfant terrible*, the magical transformations."[33] But he is to be faulted here for not supplying motif numbers.[34]

Finally, Lindfors pursues another link between folklore and Tutuola's fiction through intermediary literary influences. Writers sensitive to oral folklore may also be kindled by their reading of legends, as was Hawthorne, who profited both from his own direct recording of New England traditions in the nineteenth century and from perusing seventeenth-century versions in Cotton Mather's *Magnalia Christi Americana*. Examining Tutuola's reading, Lindfors sees some possible debts to John Bunyan's *The Pilgrim's Progress* and Edith Hamilton's *Mythology*, whose accounts of heroic adventures and trials with monstrous creatures echo in the Nigerian's later novels. But he finds the most direct influence in the highly popular vernacular novels of Daniel O. Fagunwa, like Tutuola a relater, though with more Christian gloss, of Yoruba folktales. Tutuola's descriptions of monsters closely parallel the loathsome figures sketched by Fagunwa. By a usual process of folklore, although one not perhaps anticipated for Africa, the folklore-based fiction of Fagunwa entered grade-school readers of Nigerian schoolchildren who learned Yoruba folktales through this medium as well as from their parents and grandparents.[35]

This essay by Lindfors deserves summary because it represents so well the possibilities of folklore analysis for African literature, and stands in marked contrast to less successful efforts. In other papers Lindfors broadens the base of Tutuola's African folk sources to include sorcery and magic as well as oral art. Even a television set in a ghost's palm derives from Yoruba divination rather than from Western technology.[36]

[33] Ibid., 317.

[34] Transformation occupies a whole section of the *Motif-Index of Folk Literature* under D0–D699. *Enfant terrible* would be located within section F200–F699, "Marvelous creatures." Motifs for "The Heavens" are grouped under A700–A799.

[35] Ibid., 326, note 5.

[36] "Amos Tutuola's Television-handed Ghostess," *Ariel* 2 (January 1971): 68–77. Lindfors has also written "Amos Tutuola's *The*

A number of critics have discussed the relationship of African traditional literature to modern literature, and indeed the question is almost inescapable for commentators on the African literary scene. Their handling of folklore is usually ill-informed and weighted by emotional considerations. In a two-part article on "Transition from Oral to Literary Tradition" and "Amos Tutuola and the Oral Tradition," E. N. Obiechina, head of the English department at the Institute of Administration in Enugu, argues that West African writers who enter the European literary tradition still remain faithful to their African heritage because they at the same time utilize the West African oral tradition.[37] This attitude, he notes, marks a reversal from the anti-colonialism of African intellectuals who until the 1960s rejected interest in folklore as the "Africana exotica" of British social anthropologists and European cosmopolites.[38] The change reflects the new African rationalism, which, as so often in the history of emerging nation-states, seeks reinforcement through a presumably indigenous folklore. Those post-colonial African authors who have achieved world-wide reputations writing in English and French within European literary modes are still African in heart and spirit because, according to Obiechina, they are simply converting their oral folklore into written literature.

> The essential reality of the contemporary West African culture is that within it, oral tradition continues to exist side by side with the encroaching literary tradition. . . . Whether in the tales of Amos Tutuola, in the novels of Achebe, in the plays of Clark and Soyinka or in the poems by Okigbo, we are aware that the writers are drawing elaborately from West African folklore, traditional symbols and

Palm-Wine Drinkard and Oral Tradition," *Critique* 11 (1968–69): 42–50; "Amos Tutuola and D. O. Fagunwa," *Journal of Commonwealth Literature* 9 (1970): 37–65; "Amos Tutuola and His Critics," *Abbia* 22 (1969): 109–18.

[37] *Présence Africaine* 63 (1967): 140–61; idem (1968): 85–105.
[38] Ibid., 143, note 1.

images, and traditional turns of speech, to invest their writing with a truly West African sensibility and flavour.[39]

Tutuola, whose superstition-laden tales written in street-corner English embarrassed his fellow Nigerians when they were first published, now occupies the place of honor in West Africa's literary pantheon and receives special treatment from Obiechina. Yet for all Obiechina's grand pronouncements upon the folklore base of African writing, he refers to not one field collection of African folklore. I agree with his main thesis, as stated in a conference at Ibadan in 1965, that "traditional material of folk tale, myth and legend is so intimately connected with the life of Africa, that some knowledge of it is necessary to an intelligent understanding of certain areas of African creative writing."[40] But he does not evince this knowledge. Obiechina cites outmoded references, such as Boas' dictum that the mythology of a tribe constitutes its autobiography; he generalizes from the North American Indian trickster to the West African trickster, although these trickster types play dissimilar roles; he sometimes errs, as in saying that Anansi is known to American Negroes; and he fails even to identify tale types and motifs by the Aarne-Thompson system. His generalities about African folktales are mere *obiter dicta*, and he does not realize that African folktales mentioning automobiles and toasters can be matched with modern versions of the Grimms' Märchen, that indeed all folktales are being continually up-dated.

Writing as a non-African literary critic identified with African letters, from his then post as director of the African Studies Institute at Fourah Bay College, Michael Crowder arrives at a similar position.[41] He finds it desirable that African writers employ traditional themes to preserve the continuity and vitality of their oral literature. Crowder makes some interesting

[39] Ibid., 143.
[40] Ibid., 145, note 1.
[41] "Tradition and Change in Nigerian Literature," *Tri-Quarterly* 5 (1966): 117–24.

analyses of Nigerian schools of writing, but he does not know the basic terms of the folklorist; under traditional themes he speaks of "folklore," "the folktale," and "oral [traditional] history" as coeval, which is like equating all literature with short stories and plays. His fear that the growth of literacy and the breakdown of the traditional way of life cause the withering of oral literature is an old cliché; oral folklore simply moves into new forms, like the omnipresent joke and anecdote. In looking toward past folklore as a treasury of inspiration for playwrights, poets, painters, and novelists, scholars such as Crowder and the South African A. C. Jordan lose sight of the contemporaneity of folklore.[42] If the Ijaw festival of Ozidi lay dormant for twenty years until J. P. Clark revived, recorded, and filmed it, then it had obviously lost its function, and no revival will restore the original in its pristine form, certainly not before a motion-picture camera. But the induced revival of old folklore is one aspect of romantic nationalism, which the folklorist knows as an oft-repeated tale.

FOLKLORE AND ANTHROPOLOGY

To many scholars, college students, and the public at large, folklore and anthropology are closely interrelated, and for Africanists the ties seem especially intimate. Where does the one begin and the other leave off, is a question continually asked of the folklorist, whose field is often considered a branch of anthropology. Yet while they meet at some points, the history and methods of the two subjects are quite independent. The anthropologist is at most an incidental collector of folklore. The *Dahomean Narrative* of Melville and Frances Herskovits, published twenty years after their field trip and lacking in comparative annotation, was a by-product of their ethnography on Dahomey. Evans-Pritchard's *The Zande*

---

[42] A. C. Jordan, "Towards an African Literature," *Africa South* 1 (1957): 90–101.

Trickster is a ragbag of leftovers and follow-ups from his fieldwork among the Azande, with less than satisfactory texts and notes. The business of the cultural anthropologist is the study of the whole culture of a non-literate society. The business of the folklorist is the comparative study of folk tradition in non-literate and literate societies.

Anthropologists and folklorists agree that "oral literature" or "verbal art" constitutes folklore, but they fall out when it comes to extending folklore to such central matters in the culture as religion and medicine. Can one speak of folk religion and folk medicine in a tribal culture? Perhaps not. Ordinarily the folklorist considers magic, witchcraft, sorcery, and demonology as his prime topics, because they lie in the shadows of the high civilization proud of its science, engineering, education, and theology. But when they infuse the central institutions of a tribal culture, they are better studied by the anthropologist. The methods of the folklorist are directed toward the esoteric, the fragmented, the little-observed parts of the culture. He is a sleuth and a ferret. Vance Randolph, the assiduous collector of Ozark folklore, has said that it is easier to sleep with a girl in the Ozarks than to extract her confession of a belief in witchcraft. But Evans-Pritchard did not face such a problem among the Azande, where witchcraft, to use the English term, is publicly accepted throughout the society.

Ifa, the divination system practiced among the Yoruba, may serve as a case example of the distinction between anthropology and folklore. This is an orally transmitted system, painstakingly taught over a period of years by Ifa priests to apprentices. Ifa involves interpretation of the future through supernatural means, yet I would not call it folk belief or folk religion. In his intensive study of *Ifa Divination*, William Bascom cites a long string of travelers and ethnologists who have reported, with varying accuracy, the practices and concepts of Ifa.[43] There is no mystery about the existence and centrality of Ifa, although there are subtle

[43] William Bascom, *Ifa Divination; Communication Between Gods and Men in West Africa* (Bloomington and London, 1969), ch. 2.

questions about its mechanisms and philosophy, as there are with all well-developed religious cults. Definite and elaborate procedures govern the worship of Ifa, the Yoruba god of divination, and the actions of the professional diviners who recite folktales to their clients according to the fall of palm nuts or seed shells from their hands. The clients then apply the content of the tales to their personal problems, usually by making appropriate sacrifices. Ifa is a learned, highly institutionalized, formalized, official system, and Bascom's explication of Ifa is mainly an anthropological treatise, in its subject matter and in its ethnographic methods.

Folklore is involved, through the circumstances that diviners must know and relate the corpus of Yoruba folktales, but Bascom is not studying or collecting these tales as an end in themselves. By contrast, Vance Randolph's *Ozark Superstitions,* or Harry M. Hyatt's compendious two volumes of tape-recorded interviews with American Negroes, *Hoodoo, Witchcraft, Rootwork, Conjuration,* represent the very heart of folklore. Here are splintered beliefs in magic and metamorphosis held by the anonymous underclasses, little known and unsuspected by members of the elite culture. The hoodoo doctors are underground, not stage center like the Ifa diviners. Looking at the Negro church in the United States, I would say that the First Baptist Church which I attended in Gary, Indiana, with its programs of the service, hymnbooks, sedate sermon, and decorous congregation, is a middleclass institution, while the Calvary, Trinity, and Primitive Baptist churches, which I also attended, with their chanting preachers, responsive parishioners, spontaneous singing and testifying, and catatonic cases, are folk institutions. A prizewinning study by Bruce Rosenberg based on analyses of taperecorded sermons of Negro chanting ministers is titled *The Art of the American Folk Preacher* (1970). The division between religion and folklore is of course tricky ground. A Mormon folklorist I knew was perfectly willing to study the folk beliefs of Roman Catholics but vigorously resisted any suggestion that Mormon doctrines could be subjected to the folklorist's scrutiny. There are folk counterparts to the official theologies, there are folk versions of Mormonism, Catholicism, evangelical Protestantism that revolve around saints' legends, miraculous cures, apocryphal tales, and the power of the Devil. The anthropomorphic religious system of the classical Greeks had its less sophisticated side in what Martin Nilsson has called *Greek Folk Religion*. Nigerians who purchase ju-ju amulets in the marketplace for luck and fortune—such as the taxi driver who drove me into Lagos from the airport—immediately attract the folklorist.

One title in the Oxford Library of African Literature series, *The Medicine Man, Swifa Ya Nguvumali*, by Hasani bin Ismail, does deal with magical beliefs at the informal or folk level, and is properly a folkloristic study.[44] This unusual work impinges on folklore in several ways. It contains the text in modern Swahili and English translation of a ballad composed by the Tanzanian poet Hasani bin Ismail, which he sang often in public but never wrote down until Peter Lienhardt recorded it from dictation. The song follows the well-known Swahili traditional verse form of the *utenzi*, a popular vehicle for historical, legendary, and topical themes. The event on which it was based had evoked excited talk in the village area of Mteniyapa along the coast of Tanzania and assumed the proportions of a local legend. A woman of the village, Salima binti Hanifu, herself sister and daughter-in-law of two sorceresses, was lured into the bush and murdered by a coven of sorcerers; the villagers then invited the medicine man Nguvumali to detect the culprits with his medicines, charms, and drugs, which he did successfully, even getting the coven leader to confess. The *tenzi* thus revolves around a feat of Nguvumali, who appears to be a folk hero in his own right, outside the ballad, with a "great reputation for supernatural powers,"[45] so much so that he was banned from practicing in Dar-es-Salaam by the authorities. Finally, the ballad of Hasani, the commentary of Lienhardt, and the appendix Lienhardt supplies of two court cases in Tanganyika involving murder by alleged sorcery, deal in intimate detail with magical practices lying in the

[44] Edited and translated by Peter Lienhardt (Oxford, 1968).
[45] Ibid., 73.

limbo between the tribal and national cultures. The tribe no longer manages its own business, for policemen and judges from the state interfere, and legislation in the form of the Tanganyika Witchcraft Ordinance punishes the people who employ the services of a medicine man. All these elements —ballad, legend, hero cycle, sorcery—separately and collectively are subjects of folklore investigation. But the anthropologist limits his concept of folklore to "verbal art." Many widespread folk motifs appear in the memorats about sorcery produced by Lienhardt. Some are similar to hoodoo experiences I have collected from American Negroes, such as the attribution of impotence to sorcery, the driving a disease back upon the enchanter by ritually hammering a nail into a tree, and even the explanation of hoax effects achieved by medicine men, given not by skeptics but by believers in sorcery.[46] The typology of the folk magician is again a matter for folkloric analysis. Lienhardt follows Evans-Pritchard in distinguishing between the psychic actions of the witch and the physical apparatus of the sorcerer, and he recognizes the spectrum extending from professional sorcerers such as Nguvumali to lively amateurs such as the football players who consider the outcome of the game dependent upon their magical rather than their athletic prowess. What I would call folk Islam, the counterpart of folk Christianity, also enters into Hasani's ballad and Lienhardt's commentary, and reinforces the magic beliefs already present in Swahili culture. "In coastal East Africa," observes Lienhardt, "the popular mind does not readily distinguish religious learning from supernatural power."[47]

When anthropologists comment and theorize on their collected folklore, they often describe the functions or value reflections of a given genre in the particular tribe of their fieldwork. Such studies can be cited for riddles among the Venda, among whom a knowledge of riddles and other verbal

[46] Ibid., 68–74; Richard M. Dorson, *American Negro Folktales* (New York, 1967), 193–95 (hoax), 205 (nail in tree); *Negro Tales from Pine Bluff, Arkansas and Calvin, Michigan* (Bloomington, Indiana, 1958), pp. 215–16 (impotence).

[47] Lienhardt, p. 50.

skills brings popularity and honor;[48] for proverbs among the Banyaruanda and the Fante, which are said to reflect Fante institutional values such as the importance of litigation and the clan, and Banyaruanda ethical values such as caution and practicality;[49] for drama among the Anang, used to ridicule and satirize individuals and groups—corrupt diviners, separatist churches, adulterous wives, Hausa traders, colonial administrators—considered inimical to Anang values.[50] From a folklorist's point of view, these often valuable studies run the risk of emphasizing a mirror relationship between the folklore and the culture—the Boasian concept—through emphasis on a single genre within a single society.

An example of this anthropological-sociological approach to African folklore is afforded in studies by Thomas O. Beidelman of hyena and rabbit tales among the Kaguru of East Africa.[51] Beidelman states explicitly the premise of the great majority of anthropologists when they deal with folk materials: "I begin my analyses of them (the tales) with the assumption that any such popular tale must owe its popularity to the fact that it reflects certain important beliefs and values held by the society."[52] This fallacy of correlating folklore with values is the particular blind spot of the social anthropologist, guilty, in Herskovits' phrase, of "secondary ethnocentrism" in the possessive attitude he maintains toward *his* tribe. Some folklore does indeed reflect cultural values, but again the same folkloric item may be found in many different and quite dissimilar cultures. The mirror approach

[48] John Blacking, "The Social Value of Venda Riddles," *African Studies* 20 (1961): 1–32.

[49] Alan P. and Barbara W. Merriam and Robert P. Armstrong, "Banyaruanda Proverbs," *Journal of American Folklore* 67 (1953): 267–84; James B. Christensen, "The Role of Proverbs in Fante Culture," *Africa* 28 (1958): 232–42.

[50] John C. Messenger, "Anang Art, Drama, and Social Control," *African Studies Bulletin* 5 (1962) no. 2: 29–35.

[51] "Hyena and Rabbit: a Kaguru Representation of Matrilineal Relations," *Africa* 31 (1961): 61–74, and "Further Adventures of Hyena and Rabbit: the Folktale as a Sociological Model," *idem* 33 (1963): 54–69.

[52] *Africa* 33 (1963): 62.

may work if it is joined with the comparative approach. Thinking comparatively, the folklorist wants first to establish the chain of variation of the texts he considers.

Beidelman gives two quite simple tales which he then relates to the system of Kaguru matrilineages. During a famine time, Hyena proposes to Rabbit that they kill their mothers. Hyena kills his mother and sells her meat. Rabbit substitutes the meat of a bushbuck for his mother, whom he hides in a cave. In the evening he goes secretly to visit her and eats with her. The famine continues, and eventually Hyena dies. Rabbit lives happily with his mother.

In his exegesis of the story, Beidelman discusses in some detail the kinship relations within a matrilineage. He presents diagramed models of such relationships to demonstrate his point that the authority of Kaguru men within a matrilineage depends upon reciprocal support between men and their sisters' sons. Since Hyena is the brother of Rabbit's mother, these two characters and their mothers constitute a matrilineage. The moral of the tale emerges as Rabbit's gaining power in the matrilineage through Hyena's immoral act and death.

No variants of the given text are noted, although the search for them is the first step a folklorist would take. In his second article Beidelman does cite a close variant that had meanwhile come to his attention, in so obvious a source as Alice Werner's *Myths and Legends of the Bantu*. This text ends with Hyena discovering Rabbit's deception and killing Rabbit's mother, reversing the previous denouement and invalidating Beidelman's intricate argument. The folklorist will ask, why not emphasize the filial loyalty of Rabbit to his mother, a world-wide culture trait? The celebrated Japanese legend of "The Mountain of Abandoned Old People" turns on this theme.[53] In an impoverished mountain village, children carry their parents when they reach sixty to a peak, where they leave them, since the village cannot feed them. One text recounts how on the mountain the father, being carried in a basket, breaks branches so that his sons may find their way

[53] Richard M. Dorson, *Folk Legends of Japan* (Tokyo and Rutland, Vt., 1962), pp. 222–25.

back by the broken twigs. Overcome by his love, they ignore the edict, take their father back home, and hide him under the house. While he is in hiding, the lord of the province issues an order, sometimes on threat of invasion from a neighboring lord, to have a rope of ashes brought to him. No one can produce such a thing. The old father under the house hears his children talking, and advises them: "Moisten straw with salty water and make a rope of the straw; then, after it is dried, burn it and present the ashes to the lord in the shape of a rope." His sons do so, to the great gratification of the lord, who inquires the source of their wisdom. When he learns about their father, he rescinds the decree ordering abandonment of the aged.

The Kaguru and Japanese tales are obviously distinct, but they are united by a common theme, the question of whether to eliminate old parents in times of hunger, and the answer of the filial son whose love for his father or mother wins over his fear for his own existence. The parent then saves the son, by feeding him or solving an enigmatic task. Counterparts to the Japanese legend (type 981 "The Old Man Hidden Under the Earth") are known in Asia and Europe from the Middle Ages on, and an African example was collected among the Wala of Wa, in Ghana, by Mona Fikry in 1968. In the Wala version a wicked chief orders all sons to kill their fathers. One filial son hides his father in a hole he digs for him. The chief then sets a task for the young men, to bring him the sweetest and bitterest part of a cow. Only the hidden old man knows it is the tongue, and so saves the youths. (See Part III for the complete text.) Rather than fastening on the local and unique tribal values of the Kaguru tale, a folklorist would pursue the universal elements.

In both his tale analyses Beidelman explains the character of Hyena as exemplifying the Kaguru concept of a witch. Hyena perverts his ritual authority, engages in murder, cannibalism, and incest, and even acts against his own self-interest, as does a witch. But why would the Kaguru need to symbolize Hyena as a witch when assuredly they tell direct experiences of witches? Here is another limitation of the anthropologist who ordinarily restricts his collection of oral narratives to fiction, while the folklorist recognizes that the national, regional, and tribal repertoires include many kinds of "true" stories. Comparably, a number of critics regard Rabbit in United States Negro folktales as the symbol of the crafty, underdog slave or black man, unaware that American Negroes possess a considerable body of overt protest tales. Local and universal symbolisms may infuse the same tale, but a full interpretation should consider both sets of symbols.

That an anthropologist working within one African culture can see folklore in a larger context is demonstrated in a brief but remarkable paper by James W. Fernandez, a contributor to this volume, in which he writes of "Folklore as an Agent of Nationalism."[54] Fernandez sets the stage for his discussion of a single Fang legend in a broad context by pointing out how cultural pan-Africanists and the new generation of African nationalists looked to folklore traditions for an assertion of negritude and African personality, and as a substitute for written history. He then turns to a Fang migration legend of northern Gabon and southern Cameroun, which recounts how the ancestors crossed a treeless savannah, chopped a hole through a great tree blocking their way, and passed through it into a dense rain forest inhabited by pygmies, who instructed them in techniques of forest living. After various family quarrels, groups broke off to form the present settlements of the scattered Fang. Whatever the historical truth of the tradition, it pleases the Fang, giving them a sense of community and accounting for their dependence on the pygmies. When the clans in three states—Cameroun, Gabon, and Spanish Guinea—sought to regroup in the 1940s and '50s, their leaders relied heavily on the legend, even to using it as a password. A version published in 1955 traced the ancestors back to Egypt, whence they crossed the Red Sea in biblical fashion; in spite of the opposition of officials in Spanish Guinea and Gabon, the booklet circulated widely among the Fang villagers and replaced traditional versions. Fernandez concludes, "As we expect

[54] *African Studies Bulletin* 5 (1962) no. 2: 3–8.

to find in all folklore, the migration legend gives voice both
in its traditional and modern forms to the uncertainties and
frustrations of the times while in the same breath offering a
message of integration and stability."[55]

Several points should be noted. Fernandez uses the term
folklore and not any pallid euphemism such as oral art. He
recognizes the interaction between oral and printed texts
that continually operates in the transmission of folklore, even
in supposedly non-literate societies (as in the instance, already
remarked, of the novels of Fagunwa). And he perceives the
present-mindedness of folklore, in reflecting not the old culture of the tribe, as Boas would have it, but contemporary
anxieties and hopes.

Between 1967 and 1970 two noted anthropologists have
signified their break with conventional social anthropology
in five books on African folklore and ritual. Both the Belgian
Daniel P. Biebuyck and the Englishman Victor W. Turner,
who presently teach at American universities, have left on
record their conversion experience, as it were, from the pre-
occupations of their teachers with social structure to a new
interest in the expressive behavior of African peoples. Biebuyck, a contributor to the present volume, tells how he
was engaged in field research in 1956 among the Kisimba
group of the Nyanga, deep in the Belgian Congo ". . . doing
the routine work of taking village censuses, writing down
genealogies, collecting information on descent groups, on kinship patterns, on political structure, on religion, and the
like. . . ." Then he met an epic bard, Shé-kárjsị Rureke
in the village of Bese, who for twelve days sang, narrated,
danced, and mimed the great Mwindo epic. "These days
represent a great and memorable time in my life," he recalled, "one of the highlights of my long fieldwork in the
Congo."[56] In 1969 he published the great Mwindo epic,
with the collaboration of a former Nyanga student, Kahombo
C. Mateene. From the same field collections he also brought

[55] Ibid., 8.
[56] *The Mwindo Epic from the Banyanga* (*Congo Republic*),
ed. and trans. by Daniel P. Biebuyck and Kahombo C. Mateene
(Berkeley and Los Angeles, 1969), p. vi.

out, in 1970, with the same coeditor, an *Anthologie de la littérature orale nyanga,* sampling his hoard of eight hundred tales and legends, two thousand proverbs, a two-thousand-page autobiography, and numerous songs, riddles, praises, dreams, and prayers.[57]

Turner writes in a similar manner about his circumscribed interests in following his predecessors at the Rhodes-Livingstone Institute for Sociological Research, at Lusaka, in Northern Rhodesia, now Zambia, from where he conducted field research among the Ndembu in the 1950s. "For the first nine months of field work," he recalls, "I amassed considerable quantities of data on kinship, village structure, marriage and divorce, family and individual budgets, tribal and village politics, and the agricultural cycle. I filled my notebooks with genealogies; I made village hut-plans and collected census material; I prowled around to catch the rare and unwary kinship term."[58] But Turner felt a curious uneasiness, as of an outsider peering in but ignorant of the goings on. Drums boomed near his camp, and people continually left the village to take part in strangely named rituals. Finally he overcame his instilled prejudice against collecting ritual and embarked on the course that culminated in three subtle works: *The Forest of Symbols* (1967), *The Drums of Affliction* (1968), and *The Ritual Process* (1969).

In effect Biebuyck and Turner freed themselves from the straitjacket of the "hard data" approach and turned to the materials of folklore and ritual, not as incidental collectors but as theorists and interpreters of Nyanga and Ndembu life. In his Introduction to *The Mwindo Epic,* Biebuyck gives a splendid list of indigenous categories of oral folklore far more meaningful than the tired rubrics of myth, folktale, and legend. The term *mushíngá,* for instance, applies to "a tale where the supernatural element, produced by the intervention of divinities, celestial bodies, monsters, and forest specters, stands in the foreground."[59] All kinds of animals appear in the *mushíngá* except, Biebuyck notes, for the most sacred

57 (Brussels, 1970).
58 Victor W. Turner, *The Ritual Process* (Chicago, 1969), p. 7.
59 *The Mwindo Epic,* p. 9.

animals, a point unsolved by folklorists, as to why some beasts and birds become *dramatis personae* in folk narrative, and others, equally common, never do. The category *nganuriro,* or true stories about remarkable personal experiences, usually of hunters and trappers, approximates the memorat, a term recently incorporated into the lexicon of folklorists. For *kishámbáro,* coherent statements on the problems of the country by elders, and *ịhano,* stereotyped instructions to youths about special skills, techniques, codes, the analysis of omens, descriptions of taboos, and such counsels, we have no English labels, and indeed, folklorists are just beginning to look beyond the conventional genres of tale, song, and proverb for expressions of stereotypical attitudes, prejudices, and sentiments. *Kárịsị* denotes the epic and also the epic bards and as well a male spirit who inspires the bards; most of the shorter prose and poetic oral genres of the Nyanga converge in the *kárịsị.*

The recording and publication of *The Mwindo Epic* represent a high-water mark in the anthropological contribution to African folklore studies, by making available a full-length text of an African oral epic, a form that has been reported for a number of African peoples but usually in a tantalizingly incomplete or unsatisfactory rendition.[60] Just to capture an epic is a major feat, considering the length of the narration: the bard, Shé-kárịsị Gandi Rureke, said he had never before performed the story in its entirety at one time. And after the recording come the chastening tasks of translation and glossing. What we call epic is a glorious, multifunctional, multigenre, day-and-night-long African expression. As Biebuyck writes, "It is music, rhythm, song, dance, movement, dramatic entertainment. It is feasting and gift-giving. . . . It is group solidarity and mass participation. For the bard himself, the act of narrating the story has religious significance."[61] Through his performance, the bard hopes to obtain the strength the hero Mwindo derives from songs.

In its scholarship the presentation of *The Mwindo Epic*

[60] See Jan Knappert, "The Epic in Africa," *Journal of the Folklore Institute* (1967): 171–90.

[61] *The Mwindo Epic,* p. 14.

delights the folklorist in almost all respects. There is the lucid, informative Introduction, giving crisp details of Nyanga society and oral genres, the character of the bard, and data on versions of the epic. There is a topical synopsis of the narrative themes in Rureke's version. There is the splendid text of the English translation, backed by the Nyanga original, with full explanatory and analytical glosses. There is a subject index. A folklorist would ask only for appropriate motif numbers to be attached to the topical outline, and for the printing of other recorded versions, even the fragments. He appreciates the shrewd exegesis of Mwindo's complex character.[62] And he sees in the rich tapestry of the epic narration many possibilities for comparative treatments. Mwindo's fight with the dragon brings to mind the classical syndrome of a hero's battle with fierce monsters, elaborately traced by Joseph Fontenrose in his *Python.*

Victor Turner has not moved into the domain of folklore proper, as has Daniel Biebuyck, but his highly sophisticated work with Ndembu ritual symbolism has attracted younger American folklorists interested in expressive behavior. Reviewing *The Forest of Symbols,* Dan Ben-Amos asserted, "It could well be one of the most significant contributions an anthropologist has made to folklore studies in the past decade."[63] What appeals to Ben-Amos, and undoubtedly others of what I have called the contextual school,[64] is Turner's choice of subject matter and method of explication. Turner fastens on two great bodies of ritual: what he calls rituals of affliction, in which cult associations seek to cure the ill or the tormented from the malice of ancestor spirits, witches, or sorcerers; and the life-crisis rituals, such as boys' circumcision and girls' puberty rites.[65] He conceives that each ritual constitutes a system of symbols, not fully comprehensible even to its participants, and he endeavors to penetrate into the meanings of symbols and rituals at a suc-

[62] Ibid., 20, 33, 145.
[63] *Western Folklore* 29 (1970): 134–36.
[64] *Folklore and Folklife, an Introduction* (Chicago, 1972), pp. 45–47.
[65] *The Drums of Affliction* (Oxford, 1968), pp. 15–16.

cession of levels, from rigorous ethnographic observation to sympathetic elicitation of interpretive comments from the Ndembe, such as from his talented doctor/informant Muchona, on to brilliant conceptualizations of his own theorizing. The essay *"Mukanda:* The Rite of Circumcision" is a small monograph exploring the ritual in all its sociological, symbolical, and metaphysical aspects.[66] As Ben-Amos suggests, Turner's work scatters fruitful suggestions for folklorists, as in his revision of Evans-Pritchard's oversimple dichotomy between witchcraft and sorcery,[67] and his elucidation of the ritual powers of the weak—liminality is his term—through the example of the hippies.[68]

Turning from theory to taxonomy, one should note that anthropologists interested in African folklore have expressed some pique at the neglect of Africa in Stith Thompson's *The Folktale* and *Motif-Index of Folk-Literature.* The admitted gaps in the classifying of African oral narratives are slowly being filled by the indexes of May Klipple for European analogues of African tales, Kenneth Clarke for the Guinea Coast, Ojo Arewa for the northern East African cattle area, and Winifred Lambrecht for Central Africa—all, alas, unpublished doctoral dissertations, done at Indiana University and the University of California at Berkeley between 1938 and 1967.[69] In addition, Daniel J. Crowley, who derived his interest in African and New World Negro folklore as a doctoral student in anthropology under Melville Herskovits, is engaged on a master catalogue of African tale types. The fact remains that to date anthropologists, in Africa and elsewhere, have largely ignored the available classificatory indexes.

[66] In *The Forest of Symbols* (Ithaca, N.Y., 1967), pp. 151–279.
[67] Ibid., 118–27.
[68] *The Ritual Process* (Chicago, 1969), pp. 112–13.
[69] May A. Klipple, "African Folktales with Foreign Analogues" (Indiana University, 1938); Kenneth W. Clarke, "A Motif-Index of the Folktales of Culture-Area V, West Africa" (Indiana University, 1957); E. Ojo Arewa, "A Classification of Folktales of the Northern East African Cattle Area by Types" (University of California, Berkeley, 1966); Winifred Lambrecht, "A Tale Type Index for Central Africa" (University of California, Berkeley, 1967).

FOLKLORE AND ORAL HISTORY

If the community of scholars tend to overassociate the folklorist and the anthropologist, they usually underassociate the folklorist and the oral historian. In the past decade, the historians of Africa, located in Europe, the United States, and the new African nations, have developed techniques of oral history to tap the streams of tradition and expand the meager resources of colonial records and Arabic documents. These techniques emulate the field methods of anthropologist and folklorist in the use of direct interviews and tape recorders. At Makerere University, the head of the history department, J. B. Webster, a ruddy, energetic Canadian, explained to me in March 1970 the new "History of Uganda" project he had organized and directed as an oral-history enterprise. It was refreshing to hear this lively account of a historian boning up with his students on oral traditions, driving off into the bush, making contact with the local authorities, meeting the elders and other villagers in group interviews in open assembly, flanked by an interpreter and assistant, shooting the questions at the elders and other knowledgeable persons, some critical of the elders, until the beer break in early afternoon, when the formal interviewing melted into friendly socializing. Points that Webster made have a familiar ring to the folklorist: how old men "blossom into excellent informants" as they strain to open the floodgates of their memories to precolonial times (Webster remarked on a parallel experience interviewing his eighty-five-year-old grandfather about his pioneer youth in Canada); and the rumors among the Teso people that Webster and his group were missionaries of a new religious sect or propagandists for a new political party.[70] I asked Professor Webster if he collected any folklore during his interviewing. "I wouldn't know what to do with it," he replied candidly.

[70] See J. B. Webster, "Research Methods in Teso," *East Africa Journal* 7 (February 1970): 30–38.

A number of oral historians, as can be seen from recent articles and reports, do not know what to do with folklore or simply disregard it, but whether they wish to or not, they are inescapably handling folk traditions, unless they are interviewing public personalities on national issues, as do the oral historians in the United States, and occasionally in Africa too.[71] A distinction may be made in theory between oral tradition and oral folklore, but in actuality, that is to say in the field situation, the line is hard to draw and is continually being crossed by the bearers of what Jan Vansina, or his translator, calls "testimonies" (*témoinage* in French) in his pioneering work *Oral Tradition, a Study in Historical Methodology* (published in French in 1961 and in English translation in 1965).[72] Oral historians who are concerned exclusively with establishing the validity of oral historical traditions fail to recognize, first, that every oral tradition will in due course incorporate folk elements, and second, that folklore materials can shed light on the historical past.

Vansina does recognize these points. He writes as a trained historian and anthropologist who is also aware of folklore methods and concepts, although not to the same degree of sophistication he possesses for his two major fields. It is his sound contention that the historian can employ oral sources as confidently as written sources, provided he scrutinize them with equal care and a different set of criteria, which Vansina proceeds to expound. He directs his attention almost entirely to oral tradition in non-literate societies, and of these, primarily in African societies, largely the areas of his own field research among the Rwanda and Burundi in the former Belgian Congo. The testimony—a happy term for what folklorists would call a text—is distinct from an eye-witness report or a rumor, in proceeding from its originator through a "chain of transmission" to its final stage, when it is written down by

71 This is the point of view in "Oral History in Africa," by Gwendolen M. Carter et al., *African Studies Bulletin* 8 no. 2 (September 1965): 1–25.

72 Thus the Rundi do not distinguish between folktales and history (Jan Vansina, *Oral Tradition*, London, 1965, p. 49; translated from the French by H. M. Wright).

the collector. Vansina considers all possible kinds of testimonies, whether in fixed form as handed down by court chroniclers and praise poets, or in free form as told informally by casual storytellers. What he calls a "commentary" is an independent statement by an informant, not narrative, providing cryptic historical information on some aspect of the culture. Commentaries are traditional, or convey traditional beliefs and wisdom. Folklorists sometimes call them "asides," and now they are beginning to seek them out as interpretations by the tradition bearer, which gloss the texts and are invaluable adjunct texts in their own right, also subject to variation. Thus in an example Vansina gives of a Rundi proverb, "It is cracking at Nkoondo," one commentary states that the regent Ndivyaariye defeated the rebel Twaarererye at Nkoondo, but variant commentaries name other victors and vanquished.[73]

In this admirable treatise Vansina falls short in two respects. First, he does not give sufficient clues to the oral historian as to how to identify folklore themes in testimonies. While referring to "stereotypes" that intrude into allegedly historical accounts, he fails to pin them down with motif numbers from Stith Thompson's *Motif-Index of Folk Literature*, the surest way to establish the folkloristic nature of any narrative element. He does not even mention the *Motif-Index* specifically. Yet he criticizes Eva Meyrowitz for neglecting in her monograph on the Akan to investigate the stereotypic nature of a quarrel between a son of the king of Beeo and a son of the Moslem chief of Nsoko over a girl, which led to their cutting her in half, each taking a portion, and so to civil war. This is indeed a folk legend, and I collected it myself in the Upper Peninsula of Michigan in 1946, in a closely parallel narrative of a war that ensued between Ojibwa and Iroquois after a warrior from each tribe met on the ice of the Straits of Mackinac and chopped in half a girl both were dating.[74] As in the Akan tradition, each suitor took half, and one camp destroyed the other in bitter battle.

---

[73] Vansina, p. 162.
[74] Ibid., 16; and Richard M. Dorson, *Bloodstoppers and Bearwalkers* (Cambridge, Mass., 1952), p. 41.

In the *Motif-Index* this episode can be placed under "Revolting Murders or Mutilations" (S100). To make his point, Vansina should have pursued the stereotype.

A second flaw the folklorist can find is Vansina's inattention to possible literary interferences in the chain of oral transmission he postulates. We have seen that even in African societies, such as the Fang, on whom Fernandez reports, printed versions of historical traditions affect oral retellings.

On balance the folklorist is highly pleased with Vansina's *Oral Tradition* as pointing the way to a synthesis of oral history and folklore techniques. The discussion is all about field methods, the quality of informants, the techniques of recording, the categories of oral forms, the comparison of history-oriented with history-poor societies (the Rwanda are strong in official chroniclers, the Burundi have only casual transmitters of tradition).

One historian who does cite the *Motif-Index* and cast the questions of African oral-historical traditions in a comparative context is Daniel F. McCall, in *Africa in Time-Perspective*, in which he devotes a whole chapter to "The Heritage of the Ears." McCall calls folklore an "omnibus term" and states flatly, "I eschew the word folklore," preferring oral tradition, but his rather journalistic commentary deals entirely with folklorists and their works. Briefly reviewing the theories of myth and the rejection by various scholars of a historical content in mythical traditions, he seeks to restore the status of these traditions, and notes, commendably, the need for a comprehensive African index of stylized elements to aid the oral historian in winnowing stock themes from actual incidents. He boldly compares the Iliad with the Malinké epic of Sundiata, and Homer with the Balla Fasseké, Sundiata's *griot*. A historical base may underlie both heroic epics, with conditions even more favorable to the veracity of the Sundiata tradition, since it did not, like the Homeric, pass through a period of changing culture.[75] McCall is naturally sympathetic to the approach of Vansina, whom he

[75] Daniel F. McCall, *Africa in Time-Perspective* (Boston and Legon: Boston University Press and Ghana University Press, 1964), pp. 38–61.

regards as stronger on tribal than on mythical traditions. But in a joint statement in *The Historian in Tropical Africa*, Vansina has asserted that "myths contain historical data" as well as valuable reflections of African attitudes, not simply in their pristine forms but, too, in their revived and modernized molds.[76]

Some oral historians in Africa find Vansina's systematic analyses and tables of little use in segmentary or non-centralized societies, which lack an encompassing political structure to serve as a frame for a general traditional history. An active oral historian in Ghana, Kwame Y. Daaku, has conducted a series of field expeditions with students from the University of Ghana and found Vansina's elaborate methodology of little use. His field method to some extent resembles that of Webster's in Uganda, except that as a native Ghanaian he enjoys far closer rapport with the chiefs and elders he interviews. In his recorded interviews with Akan chiefs, a considerable amount of folkloric material comes to the surface as the chiefs respond to broad questions about clan history.

Q. How did the clan acquire the name Asakyire?
A. There is a bird of prey called the eagle. Whenever it caught an animal it would give it to the vulture to feed on. This made the eagle inform the vulture that they should consider each other as brothers. Anytime the vulture found our people approaching, it would leave the meat and fly away. Thus the people realized that the eagle and the vulture were the only birds of prey. Again, the vulture put a gold nugget on the feet of its young one. One day when it went to ease itself, the nugget fell down and was later picked up by an old woman. This gave rise to the saying "Kokosakyi, odi amanade" (literally "vulture the scavenger"). It is this our clan which "eats the

[76] *The Historian in Tropical Africa*, ed. J. Vansina, R. Mauny, and L. V. Thomas (London, Ibadan, Accra: published by the Oxford University Press for the International African Institute, 1964), pp. 78–80.

excrement of the land." Again, the Asakyire clan was the first to be created.[77]

Q. How did Tuesday become the day of the Offin River?

A. You see, fishhooks are for catching fish. One Tuesday a man instead hooked a mat. On continuing he hooked a small baby. He died immediately on telling of his experience. Hence we looked on the day as the river god's.[78]

In these two replies to straightforward historical inquiries, Daaku received a myth attached to a tribal name and incorporating a proverb, and a legend connected with a taboo and, presumably, a rite. Further questioning would certainly have elicited variants and additional details concerning the origin of the Asakyire clan and the worship of the Offin River god. Elsewhere in his report Daaku records more elaborate mythical/historical traditions. A testimony about the origin of the Aduana clan tells how the ancestor Nana Gyebi learned from a deer that most of the people who came to the marketplace at Asumegya were animals. Gyebi followed the deer's advice and told the animals to go home and settle down and not change into animal shapes. When they did so, the original inhabitants, now at peace, "found themselves with the problem of population explosion." The elders thereupon decided to rid the town of Nana Gyebi for causing the situation, but the Asantehene discovered the plot, executed the elders, and reinstalled Nana Gyebi. As a tribute to Gyebi the Aduana still today enjoy exemption from defaulting oaths and paying tolls, granted to his son's clan by the Denkyirahene, Kwadwo Tibo, who married Nana Gyebi's sister's daughter.[79]

An oral historian in Africa inescapably encounters tribal histories that mingle references to real persons and places with universal folklore motifs such as the transformation of

[77] K. Y. Daaku, *Unesco Research Project on Oral Traditions: Denkyira No. 2* (Legon, Ghana: Institute of African Studies, University of Ghana, September 1970; xiv, 287 pp.), p. 72.

[78] Ibid., 110.

[79] Ibid., 222-23.

men into animals (D130). He will need to identify these motifs and separate them from the historical residue. Conversely, the folklore collector seeking fictional tales catches in his net many origin and migration legends, since Africans, and other peoples, even in literate societies, often do not segregate historical from folk tradition.[80]

The oral historian in the field learns about the processes as well as the products of folklore. A variety of social mechanisms govern the transmission of the lore. In his fieldwork with the Denkyira, Daaku learned that grandfathers did not customarily impart the histories and traditions of the land to their grandsons, for a child with too free a tongue could release esoteric knowledge that might destroy the family. Accordingly the seniors kept their eyes open for a smart boy who could hold secrets. Finding one, an elder instructed the youth to remember a particular ritual and its associations, and to keep a piece of skin of the sheep sacrificed on the occasion. At the death of a chief, the candidate who could best tell the stories of the sheepskins would be enstooled as his successor. This situation gave rise to the saying "The boy knows skins" to describe brilliant school children.[81] Here the informant has relayed unusual information about the disbursal of traditions, for they are entrusted to the close-mouthed rather than to free and easy talkers. One notices, too, the association of sheepskin with learning, as in Western civilization, where the college graduate is awarded a diploma, or "sheepskin," although his learning is based on the printed word.

This notion of secrecy as a necessary precaution to safeguard family history, and consequently family or lineage values and power, is common to a number of African societies. In an excellent essay on the concepts of history among the Gola, of northwestern Liberia, the anthropologist Warren d'Azevedo sets forth their pragmatic use of secrecy and re-

[80] See e.g. S. Jangaba M. Johnson, *Traditional History and Folklore of the Vai Tribe* (Monrovia, Liberia: The Bureau of Folklore, n.d.).

[81] Daaku, op. cit., 138.

lated attitudes toward the past.[82] To the Gola, the family elders and ancestors control historical knowledge. Whatever public consensus may be arrived at among elders of different families as to an origin or migration account, within a given family the private version remains "the truth for grown men that will make them kings in the world," and the public version is derided as "the proper truth for children and strangers." Inconsistencies and contradictions do not disturb the Gola; they reconcile "very deep history" of pregenealogical times with recent events of immediate concern; they blend the marvelous and supernatural with the realistic and prosaic; they assimilate the new, written history of Europeans into their own spoken traditions. History serves their purposes of providing moral lessons and supporting family status; and to them its instrumental utility, not its objective rigor, is what counts. For the Gola, history is local, personal, and experienced, either at first hand by the elders or transmitted to them through the ancestors. Actually the Gola have no word for history; the closest term, *kabande,* applies to a series of episodic stories offering moral comments on human behavior. A Gola elder reproved D'Azevedo, who was questioning him closely about conflicts in the genealogies of two families, with an apt *kabande:* The speaker's father's uncle, a great man, brother of King Gaya of Mana, accused one of his many slaves of stealing rice from the kitchen. The slave knew nothing about the rice, but agreed with his master's charge and was whipped. It was not for him to disagree with his master, with whom he had to live. Perhaps his master had some reason for making the charge, which the slave would learn about in time, or perhaps he had eaten the rice in his dreams.

Thus the *kabande.* It imparts a lesson, it is anecdotal, it claims a historical association. The *kabande* encompasses all forms of oral narrative, covering the well-known genres of myths, legends, animal tales, memorats, anecdotes. Although the Gola distinguish between historical and mythological *kabande,* both classes of narrative abound in the miraculous. It is just that the first group is validated by the elders and

[82] "Uses of the Past in Gola Discourse," *Journal of African History* 3 (1962): 11–34.

ancestors, and the second is shrouded in antiquity. Gola history is always presented in story form, and the stories are filled with folklore themes and supernatural beings. It is apparent that the oral historian working with the Gola, as with other African peoples, must be trained also as a folklorist if he is to succeed in his research.

Some of the same points are made by Ian Cunnison who, in his *History on the Luapula, An Essay on the Historical Notions of a Central African Tribe,* likewise considers indigenous concepts of oral-traditional history.[83] Again there is the distinction between personal, subclan history and impersonal, universal history (with the Luapula Valley between Northern Rhodesia and the Belgian Congo as the universe). There is the loose sense of history—*ilyashi* in Bemba, meaning something like "affairs"—permeated with mythical and supernatural episodes, and yet tied to practical ends. History is indeed as non-rational to the clans as witchcraft is to Europeans, and historical and magical beliefs reinforce each other in the Luapula Valley. Many of the clan and subclan histories establish claims of land ownership on the basis of incidents widely repeated among different tribes. So a history told to Cunnison by Chisamamba, a subclan head of the Drum Clan, of how his brother, Muonga, relinquished his land to Makungu, begins with a scene of young girls washing; one throws a wooden doll in the water, and in anger the doll's owner throws a real child of the other girl into the water. Payment is demanded by the mother and refused by the owner of the doll, who then leaves the country. Cunnison located this story among five other groups, who related it as their reason for leaving their ancestral home to come to the valley.[84] He refers to other such stock events, which he terms mythical (he does not use the term folklore) but, like other non-folklorists, he does not categorize them in any systematic way and sometimes is reduced simply to saying, "The story given above sounds unlikely."[85]

[83] (Cape Town, London, New York: Oxford University Press, 1951; Rhodes-Livingstone Papers No. 21), 40 pp.
[84] Ibid., 11–13.
[85] Ibid., 19.

The processes as well as the themes of folklore come to light in Cunnison's essay on Luapula history. A folk explanation for the magical wonders of olden times given by the Lunda and Shila is that their ancestors possessed such powers before the Europeans came and weakened the Africans.[86] In my own fieldwork among the Ojibwa Indians in northern Michigan I heard exactly the same idea applied to the loss of Indian magic power with the coming of the white man. Hence, African and Indian alike can place credence in the marvelous history of yesteryear. Besides, marvels still exist and enter into newly forming realistic traditions. "In the Luapula Valley, myths are arising daily."[87] After living in an ambiance of African gossip, Cunnison found himself matter-of-factly pursuing a monster of Lake Mweru who led spawning fish out of the lake and up the Luapula River every January. This contemporaneity of folklore is little recognized by collectors of presumably archaic traditions.

Another aspect of the myth-making and myth-retaining process, alluded to by Cunnison, might be called reinforcement, namely the mnemonic association of traditions of persons and places with natural phenomena. If the Luapula Valley were flat and unbroken, the store of local legends of its peoples would be leaner, but it possesses a variety of ecological features, all visible in one sweeping glance: green jungle vegetation, grassy valleys, swamps with land patches, lagoons, streams, islands, and man-made landmarks such as ditches and pathways. Such features help keep alive memories of events occurring at or near them. Every time Cunnison passed Chalalankuba, on the Luapula, a stream named from the adventure of the Shila hero Nkuba who hid there, some companion repeated the tale to him.[88] Footprints on rocks at Kazembe, by the Ng'ona River—perhaps grooves worn by early men sharpening metal instruments—recalled a tradition of men created by God who roamed the world and the valley "when the rocks were still mud." This tradition of

[86] Ibid., 21.
[87] Ibid., 3.
[88] Ibid., 24.

the indelible footprint occurs among many peoples living near such indentations.[89]

A specific examination of the interplay of history and folklore (again a word never used by the author) is rendered in a study by J. S. Boston treating "The Hunter in Igala Legends of Origin."[90] He finds that legends of the founding of communities among the Igala of Nigeria conform to such well-known cultural and ecological facts as the ritual prominence of hunting and the favorable conditions for game of all sorts. Yet the plausibility of these tribal-origin legends diminishes on closer examination. The hunter/hero who founds the clan turns out to be a stock figure, symbolic in "the context of political organization rather than in the sphere of history."[91] In Igala society the hunter is more than a successful killer of game, he is the ritual and magical specialist, expert in combating the sorcery and witchcraft that account for failures in the hunt. Accordingly the hunter assumes the role of a culture hero, skilled in medico-magical compounds, wise in the properties of herbs, shrubs, and trees. Anecdotes of the hunt constitute a favorite form of Igala oral narrative, and Boston notes the repetitive appearances in different villages—what the folklorist would call variant texts—of the same incidents: how the hunter Otigba stalked and killed a great number of antelope and bush cow, slept in a tree, drove away a leopard, and made his home at the edge of a rocky hill where he recorded his hunting triumphs by building a shrine from skulls of animals he had killed. Another set of variants explains why the wandering hunter departed from his home town, usually because of a personal quarrel involving an act of adultery on his part. What the folklorist can clearly see operating here is the intrusion of standard oral legends of hunting episodes into a purported history of clan or lineage origin. The histories do not indicate the existence of any indigenous population before the arrival of the hunter, and often deny their existence. The next step

[89] Motif A972.1, "Indentions on rocks from imprint of gods and saints."

[90] Africa 34 (1964): 116–26.

[91] Ibid., 125.

would be to typologize the recurrent episodes and characters, within the framework of the existing indexes. Then the folk elements can be clearly culled from the historical narratives, rather than noted with vague, general references.

Only rarely will the oral historian recognize that oral tradition conveys a folk point of view toward historical events that is itself worthy of record. Where the professional historian eschews folk supernatural ideas in presenting his documented record of the past, the oral chronicler transmits those ideas. A study by C. G. B. Gridley reconstructing a battle that took place in northern Nigeria in 1898 accommodates historical truth to the folk mentality. Only one printed scrap bore witness to the battle of Tattawara between the Sultan of Damagaram and the Emir of Kano, until the oral sources reported by Gridley fleshed out the campaigns.[92] The conflict itself was sparked by a curious mishap, when the Sultan Amadu sent two letters to the new Emir of Gumel, a dependent of the Emir of Kano. One letter, to be read publicly, offered congratulations; the other, for private perusal, reminded Gumel that Damagaram was more powerful than Kano. But the messenger inadvertently read it in the presence of a messenger from Kano, who reported back to his Emir, Aliyu. The incident provided a *casus belli*. Aliyu wrote strongly to Amadu, who promptly led an army against Kano. Throughout the fighting both sides relied heavily on soothsayers. When the two forces faced each other north of Damargu, the Kano soothsayers dissuaded Aliyu from joining battle, on the grounds that the signs in the heavens were inauspicious; and it is known that an eclipse occurred about this time. Nevertheless the Emir felt compelled to fight, suffered a severe defeat, and fled back to Kano. Amadu pursued him, but now his soothsayers advised him not to lay siege to Kano, saying that the tombs of many saintly men buried within the city gave it a protective sanctity. Amadu accordingly pulled back, giving Aliyu a chance to slip into Kano. There Aliyu called together all the mallams and commanded them to throw a spell on Amadu, who fell ill and,

[92] C. G. B. Gridley, "Mantanfas, a Study in Oral Tradition," *African Language Studies* 6 (1965): 32–51.

following the counsel of his soothsayers, returned to his base. This account sounds like a contest between two magicians, a familiar folktale and ballad motif (D1719.1, "Contest in magic"). Heavenly signs as omens preceding battles is also a world-wide motif (D1812.5), occurring even in colonial American wars.[93] A Western historian would never present the campaign in terms of magic power rather than firepower, but the oral chronicler has clearly captured the mental view of the participants.

Another relationship with folklore in this affair appears in the ballad of Aliyu that has circulated in variant form since the battle of Tattawara. The ballad departs from the oral narrative in its chronology and its glorifying of Aliyu, who is given credit for a triumphant flight; but it, too, is a source for popular attitudes. Thus it contains a well-known Hausa saying, "There is a Tuareg in Kano," referring to the disguise of Tuareg clothes put on by Aliyu to make his escape when the forces of Amadu cut his army down to six men. Just where this episode occurred is a matter of dispute, but its historicity is accepted, and the ballad makes the Emir to be a strong and clever hero outwitting his enemy when his own warriors prove feeble.

The studies so far considered deal with folk elements in oral-traditional history. They grapple with the question of the historical validity of oral tradition, a matter that has received considerable and heated discussion in many scholarly circles. Another approach concerns the possible historical content in folklore genres, and this approach has largely been ignored.

One scholar conscious of both these interrelationships of history and folklore is the Nigerian historian Ebiegberi Joe Alagoa. In the *Journal of African History* he has discussed the processes of oral-traditional history among the Ijo of the Niger Delta, and recognized the presence of "clichés" and "stereotypes" in this history.[94] The need for each Ijo to know

[93] *America Begins*, ed. Richard M. Dorson (New York, 1966), pp. 158, 159, 412.

[94] "Oral Tradition Among the Ijo of the Niger Delta," *Journal of African History* 7 (1966): 405–19.

his origins is so demanding that a proverb demeans the person ignorant of his genealogy: "He's of goblin ancestry who knows not whence he came." Such an individual can derive only from the *Nondo,* an ape man inhabiting the mangrove swamps in a distant past. Accordingly the Ijo do trace back their past and usually to Benin because of its prestigious kingdom. Their annals state that the peoples in question fled from Benin to the safety of the inaccessible delta. Alagoa credits as convincing only those traditions dealing with internal movements within the delta. Very few peoples claimed autochthony, but the Ke assert their founders dropped from the sky. In only two cases did Alagoa find corroborating evidence, through personal names and bronze artifacts, to support the contention of Benin origins in the oral traditions. The Oporoma actually shifted their autochthonous-origin myth, first recorded in 1931, to a Benin-origin myth, seven years later. Clearly at work is the folkloristic phenomenon of fantasizing illustrious origins.

Within the origin and migration traditions appear repetitive episodes that Alagoa terms stereotypes. These episodes explain why the people moved within the delta after leaving Benin. A family quarrel leading to bloodshed was a commonly given reason; the side with the fewer losses fled to avoid handing over the required number of its own members for restitution. This tradition fits into the pattern of the "family saga," which maintains the esteem of the family or clan group through formulaic incidents.[95] The fleeing party is held up as the victors rather than the vanquished—as in the ballad just mentioned making a hero of Aliyu. Another stereotype accounts for the decline of a once proud community for some sin of *hubris,* such as their trying, godlike, to hold up a falling silk-cotton tree. Pride goes before a fall, in the history of Romans or of the Ijo. These migration legends, or *Wandersagen* in Vansina's terminology,[96] reveal not the facts behind the migration but rather the area of migration, which

[95] Mody C. Boatright, "The Family Saga as a Form of Folklore," in Boatright et al., *The Family Saga and Other Phases of American Folklore* (Urbana, Illinois, 1958), pp. 1–19.

[96] Vansina, op. cit., 74–75, quoted in Alagoa, 418.

can be plotted according to the spread of the stereotypes. Like his mentor Vansina, Alagoa has not progressed to the detection of folk motifs.

In the *Journal of American Folklore*, Alagoa considers ways in which Ijo proverbs cast light on the historical record.[97] The proverbs are compact and cryptic and require considerable exegesis, but when this is available they yield fruit for the historian. "That was how Okponga flattered Kulọ" is a saying used to puncture sycophantic praise. In the more formal oral chronicles of the Nembe kings, great respect is accorded King Forday Kulọ, who reigned in Ogbolomạbiri during the first half of the nineteenth century. But the humble proverb recalls a house slave named Okponga who stood at the king's side during mealtime and purred, "His Excellency is such a light eater, I fear he will leave most of these nice dishes untouched." Pleased at this tribute to his self-control, the king rose, leaving much of his meal behind him, to be devoured by the wily Okponga. The proverb memorializing this incident thus shows a streak of vanity in a supposedly heroic ruler. Alagoa also uses proverbs to support his thesis that the monarchies of the eastern Niger delta were fairly democratic, and not, as K. O. Doke contended in *Trade and Politics in the Niger Delta*, autocratic and divine. "The king is a rubbish dump" suggests that the king bears the blame for all the troubles of the community. Rather it was the chiefs of the lineages in the delta states who ruled despotically, as indicated in the proverbs "A chief never does wrong" and "A chief's fart does not have an evil smell." These Nigerian delta proverbs stand in contrast to the English proverb signalizing the might of divine-right monarchy, "A king can do no wrong." As Alagoa demonstrates, proverbs are a kind of non-narrative folklore from which kernels of history may be extracted.

[97] "The Use of Oral Literary Data for History: Examples from Niger Delta Proverbs," *Journal of American Folklore* 81 (1968): 235–42.

FOLKLORE STUDY AS AN END IN ITSELF

One group of sophisticated scholars is presently engaged in research into African folklore on its own merits, and not as subsidiary to literature, anthropology, or history. They formally organized in Paris in May 1969 as the Research Group of African Oral Literature, supported by the French National Center of Scientific Research, under the Ministry of Education. Their eleven members are affiliated with the Center, or the École Pratique des Hautes Études of the Sorbonne, or the National School of Living Oriental Languages in the Sorbonne; they possess backgrounds in anthropology and linguistics; they have done extended fieldwork in Africa; and they feel a need to talk about African folklore. They meet bi-weekly to discuss common and individual projects, and they also attend seminars directed by their two most active and productive senior members, Denise Paulme and Geneviève Calame-Griaule, daughter of the eminent French anthropologist Marcel Griaule. In their various publications, singly or as a team, the group employ the term *littérature orale*, although they do link it with *folklore* in one issue of a journal devoted to their work with African folktales.[98] While these French scholars use "oral literature" and "oral art" in their English writings, their sense differs from the literary bias of Finnegan and the ethnological bias of American anthropologists. Paulme and Calame-Griaule are applying the methods of folklore to the materials of folklore, within the African scene. Never having cared much for the word *folklore*, as being an English coinage, the French call their folklore journals by such titles as *Arts et traditions populaires*.

The folkloristic emphasis of the Research Group of African Oral Literature is immediately evident in their published and

[98] *Cahiers d'Études Africaines* 30 vol. 8 (1968), titled *Littérature orale et folklore africains*.

projected studies. Their statement of work in progress covers investigations of (1) literary and stylistic aspects of oral poetry and narrative, (2) theoretical and methodological problems of formal analysis, and (3) sociological questions of oral art as a sublimation and reflection of social tensions and psychical constants.[99] This is a broad platform, encompassing much of the ground covered by current schools of folklore theory. As soon as one turns to the essays and monographs of the French Africanists, he perceives the world of difference in their approach from that of non-folklorists treating similar materials. They refer familiarly to the Aarne-Thompson indexing and Propp morphological-analysis systems, they deal specifically and confidently with field-collected texts and variants, they interpret their materials on several levels of sociological and symbolic analysis, and they follow the comparative trail from one culture to another and from Africa to other continents. Their basic method, reminiscent of the great English folklorists of the nineteenth century, is the serial presentation of related versions in a family of tales, with interspersed commentaries by the authors pointing out the stable and the novel elements in each text, until the full narrative structure is revealed. But where the Victorians compared texts to find survivals of prehistoric ideas and customs, and the Finnish historical-geographical school compares texts to determine a hypothetical original, the French Africanists seek the inner symbolic meanings of their *contes*.

A representative essay is Calame-Griaule's "The Oral Tradition as an Art Form in African Culture." In this piece she deliberately eschews folk narrative to treat less-well-known genres, though she does refer to stories as "a sort of privileged mould where we find all the elements of the culture smelted together, and ready for analysis on every level —psychological, social, moral, mythological—being a mirror

---

[99] From a handout, "Note on the Research Group of African Oral Literature (Paris)" prepared and distributed by Veronika Görög-Karady at the Indiana University African Folklore Conference, Bloomington, Indiana, July 16–18, 1970.

of a conception of the world and of man."[100] Here she turns her attention to songs, enigmatic expressions, jokes, and riddles used in teaching. Her examination of a Bambara folk song first collected in Mali in 1956 and found in variants in many villages, always attributed to a local author, is exemplary. Glossing the folk song, she points out the artistic use of conventional images; the substitution of modern political figures for older, legendary heroes; the cluster of associations with the legendary antelope; the mythical origin site of West African peoples; the concluding proverb containing a subtle pun and a subtle link with the reference to the antelope; the employment of enigmatic expressions and allusions. What the folklorist appreciates here is Calame-Griaule's recognition that she is dealing with a folk song, even though her informants thought it a composed song; and her explication of the song's content in terms of other folklore genres, such as legend, myth, proverb, joke, dilemma tale, and riddle. She can and does discuss stylistics as skillfully as any oral-literature critic, but above all she is concerned with folk ideas and folk genres. Her overriding theme is the mastery of language, admired by Africans and exhibited in their sensitive handling of metaphors, images, proverbial riddles, and covert jokes. One thinks of the "man of words" now recognized as a culture hero of American Negroes.

In a complementary paper written with Z. Ligers, Calame-Griaule concentrates on one narrative type widely told in the Sudan about a hyena man, comparable to the werewolf in European tradition.[101] This kind of tale is usually overlooked by collectors in Africa since it often takes the form of a believed personal experience, or memorat, rather than a conventional folktale. The authors juxtapose a dozen texts in which a hero or heroine engages in combat and slays a monstrous creature, usually half human half hyena, who has been terrorizing the countryside. By noting common and special features in the texts, which range from eye-witness re-

[100] *Présence Africaine* 19 (1963): 197–214. The quotation is on p. 200.
[101] G. Calame-Griaule and Z. Ligers, "L'Homme-Hyène dans la tradition soudanaise," *L'Homme* 1 (1961): 89–118.

ports to well-structured *contes*, they arrive at what they consider the complete tale type. The narrative falls into two halves, a negative part depicting the destructive exploits of the anti-hero, or monster, and a positive part glorifying the victory of the liberator-hero and the re-establishment of order. Calame-Griaule and Ligers carry through the series of oppositions, in the manner of Lévi-Strauss, whom they cite, to uncover behind the tale a myth that sets the village against the bush, human society against the beast, love and fecundity against sterility. They stress in one tale variant the curse of impotence that the dying hyena man pronounces on his slayer. But the oppositions meld in a Hegelian synthesis. The hero is sometimes a woman and betrays androgynous characteristics, as in using weapons replete with female symbolism; the monster sometimes eats, that is to say ravishes, the woman; the hero and the hyena/monster are seen as two aspects of man, representing principles of order and disorder, one yielding to another in a recurrent cycle of death, rebirth, and renewal. Woman and the right of procreation are the stakes of the combat. The tale/myth expresses the philosophy and world view of the Sudanese, who are strongly involved with the sexual symbolism of objects in daily life.

This majestic interpretation suggests the comparable exegesis of classical hero-dragon encounters by Joseph Fontenrose, in *Python*. Fontenrose, too, perceives one all-enveloping myth behind these death struggles, centered on a conflict between Cosmos and Chaos. Whatever one may feel about symbol readings, and I am not too keen on them, he must acknowledge the worthy endeavors of Calame-Griaule and her associates to interpret and not simply collect African folklore.

Others of these endeavors should at least be noted. Two seminars on persistent themes in oral narratives of black Africa have resulted in substantial publications. Denise Paulme conducted one seminar on the theme of the impossible restitution or marvelous gift, and introduced the symposium with her own comparative study of three African tale texts, from the Bete, the Dogon, and the Kikuyu, bearing on the theme.[102] In the manner of the French school following the functional structuralism of Propp, she asserts that the dissimilar Bete and Dogon narratives (the Kikuyu is a close variant of the Dogon, but with an added etiological element of the origin of fire) reveal the same fundamental pattern. A borrowed object is lost; the borrower sets off on a voyage to the other world, and brings back a marvelous object—in one case the moon, in the other "une chose" from the dead—that excites the admiration of all, while the losers of the objects are blamed. Paulme ascribes differences in detail in the two stories to differences in culture between the agricultural Dogon and the woodland Bete, but at the core finds the identical myth of the hero's descent to hell and his return with blessings for mankind. Other contributors add their commentaries and texts, and one, Anne Retel-Laurentin, embarks on her own voyage into the intricacies of structural and symbolic analysis to demonstrate, with tables and diagrams, the pan-African character of the basic theme.[103]

In the second symposium, Calame-Griaule directs attention to the theme of the tree in African folktales.[104] She sees it as a cosmic symbol, standing between heaven and earth; as a feminine symbol of the protector and nurse; and as a phallic symbol, signifying death and rebirth. These ideas are illustrated in individual studies: of the tale type with negative and positive heroes who seek treasure in a tree; of symbolic attitudes toward the sorcerer's tree which the Evuzok in the southern Cameroons associate with fecundity, power, and wealth; and of Haitian tales about deified trees.

The French African folklorists are eclectic, happily accommodating Frazer, Freud, Propp, and Lévi-Strauss to their interpretations, which, like the monistic theories of the great nineteenth-century mythologists and survivalists, always come

[102] Denise Paulme, "Sur trois textes africains (bété, dogon, kikuyu)," *Cahiers d'Études Africaines* 30 vol. 8 (1968): 190–200.

[103] "Structure et symbolisme: Essai méthodologique pour l'étude des contes africains," *idem* 206–44.

[104] *La thème de l'arbre dans les contes africains* (Paris: Société pour l'Étude des Langues Africaines, 1969).

out the same way. As Paulme puts it: "Origin of death, origin of marriage, origin of agriculture, these have the same explanation and tell the same tale: to die in order to be reborn, to give so as to receive. It is both a very simple and an inexhaustible tale, precisely the one the *Golden Bough* tells over and over again."[105] By allowing different levels of interpretation, Paulme and Calame-Griaule can have their rebirth, their sexuality, and their binary oppositions. Not all the French school follow their symbolic lead. Analyzing thirty-seven African tales of the origin of the inequality of races, Veronika Görög presents her findings at the face value of the texts.[106] The large majority accept the European value system and acknowledge with an ideology of resignation the superiority of the whites in consequence of a grave fault committed by the blacks. A smaller category displays an ideology contesting white superiority through reform rather than revolution.

If the French school are boldly committed to theory, they have not neglected the necessities of bibliography and indexing, so vital for comparative folklorists. Görög has outlined an ingenious system for an analytic bibliography of African folklore intended to avoid shortcomings in the well-known systems of Aarne, Thompson, and Propp—the first two being too variable, and the third too rigid. Her plan provides a listing of the main thematic concepts and actors, with their spheres of action, for a given tale.[107]

While the Paris school is clearly dedicated to the study of folklore, whether or not they use the word, they have not yet moved into modern areas of folklore research. Theirs is still the folklore of the tribe in the bush, just as until recently European folklorists went after the peasant in the country-

[105] Denise Paulme, "Two Themes on the Origin of Death in West Africa," *Man* 2 (1967): 51.

[106] "L'origine de l'inégalité des races, Étude de trente-sept contes africains," *Cahiers d'Études Africaines* 30 vol. 8 (1968): 290–309.

[107] Veronika Görög, "Pour une méthode d'analyse de la littérature orale africaine: introduction à une bibliographie analytique sélective," *Cahiers d'Études Africaines* 30 vol. 8 (1968): 310–17.

side and American folklorists tracked down the mountaineer in Appalachia. But newer and broader perspectives are taking the fieldworkers into the cities, the factories, the entertainment world, the schools and universities. No one has scratched the folklore in African cities, where tribal peoples commingle and urban cults of magic and ju-ju flourish in the marketplaces amidst whizzing autos. How potentially rich are the traditions of modern Africa can be seen in a vivacious report by a young American student, John Vlach, currently a doctoral candidate in folklore at Indiana University, who noted evolving folk traditions at the University of Ghana in Legon.[108] These traditions clustered most densely around Commonwealth Hall, a residential building opened in 1958 which acquired a clientele of spirited youths from the regional secondary schools who took pleasure in shocking their older colleagues in the other halls. Taking to themselves the name of "Vandals," after a reproof from a senior associate, "Quiet, you Vandals," the students in Commonwealth consciously nurtured a spirit of Vandal vitality expressed in studies, sports, and scatological behavior. As a ritual expression of the Vandal spirit, the residents of Commonwealth organized a four-day orgy each fall term honoring their patron deity, Father Bacchus, with prolonged drinking, speechmaking, singing, and parading, all heavily larded with obscenities. Returning alumni, now men of distinction, regale the collegians with memories and traditions of their own vandalizing. On Vandals' Day the celebrants sing obscene songs, now traditional, combining Ashanti chants with Christian hymns.

Bend for me to look at your vagina.
Bend for me to look at your vagina.
Your vagina, your vagina is like palm oil,
Your vagina is like palm oil.
Lover, let me come do the job.
She will open up her vagina and show me the red part.
Insert it!
Insert it!

[108] "Father Bacchus and Other Vandals: Folklore at the University of Ghana," *Western Folklore* 30 (1971): 33–44.

The orgiasts march to other halls shouting "Your anus" and "Your mother's vagina," urinate in the pond before co-educational Mensah Sarbah Hall, and end at all-girls Volta Hall, where they brandish sticks at the inmates while hollering in Twi, "Your vagina." These are but the highlights of a ceremonial schedule that finds its counterpart on university campuses in other parts of the world. Gross contests, in which fraternity brothers try to outdo each other in disgusting and revolting acts, are an undercover feature of American university life.[109] At Harvard I often heard the expression "My sister's ca-nary" pronounced so that it seemed to be coming out "cunt." The large undergraduate repertoire of obscene parodies of popular songs is now well documented in the folklore archives of American universities.

This original report by Vlach illustrates how African tribal traditions of chanting and festivity may take modern forms. As the tribal cultures move into national settings, the old traditions will find new expression. This process is especially apparent in the field of drama, where traditional theater has contributed to the evolution of modern theater.[110] In a comprehensive study of the folk, popular, and literary expressions of African drama, Anthony Graham-White indicates the complexities of African theatrical forms, in which traditional drama impinges on dance, song, ritual, festival, masquerade, and storytelling, and is often difficult to distinguish from the dramas written by playwrights.[111] He states that the role of the individual creator may loom as large in folk as in literary and popular drama.[112] Speaking of folk opera, Graham-White points out its double debt, on the one hand to the adages, metaphors, and parallelisms of oral literature,

[109] "Scatological Lore on Campus," *Journal of American Folklore* 75 (1962): 260–62.

[110] Nicholas S. Hopkins, "The Modern Theater in Mali," *Présence Africaine* 53 (1965): 190.

[111] Anthony Graham-White, "West African Drama: Folk, Popular, and Literary" (Stanford University dissertation, Department of Speech and Drama, June 1969).

[112] Ibid., 76.

and on the other to modern elements such as biblical episodes derived from entertainments staged by separatist
African churches.[113]

Surely there is no more exciting place in the world today
for the training of the folklorist than the nations of Africa.
This new scholar will be grateful for the work already done
by the oral-literature critic, the cultural anthropologist, and
the oral historian, but he will depart from their concerns with
stylistics or kinship systems or concepts of time and dating.
He will be looking at traditional cultures hidden under and
penetrating into modern ways, and he will see these covert
traditions throughout the Africa that has come to nationhood
in the 1960s.

[113] Ibid., 221–22.

_____

PART II

Papers of the African Folklore Conference

TRADITIONAL NARRATIVE

DESCRIPTION IN GBAYA
LITERARY ART

Philip A. Noss

INTRODUCTION

African oral traditions, collected most often by those interested in civilizing a people or in recording their autobiography, have been considered for many years in the Western
world as naïve tales of grotesque monsters and simplistic
accounts of man's origin in a world where his existence appeared indistinguishable from the world of nature that surrounded him.[1] Only relatively recently have Western critics
and students generally begun to discover that African tales,
although combining the twin functions of entertainment and
didacticism, are above all an art form with a full complement
of aesthetic standards.

One of the primary factors in blurring the aesthetic qualities of the African tale has been the belief that good literature
has dimension and depth while the African folktale lacks
description and therefore dimension. When the Western

[1] The original research on which this paper is based was made
possible through a grant from the Foreign Area Fellowship Program in 1966–68. Additional work was made possible through the
assistance of Mr. André Abari and grants from the African Studies
Association and the American Philosophical Society during the
summer of 1970.

reader thinks of literature, he thinks of the short story or the novel, in which description is a conscious art with paragraphs and chapters devoted to the embellishment of setting, event, and character. Or he may think of poetry with its metaphors and similes, whose principal purpose is that of description. When one reads tales that are meant to be presented orally, usually in a language other than the original, with little awareness of the cultural setting or the aesthetic principles and assumptions underlying the tale, it is not surprising if he concludes that the tales are merely action-packed episodes involving stock characters whose only dimension may be comic. Yet, to the audience for whom the tale is created, every dimension is explicit. The performance is a complete living event.

The Gbaya people of Cameroun and the Central African Republic were traditionally semi-nomadic hunters and farmers. They developed what they called *to*, an art form that was oral and dramatic. It was performed by an artist through the medium of the spoken word. When the printed word is the medium of expression, it alone must evoke whatever imagery exists; it alone must create dimension. The spoken word in contrast has many dimensions. It is heard and seen and felt; it is experienced as the narrator becomes a one-legged swinging creature, a character with a long nose or with two noses, or an ugly old lady with mattery eyes and black mushrooms all over her back, or when he is simply Wanto receiving a richly deserved beating at the hands of his wife. With varying degrees of animation, body movement, facial expression, tone of voice, and rhythm of speech, the narrator presents the character and his plight.

The narrator's audience must be attracted and held; it is not captive. The easiest way to hold the listener's interest is through action, and the Gbaya language is grammatically well suited to the rapid development of plot. Sequences of three or four verbs are quite common, as in the sentence "The baboon wandered coming came arrived found them (II, 7)."[2] But narrative action that may lead to speedy reso-

[2] All tales are identified from my recorded collection by tape and item number.

lution of the plot cannot alone sustain the attention of the listener. He wants to know not only what is happening, but what kinds of characters are performing the actions, what kinds of environments and circumstances they find surrounding themselves, as well as details such as the time of day and the darkness of the night. The oral performer must weave these details into his story just as the novelist does, but with considerably less leeway for error. Unlike the reader, who puts the book down for an hour or who skips to the next chapter, the audience either begins disrupting the performance or simply disperses. Thus the oral performer, like the poet, must create new ways of describing his people and their places and actions. His tale must be imaginative, concise, and beautiful.

Inherent in the development of the *to* was the establishment of aesthetic principles. Methods of description were required in order to provide the dimension necessary to a complete performance. Thus, the following descriptive techniques occur in the Gbaya tale as it is performed today:

1) Ideophones
2) Names
3) Imagery
4) Narrative Description
5) Allusion

1) *Ideophones*

It is perhaps misleading to single out one descriptive technique above all others, but the one that is most pervasive, and in that sense the most important, is the ideophone. The ideophone is a descriptive word that, unlike the verb (which merely states action) and the adjective (which only describes an item), creates an emotion. It creates a picture; it is sensual, enabling the listener to identify a feeling, a sound, color, texture, expression, movement, or silence through his own senses. The ideophone is poetic; it is in the purest sense imagery.

I have selected two tales to demonstrate the occurrence of the ideophone within its context. Both tales are presented in summary form, with the result that the ideophone appears in a more prominent position than it in fact holds in the full form of the tale.

The first tale is an account of action, the classic conflict of brain versus brawn, as Rabbit, or Hare, meets Lion (II, 43). The tale was told by Daniel Ndanga of Bétaré Oya, Cameroun, a man about thirty years of age, of little or no formal education, but highly trained in the traditions of his people. He is an outdoorsman—a hunter and trapper. In his ten-minute performance ideophones occur forty-one times.[3]

Rabbit customarily wanders about the country looking for food, until one day he is warned of a place that he should not visit. The king of the animals lives there and eats animals that come close. Surely a king should be visited by his subjects, Rabbit decides, but when he learns that his life would be in danger were he to visit the king, he determines to challenge Lion. He takes some eggs, fashions himself a great bell, and goes to hide in the reeds *Mɛk Mɛk Mɛk Mɛk Mɛk Mɛk*, where Lion sends his underlings for water. Soon Fox comes along *kirik kirik* and begins to wash out his water pot *hokoro hokoro*. At that, *Gbévévévévévévé!* Rabbit rings his great bell and sings a hunting song siccing his great imaginary dog onto the game. Fox tries to run away and rolls *kiliwili*. As he gets up, *tɑqq*, an egg comes flying to hit him on the head *lôp*. The egg is rotten and the hidden Rabbit now sings telling him to touch his head and smell it. He does and, deciding that he is losing his brains, he races back *bakatak bakatak* to his king. Lion does not believe the story and sends Hyena, who hears the same bell, turns to run *zak vakdilak*, and is hit *lôp* with the rotten egg. *baDambang baDambang baDambang baDambang baDambang baDambang* he runs back to burst *púrúp* into the king's courtyard.

Lion decides that since no one else can face this hidden danger, he the king must go. He approaches, roaring *pufufuk kpinggim!* and then stops to peer around *ngɛ ngɛ ngɛ*.

He roars again *tukpik kpinggim! tiktik kpinggim!* Rabbit wonders to himself what that strange noise could be, "Hm, my bell sounds louder than that," *gbévévévévévé!* and as Lion turns *ngalDak* to flee, *lop lop,* he is hit by two eggs.*
baDambang baDambang baDambang baDambang baDambang baDambang, púrúp, he bursts into his compound. The women are already packed and everyone scatters in headlong flight *pamdal.* The tale continues through another episode until they are completely and forever dispersed and Rabbit returns to Lion's former home to settle down *Deteng.*

Many of the ideophones in the tale are onomatopoeic, such as *hokoro hokoro* for the rattling pot and *gbévévévévévé* for the ringing bell, but the running of Fox *kirik kirik* is not merely the sound of steps; it represents the pattering of dry paws, while *bakatak bakatak* is the slopping of paws that are wet and muddy. Associated with running, *baDambang* does not refer to sound at all. It portrays the motion of the head up and down as a great animal gallops wildly, and is usually associated with the buffalo. Here the narrator has deliberately applied a word normally identified with a larger and very different animal to a smaller animal, and in the switch he creates comic perspective. The tale ends with Rabbit making his home *Deteng,* an ideophone symbolizing permanence. With its use here Mr. Ndanga is saying "happily ever after."

The second tale was also told by a man, the late PeDangkao Michel of Bouli, Cameroun (IX, 9). He was about forty, a man of the land, a hunter and farmer, and the finest artist I met in eighteen months of research. His tale is very different from the first. Instead of having action it is about emotions, hatred, jealousy, love, and hope. It is a serious account of brotherly conflict and wifely loyalty, and in twelve minutes ideophones occur only twenty-three times.[4]

The story is of two brothers, the younger successful and rich, the elder a failure, jealous of his younger brother and eager to kill him to inherit his wives, cattle, goats, garments,

---

* The tonal difference between *lôp* and *lop* depends on the performer's intention.

[4] See Appendix, Table Two.

and money. The tale begins with a hunting trip and is told in a serious tone with little embellishment until the elder brother sends the younger to pick some fruit that is growing on a vine high above the hot springs. Having eaten his fill, he suddenly reaches for his machete and cuts the vine *ndúng* to leave his brother suspended *ngileng* high up above the water *wɛ́ɔ́*. He then returns to town *wɔkɔkɔ* explaining that his brother was going to return another way and must be lost. Time passes and the loss is accepted by all except the younger brother's first wife. There are no ideophones as she searches day after day until *kpáɔ́* she stops and gazes at something that she recognizes as her husband high up on the vine *ngɑ̀ɔ*. She doesn't know how to get him down until she happens to stub her toe *kpút* on a root that tells her what she must do. A short while later the vine extends down toward her with her husband, who is by this time as thin as a chameleon *kɔ́nggɔ́Dí*. She picks him up *káBák* and carries him home in the evening when it is *ndiying*. She hides him and secretly nourishes him back to life until he begins to put on weight and his stomach begins to protrude a little *Dɔ́lɔ́k*. Soon *Buturu* he is well again, a healthy and strong man, and the tale ends when she reveals to the town the treachery of the elder brother.

In this tale ideophones are used sparingly, occurring only at those points where the narrator wishes to be dramatic. The first ideophone is found at the point of the treacherous blow when the vine is cut with a single swift chop of the machete. *ndúng* unites the swinging motion of the arm and the machete with the separation of the two parts of the vine. The younger brother is then depicted as a weight suspended and swinging in the air *ngileng*. *wɔkɔkɔ* describes the elder brother's return to town. Earlier in the tale, the men's hunting gear had been described. *wɔkɔkɔ* is the walk of a man encumbered with lots of gear. Not only does he return carrying his own weapons but also carrying his brother's gun and other equipment, explaining that his brother had lent it to him. When the wife sees her husband up on the vine, *ngɑ́ɔ́* indicates that the vine and its leaves are completely dried up, and *kɔ́nggɔ́Dí* not only describes his emaciation but also shows him to be shriveled and curled up. As his wife picks him up *káBák*, the listener further learns that he is almost weightless, for only that which is very light can be snatched *káBák* to oneself.

Thus, from these tales it is evident that the ideophone is a means of description. It is also a concise way of adding additional dimension to that which has been described in simple action. Further, there is the possibility for creativeness in stretching the range of meaning associated with a given ideophone to create original and unique imagery in the manner in which a poet combines words to form the uncommon from the common.

2) Names

In any literary tradition, names may be a device for telling the reader something about the character bearing the name. This is particularly true of the African traditions of praise names and praise singing. In Gbaya tales, three categories of name and usage may be observed: a) proper name, b) descriptive name, and c) praise name.[5]

The most obvious proper name is that of Wanto himself, the major character in Gbaya tradition. His name means "spider," a fact that may lead to an overly simple characterization as the Trickster. The name is also a compound of two words, *wan* "master" and *to* "tale," meaning "master of the tale." Wanto is the master of the tale, frequently defeated but never vanquished. His children are named Papɔlɔ "cassava stick," Tikìn "cassava stirring stick," and Gong, or Gondo, "cassava scoop" (IV, 49). In another tale (VIII, 2), the names are those of his older brothers, but in either case they reflect Wanto's character, his insatiable love of food. Wanto's antagonist is called Gbasɔ, which means "great god." The name is ironic, because it suggests a being that is suprahuman but in a monstrous sort of way. Gbasɔ is also known

[5] See Appendix, Table Three.

as *gba-yɔng-wí* "great man-eater," a more apt description of his nature.

There are lesser characters, who occur only in a limited number of tales, and many are given descriptive names that depict something of their physical characteristics. There is *té-doko* "leprous body," the name of a clan of lepers; *kpa-mɔ-nɛ-ngíndá* "get thing with the stump," a clan of one-legged creatures who remove their one leg to swing in the trees along the river; *gba-yɔng-wí* "great man-eater," a name for Gbasɔ and also for a clan of man-eating people; and *zɔɔ-né-ndíá* "honeycomb nose," the name Wanto gives himself when he is disguised in dry leaves with globs of honey beside his nose to deceive Crocodile. Dogs may also be given meaningful names such as *ngá-dìla* "powerful lion" and *mɔ-nɛ-ngai* "things with force," the former comparing the dog to a lion, the latter proclaiming that the dog does everything with great power and force.

Praise names are general terms or formulas that may be applied to anyone the narrator wishes to describe, unlike proper names and descriptive names, which are used only with reference to specific characters. The initial item of the compound name is *yaá*, meaning "one who is, one who does," as *yaá-zɔ́ngá* "maiden one," a young girl, and *yaá-ngai* "strength one," a young man. The baboons sing the name *yaá-de-dé-mɔ* to Wanto, who has unwittingly given them his honey food. When he learns of his mistaken generosity, he plots to kill them for eating his food; meanwhile they praise him, singing, "The One Who Does Good!" The girl whose hair is beautifully woven in long braids is called *yaá-kara-zu-nɛ-bójạ* "long braided hair one." The girl being praised for her black skin is called *yaá-tú-zɔmɔ* "black tree one" and the brown-skinned girl is called *yaá-gbɛ-ndaka* "red dye one." A second praise-name formula uses *zɔ́ngá* "maiden" as the initial item. *zɔ́ngá-lande* "yarn maiden" is sung to a girl bedecked in finery made of yarn, and *zɔ́ngá-yére* "buffalo maiden" is sung to the girl who appears from a buffalo hide. Thus any character may be identified for the quality, whether good or bad, to which the narrator wishes to draw the attention of the listener.

Puns and plays on words are relatively rare in Gbaya narrative tradition although very frequent in songs, but one tale includes the motif of Homer's No Man. Bat challenges Elephant to a game of hide-and-seek, and Elephant foolishly agrees to play (I, 26). First Elephant hides and Bat has little difficulty trailing him through the thick underbrush to find him. When Bat hides, his big friend looks everywhere and finally begins to call, "Ká-mɔ! Ká-mɔ!" From over to the side he hears an answering "Yéo!" It is his ear answering and he says he's not calling Ear, he's calling Ká-Mɔ! He calls again and gets the same response. Finally Bat comes out from his hiding place by Elephant's ear. His name, *ká-mɔ*, means "beside thing" and each time he answered, Elephant thought it was his own ear. Bat does, of course, often hang beside or from something.

3) *Imagery*

Imagery is not common in Gbaya narrative, although it occurs extensively in songs. Occasionally, however, a performer may use a metaphor or a simile.

In a certain tale Wanto and Tortoise set out together taking their marimbas to entertain the people in town with their song and dance (IX, 21). Along the way, Wanto suggests that they test their instruments, and it is immediately apparent that Tortoise's song is the more lyrical, his melody the more rhythmic. Wanto tricks Tortoise, catches him, drills a hole through the edge of his shell, and hangs him by a cord up in a tree. Some hours later a woman passes by on her way to draw water and sees "Tortoise riding a bicycle" in the tree. The narrator elaborates on the image of the bicycle rider, saying that Tortoise was hanging, waving his legs helplessly *yɑtųɑ yɑtųɑ yɑtųɑ*.

The clearest image is one in the formula that may precede a performance. As a storyteller is about to begin his tale, the audience may chant,

Your throat is a bell, your body a locust,
Bring it here for me to roast lest the slave eat it.

The audience likens the performer's voice to a gong that
sounds above all other instruments at a dance. The narrator's
voice will now be heard above the noise of the crowd. He
is then likened to a locust, a *nduluk*, which has a small body
and a large head. What is important now is not the performer's body, but his head, from which the story comes.
Then the formula shifts to the tale, i.e., bring it here that we
may roast it and eat it as we do the locust, lest some other,
less deserving person, such as the slave, hear it and benefit
from it.

In a tale of the Frog and the Toad (IX, 1), a simile is
used. The narrator wishes to describe two characters, the
smooth-skinned and attractive Frog and the ugly, dark-
skinned Toad. The Frog is like the Fulani, the Toad like the
Gbaya, the Gbaya narrator says, and he asks, "Isn't the Fulani
more beautiful than the Gbaya?" The story about the two
suitors continues as the Frog is accepted and receives the
girl in marriage. But the real test comes when he must provide food for his bride and her family. On the day of the
great hunt, it is only Toad who makes a kill, an elephant,
which he proudly drags through the village of his rival to
his own home.

In the tale of the hunter fleeing his wounded quarry, the
image occurs in the song he sings to his sister (IX, 44):

kponggo-ye, kponggo on iron,
    open the door for me!
kponggo, my neck is the neck of the antelope,
    open the door for me!

The boy sings *kpónggó*, an ideophone that represents the
sound of the metal door as he bangs on it calling to his sister

to let him in. He describes himself with the image of the cob, an antelope that has a long, slender, reddish neck.

A second performer sings the same song but applies the image to the girl inside the house (IX, 15):

> kponggo, kponggo iron,
>> open the door for me, kponggom kponggom,
> my sister with the antelope neck,
>> open the door for me, kponggom kponggom,
> the spear flew over the orobi
>> and hit the buffalo bull, kponggom kponggom,
> my sister with the urn neck,
>> open the door for me, kponggom kponggom.

He says first that his sister's neck is like the neck of the cob antelope; then he compares it to the thin, smooth neck of a large water urn. Both images are symbols of beauty in Gbaya tradition.

In another tale a mother and son sing antiphonally as girls approach to offer themselves in marriage. The mother sings first, introducing the girl to Ndúmé Yɛnggɛ, her son (II, 29):

> Ndumɛ Yɛnggɛ! Ndumɛ Yɛnggɛ!
> A little girl is calling you!
> Ndumɛ Yɛnggɛ! Ndumɛ Yɛnggɛ!

The boy answers:

> Mother Boye, tell her I don't want to,
> Ndumɛ Yɛnggɛ-ye, Ndumɛ keng!
> Mother Boye, tell her I don't want to,
> Ndumɛ Yɛnggɛ-ye, Ndumɛ keng!
> My body is white cassava flour,
> Ndumɛ Yɛnggɛ-ye, Ndumɛ keng!
> My legs are banana stalks,
> Ndumɛ Yɛnggɛ-ye, Ndumɛ keng!

> My teeth are fine fish teeth,
> Ndumɛ Yɛnggɛ-ye, Ndumɛ keng!
> My eyes are kɛlɛlɛ,
> Ndumɛ Yɛnggɛ-ye, Ndumɛ keng!

The boy sings, rejecting the girls and praising his own beauty, his fair skin, his strong legs, his fine clean teeth, and his clear eyes and face. Each phrase is a metaphor with nouns until the last, where he uses an ideophone *kɛ́lɛ́lɛ́* to signify clearness and smoothness. The *kɛ́ng* at the end of each refrain represents firmness, his determination not to accept any of the girls before him.

4) Narrative Description

Any person, event, or place may be described very simply in narrative fashion with the use of adjectives and adverbs, but the effect is not generally accepted by listeners as creative or aesthetically pleasing. The use of adjectives serially is acceptable neither by artistic standards nor by grammatical convention.

Tales begin simply, with no more than an introductory comment,

> There were two orphans, one little boy, one little girl; their mother died, their father died (II, 7).

Another tale begins about a girl:

> There was a certain maiden, she was very very very very beautiful; here on earth, there was not another maiden like her (VIII, 7).

Her beauty is never again described until the end of the tale, where she is freed *geDeng* from the python that had swallowed her. Drawing special attention to her height, *geDeng* shows her to be a comely girl.

One tale tells of Wanto's quest for food during a time of hunger (VIII, 9). Each day, he wanders about looking for wild yams until one day he happens into a valley that he has never visited before. A strange woman lives in the pool in the valley, a woman with many wonderful things on her body. Wanto devises a lure, a delightful song that the woman cannot resist, and

> . . . then the woman rose out of the water there *Bet*,
> and the huge thing came up like lightning *gɛgɛgɛgɛgɛ*,
> when you looked at her body, the names of the crops
> that covered it *wasawuzuu*, squash *Bilong Bilong
> Bilong*, corn, all different kinds of things. . . .

The performer here combines narration and names with action and ideophones to present a composite whole. The woman rises abruptly from under the water *Bet*, she is a monstrous creature resembling sheet lightning that flashes *gɛgɛgɛgɛgɛ* all across the sky, her body is covered with every plant that a person can name including squash and corn, the leaves wave *wasawuzuu* around her body as she walks, the squash bumps *Bilong Bilong Bilong* as she moves.

A further development in descriptive narrative is the description of one character through the actions of a second. In PɛDangkao Michɛl's tale about the two brothers, after the younger brother's wife has nursed her husband back to health, she prepares a great feast, ostensibly to perform a sacrifice for her lost husband. She invites the entire town, and when all are gathered and seated, she explains that the celebration is for her husband's death. Do they know how he died? They do not, and she asks to be excused for a few moments.

> Then she went and took her husband, *Birawandu*, she
> took this great robe, *Birawandu*, this trouser and
> slapped it on his feet, *Birawandu*, she put on shoes,
> she put on socks, *Birawandu*, she slapped on this
> white robe, she slapped on that white robe, she took
> a fez and set it on *Déng*, she wrapped a turban on
> her husband *zekeke* like a chief. Then she came back
> and got a big iron chair that her husband sat on, she
> came and took it like this and came and set it *mgbem*
> alongside the gathering next to the chief.

At this point in the tale as the narrator leads toward the
climactic revelation of the elder brother's treachery, he
creates a setting with a focus on the actions of the faithful
wife. But as the narrator recounts the manner in which she
prepares her husband for the confrontation with his brother,
the focus is subtly shifted so that her actions depict his appearance. Through the account of her actions in dressing
him, the figure of an impressive and noble man emerges.
His stature, for a time reduced to that of a shriveled chameleon, is important, but the unusual role of his wife, her
strength, courage, and love symbolized in her recreation of
her husband, are no less significant. In keeping with the
seriousness of the situation, the narrator uses the oath *Birawandu*, "son of a bitch," four times, he uses many verbs,
but he uses only three ideophones.

5) Allusion

The final category of description is perhaps the simplest
from the point of view of the performer, but it is that which
requires the most of the audience. It requires that they be
familiar with what is alluded to and that through the allusion they supply their own dimension to the tale.

The world of the tale is normally the immediate world
of the people for whom it is told. Rarely is the tale about

distant places and persons. The performer may accordingly allude and imply with much greater freedom than the writer, who must describe his scenes in careful detail. When the narrator mentions Wanto, his listeners need no further description. They have heard tales about him from earliest childhood and in their own minds they have a complete image of him. He is never described except in such general phrases as "Nothing ever gets by Wanto," or "Wanto is never one to let something go." In writing, Wanto appears devoid of dimension, but the audience knows him intimately as a unique stock character.

Animals may function as stock characters. The lion is a king of animals, the hyena is a despicable eater of rotten meat, the baboon is a stupid and ugly brute, the tortoise is the embodiment of cleverness.

There are stock places. When the storyteller observes that Gbasɔ lives on the plain, not only has he described the location but the character as well. In land where there are gallery forests with springs of running water, the dry plains stand in unwelcome contrast. There is no water, there are few shade trees, the ground cannot be cultivated, the plain is uninhabitable. A creature living there can be only an enemy of man.

In direct opposition to the plain is the valley, where outcasts and orphans are often found in tales. The little cove beside the stream is well known to the Gbaya, who build temporary hunting and fishing camps. But it is not a place where they normally live. Only those who have been driven from society or who have gone into hiding live there. The valley needs no more description. To the Gbaya listener it is vivid both in its appearance and in its significance.

The corollary of the stock figure is the character selected from the audience, "the way Brother Pierre has two children, Jean and Jacqueline," and the tale about Jean and Jacqueline begins (III, 23). Or, another one:

Listen, once there were some people. I can give an example, like Elie Barbou and his wife. They had no children. (IV, 53).

From its knowledge of the people referred to, the audience provides the character of the tale with dimension. The first tale is about the abduction of a sister, who is taken to a distant city to be married to someone who has not made the usual arrangements with her family. Just as Jean and Jacqueline are brother and sister, the brother in the story must go in search of his sister to return her to her family. The ancient theme is given life through the artist's use of characters from his audience.

A second manner in which the narrator may draw upon the imagination of his listeners is by compelling them to imagine what he is describing by using exclamations such as *kâi!* "no sir-ee!" *siidi!* "wow!" or the oath *Birawandu!* "son of a bitch!" Such interjections signal only that the event is in some way remarkable or extraordinary. It is left to the listener to picture exactly how.[6]

In addition to the exclamations of indescribability, the performer may even say that something cannot be described. He begins telling about himself and two friends as they travel to the country's capital (VIII, 13). Along the way storm clouds suddenly blow over.

> Then, as we were coming back, rain threatened like this; the way the rain threatened, it's not something to be described. And then it was about to rain. . . .

This technique at first appears to be an easy way for a narrator to avoid the difficult task of describing precisely and succinctly something that he wishes his audience to believe is quite uncommon. The best performers, however, use this device. They use it not because they are at a loss

---

[6] The frequent use of these items by some narrators suggests that they may be useful devices for gaining time to think of what comes next. They are, of course, means of affecting the tone, rhythm, and emphasis of the tale.

for ideophones, exclamations, or oaths, but because they wish to involve the audience in the narrative. By failing to describe the scene in every detail, they compel the listener to imagine what is being spoken of.

PɛDangkao Michɛl, in a second tale (VIII, 1), describes the power of Guwɛ, an Enfant Terrible who was born with a blacksmith's hammer in his hand. Guwɛ wants to challenge Rain over the drums that he needs for his sister's dance, but his father remonstrates with him:

> "No! No! Listen! The owner of the drums is Rain. Rain is so powerful that if he should thunder even from where he is now, you and I and all of us would be dead *lóe*, no one would live. Can you handle that?" Guwɛ told his father to take his advice off in that direction, but his father said, "Oh, come off it! You don't pay any attention to my warning, you'll end up in the darkness of death yet!" When his father said that, Guwɛ pointed his little finger, his left one, "Father, you get over there!" and a great big hernia stretched out from his father *Déngng* too big to talk about.

The hernia is dismissed, it has hardly been mentioned, it is barely described, but the audience is left to ponder its monstrousness. Fortunately for his father, Guwɛ taps the hernia with his club and it recedes, but a little later Guwɛ again needs a hernia and this time the narrator says that the hernia is as high as the house in which the audience is sitting.

In a blending of all descriptive devices, the narrator may combine the exclamation with silence, with adjectives, with ideophones, and perhaps even with a praise name. A young boy lives alone hunting wild game for food and for sale (VIII, 4). He kills buffaloes, dries their skins, and hangs them up in his house to await sale. One day as he returns from the hunt, he enters the house to find a meal prepared and set out in perfect order for him. In his absence a red buffalo hide had turned into "a beautiful woman like this

Birawandu." Through a root that performs the function of *deus ex machina,* he learns how the woman can be kept from turning back into the buffalo hide at his appearance. (The character in this tale is in a predicament, and a root on which he stubs his toe speaks and tells him how he can overcome his difficulty.) He confronts the woman suddenly, she goes through a series of metamorphoses, finally turning into a bottle, which he smashes, and she emerges:

> . . . a beautiful woman like this, *Birawandu, géDéng* to the floor, no sir-ee! If you look at her, it's too much! Do you hear? *kpósó kpósó kpósó,* no sir-ee! It's too much! Do you hear?

The audience is given the information that the woman is beautiful, *géDéng* describes her as a tall woman, *kpósó kpósó kpósó* portrays her reddish-brown complexion. The narrator utters the oath *Birawandu,* "son of a bitch," and twice says *kâi!* "no sir-ee!" Then he challenges the audience, does it hear, does it understand? The woman is too beautiful to be described. To the listeners the description has been explicit. Buffalo Maiden, for this is her name, in the imagination of the listeners lacks no dimension.

CONCLUSION

Given the potential of the ideophone, of names, of imagery, of simple narrative description, and of allusion, the traditional Gbaya tale need not lack for dimension. In the hands of a skilled performer, the tale is not deficient in any way. It is a complete aesthetic work of art. The conflict arises when a translator or writer attempts to put on paper, through the written word, what was created for oral performance. To fault the traditional art form for being simple and shallow is at best unfair.

When a student of literature picks up a volume such as Alta Jablow's *Yes and No* to read a collection of African tales, he cannot help but be entertained by the delightfully rendered stories. But as he looks more closely at African tradition and Miss Jablow's tales in particular, he begins to wonder whether her charming interpretations are authentic.[7] He may check her sources and find the original in R. S. Rattray's *Hausa Folklore* or *Akan-Ashanti Folktales* to be quite different from her colorful and imaginative presentation.[8]

If one reads a selection of tales from *The Zande Trickster*, by E. E. Evans-Pritchard, one gains some insight into Ture's character, but little insight into Zande literary expression and form.[9] The same is true of many of the tales in A. N. Skinner's *Hausa Tales and Traditions*.[10] The tales do appear to lack dimension; the characters seem like stock figures. And Miss Jablow's collection and the work of Birago Diop in *Les Contes d'Amadou Koumba* and *Les Nouveaux Contes d'Amadou Koumba* do not greatly help in understanding the art and dimension of African oral performances, because their work is essentially part of the written tradition of the short story.[11]

[7] Alta Jablow, *Yes and No; the Intimate Folklore of Africa* (New York: Horizon Press, 1961).

[8] R. Sutherland Rattray, *Akan-Ashanti Folktales* (Oxford: The Clarendon Press, 1930); and *Hausa Folklore, Customs, Proverbs, etc.* (Oxford: The Clarendon Press, 1913).

Miss Jablow admits this in the Foreword to her book (pp. 28–29) when she writes:

> Knowledge of the creative role of the narrator has provided me with the insight necessary for the reconstruction of those tales—those which I found recorded in the earlier volumes of published folklore as bald unadorned plot sequence, as well as those which are in my notes in similar form.

[9] E. E. Evans-Pritchard, *The Zande Trickster* (Oxford: The Clarendon Press, 1967).

[10] A. Neil Skinner, *Hausa Tales and Traditions*, Vol. 1 (London: Frank Cass and Co. Ltd., 1969).

[11] Birago Diop, *Les Contes d'Amadou Koumba* (Paris: Présence Africaine, 1961); and *Les Nouveaux Contes d'Amadou Koumba* (Paris: Présence Africaine, 1962).

One obvious cause for the above problem is the fact that many early collections were recorded in writing through dictation. There was no other means of recording at that time, and the early collector is not to be faulted. But in slow dictation and writing, descriptive devices such as ideophones are in fact usually omitted. Today, with the availability of full sound and photographic equipment, they can be obtained.

The second problem is more difficult, because it involves not mere technology, but rather the art of translation. Efforts are being made to reduce translation to a science, and answers may be forthcoming.[12] But in the meantime the problems of translating the ideophone, the image, and the name remain with us.[13]

A. The Ideophone

The translator of the ideophone has three clear options:

1. He can translate the ideophone into its nearest English equivalent such as "splat" for *lôp*, "rattle rattle" for *hokoro hokoro*, and for *gbévévévévévévél* something like "ding ding ding" or "ding dong." English does have ideophones, but to use them in this manner would, I think, significantly modify the tone of the African tale.

2. He can translate the ideophone into a descriptive phrase of adjectives and adverbs. In this manner the basic sense of the ideophone can be captured and conveyed, but the character of the original tale would be drastically changed. The tale would lose its concise crispness and would enter the realm of the short story.

[12] See J. C. Catford, *A Linguistic Theory of Translating* (London: Oxford University Press, 1965) and E. A. Nida, *Toward a Science of Translating* (Leiden: E. J. Brill, 1964).

[13] Students of phonetics and music have devised complex symbols and codes to represent sound in writing. It is not impossible to transcribe a tale using those systems, but the resulting transcription would not be meaningful for classroom students and nonprofessional readers.

3. Finally, the ideophone may be included as part of the translation. This may be unfair to the reader, because it requires that he pause and attempt to learn something of the sound system of the African language and its semantics as he tries to read it in translation. But this approach seems to be the best. The serious reader will begin to understand the ideophone and will then begin to comprehend the dimension of the original tale.

B. The Image

The image may be equally difficult to translate although literally it may be quite translatable. The significance of "My legs are banana stalks" may not be entirely clear, but the image even in English is acceptable. However, to speak of a girl's water-pot neck, even using the classical urn, does not convey the beauty of the girl.

C. The Name

Evans-Pritchard has noted the difficulty of names in translation.[14] Perhaps here, as with imagery, the translator must practice his art. Certain names can be translated, such as Buffalo Maiden and Honeycomb Nose, but others have misleading connotations in English. The *bíá* is a large rodent, but "Rat" means something very different from the delicacy the Gbaya thinks of at the mention of *bíá*. If one is to try to preserve tone and rhythm, the task becomes difficult indeed. "Get thing with the stump" may translate *kpa-mɔ-nɛ-ngíndá*, but the rhythmic effect is quite dissimilar.

In conclusion, I would suggest that for the student of African oral literature there are two requirements. The first is a thorough knowledge of the linguistic and artistic tradi-

14 E. E. Evans-Pritchard, p. 26.

tion of which the tale is part, including the formal and aesthetic principles of the art form. The second is an imaginative creativity that will enable him to capture in English the dimension of the original performance without violating the piece of art that it is.

APPENDIX

*Table One: Ideophones in "Rabbit and Lion," by Daniel Ndanga**

1. he went into the thick growth of reeds *Mɛk Mɛk Mɛk Mɛk Mɛk Mɛk*
   The thickness of the reeds.
2. when the sun rose *ser*
   The rapid early rise of the sun to about 8 o'clock.
3. here came Fox *kirik kirik*
   The leaping bounding run of the fox.
4. just as he began to wash out the water pot *hokoro hokoro*
   A rattling sound as a dried skin or something hard scraping against the clay pot.
5. *ghévévévévévé*
   The loud ringing of a great bell.
6. the grassfork *vem*
   The way tall grass looks when it has been flattened by a fork, a large animal, or the wind. Here it represents the manner in which everything is flattened before Rabbit's imaginary hunting dog. It occurs repeatedly as part of the refrain.
7. then he ran *kiliwili*
   The rolling of a large object on the ground, as a barrel or a person falling and rolling.
8. an egg flew *tǫqǫ*
   The whistle of a small, hard, thrown object.
9. *lôp*
   The splat of the egg as it hits Fox's head.
10. *fé*
    The sound of the whistle blown by hunters returning from a successful hunt. Here used ironically as the sound of defeat instead of victory. It occurs repeatedly as part of the refrain sung by the animals as they flee Rabbit.

* The translated phrase containing the ideophone is given first, followed by an explanation of the words in italics. These symbols are used: M for a double nasal, B for the implosive "b," D for implosive "d," and V for the labiodental flap. The acute-accent mark indicates high tone, unmarked syllables are low tone, the circumflex is high falling. Vowels with subscript comma are nasalized. ɛ is a lower front vowel as in "pɛt"; e is an upper front vowel as in "bit"; ɔ is a lower back vowel as in "fɔught."

11. *bakatak bakatak bakatak*
    The splatter of wet muddy feet as an animal runs.
12. and then Hyena ran *hɔVɔVɔvɔ*
    The sound of the leaves and branches as Hyena crashes wildly through the brush.
13. *gbévévévévévévé*
    See 5 above.
14. as he tried to run *zak vakdilak*
    An abrupt turn to run away.
15. *lop*
    See 9 above.
16. *lôp*
    See 9 above.
17. *baDambang baDambang baDambang baDambang baDambang baDambang*
    The up-and-down movement of the head of an animal such as the buffalo as it gallops.
18. *púrúp*
    The sudden motion of bursting into something, here into the courtyard.
19. *pufufuk kpinggim*
    The roar of the lion. *kpinggim* alone describes the crash of a heavy weight as a gravel truck bouncing over rough road.
20. I take the buffalo and throw it *ringgim*
    The falling sound of a large animal or any large object.
21. throw it *ringgim*, throw it *ringgim, rim, rim*
    rim also describes the sound of a crashing falling object, but here combined with *ringgim* to represent the rhythm and sound of Lion's roar.
22. then he stretched his neck forward *ngɛ ngɛ ngɛ*
    The manner in which Lion bares his teeth as he peers about for his hidden enemy.
23. *tukpik kpinggim*
    The sound of Lion's prey as it falls, here Lion's boastful roar.
24. *tiktik kpinggim*
    The falling of prey, again Lion's challenging roar. *tiktik* normally describes a man raising his clenched fists in a threatening motion.
25. *gbévévévévévévé*
    See 5 above.
26. as he started to run *ngalDak*
    The sudden movement to turn around and flee.

27. *lop lop* it hit the head of the great man (Lion) there twice

    The splat of two eggs on Lion's head, normally used of the sound of dripping liquid.

28. *baDambang baDambang baDambang baDambang baDambang baDambang púrúp*

    See 17 and 18 above, here combined for one continuous act.

29. and then it was nothing but flight *pamdal*

    The headlong scattering in all directions of frightened people or animals.

30. then they stopped abruptly *ríp*

    From headlong flight suddenly stopping and standing still.

31. young men, stand still *sém* a minute

    sém is motionlessness.

32. and then the strong person (Hyena) ran *hɔVɔVɔvɔ*

    See 12 above.

33. Rabbit climbed right up *hárrr*

    Climbing rapidly up a tree as a squirrel or other small, agile animal.

34. and he stood quietly *sém*

    See 31 above.

35. then he stood perfectly still *sémm*

    See 31 above, here lengthened for emphasis.

36. Hyena ran *hɔVɔVɔvɔ*

    See 12 above.

37. then he hit the bag *kpikirik kpikirik* with Rabbit inside

    The rattling sound and slow swing of the heavy leather bag as Hyena throws things at it to knock it down from where it is hanging in the tree.

38. *gbévévévévévévé*

    See 5 above.

39. *mgbot* it broke and fell to the ground with him inside

    The sudden snap of the cord as it breaks and the bag falls.

40. then he came back *horr*

    Quick movement as the Rabbit here is scurrying back to the place abandoned by Lion and his people.

41. he just made his town there *Dɛtɛng*

    Indicates permanence. Rabbit settled there to live happily ever after.

Table Two: Ideophones in "The Tale of Two Brothers," by PɛDangkao Michɛl

1. he just cut it right off *ndúng*

   The single motion of the machete and arm together with the separation of the vine.

2. the vine swung back and hung up there over the middle of the water *ngileng*

   The swinging of a weighty object suspended in the air.

3. the vine swung back and hung up there over the middle of the water *ngileng*

   See 2 above.

4. and he left his brother up in the tree over the middle of the water *wɛ́ɔ́*

   A great distance up in the air.

5. he arrived in town *wɔkɔkɔ* and entered his house

   The noise of his gear as he walks.

6. *yaa* Ngɛɛsí didn't arrive

   yaa is emptiness and nothingness.

7. she stood *kpá̤ɔ̤*

   Standing still peering carefully in search of a lost item.

8. the vine had dried up together with him *ngą̀ǫ̀*

   Refers to the dried leaves on the vine.

9. then *kpút,* she stubbed her toe

   The sound of stubbing one's toe on a root or stump.

10. he was thin like a chameleon *kɔ́ngg5Dí*

    Something very thin and twisted, shriveled up.

11. she took her husband *káBák*

    The quick easy motion of picking up and taking to oneself something that is nearly weightless.

12. when it became *ndíying*

    Twilight darkness when a person can barely see.

13. her husband's stomach was getting a little fat *Dɔ́lɔ̀k*

    A person's stomach that begins to protrude as a man puts on weight.

14. *Buturu* her husband became healthy and strong

    A man who is fully mature, healthy and muscular.

15. he argued with the wives *sókɔ́lɔ́kɔ́ɔ́*

    The sound of heated argument as voices rise over each other and no one listens to what another is saying.

16. she swept outside the door *pém pém pém pémpém*
    Clearing a large area of ground as when clearing weeds or sweeping up refuse.
17. she put them all in the storehouse *rík rík*
    Arranging objects side by side in order and in quantity.
18. they put down skins on the ground *fík fík fík fík*
    Placing skins or mats side by side on the ground in such a way that the entire area is covered.
19. and they all sat on the chairs *rík rík rík rík*
    See 17 above.
20. she set it *Déng*
    Setting something small on top of something larger, here the fez placed lightly atop the husband's head.
21. she wrapped a turban on her husband's head *zekeke* like a chief
    The curving bulk of a large turban worn by a great man.
22. she set it down *mgbem*
    Setting a heavy object on the ground with a solid thud.
23. night fell *tírr*
    The arrival of night while people are still engaged in an activity, as the feast here continuing into the night.

Table Three: Names Occurring in Gbaya Tales

A. Proper Names: Common Characters
   1. wanto   "spider; master of the tale"
      The main character in Gbaya tales.
   2. papɔlɔ (IV, 49)   "cassava stick"
   3. tikìn (IV, 49)   "cassava stirring stick"
   4. gondo (IV, 49)   "cassava scoop"
      The preceding three names are Wanto's children, their names symbolizing his love of food. Occasionally they may also be the names of his elder brothers (VIII, 2).
   5. gbasɔ   "great god"
      The antagonist in Gbaya tradition.

B. Descriptive Names: Specific Characters
   1. Bua-gɔ́n-bárá (IV, 53)   "mushroom on hard earth"
      A girl that appeared from a mushroom.
   2. gba-yɔng-wí (II, 36)   "great man-eater"
      Another name for Gbasɔ, describing his usual character; also the name of a man-eating family of creatures (X, 3).

3. gbak-tɛ-nɛ-pondo (IV, 14)   "help oneself with pondo leaves"

A man who identifies himself with the edible *pondo* leaf and who provides clothing and disguise to the leper who goes to win a wife (see 12 below).

4. gér-mé-dande (II, 23)   "neck like an urn"

A beautiful woman who is described with reference to her neck, which is compared to the slender, smooth neck of a water urn.

5. ká-mɔ (I, 26)   "beside thing"

The name that Bat gives itself in its game of hide-and-seek with Elephant.

6. kpa-mɔ-nɛ-ngíndá (II, 34)   "get thing with the stump"

A one-legged people who remove their single leg to swing in trees by the stream.

7. kúl-Bíʼɛ (II, 22)   "bank over here"

The name of a character destined to leap forever back and forth from one bank to the other.

8. kum-yɔng (I, 16)   "finish eat"

A person who eats everything he can find but who never gains weight.

9. mɔ-nɛ-ngai (X, 8)   "things with force"

The name of a dog, indicating that it does everything with great strength.

10. ndáng-nánga (VII, 13)   "one foot"

A name given to Man by the animals.

11. ngá-dila (II, 43)   "strong lion"

A name given to a dog reflecting its hunting prowess.

12. té-doko (IV, 56)   "leprous body"

A people who are all lepers.

13. wí-de-tom (I, 22)   "person-do-work"

A laborer.

14. zɔɔ-né-ndíá (II, 26)   "nose is honeycomb"

The name Wanto gives himself when he is disguised with dry leaves over his body and blobs of honeycomb on his nose.

15. zɔɔ-yíítoo (X, 4)   "two noses"

A people characterized by their two noses.

C. Praise Names: General Characters

1. yaá-de-dé-mɔ (IV, 24)   "one who does good"

Wanto's name after he has unwittingly been very generous to the baboons.

2. yaá-gba-mbɔ́yá (II, 3)   "great fatigue one"
   Rabbit's praise name for himself as he beats the large animals with a club.

3. yaá-gbɛ-ndaka (X, 4)   "red dye one"
   A name for a girl who has beautiful brown skin.

4. yaá-kara-zu-nɛ-bɔ́ia (IV, 13)   "long braided hair one"
   A girl who has long braided hair.

5. yaá-ngai (I, 33)   "strength one"
   A young man in the prime of life.

6. yaa-tú-zɔmɔ (X, 4)   "black tree one"
   A woman with dark skin like the *zɔmɔ* tree.

7. yaá-zɔk-Dóng-mɔ-ná (IX, 13)   "one who doesn't look after something"
   A person who cannot let anything pass without joining in or without doing the same and who ignores the advice and example of others.

8. yaa-zóngá (I, 33)   "maiden one"
   A young woman.

9. zóngá-lande (III, 19)   "yarn maiden"
   A praise name sung by girls to each other in reference to their jewelry and other finery of yarn.

10. zóngá-yére (II, 18)   "buffalo maiden"
    A girl that appears from a buffalo hide.

TWO BENIN STORYTELLERS

Dan Ben-Amos

Laments are premature about the disappearance of traditional storytelling in Africa. The forces of change, such as
the emergence of modern urban life, the spread of Islam
and Christianity, and the increased volume of mass communications media may affect oral literature, but they have
not eradicated it. In spite of all predictions to the contrary,[1]
folklore continues to be viable in both rural and urban Africa.
Its persistence in a situation of cultural change hinges not
only upon the number of traditionally functioning narrators
and singers, but also upon the ability of these artists to respond
creatively to novel and foreign cultural elements. Their reaction to films, radio, and records is not imitative but innovative. They switch principles of narrative-art performance,
blend genres of folklore, and form new kinds of actions of
artistic communication.

The delineation of these modifications is not an easy task.
The comparative analyses of traditional and modern oral
texts, or even photographs of different storytelling situations, are insufficient. At most, these are documentations of
the end results of gradual transformations in verbal art, the
dynamic ingredients of which it is still necessary to uncover.
Furthermore, as in any comparative folklore study, the estab-

[1] Michael Crowder, "Tradition and Change in Nigerian Literature," *Tri-Quarterly* 5 (1965): 117–28.

lishment of equivalent categories is essential. What aspects in modern African culture could we legitimately consider to be continuations of traditional elements? What are the dynamics of change in folklore performance? The complexity of these problems becomes immediately apparent to whoever researches the folklore of modern Africa.

In 1966 my wife and I spent almost a year in Benin City, in Midwest Nigeria, during which time I studied the traditional communicative forms and techniques of the Edo people. I recorded and interviewed traditional professional storytellers, both in the urban center and the rural surroundings of Benin.[2] In Bini,[*] as in many African languages, though by no means all, there are names for folkloric events. These terms are descriptive and epitomize the attributes of storytelling, singing, and dancing situations from the speaker's point of view. The Bini of Midwest Nigeria conceive of two kinds of communicative events in which storytelling is likely to take place: *ibota* and *okpobhie*.[3] The first is a family evening entertainment, as the term *ota*, "evening," indicates.

[2] This research was conducted in 1966, under a grant from the Midwestern Universities Consortium for International Activities, to whom I am grateful. I also would like to thank my helpful assistants in the field, Samuel Idah, Robinson Ahanon, and Solomon Amadasu, and Dr. Rebecca Agheyisi, who read and commented on this paper.

[*] The terms "Benin," "Bini," and "Edo" are all found in the literature. The first two, possibly of Yoruba derivation, are used by Westerners. The former commonly refers to the city and the kingdom, the latter to the tribe and the language. "Edo" is the term the people themselves use for their capital city, kingdom, language, and the tribe.

[3] The concept of "communicative event" has been developed by Dell Hymes in "Introduction: Toward Ethnographies of Communication," in *The Ethnography of Communication*, ed. John J. Gumperz and Dell Hymes, special publication of *American Anthropologist* 66 (1964) No. 6, Part 2: 1–34. In this connection see also the model for the particular event of storytelling as developed by Robert A. Georges, "Toward an Understanding of Storytelling Events," *Journal of American Folklore* 82 (1969): 313–28.

In the early evening hours after the daily work has been completed, the family may gather in the *ikun*, the central room in the house, and discuss household matters, tell traditional narratives (*okha*) and sing songs (*ihuan*). Once gathered in the *ikun*, the members of the family take their seats according to their age and sex. The head of the household usually sits near the ancestral altar, the children congregate in one corner on the floor, and the rest of the family sit on the mud benches along the wall. No restrictions or rites are involved with telling stories in the *ibota*. Whoever wishes may tell a story or start a song. However, two or three people often tell most of the narratives. The head of the household assumes a rather passive role as listener in the *ibota* and allows his wives and children to display their knowledge of Benin oral tradition.[4]

The head of the household may extend an invitation to a professional narrator to entertain the family during an *ibota;* however, this is rather unlikely. The presence of such an artist would involve subsequent modifications in the basic attributes of the situation which would transform it into the second folkloric event, *okpobhię.* This term consists of two elements: The first, *kpe*, means to play a musical instrument as in *kpema*, "to drum"; the second element, *mwię*, means "to sleep." Combined, the term conveys the notion of playing or "drumming while others are asleep."[5] *Okpobhię* usually takes place in the context of large festive occasions. These could be either rites of passage such as naming a newborn (*iheni*), a wedding (*irhioha*), or burial ceremonies (*iṟoṟinmwin*), or the annual family sacrifice to the ancestors (*eho*). The general festivities that engulf Benin in conjunction with the celebration of *igwę*, the annual ritual in honor of the

4 See Daniel Ben-Amos, "Storytelling in Benin," *African Arts/ Arts d'Afrique* 1 (1967): 54–59.
5 Hans Melzian, *A Concise Dictionary of the Bini Language of Southern Nigeria* (London, 1937), p. 143.

Oba's (the king of Benin's) ancestors, also serve as frame occasions for the *okpobhię*. The *okpobhię* is an open-ended and multimedia event in which a wide range of play activity is permissible. Traditionally, professional storytellers, singers, and dancers could provide entertainment for the participants. If space allows and the crowd is sufficiently large, several kinds of artists can provide amusement simultaneously "until daybreak."

Thus the *ibota* and the *okpobhię* differ from each other in their initial causes, duration, composition and size of audience, narrative skill of performers, and consequently in the span of attention the listeners devote to a performer. While they listen all night long to a single storyteller during the *okpobhię*, they diffuse their attention among several narrators during the *ibota*. Further, while the *ibota* is, by and large, an event of relaxed conversational exchanges, the *okpobhię* can include a wide range of possible entertainment including singing, dancing, and music playing. Those occasions in which the main activity centers around a single professional storyteller share in common with the *ibota* the basic repertoire of traditional Benin narratives.

The Bini enjoy stories about their past, and for good reason. The Benin kingdom was one of the main West African empires and its traditional history is abundant with tales of intra- and intertribal warfare, conquests, and victories. The Benin empire reached its political peak in the fifteenth and sixteenth centuries, during which time the sovereignty of the Oba was respected as far west as Lagos. The territorial nucleus of this historically mighty empire is limited by comparison to these historical boundaries. It corresponds roughly to present-day Benin Division, and consists of Benin City, its preindustrial urban center, and "several hundred compact villages ranging in size from less than 20 to more than 6000 souls. The great majority of the villages had populations of less than a thousand; four or five hundred may be taken as typical."[6] The Oba is certainly the political, religious, and

[6] R. E. Bradbury, "The Kingdom of Benin," in *West African Kingdoms in the Nineteenth Century,* ed. Daryll Forde and P. M. Kaberry (London, 1967), p. 8.

social center of Benin culture. Yet, throughout its folklore, art, beliefs, and even its political system, there are undertones of tensions between the rural areas and the court. Benin is basically a village society with a superposed or inner-grown urban, royal structure. The cultural tension between the two segments of the population has never completely subsided.

Transformations that occur within the *okpobhię* can best be demonstrated comparatively by our focusing on the storytellers. For that purpose, let us examine two narrators, one traditional and the other innovative, in terms of their acquisition of narrative skill, instrumentalization, degree of dramatization, belief system, and conception of selves. These are the areas in which change was most pronounced and which most significantly altered the nature of the *okpophię*. Neither of these professional artists is representative of the average storyteller in his generation. Both achieve a high degree of excellence in their performances, and their reputations are widespread. The effective introduction of any innovation requires the persistent efforts of a capable artist. For comparative purposes his traditional counterpart should be equally prominent as a narrator.

Such a storyteller is Aimyekagbọn. During our stay in Benin City, I became a close friend of his. In times of trouble, he often turned to me for help and confided intimate personal matters to me. Originally, Aimyekagbọn was from the village of Erua, some twenty miles east of the city, but at the time we met he lived in Benin. He had resided there for a couple years after spending most of his artistic life in the rural parts of Benin Division. No one either in his nuclear or extended family was a professional storyteller. His father was a common villager who did not hold any significant position in the rural society. Aimyekagbọn's motivation in learning the art of storytelling was purely economic, at least in his retrospective view. At first he had made several unsuccessful attempts at other occupations: He helped his brother to farm palm trees but had an accident and could not continue in this work. He began to treat the sick with medical herbs but could not earn his livelihood doing so. At that point of frustration, Aimyekagbǫn happened to listen to a performance of a professional storyteller who visited his village. As he watched the artist and the audience's reaction to his narration, Aimyekagbǫn realized the esteem the Bini had for their traditional tales about the glorious past. "A narrator will never starve among them," he said to himself and decided to learn the art of storytelling.

Aimyekagbǫn's training period lasted a year, during which time he learned to play the *akpata* and acquired a substantial repertoire of tales and songs. His teacher also passed on to him some professional secrets, that is, several cautionary measures a narrator must take in order to ensure his safety.

The search for economic security also motivated Erhengbo, the younger and innovative narrator, to learn the art of professional narration. But here the similarity between the two ends. They differ completely in the next stages of their artistic development in terms of actual exposure to Bini tradition, acquisition of narrative skill, and accumulation of tale repertoire. While Aimyekagbǫn learned mostly the rural versions of Bini tradition, Erhengbo heard these stories at their most "authoritative source," namely the royal palace. Since the age of ten he had lived in Benin, after his family moved to the city from the nearby village of Ofunmwegbe, where he was born. His father, who was active in the social and political life of the court, took his child along with him to the various official functions and social gatherings at the palace. These occasions provided Erhengbo with the necessary exposure to Benin traditional narratives. Particularly attractive to him were the details about the Oba's wars of conquest. While as a child Erhengbo was content with passive overhearing of tales, as he reached adolescence he became inquisitive and began to ask deliberately for explanation of palace rituals, meanings of symbols, and functions of institutions. He no longer accepted tales at their face value. Contradictions had to be reconciled, obscure points needed clarification, and any tale required satisfactory verification by at least two sources. Thus, while Aimyekagbǫn formally apprenticed himself to a single master and followed the Benin pattern of acquisition of a specialized skill, Erhengbo learned the traditions of Benin in a customary accumulative process of obtaining general knowledge. It was only in the last stage of his development that he turned this information into art.

This transformation did not take place without the introduction of new symbols into the storytelling event, the most important of which is the change in instrumentation. Professional Bini storytellers accompany their narration with the *akpata*, a musical instrument widely known in Africa. It is a seven-stringed bow-lute (*pluriarch*) made out of a triangular resonant box with seven rods attached at its bottom. The seven strings, which are made from either metal wires or palm-tree fibers, are wound around the rods on the one end and tied to a bar on the resonant box on the other. The distributional center of the *akpata* seems to be the Congo, and Benin serves as the utmost northwestern limit of the area.[7] Regardless of this ethnographic fact, the Bini consider two traditional figures as the inventors of the *akpata*: Arhuanīan (fifteenth and sixteenth centuries)[8] and Oba Ẹwuakpe (seventeenth century).[9] Both were folk anti-heroes, tragic figures who were part of the king's family but failed to live up to their royal status. Arhuanīan, a foolhardy giant, was the son of Oba Ọzọlua and the brother of Oba Ẹsigie. In spite of his right of succession to the throne according to the primogeniture rule, his brother cleverly deceived him and ascended to the royal position himself. After his defeat Arhuanīan committed suicide by drowning. The Bini say: "You can still hear him play the *akpata* in the lake." Oba Ẹwuakpe, the second mythical inventor of the *akpata*, did ascend to the throne, but the Bini rebelled against him by

[7] See J. S. Laurenty, *Les Cordophones du Congo Belge et du Ruanda-Urundi.* Annales du Musée Royal du Congo Belge Tervuren. Sciences de l'Homme, n.s., Vol. 2 (Tervuren, 1960). Also Bertil Södenberg, *Les Instruments de Musique au Bas Congo et dans les Régions Avoisinantes: Étude Ethnographique* (Stockholm, 1956), pp. 169–76.

[8] There is, of course, a great uncertainty about the actual dating of the Benin kings. These dates follow J. Egharevba, *A Short History of Benin*, 3rd ed. (Ibadan, 1960), pp. 27, 38–40.

[9] For a modern literary interpretation of this tragic figure see Emwinma Ogieriaikhi, *Oba Ovanramwen and Oba Ewuakpe* (London, 1966).

withdrawing all social and economic support. They paid him neither visits nor taxes. In these dire hours of poverty and isolation, Ẹwuakpẹ invented the *akpata* and played to relieve his grief. These myths of origin represent the symbolic meaning of the *akpata*. The instrument stands for suffering, social rejection, and defeat. Although the Oba himself, center of all Benin knowledge, learns to pluck the *akpata* in his youth, any other narrator who plays it in the palace is bound to suffer misfortune.[10] To avoid it he must break the instrument he played before the king. Thus the *akpata* stands in direct contrast to the established order and further symbolizes the marginal and deprived people in Benin.

The contrary is true of Erhengbo's musical instrument, the drum, *ema*. Drums are put to multipurpose use in Benin; they accompany dances in family rites, cults, rituals, curative ceremonies, and entertainment. They are at the center of social and cultural life in Benin. Hence the substitution of an *akpata* by a drum has a symbolic and not simply musical implication. It introduces cultural conformity to the communicative event of storytelling.

In his performance style, Erhengbo carries this symbolic transformation of the event even further. Traditional Benin narrators such as Aimyekagbon tell their stories in a reserved manner, letting the words, not their mimicry, impress the listeners. In contrast, Erhengbo has increased the degree of dramatization of his narration. He and his assistants enact face-to-face combat and other battle scenes of the tales, in all of which Erhengbo personifies the winning protagonist. A casual observer may suspect that modern movies inspired this dramatization of narratives. Indeed, it is quite possible that they triggered Erhengbo's transformation of the storytelling situation into a folk drama. However, the performance itself draws upon the central ritual in Benin culture, *igwẹ*, the annual celebration of honor to the Oba's ancestors.[11]

---

[10] Jacob U. Egharevba, *Benin Law and Custom* (1946), p. 71.
[11] See R. E. Bradbury, "Divine Kingship in Benin," *Nigeria*, No. 62 (1959): 186–207. A documentary color film describing this royal ritual was prepared by R. E. Bradbury, *Benin Kingship Rituals*, University of Ibadan, 1962.

This ritual culminates ten days of festivities, in one of which, *iron*, there is a dramatization of the ancient conflict between the Oba and the Uzama, the seven hereditary chiefs in Benin. The Uzama challenge the Oba and a battle between them and the Oba's defenders ensues. The struggle rages back and forth four times until the Uzama admit defeat. In that respect Erhengbo's innovation is twofold: first, he deritualized *iron* into drama by delocalizing and detemporalizing the event; he moved it from its central position both in space —the square in front of the Oba's palace—and in time—the beginning of the New Year—and moved it into the homes of the Bini, where it serves particularly the purposes of amusement. Secondly, by the very same process, he extended the range of possibilities of the *okpobhie*, a secular entertaining event, by introducing into it symbols of royalty. The court tradition also manifests itself in Erhengbo's art in his selection of repertoire. In his tales of the past, obas are the protagonists, not the antagonists as is the case in many narratives told by *akpata* players.[12]

In conjunction with these transformations in the narration situation, there is a complete change in the belief system that the artists associate with their performances. Aimyekagbon, perhaps more than any other traditional narrator, is preoccupied with the mystique of *akpata* playing. He rigidly follows the temporal rules of musical-narrative entertainment; he tells stories only at night. For him the art of accompanied narration has absolute fascination. Once a storyteller starts he is spellbound by his own art, completely removed from the tribulations of daily life. Consequently, he is likely to neglect all his other duties. According to Aimyekagbon, such an intrusion of the nightly relaxation into the working hours of the day can cause insanity. Other dangers are awaiting the narrator at dark: his melodies and voice attract the *eniwaren ason*, the night people, and the *azen*, the witches. They constitute an elusive audience, whose re-

[12] See for example Joseph D. Sidahome, *Stories from the Benin Empires* (London, 1964). These tales are narrated by the Ishan narrators; however, they bear similarity to the narratives of the Benin *akpata* players.

sponse is unpredictable. Whereas the human audience constantly responds by joining the narrator in the songs interspersed in the tale, the *eniwaren ason* and the *azẹn* do not voice any reaction to the narration. While the artist plays, they are dancing, yet he cannot see them. If he tires out and stops playing while they are in the midst of their dance, they might hurt him either by cutting the strings of the *akpata* or even by blinding him. In order to avoid these dangers, the *akpata* players have to devote the first melody of each performance to the night people, and later they have to offer them cola nuts and wine. Aimyekagbọn resorted to more strict protective devices: he constantly wore a white robe whenever he played the *akpata* to signal the night people of his affinity with them.

None of these beliefs and fears does Erhengbo associate with his performance. Two reasons could account for this elimination. The first is factual and biographical; the second is cognitive and symbolic. Traditional *akpata* players learn from their teachers about the possible dangers of their art and the protective measures that they have to take to ensure their safety. Since Erhengbo did not go through any formal apprenticeship and did not have a single instructor, he remained completely uninformed about the possible traditional hazards of his profession. Furthermore, such a belief system would no longer be functional within the new *okpobhiẹ*. The substitution of the *akpata* and the musical narration by the drum and the dramatic representation of tales involve also the replacement of the artist's notions of suffering, tribulation, and social rejection by a sense of order, security, and social confidence. A narrator who is well entrenched within the social system need not fear the dangers that hover at its margins.[13]

If for nothing else, Erhengbo could feel confident economically. When I met him in 1966 he used to perform in *okpobhiẹ* three times a week: on Mondays, Wednesdays, and Fridays. In fact, his busy schedule prevented us from establishing as close a friendship as I had with Aimyekagbọn

[13] See Mary Douglas, *Purity and Danger* (London, 1966).

and, consequently, at times the reconstruction of his artistic growth is indefinite. It was his assistant who told me about the economic aspects of his work. Erhengbo's charge per performance was four to eight pounds, which he shared with his three or four assistants. The variation in price depended on the length of his performance. He also appeared before Bini associations in Lagos, Ibadan, and Port Harcourt. In 1966 the admission fees for an evening of "Erhengbo and His Group: Concert and Dance" were five shillings for a double ticket. Aimyekagbọn could not envision such an economic success even when he was at the peak of popularity. Aimyekagbọn said that he used to appear from two to four times a week, and also that he traveled as far as Ibadan and Lagos. During the political campaigns in Nigeria in the 1950s and 1960s, the parties recruited him to provide entertainment for their village rallies. Nevertheless, he could not rely on storytelling as his single source of livelihood. At all times he also was either a farmer or a native doctor. His narrative skill served as an essential, yet not exclusive, element for his social identification. Erhengbo, on the other hand, does not have any other professional involvement aside from his narrative-dramatic performance. Furthermore, he has a new conception of self. Whereas traditional storytellers regard themselves as narrators and *akpata* players, *okp'akpata*, Erhengbo considers himself to be an actor.

The role of a professional actor is hardly traditional in Benin culture. Quasi-dramatic performances take place only within ritualistic contexts in which they function in a religious-political rather than a theoretical capacity. Hence, Erhengbo probably derived the notion of acting as a profession from external sources, either the Western or Indian films popular in Benin or the Yoruba dramatic performances with which he might have been familiar. In either case, the external influence at most just triggered a change. For the substantive modifications in the performance of storytelling, Erhengbo delved into traditional Benin cultural resources and his own recollections of childhood and adolescent experiences.

Thus a combination of both external and internal factors effected these transformations of the communicative event of *okpobhię* and the cultural conception of *okpobhię.* So far, the extent of these changes is relatively limited. Dramatic narration has not made musical narration outmoded. Every professional storyteller I interviewed, including Aimyekagbǫn, mentioned at least five pupils he had taught in the previous few years. The general appeal of the *akpata* is not fading away, though it may be more pronounced in the villages than in Benin City itself. Such a decline in its popularity may be due to the emergence of new modes of entertainment and the increase in the number of possible alternative performances within the *okpobhię.* Consequently, the share of traditional storytellers in these events dwindles somewhat. Furthermore, the invitation of a professional entertainer to an *okpobhię* generates some prestige and social appreciation toward the host. Since the hiring of a dramatic troupe costs more than the engagement of an *akpata* player, he has lost some of his prestige value. Yet, in spite of Erhengbo's success, he does not have any disciples. The youths who assist him in his performance do it mostly for the economic benefit and do not intend to become actors. In that respect, Erhengbo is, so far, a singular innovator who extended the capabilities of the *okpobhię* and modified the symbolic meaning of the performance in this event. Whether such an innovation will become stabilized in Benin culture remains to be seen.

Yet, the very possibility of introducing changes into the *okpobhię,* even if they are only idiosyncratic for the time being, is indicative of the cultural conception and definition of this communicative event. The *okpobhię* lacks religious sanctions and rigid social regulations. Traditionally, variety was one of its basic attributes, as both singers and narrators could have equally been its valued entertainers. Probably this very intrinsic flexibility of the event made innovation desirable, even inevitable. Hence, Erhengbo could creatively change the kind of performance and the content of the *okpobhię* without violating the cultural, artistic, and behavioral rules of this event.

THE ART OF
NONGENILE MAZITHATHU ZENANI,
A GCALEKA NTSOMI PERFORMER

Harold Scheub

The Xhosa *ntsomi* is the objectification of ancient songs,
chants, and sayings, the creation of a dramatic narrative
whose conflict and resolution are derived from these remembered core clichés and shaped into a plot during performance.
The *ntsomi* is performed potentially by every member of
Xhosa society—there are no professional entertainers—and various people approach the venerable images in various ways.
Storytellers merely link the core clichés together, repeating
them as often as necessary to push the plot forward to its
denouement. Performers, however, while they also utilize
the core clichés to move the plot forward, incorporate many
non-verbal elements as well, developing unique styles of performance, reining in and channeling Xhosa song and dance to
give *form* to the narrative-plot—song, controlled and con-
tributing both to the core cliché and to the poetic rhythm
of the production, and dance, also controlled and finding form
in body movement, gesture, and mime.

Of the many artists whose productions I have witnessed,[1]
one of the most brilliant and talented is Nongenile Mazithathu

[1] During my research in South Africa in 1967–68, I witnessed
and taped 3946 such performances by 2051 Xhosa and Zulu artists
in the Transkei and Zululand.

Zenani of the Transkei. Her home is on the slope of a lazy hill some thirty miles from the Indian Ocean in Willowvale District in the Transkei; she is about fifty years old, a member of the Gcaleka state of the Xhosa nation. She became a diviner some years ago, and she is a good if somewhat forbidding one. She is also an expert creator of Xhosa *ntsomi* performances. Her neighbors consider her a difficult woman, and she is feared by some, insulted by others. But Mrs. Zenani is in no way cowed by their attitudes toward her. This tall, erect woman, her face a mask of disdain, regal in her bearing, is seemingly bored with and contemptuous of the members of her audience. She pulls her red ochre blanket around her, ignores the audience and its banter, and proceeds to detail the colorful world of the *ntsomi*. She is not given to broad outward dramatic gesticulation, and one is apt to miss the extraverbal elements of her production if one does not watch her carefully. One might also fail to note the developing and warming closeness between the artist and her audience during the process of the performance, and the skill with which Mrs. Zenani exploits the considerable tension that arises between her and its members. Slowly and calmly she moves into the narrative, usually a long one, pronouncing the opening formula in a yawning, casual manner, concealing the seriousness with which she is about to create her images. She initially provides motivation for the crisis that lies in the future, avoiding the eyes of those in her audience, seeking beyond them for the ancient clichés and the creative tools that will conspire to create her work of art. Her art is subtle, and understated even when it is most bombastic. Her face and body are constantly in harmony with the developing production: a slight grimace, a flash of fear, anger, joy. Her hands work softly, calmly, deftly, molding the performance, giving a nuance to this character, adding depth to that one, her red blanket shimmering slightly and continually as her body moves rhythmically to the poetry of her narrative.

She has known these stories for years, she told me. She learned them in no formal way, for the *ntsomi* tradition, with its dependence on the core clichés for transmission through the generations, requires no apprenticeship. She learned her craft the way all performers do: she heard a plot here, another there, she witnessed a performance presented by an aunt, by a grandmother, an old friend of her parents; she picked up a detail here, a stylistic device there. She found elements of production that she appreciated when she was a member of an audience, that she cherished and remembered, then made her own. Mrs. Zenani is an amalgam of all the performers she has met; her productions have their roots in the countless productions she has seen, as a child and as a mature woman. But she is more than that, of course; she wants one to know that she is also an artist, that she has great ability to work with these *ntsomi* images, to transform them into unique, glimmering, evanescent moments of color and movement. Under her guidance and control, the images become reflections of her society, and of her own opinions and thought. Her own personal sorrow and her proud profession are frequent themes in her performances.

She utilizes the finite number of images in the *ntsomi* tradition as a poet uses language. She is faithful to the traditional images, to a controlling metaphor that stresses a society of order, of an equilibrium best exemplified by symbols of nature, but she is in no way confined by them. Her art demonstrates how wide indeed are the curbs of the tradition, how a competent artist can make the tradition work for her. Like any poet or artist, she is tied to the artistic traditions of her time. Her basic equipment consists of the ancient mythic images, and her genius is in the way that she brings them together, into new combinations; more than that, she gives the images new interpretations—a deepened tragedy, a novel ribaldry, a splendid insight. Even her many detractors, those who dislike her personally, are silent, emotionally involved in the *ntsomi* image when she is in the midst of her performance; many of them participate against their wishes, taking their cues from this artist who has ultimate control over the production, and so they become psychologically and rhythmically a part of the performance. *Ntsomi* productions are not simply for children, and Mrs. Zenani's audiences are most often composed of adults, for hers are adult performances. Many of the men who condemn the *ntsomi* tradition because it has relevance only to the oral-aural societies that are rapidly giving way to the new institutions of literate cultures will participate in the performances. They, too, have heard the narratives many times, but in form and development of theme they know that there are few artists of the stature of this one.

In her use of the various traditional elements of *ntsomi* production, Mrs. Zenani suggests the possibilities of the art form. One of the most direct and obvious ways in which she distinctively develops her *ntsomi* images is through her use of detail, particularly in the delineation of character. Her eye is generally on the character rather than the action, the latter being important only in so far as it reveals character. In fact, she seems to enjoy seeing a human in an utterly incongruous situation—putting him there, and then carefully detailing the way he reacts.

A woman gives birth,[2] but she does not again become pregnant. "Her heart was pained," Mrs. Zenani comments, "because she could not become pregnant, she was growing old and she had no child." Finally, she discovers a person who can give her some medicine that will cure her barrenness, so she sends her son to get it, with the admonition, "Don't you dare drink it yourself!" The boy gets the medicine, and, of course, he drinks it. Compare now the use of details in these three excerpts from three versions of this image by three different artists:

> 1. When she had gone, this boy took the medicine and drank it. When he had drunk it, he went to the river, and when he got to the river, he gave birth to two children, because he had consumed the medicine. One child was a boy, the other was a girl. The boy remained there at the river with these children. Whenever he wanted to suckle them, he said, "Breasts,

[2] For a fuller discussion of the use of details in *ntsomi* productions, see chapter six of my Ph.D. dissertation, "The Ntsomi: A Xhosa Performing Art" (University of Wisconsin, 1969).

breasts, breasts, be full!" And a breast would appear. Then he would suckle the children at his breast.[3]

2. When he returned, along the way he drank from the bottle. He was now in a certain place, and this boy became pregnant. He bore a child there, and he put it there in that place. . . . In the morning, the boy returned to where he had left the child. . . . As he was approaching, he said, "Breasts, breasts, be full! . . . Breasts, breasts, be full!" Well, the child appeared, and he nursed it with this milk, he nursed it with this milk.[4]

Finally, this is Nongenile Mazithathu Zenani's version of this part of the narrative:

3. When he found that his mother was gone, he looked at the medicine and said, "This medicine looks good! It probably tastes sweet!"

He put the medicine into the hearth, it was cooked, and then he drank some of it. Then the boy waited, and finally his mother arrived. He gave the medicine that remained to his mother.

"But why did he prepare such a small amount of medicine?"

"Well, I don't know! This is what he gave me! He said that you should put it into the hearth, and then drink it."

So the mother of the boy put it into the fire, and then she drank it.

---

[3] Performance 2005 in my collection. The *ntsomi* was performed on November 14, 1967, at about 1:30 P.M., in a home in Nyaniso Location, Matatiele District, the Transkei. The performer was a thirty-year-old Hlubi woman, and her audience was composed of twenty women, fifteen children, and six teen-aged boys.

[4] Performance 2040 in my collection. This performance took place on November 15, 1967, at about 12:30 P.M., in a home in the kraal of Headman Thandela in Nyaniso Location, Matatiele District, the Transkei. The performer, a Hlubi woman of about fifty-five years, produced her work before an audience consisting of three men, five women, one girl, and two boys.

Time went on for the boy, time went on, time went on, time went on—and he noticed that breasts were developing on him! The boy saw that breasts were developing on him, and from time to time he felt the breasts with his hand.

"Oh, I'm developing breasts!"

As he was developing these breasts, his stomach became bigger. Oh, the boy was pregnant now! He carried on in this state of pregnancy then, constantly afraid of what was happening. Now he wrapped himself up, he fastened his blanket together in front of him, he was afraid of these breasts of his and his stomach, which continued to grow larger. Time went on, time went on, time went on for the boy, the months came and passed, and the boy's stomach became bigger and bigger. He remained by himself, he didn't keep company with the other boys because his breasts kept growing. He remained a boy who kept apart from the others. The boy carried on like that, and the months followed one another. Ah, now this boy was truly heavy, and when the boy saw that he was so heavy with a child, he began to feel birth pains.

When the boy first felt the pains, he was away on the veld looking after the livestock, and he exclaimed, "What might have gone wrong with me?" And all this time, he was feeling the movement of the child here in his stomach. But he kept quiet, he did not speak about it, he hid it from the people. He felt that there was indeed something moving here in his stomach. He carried on like that, and when he was going through the pains, he started digging, he dug in the ground, he dug, he dug, he dug, he dug, he dug, he dug, he dug, he dug. He made a house, he made it well. He scooped out a hole, he scooped out a hole, he dug it, he dug, he dug, he dug into an ant heap. And the boy felt these birth pains. When he at last felt that the pains were especially intense, he went into the ant-heap house, and gave birth, he gave birth to a girl. . . .[5]

---

[5] Performance 626 in my collection. Mrs. Zenani produced this *ntsomi* on September 13, 1967, at about 6 P.M., in a kraal in Mboxo (Nkanga) Location, Willowvale District, the Transkei. Her

Her concern is for character, for verisimilitude of character and motivation of actions. Through the use of details, Mrs. Zenani here develops the boy's plight, and she does not fail to reflect the grim humor of his developing pregnancy, exploiting his agony. Moreover, these details, which may seem merely descriptive here, become more vividly expressive in performance. With gestures and body movements, the artist portrays the boy's enlarging body, his attempts to shield his developing breasts from the other boys, his frantic digging motions. The details provide a strong motivation for the boy's anguished question, "What might have gone wrong with me?" the question basic to many of the conflicts in the *ntsomi* tradition.

Through details, Mrs. Zenani enhances the unreal. The bizarre elements of the plot are made the more bizarre because of the concentration on the atmosphere of realism elsewhere (the long period of pregnancy, for example, and the boy's relations with his fellows). This is one of her primary artistic techniques: she achieves humor, surprise and terror by means of this detailed and curious juxtaposition of the real and the fantastic. She casts the fantastic in a known milieu, providing detail after detail about the realistic activities, most of which the audience knows well. This artist communicates her fascination with what occurs when the unknown penetrates the real. And she does this for artistic reasons. She is not attempting, in the narrative dealing with the pregnant boy, to make the boy's condition logical and in any way scientific; she makes his awkward situation more incredible by making him so real. She thus grafts onto her immediate society the activities of the *ntsomi*, no matter how strange they might be, and she is thereby able to support the basic and controlling metaphor of the tradition.

Mrs. Zenani's concern for details of character extends to actions, in the sense that she is at pains to carefully motivate

audience was made up of about thirty-five children and fifteen women.

them. Consider her use of details in this short narrative about a terrible drought:

> In a certain broad village were some men who possessed great amounts of livestock—small livestock such as sheep. And they had cattle—all kinds of livestock, including horses; all kinds of livestock, including donkeys. Everything that is raised, they had.

Thus does she set up the contrasts that will become important as the conflict is introduced into the performance: great men, for their fall will be the mightier. They are men with much to lose. And so she introduces the conflict:

> Time passed, time passed, and at this time there was a great drought. The grass was finished, everything dried up. The livestock could find nothing to eat, the rivers dried up, the pools dried up, the springs were dry, wilderness. Then it was that the people ate roasted things, they drank urine because the water was gone. They learned that this drought was also plaguing other countries.

Mrs. Zenani is preparing the way for her heroine, the young girl who will become the savior not simply of her own people but of all mankind:

> Someone said, "We have heard that there's a bird that is called *Ntakanankulu* [Great Bird]. It is said that if it drinks in the river, the river will dry up; if it drinks in a pool, the pool will dry up. This is why we must learn what we can do about it, because there is death now on every hand. A person unable to drink becomes parched, he will die! The livestock is dying! Nothing will be left! Let's seek this bird, we must try to kill it."

A large meeting was then assembled to discuss the matter. The men got up and spoke in turns, each speaking his mind:

Someone said, "What else can we do? It's said that this bird is huge, it's huge and it always causes difficulties. Perhaps it'll be too much for us!"

Another man got up and said, "Well, we must head for Embo and seek some weapons, weapons that will enable us to get at the bird from a distance, without coming too close!"

There was general agreement to the man's suggestion, and all the men then gathered together.

Then the women said, "We must not be left behind, because it is said that even if the bird *sees* a person, it eats him, it kills him! We must travel also when they go off to Embo, because Embo is far away, and they won't return for a week!"

The men agreed then that they would travel with their wives and children.

As always, Mrs. Zenani is greatly concerned about plausible motivations for all actions in her performance. Nor does she simply depend on the members of the audience and their intimate knowledge of the *ntsomi* images to provide the motivation for her. Her narratives are carefully constructed, and actions are consistently correct within the developing plot and the frame that it sets up. In this narrative, she has taken great care to depict the strength and awesomeness of the Great Bird and the fact that it is too powerful for most humans. The artist thus assures that the villain's entrance will be a grand one—and she simultaneously prepares the way for the superior wit of the hero. It is time now to introduce that hero:

There was a child who would be left behind. This child said, "Well, friends, *I* don't know how to walk!"

Not a very promising heroine.

And yet this child was a big girl! She said, "Shut me up here in the house, so that it can't get in. Tie the doors of all the houses together, tie them together here, fasten them so that it won't know how to get in. I'm staying here, inside."

"Oh! How can we deal with this child?"

"How can this child say that she should be left behind?"

"Alone!"

Well, the child does not agree to travel, so it was said that the thing should be done, this thing spoken by the child should be done because [and here again Mrs. Zenani is preparing us for what is to come] it sometimes happens that a child has a certain sagacity when she speaks.

Well, the doors of all the houses were tied together, they were laid over each other, one on top of the other, one on top of the other, they covered the distance from the door to as far away as that, they were packed together and then they were stood upright. Now the others departed.

With that, the introductory section of the narrative is at an end. Motivations for future actions have been established; we have been fully prepared for the crisis of this *ntsomi*, the arrival of the Great Bird and the resulting conflict with the child. Other performers would have abbreviated this section considerably.

But the Xhosa *ntsomi* is *not* developed by means of details. The structure of the performance depends on the basic building unit of the narrative, the expansible image.[6] We have seen that the *ntsomi* has as its dynamic center a core cliché, an easily remembered song, chant, or saying about which the narrative is constructed. The movement between conflict and resolution takes place structurally through the

[6] See my article "The Technique of the Expansible Image in Xhosa *Ntsomi* performances," *Research in African Literatures* 1 (1970) No. 2: 119–46.

continued repetition of the core cliché. The cliché and associated details and image segments combine to form the expansible image, because the core cliché and allied details can be repeated any number of times. But the repetition is never gratuitous. It has a very practical value: it is through repetition that the plot of the *ntsomi* is developed, that the action moves from conflict to climax, or from conflict in one image to conflict in another. It also has aesthetic value, for repetition is deeply involved in the form of the *ntsomi*.

The expansible image in the narrative we are considering is a chanted, formal conversation between the Great Bird and the child:

When they had departed, at the time of the second week, during which they were to return, the bird was heard, it was heard approaching, even the earth quaked as it approached. The child here in the house was frightened, the child trembled with fear. She went to the upper side of the house, she went here, there, now crouching under something, now getting up again, afraid of this bird.

The bird arrived. It arrived and stopped, it stopped at the end of the row of doors. When it stood at the end of these doors which were packed together, it said [the expansible image follows],

[chanting] The people! The people! Where are they? Inside, the child answered and said,

These people, these people, they have gone to Embo!

The bird said,

There at Embo, there at Embo, what have they gone there for?

The child said,

There at Embo, there at Embo, they have gone to seek weapons!

The bird said,

These weapons, these weapons, what will *they* do?

The child said,

      These weapons, these weapons, they will kill the
         Great Bird!
The bird said,
      This Great Bird, this Great Bird, what has it done?
The child said,
      This Great Bird, this Great Bird, it's the one that
         drank up the water in the rivers!
   Then the bird got up and it broke off four doors and
hurled them over there! Yes! And again, it said,
      I say, These people, these people, where are they?
The child said,
      The people, these people, they have gone to
         Embo!

And so it goes, the bird ripping off four more doors at the
end of this repetition of the core cliché. Had Mrs. Zenani
desired, she could have had the bird tear off but one of the
doors at the end of each chant, thus expanding the image
even further. Note that with each repetition of the core
cliché, the plot is inched forward, the suspense heightened
as the bird progressively gets closer and closer to the child.
Now, however, the performer alters the cliché somewhat,
demonstrating the flexibility of the expansible image. Through
this slight alteration, the artist is able to further characterize
the heroine, to reveal without stating it the child's bravery
in this tense situation, as she simultaneously brings the plot
to its crisis:

The bird again said,
      I say, These people, these people, where have
         they gone?
The child said [mocking the bird],
      These people, these people, where have they
         gone?
The bird:
      I said, These people, these people, where have
         they gone?
The child said,
      Nyi nyi nyi nyi nyi nyi . . . nyi nyi nyi nyi nyi nyi!

Kwok! The bird was angry! It threw a tantrum, it ground its teeth, it backed off, it was furious, it was enraged. And again it said,

> I say, These people, these people, where have they gone?

The child said,

> Nyi nyi nyi nyi nyi nyi . . . nyi nyi nyi nyi nyi nyi!

Kwok! Again it was angry, and again it threw a tantrum. But the people were now not far off. They were coming. And again the bird:

> I say, These people, these people, where have they gone?

This child said,

> Nyi nyi nyi nyi nyi . . . nyi nyi nyi nyi nyi!

The bird went to the back of the house, it was furious, it ground its teeth, it again returned and stood on the door. The people were coming behind the homestead, they surrounded the homestead, the men carrying the weapons they had brought from Embo. . . .

Thus, with the assistance of the expansible image, Mrs. Zenani establishes the suspense that is at the heart of this *ntsomi:* the endangered child inside, the enraged bird without—and the taunting of the bird by the child as the bird becomes angrier and angrier, and the people come closer and closer to the rescue. It is the classic chase sequence, its structure the expansible image, and, of course, the bird is destroyed:

The men shot it, they shot it with their weapons, and they hit it. The bird died, and when it died much water flowed out: the rivers filled, the ponds filled, and the walls of the homes collapsed because of the great amount of water that came out of this bird. Then they took the bird and threw it away, for they had no use for it, there was nothing that they wanted with this bird.

They turn then to the girl, praising the

> great work that she has done, she has helped all mankind, all of it, because we had no livestock here, we were already bereaved of many people because of the drought, because they had no water to drink.

The people of the village prepare a large reward for the child,

> And now they began dipping water, the people washed, they drank, they cooked, they ate. The grass started to come out, and the livestock became healthy, they drank—those that were as good as dead, those unable to walk, those who were lean because of the lack of water and food—everything rose again because of this child.[7]

The use of the expansible image here is obvious: the repeated attempts of the Great Bird to get into the house, to the girl, form the crux of the performance—all else is introduction and winding up. The structural aspects of the expansible image are also obvious in this performance: it forms the very backbone of the *ntsomi*. And, in its creation of suspense, in the alteration of its shape, in its formal movement, it also has aesthetic value. With the aid of interlocking details and image segments, one or more additional expansible images may be added to the original image. The plot of the narrative is suggested by the core cliché, and often it has its existence purely on the basis of the repeated core

---

[7] Performance 650 in my collection. This *ntsomi* was performed by Mrs. Zenani on September 15, 1967, near her home in Mboxo (Nkanga) Location in Willowvale District. She produced it in the morning, at about 10 A.M., before five women and fifteen children.

cliché with very few added details. Action is produced by the continued expansion of the image, and character and atmosphere, too, are deepened through the repeated image (the core cliché of which is not always as obvious as it is in the narrative just discussed). The traditional wisdom of the Xhosa people is communicated by means of the expansible image—thought and structure cannot be separated.

The expansible image doubtless has a mnemonic function: the core cliché is readily remembered, and it calls up the associated details that make it possible to project the *ntsomi* image. But the expansible image is also at the very heart of the structure of the *ntsomi* performance, and it is a key aesthetic principle. A Hlubi performer, Mrs. Emily Ntsobane, creates the Cinderella story (which her child, a pupil in a Xhosa grammar school, told to her after hearing the Western version at school) in the *ntsomi* tradition, completely recasting it, and in so doing incorporating two expansible images. In the first part of the performance, the rejected stepdaughter returns to her mother's grave on the several occasions that a dance is held, and the dead mother assists her daughter, providing her with the things necessary for attendance at the festivities. The core cliché is a chant, repeated during each visit to the grave: "Mama, Mama, come out, come out, I'm troubled!" In the second part of the narrative, the expansible image is an action cliché, involving the repeated visits of the young chief to the girl's home in his attempts to discover the owner of the slipper. Each time he visits, one or another of the stepsisters tries to get the slipper on, but to no avail, even when they cut off the flesh from their feet. Finally, at the last repetition of the cliché, the right girl is found. There is no mnemonic function as far as the expansible image is concerned here; the European Cinderella story has simply been brought into structural and aesthetic harmony with the *ntsomi* tradition.

In Mrs. Zenani's performance treating a barren senior wife who, jealous of a child-bearing junior wife, seeks to destroy her,[8] the expansible image again has a structural and stylis-

<hr>

[8] Performance 652 in my collection. The performance took place

tic function. There is no song or chant in the production, the expansible image having as its core cliché an episode—the attempt to kill the co-wife. The force of the *ntsomi* and the revelation of character are achieved not through detailed description, but through the quietly expressed, unemotionally related repetitions of the murder attempts, each attempt becoming the more frenzied, until finally and quite suddenly the audience is made aware of the profundity of the senior wife's hatred, of the depths of her agony, the frustration and jealousy that drive her.

Here is the opening of the performance and the first use of the expansible image (an action cliché):

Now for a *ntsomi*.

There was a fellow who married two wives, a senior wife and a junior. It happened that this junior wife was envied by the senior wife, the senior wife being excelled by the junior. This senior wife wanted those things that would enable her to surpass her junior. Then this younger wife was pregnant, and she gave birth. While she was still nursing her child, her senior went calling on others, asking, "What can I do with this woman? I want her dead! She's loved by my husband, and this annoys me!"

The one to whom she was speaking said, "Get a pumpkin for her, then cook it and tell her that this plant will make her breasts yield much milk. You want her baby to grow! You must prepare it yourself, but don't *you* taste it! Dish it up for her so that she can eat it."

This woman did this thing. She journeyed all day, looking in the forest, seeking this plant. But she couldn't find it! She returned. On the following day, she again went to her brother.

She said, "In which forest exactly is this plant? because I looked a long time in that one over there! But I didn't find it. I went all around that forest, I went

on September 15, 1967, at about noon. The audience consisted of about five women and fifteen children.

all around seeking this plant, but I couldn't find it! In which forest is it?"

The other said, "Go to that great forest, and look just beneath a cliff over there. It'll be there!"

She went then to that place, that woman, and she arrived. She looked, she looked and looked. She found a pumpkin, and she picked it. When she had plucked it, she went home with it. She arrived at home, and she worked at it, she worked at it, she worked at it. She cooked it. She ground it into meal, she poured it out, she made it simmer, saying, "You see, then, my sister, today I'm coming to you with some food that makes the blood of a child healthy! so that your child will grow! so that your child will be satisfied! because this plant will help your breasts to provide milk!"

Oh, the young woman was happy about this. "Yes, you are helping me, Sister!"

"Sister" is what she called this wife of her husband whenever she spoke to her, because she was the elder woman.

She had done this thing then—she took it out of the pot, and poured it nicely into a dish. When she had poured it into the dish, she cooled that food so that this woman might eat comfortably. When she gave it to her, the young mother ate it.

Kwok! It was good! "This is the best food in the world! It's the first time I've tasted it! I've never tasted such food!" She said, "Sister!" She said, "Sister, this food, where did you go to get it for me?"

"Well, I went to get it for you over there. I heard from someone else that a nursing mother should be fat so that her baby will grow!"

The young mother was fed that food. "Sister, what's this food called?"

"Well, it's a pumpkin. Its name—oh, it's a pumpkin, yes!"

"Yo yo yo! It's good! Say, Sister, please! *you* taste it, too!"

She said, "No! No, I'll not eat with you now, not from the first pot. I'll eat with you from another pot!"

And yet she spoke knowing that when the young mother finished, she would die. And this senior wife did not want to put this food into her own mouth!

The nursing mother finished—and she did not die!

In the morning she had not died, she did not even have a pain! She felt nothing at all! She felt fine! And the milk in her breasts increased.

"Oh, Sister, when will you go to get some more of that food?"

She again went; she passed on to him, to her brother. She said, "Now look! I gave her the food, I prepared it for her, and she hasn't said anything yet!"

"Does she say that she felt nothing?"

"No, she hasn't felt a thing!"

"Doesn't she say that she feels any pain at all?"

"No, not yet!"

"She doesn't even have pains?"

"No!"

"She doesn't even have dysentery?"

"No!"

"Well, friend, you probably picked a fresh one that's not potent yet! You must go and find a big one that seems to be mature! Don't pick a fresh one!"

She returned, determinedly going to that forest. . . .

And so she returns to the forest to find an older pumpkin—but again the younger wife thoroughly enjoys it. On her fourth trip to her brother, she is told that she must mix the plants together. She does so, and the co-wife enjoys the food even more than previously. On her fifth visit (note the continuing expansion of the basic cliché), her brother accompanies her to the forest, and they learn from others that the plant is not at all poisonous, that on the contrary it is good for the blood. The senior wife makes a final, desperate attempt to kill the younger woman, now with a poison that she puts in the other's blanket. But voices come to that woman and warn her not to sleep in the blanket. Then the senior wife simply gives up.

It is a deceptively simple narrative, with what appears superficially to be a rather boring repetition of murder attempts. But the power of the performance lies in the quiet style of delivery, the calm description, the deft incremental development of the senior wife's hatred and jealousy. And in this highly sophisticated use of the expansible image there comes a moment of revelation, when the members of the audience are suddenly sharply aware of what the older woman is going through, of the true torment of barrenness. Mrs. Zenani is not primarily concerned with the continued efforts to kill the younger wife; her interest as an artist and perhaps as a human suffering the same tragedy focuses on the developing viciousness of the senior wife, reminiscent of the monk's hatred of Brother Lawrence in Browning's *Soliloquy of the Spanish Cloister*. This revelation of character emerges not from descriptive details. Indeed, the performer seems almost to ignore the woman herself, concentrating instead on her frenzied actions. Character is revealed through action in the *ntsomi* tradition, and never more powerfully than in the hands of this artist who is so wholly preoccupied with character. In simple and, at least partially for that reason, potent fashion, the depravity and pathos of the senior woman are exposed; in her repeated attempts to destroy, she exposes her soul. The almost precisely repeated actions reveal her persistence, and it is in that persistence, developed by means of the expansible image, that the depths of her hatred become fearfully clear.

In *The Epic of Sikhuluma,* a performance that traces the history of Sikhuluma from his strange birth to the time he assumes his father's chieftaincy, the expansible image provides the dynamic core of each of the major parts of the odyssey, each part detailing some aspect of his growth to maturity, some rite of passage—from his success in proving himself as a youth, to his circumcision, to his marriage, and finally to the chieftainship. Two brief excerpts from the epic will illustrate the use of the expansible image as it occurs in a lengthy production. (For the first excerpt see Part III, page 528, beginning "His little brother, Sitshalotshalwana, said, "Get out! Why are you thanking him? . . ." to page 529, ending ". . . It makes no difference if I die now.") The movement of physical traveling, basic to the *ntsomi* tradition, along with the plot of the narrative, is thus created by means of the expansible image. Later in the performance, Sikhuluma steps off the grass and onto soil, so that his footprint can be found by the deadly villain, Mangangedolo, who thereupon works his magic on it.

> . . . The mouse . . . said, "Well, Sikhuluma, and now you're dying!"
>
> Sikhuluma said, "Yes."
>
> The mouse then traveled on its way.
>
> As they traveled on, Sikhuluma said, "My body feels run down."
>
> "What did you say, Chief?"
>
> "My body is run down."
>
> "How is it run down?" his wife asked. She asked him, "How is it run down?"
>
> "My body is run down, I'm weighed down by the blankets. His blanket dropped to the ground. He said, "Pick it up, pick it up, old friend."
>
> One of them picked it up and carried it. They traveled on.
>
> He said, "My head is in pain!"
>
> "What did you say, Chief?"
>
> "I said, 'My head is in pain!'" His stick dropped. "Pick it up, pick it up, old friend."
>
> Another picked it up and carried it. They traveled on.
>
> Again he said, "My back is in pain, and my legs are in pain, and my feet are in pain!" His penis cover fell to the ground. "Pick it up, pick it up, old friend."
>
> Another picked it up and carried it. . . .

The melancholy, the understated agony of the dying hero, are thus underscored by means of the expansible image.

Parallel image sets are a special and complex kind of expansible image. In their most obvious and usual form, parallel image sets are objectified, portraying positive and negative values within the society through the characters of the two humans involved. The details of each of the image sequences are the same. Each character encounters humans (frequently older women) and creatures, the first character assisting each person and animal she encounters and thus having great success, the second arrogantly refusing to help those with whom she comes into contact and therefore meeting with failure.[9]

Perhaps the finest example I have seen of the use of parallel image sets was created by the distinguished Xhosa artist Noplani Gxavu, a neighbor of Mrs. Zenani's in Willowvale District. In her lengthy production of the *mbulu makhasana* narrative, she probes the psychological motivations of her characters and the effects of their actions. She analyzes the problem of the loss of identity that occurs in the life of the young heroine,[10] and she does this by aligning parallel image sets.[11] In the first, the girl's brother destroys her sister and eats her. Then the surviving sister and her mother destroy the demented boy. In the second image set, the girl leaves the village as her mother burns herself to death, and she goes to start life anew at her maternal grandparents' homestead. Along the way, she meets the subhuman *mbulu makhasana* (its less-than-human character suggested by the fact that it lisps, that it has a tail, that it walks with a crouch and a limp), which cunningly steals her clothes and makes her wear its rags. She thus becomes the *mbulu* and it becomes the girl, and when they arrive at the grandparents' place, the *mbulu* has all the good things of life and the girl must live as a dog and with the dogs.

The subhuman qualities of the *mbulu* reflect the disharmony, the unnatural qualities of the lives these humans live. When, in the second image, the *mbulu makhasana* takes the girl's clothes and pretends to be the girl, the identity crisis that is provoked is a dramatic reflection of the tainted conditions from which

[9] See, for example, Performance 1911 in my collection.

[10] Cf. *Umkxakaza-wakogingqwayo,* in Henry Callaway, *Nursery Tales, Traditions, and Histories of the Zulus* (London, 1868), pp. 181–217. See also the version retold by A. C. Jordan in his forthcoming *Tales from Southern Africa.*

[11] See my dissertation for a fuller discussion of parallel images, Chapter Seven. Performance 608 in my collection. Mrs. Gxavu performed this *ntsomi* on September 12, 1967, at about 4 P.M., in a kraal in Mboxo (Nkanga) Location, Willowvale District, before an audience of five women.

the girl has emerged. The *mbulu* is an apt embodiment of this: the unnatural creature, human and yet not human, unable to restrain its tail when *amasi* [curdled milk] or fat are around, i.e., unable to restrain its penchant for evil, no matter how hard it tries. . . . The second image is a reflection of the first; they are the same. This is the balance of the production, the repetition, the parallelism. . . .

The girl begins the second image of the performance fresh, in the sense that she goes to be "born at home," at her mother's family's home. The first image is thus not a chronological necessity for the second, in that the second image, while it is without question an organic extension of the first, cannot exist without the first. The artist links them chronologically, the first being a motivation for the actions of the second, the first being a motivation for the girl's departure. But the connection is more than chronological. Mrs. Gxavu links the two images in many places, making the second an image of the first. . . . It is not simply that Mathula [the demented brother] can be equated to the *mbulu,* for there are areas in which parallelism is not perfect. Nor should the girl be equated with the mother. . . .[12]

The images are *parallel* sequences, the one set reflects the other, commenting on it, symbolically clarifying it. The one affirms or explicates the other, sees the other from a different perspective. There is not necessarily a one-to-one relationship between the two image sequences; rather, the second exists to speculate upon the first.

Mazithathu Zenani employs the device of parallel image sets to great comic effect in her *ntsomi* regarding a baboon that becomes circumcised. In this finely wrought production, a man is constantly being annoyed by baboons which raid his cornfields and destroy his crops. He tries various ways to discourage the creatures, and finally he confronts them: "Are you all of the same age group?" he asks.

[12] Dissertation, pp. 290, 292.

"Is there not one among you who is older than the rest? . . . Is there not someone here who is a *man* [i.e., circumcised]? Because really, a *man* would sympathize with another man, he wouldn't be such a nuisance to that man, a man would be responsible!"

A baboon asks, "What is a man?" And with that metaphysical question, the parallel image sets are established. "A man is a person who is circumcised," the man answers, "who has left his boyhood behind, who has become a man!" And the baboon wonders, "What is this circumcision?" Well, says the man, "I'll show you." He explains that

"To become a man, one must be circumcised with a knife, and then, when you've been circumcised with a knife and become a *khwetha* [that is, a circumcised lad], when you have become a *khwetha*, you have graduated from boyhood. When you have thus graduated, it is then said, 'You are a man!' You separate yourself from the boys then, and you remain with the men, and then you get married."

"But," asks the baboon, "what does this do?" The man says,

"It endows you with dignity, it gives you value. And when you're a valued member of your society, then when people speak with you, they speak to a responsible person! When you are a man, and I see you here, really, I wouldn't shoot you! I wouldn't even set the dogs on you! All I would do would be to ask you politely, 'What do you want, sir?' and you too would respond politely, and I would pick some corn for you and you would go along your way—*if* you were a man!"

The baboon then wants to become circumcised, to become a man. To assure the baboon that this affair is a proper one, the man tells the creature that he, too, the man, has not yet been circumcised. "So I'll begin with you," he says, "so that I might show you how it's done, and then you can do it for me." The baboon agrees, and they part.

Thus does Mrs. Zenani set the stage for the hilarious mixture of people and beasts, and of the sexes, that follows. She realizes that every member of her audience knows what a hallowed tradition circumcision is, and she relies on the audience to supply this unspoken and solemn knowledge as a counterpoint to her parallel image sequences—the solemnity of the one reinforces the humor of the other. She underscores this early in the *ntsomi* by speaking of the dignity of circumcision, of the responsibility that it entails—her audience ever aware of the fact that this is but a deception to keep the baboons from the cornfields. This lengthy introduction at an end, motivations now set up and actions put in motion, Mrs. Zenani introduces the first of her parallel image sets: the circumcision of the baboon, the making of the baboon into a man.

The next day the man returns with a sharp knife. He calls the baboon out of its cave, and tells it to wash its body. Then he asks the other baboons to stay far off while the operation takes place.

> He said then, "Spread your legs, spread your legs. Don't bring them together!" The baboon sat and spread its legs. The man grabbed it, he grabbed it, he grabbed it here in front, he cut it, he cut it, and put [the foreskin] down.
>
> He said, "You see, then, now say, 'I am a man!'"
>
> The baboon said, "I am a man! Kwo! I didn't realize this was such a painful operation!"
>
> The man said, "Yes, that's the way people become men in this world."

Then the man tells the baboon that it has graduated from boyhood, and that it must now remain in seclusion for two months. Moreover, it must remain by itself, and food must be brought by its own people. But it cannot join those people. Nor, of course, can the baboon raid the man's cornfields— though the man does not comment on this. After two months, the man returns, having had no difficulty with his fields during this time, and he tells the baboon that it can come out of seclusion and join the other baboons. In another month, the baboon will be a full-fledged man.

When that month has passed, the man and the baboon come together again—and for the man, the piper must be paid. The man must be circumcised. The man agrees that "A day should be set aside for my own circumcision." The baboon reminds the man to come along with his sharpened knife, and those words provide the transition between the two parallel image sets. When the man goes home, the second of the two image sets is launched. The man speaks with his wife.

"Wife!"

"Mmm, well?"

"I'm going to be circumcised over there, I'll be circumcised tomorrow. A baboon will circumcise me!"

His wife said, "*Tyhini! Tyhini!* Why are you going to be circumcised? You were circumcised long ago! Why are you being circumcised now?"

"Well, my fields would have been in danger. I deceived the baboon over there. The reason my fields are no longer being eaten is because I deceived the baboons, I said that they should be circumcised! And I said that I, too, *I* am not circumcised either. I said that they should do it first, and I'll be the last one. Now this is a touchy situation, I might be hurt!"

The man outlines his plan to his wife, telling her that *she* must go over there to the baboons wearing his trousers and coat, that *she* must go over there and pretend that she is he, and she must say that she has come to be circumcised.

> "Carry this bag of mine," he goes on, "and this pipe of mine—smoke as you go. Then you should say that you've come to be circumcised. When you've finished washing, you should sit there naked. But don't take off the shirt, lest the baboon see your breasts! Don't take off the shirt, just take off the trousers. Then you must spread your legs, spread your legs for him, and say that he should circumcise you."
>
> His wife said, "Is this a good idea? Doesn't the baboon know you? You've gone over there so often, won't it know?"
>
> "No," says the man, "it doesn't know me because I never took off my clothes, it won't know the difference between us. Just smear your face, and then it won't know you."

So the woman dresses and smears her face, and she goes off to see the baboons. The completion of the *ntsomi* demonstrates that parallel image sequences can be used for fine, if low, comic effect:

> When she came to the baboons, one of them said, "Hello!"
>
> "Hello, all of you, friends!" she said.
>
> "Yes, yes, where have you come from?"
>
> "Well, I've come so that we might do that thing."
>
> "Oh, did you bring the knife?"
>
> "Yes, I brought it."
>
> "But did you sharpen it?"
>
> "Yes, I sharpened it, I sharpened it yesterday."
>
> "All right then, go and wash."
>
> The woman went to wash, and the baboon followed her. It arrived and said, "Take off your clothes now."

The woman took off her trousers, but she left the shirt on. Then she took the knife and gave it to the baboon, sharpened. The baboon approached then, and the woman spread her legs.

The baboon said, "Yo! Yo yo yo yo yo! *Who circumcised you so badly?* Who hurt you so much? Who hacked you so *totally?* Oh oh oh oh oh! I can't bring myself to circumcise you, you're terribly mutilated, *horribly* mutilated! Go! Go, go! It doesn't matter, it doesn't matter, friend, you've been done already, *you've been done already!*"

And the woman returns to her home and reports to her husband that the baboon said that she had been done already—and thus does she rescue her husband from a difficult situation.[13]

Just as tragedy can be evoked through the use of expansible images, as in Mrs. Zenani's narratives about the jealous wife and about Sikhuluma (given in Part III), so parallel image sets can be employed for comic purposes, as in this performance. In this case, what is important is the *patterns* that have been established. The pattern that has been set up in the first image set is essential to the humor of the second. In fact, there is also the unspoken pattern already mentioned, the audience's knowledge of the tradition of circumcision—and this knowledge remains in the background throughout. Few performers, especially female performers, would dare produce this *ntsomi*, the circumcision ceremony being a very sacred matter among the Gcaleka people. (Note, too, that there are no men in the audience.) The absurdity of the circumcision of the baboon is brought into sharp focus because of the contrast with the actual rite of circumcision, its important place in the society, and the gravity with which people consider it. The very forbidden nature of the subject of this *ntsomi* (wholly forbidden as far as

13 Performance 653 in my collection. Mrs. Zenani performed the *ntsomi* on September 15, 1967, at about 2 P.M., in a kraal in Mboxo (Nkanga) Location, Willowvale District, before an audience of five women.

women are concerned) and the manner in which it is treated provide additional tension and add considerably to the humor of the production. Humor is further evoked by the seriousness with which the man goes through the entire circumcision process, even to the three months following the operation (of course, he has good and practical reasons for doing so). The absurdity of the circumcision of the woman is built in, but it achieves even further comic effect because of the patterns already set up both by the unspoken image sequence (and its special tension) and by the image of the baboon. The audience's knowledge of what has already been established in the earlier images provokes anticipatory laughter at the commencement of and throughout the final image.

The expansible image, parallel image sets, details, characters, motivation, actions, the ancient core clichés, the controlling metaphor—these are the materials that all artists in the Transkei work with. Because of her artistic genius, Mrs. Nongenile Mazithathu Zenani is able to demonstrate the exciting possibilities of the art form: for characterization, speculation, opinion, for humor, tragedy, pathos, and always for the continued affirmation of traditional Xhosa ideals.

AFRICAN DILEMMA TALES:
AN INTRODUCTION

William Bascom

Dilemma tales constitute a large, varied, and widespread class of folktales in Africa. They are narratives that leave the listeners with a choice between alternatives, such as which of several characters deserves a reward, or which of them has done the best. Sometimes they have a "correct" answer, but often they do not. Usually the narrator ends his tale with an unresolved question, often explicitly stated, to be debated by his audience. Even when they have standard answers, dilemma tales generally evoke spirited discussions, and they train those who participate in the skills of debate and argumentation. It is this function, rather than any literary merit, that makes them interesting. It is perhaps because many dilemma tales have little literary merit, a shortcoming exaggerated in my summaries, that they have been relatively neglected; or perhaps it is because American folklorists have neglected African folktales in general.

One African dilemma tale with an answer, that may be familiar to some readers, is the Liberian title tale of Courlander and Herzog's book *The Cow-Tail Switch*. The tale tells how a hunter went into the forest but did not return. His family wondered what had happened, but after some months went by, they forgot about him. Then a son was born to his wife, and when he began to talk, the first thing he said was, "Where is my father?" His elder brothers repeated his question and decided to do something about it. They searched through the forest, and each time they lost their way one of the brothers found it again. Finally they found their father's scattered bones and rusted weapons, and knew that he had been killed in the hunt. Another brother put the bones together. One covered the skeleton with sinews and flesh. A fifth put blood into the hunter's veins. A sixth put breath into his body. A seventh gave him the power of movement. And the last gave him the power of speech. After the hunter had been purified, a feast was held. He announced that he would give his cow-tail switch, which all admired, to the one who had done the most to bring him home. His sons began arguing about it, and the whole village joined in the argument. Finally, calling for quiet, the hunter gave the cow-tail switch to his youngest son, who had asked, "Where is my father?"[1] Versions of this tale have been recorded among the Temne and Limba of Sierra Leone, the Bulu of Cameroun, the Kongo of Congo (Brazzaville), and twice among the Luba of Congo (Kinshasa).

A similar theme is found in a different tale from the Grushi of Togo, in which a chief's daughter fell in love with a python that appeared in the form of a handsome man. During the night it resumed the form of a python, swallowed the girl, and carried her off to its home in a large lake. In the morning the chief ordered his people to follow, but they found no tracks. A man who could smell everywhere followed their trail to the lake. A man famous for his thirst drank the lake dry. A famous worker dug out all the mud, revealing a hole so deep that its bottom could not be reached. A man whose arm could reach all over the country pulled out the python; it was killed, but when they cut open its stomach, the girl was dead. A man who had medicine to raise the dead restored her to life. Now, which of these five men did best? Answer: They were all equally good, and the girl never married again.[2] This tale has been recorded among the Ewe of

[1] Harold Courlander and George Herzog, *The Cow-Tail Switch* (New York, 1947), pp. 5–12.
[2] A. W. Cardinall, *Tales Told in Togoland* (London, 1931), pp. 203–4.

Togo and the Kono of Guinea, and an animated cartoon has been based on an Ashanti version.

None of the eleven texts of these two tales are to be found in Aarne and Thompson's *The Types of the Folktale*. Tale Type 653 in this index is a widely distributed dilemma tale that is analyzed as follows: I. *The Four Brothers Tested*. (a) Four brothers are sent to learn trades, and return home and are tested. (b) The stargazer sees how many eggs are in a bird's nest on a tree, the thief steals the eggs, the huntsman shoots them although they are scattered about on a table, the tailor sews them up so that they can be returned. Only a red line is around the necks of the birds when hatched. II. *Rescue of Princess*. (a) A stolen princess is offered in marriage to her rescuer. (b) The astronomer finds her on a rock in a distant sea, the thief steals her, the huntsman shoots the dragon guardian, the tailor sews together the shattered planks on the boat on which they are returning. III. *The Reward*. (a) Each claims to be the rescuer of the princess and they dispute as to who shall have her. (b) The dispute is still unsettled; or (c) it is proposed that she be divided and thus her true lover is discovered; or (d) they are given half the kingdom instead. Over 270 examples are reported from Europe and Asia, 22 for the Americas, 1 for the Cape Verde Islands, and 6 for Africa.[3]

The African evidence demonstrates that Parts I and II–III are separate tale types, since each "is a traditional tale that has an independent existence."[4] As an example of the first type there is a Betsimisaraka tale from Malagasy in which a hunter, a thief, and a woodworker found some eggs. The hunter shot, hitting only one egg. The thief stole the other eggs without being noticed. The woodworker repaired the broken egg. Having shown what they knew how to do, they went home. Which of the three men was the most skillful?[5] A similar version is found among the Ewe of Togo.

[3] Antti Aarne and Stith Thompson, *The Types of the Folktale*, 2nd rev. ed. (Helsinki, 1964), pp. 228–29.

[4] Stith Thompson, *The Folktale* (New York, 1946), p. 415.

[5] Charles Renel, *Contes de Madagascar*, I–III, *Collection de Contes et Chansons Populaires*, 37, 38, 46 (Paris, 1910–1930), vol. 38, pp. 118–19.

Two versions of another Ewe tale illustrate the second tale type: a thief, a hunter, and a cobbler went by boat to rescue the king's daughter, who had been carried away by an eagle. The thief stole her from the eagle's claws. The hunter shot the eagle when it pursued them. The eagle fell into their boat and broke it, but the cobbler repaired it. Which of the three did the greatest work?[6] A similar version[7] of this tale is found among the Popo of Dahomey, and these two tales are told together by the Kongo of Congo (Brazzaville).

Another dilemma tale in Aarne and Thompson is Type 653A, which is summarized (omitting motif numbers) as follows: "A princess is offered to the one bringing the rarest thing in the world. Three brothers set out and acquire magic objects: a telescope which shows all that is happening in the world, a carpet (or the like) which transports one at will, and an apple (or other object) which heals or resuscitates. With the telescope it is learned that the princess is dying or dead. With the carpet they go to her immediately and with the apple they cure or restore her to life. Dispute as to who is to marry her." This type is reported in small numbers from Europe and the Americas, with one instance from the Cape Verde Islands, and none for Africa.[7] Actually, five of the seven tales listed by Klipple[8] under Type 653 belong to Type 653A, which is the most common dilemma tale in Africa, with twenty-six instances noted thus far.

In a Vai tale from Liberia, three brothers were in love with the same girl. One had a glass in which he saw that she was dead; one had a magic hammock, which carried them home; and the third had a medicine that restored her to life. Which one should she marry?[9]

An answer is provided in a version from the Ovimbundu

[6] Jakob Spieth, *Die Ewe-Stämme* (Berlin, 1906), pp. 595–96; and D. Westermann, *Grammatik der Ewe-Sprache* (Berlin, 1907), p. 149.

[7] Aarne and Thompson, *The Types of the Folktale*, pp. 229–30.

[8] May Augusta Klipple, "African Folk Tales with Foreign Analogues," doctoral dissertation in English, Indiana University, 1938.

[9] George W. Ellis, *Negro Culture in West Africa* (New York, 1914), pp. 200–1; repeated in Carter Godwin Woodson, *African Myths together with Proverbs* (Washington, 1948), pp. 165–67.

of Angola. A girl sent her three lovers to bring back something never before seen in her village. One brought a casket of dreams, one a bow and arrow, and one a snuffbox. The first dreamed that the girl had died; the second supplied a magic arrow on which all returned; and the third put snuff to her nose and she sneezed. The king said that their claims were equal, and he married the girl himself.[10]

The remaining twenty-four versions of this tale, which are remarkably similar, come from the Temne and Limba of Sierra Leone, the Kono of Guinea, a second version from the Vai of Liberia, the Dangmeli, Akan, Ashanti, and Adangme of Ghana, the Krachi of Togo, the Ibibio of Nigeria, the Kpe and Tanga of Cameroun, four versions from the Nkundo of Congo (Kinshasa), the Ngonde and Zigula and an unidentified source and two Swahili versions from Tanzania, the Yao of Zambia, the Tsonga (Ronga) of Mozambique, and the Betsimisaraka of Malagasy.

I have no competence in Flemish, but I believe that I recognize four versions of this tale in Hulstaert and De Rop.[11] This remarkable collection of forty-five dilemma tales from the Nkundo of Congo (Kinshasa) alone demonstrates the number and, presumably, the diversity of dilemma tales in Africa.

"Which was the Noblest Act?" Type 976 in Aarne and Thompson, is another dilemma tale that is sometimes incorporated into Type 976A; it has been reported for India, Turkey, Europe, and Spanish America. Counting Type 653 as two tale types, this gives only four in the Aarne and Thompson index, a very small number compared to the large repertoire of dilemma tales known in Africa.

Although Type 653B involves a maiden restored to life by her suitors and ends with the question "Which shall have her?" it does not fit the general pattern of dilemma tales, be-

10 Merlin Ennis, *Umbundu. Folk Tales from Angola* (Boston, 1962), pp. 89–91.
11 G. Hulstaert and A. de Rop, *Rechtspraakfabels van de Nkundó, Annales du Musée Royal du Congo Belge, Sciences de l'Homme, Linguistique* 8 (1954): 18–22, 22–25, 26–29, 56–59.

cause the answer is a clever solution rather than a thoughtful choice; apparently it has been recorded only in India.

There are a number of African variations on the theme of rescuing a lost or abducted person, of which only two others can be given here. In an Ila tale from Zambia, a woman sent her four sons in search of their missing sister. The eldest saw her in the clutches of a lion, fifty miles away. Another made himself invisible and stole her from the lion's claws. The third killed the lion, but the brothers found the girl dead when they reached home. The fourth brother interrupted the funeral preparations and, with his magic, restored her to life. The mother wanted to reward all of them with meat, but they asked that it be given to only one of them—the one who had done the most to bring their sister back alive. To whom should the reward be given?[12]

One feature of African dilemma tales is that human characters predominate; but there are some in which the principal characters are animals. In a Vai tale from Liberia, Eagle, Dog, and Otter fell in love with the daughter of a hunter who had disappeared in the forest. The girl's mother promised her daughter to the one who brought back her husband. Dog followed the hunter's footsteps to a pool. Otter found the hunter, who had been captured by the Water People, and convinced them to release him in return for a hundred monkeys. Eagle captured the monkeys and threw them into the pool. When the hunter was released he agreed to his wife's promise. But which of the three animals most deserved the girl?[13]

A number of dilemma tales involve the mother-in-law. One type is illustrated by the following example from the Bura of Nigeria. A man, his wife, his mother, and his mother-in-law were all blind. He found seven eyes and gave two to his wife and took two for himself. Then he gave one eye to his mother and one to his mother-in-law. "He had one eye left in his hand. 'Kai,' a stalling thing had happened. Here was his

[12] Edwin W. Smith and Andrew Murray Dale, *The Ila-Speaking Peoples of Northern Rhodesia* (London, 1920), vol. 2, p. 332.

[13] Peter Pinney, *Legends of Liberia* (Mimeographed, n.d.), pp. 134–35.

mother with one eye looking at him. There was his wife's mother with her one eye looking at him. To whom should he give the one eye which he had left? If he gives it to his mother, he will be ashamed before his wife's mother, and before his wife, because both of them are looking at him. If he gives it to his wife's mother, he fears the heart of his mother, because a mother is not something to be played with. . . . This is a real problem. Dare any man choose?"[14]

In a similar Mosi tale from Upper Volta a man's wife and mother-in-law each dropped an eye in a river, and he could find only one eye. To whom should he give it?[15]

A second tale type involving the mother-in-law, which concerns crossing a river, is illustrated by a Lamba tale from Zambia that Doke entitled "The Problem." A man, his wife, his mother, and his mother-in-law were attacked by a marauding band. They fled to the river, but his canoe could take only the man and one passenger. Which did he take? Doke adds, "The solving provides much merriment. Of course, *not* his mother-in-law. His wife, then? No, he can get another wife! But he could not get another mother."[16]

In an Ila tale from Zambia a man and wife and their two mothers were attacked by wild animals. They escaped to a river full of crocodiles and found a canoe which held only three people. Who was to be left to die? The man sacrificed his mother-in-law, you say. No! His wife would not allow him. She would not desert her mother, nor he his; and the elders would not forsake their children. How did they get out of their difficulty? Answer: They all sat down on the riverbank and died together.[17]

A third version comes from the Bete of the Ivory Coast. In the course of crossing a river the canoe capsized and a man

[14] Albert D. Helser, *African Stories* (New York, 1930), p. 39; retold by Alta Jablow, *Yes and No; the Intimate Folklore of Africa* (New York, 1961), pp. 52–53.

[15] René Guillot, *Contes et Légendes d'Afrique Noire* (Paris, 1946), p. 37.

[16] Clement M. Doke, *Lamba Folk-Lore, Memoirs of the American Folk-Lore Society* 20 (1927), p. 119.

[17] Smith and Dale, *The Ila-Speaking Peoples of Northern Rhodesia*, vol. 2, pp. 332–33.

found himself in the water with his sister, his wife, and his mother-in-law. None of the women could swim. Which should the man save? The narrator added the following commentary: If you save your sister and leave your wife to drown, you must give bridewealth again (to acquire a new wife). If you save your wife and abandon your sister, your parents overwhelm you with reproaches. But if you choose to save your mother-in-law, you are an idiot.[18] A fourth version of this type has been recorded among the Kono of Guinea.

Choices of this kind do not always involve the mother-in-law. In a Popo tale from Dahomey a man was crossing a river with his wife and his mother when a giraffe appeared on the bank. When he raised his gun to shoot, the giraffe said that if he shot, his mother would die; and if he didn't, his wife would die. What would you do if you were in his place?[19]

In a Vai tale from Liberia a man's helpless mother was fed by his wife. One day she bit the wife's hand and would not let go. Not knowing what to do, the man asked the judge, and the judge asked the people. The young people said, "Break the old lady's jaw." The old people said, "Cut off the young woman's hand." The judge was unable to decide. What would you do?[20]

In a Mosi tale from Upper Volta a man fell from a tree and was killed. His first wife killed herself. The second went home to take care of the children. The third kept vultures away from the two corpses. The fourth went into the forest to be eaten by a beast, but met a spirit which revived the husband and demanded one of his wives in payment. Which would you choose? Answer: None. You should demand that the spirit return you to death.[21] In a second Mosi version and

18 Denise Paulme, "Littérature orale et comportements sociaux en Afrique," *L'Homme* 1 (1961): 38.

19 René Trautmann, *La Littérature Populaire à la Côte des Esclaves, Travaux et Mémoires de l'Institut d'Ethnologie* 4 (1927): 99.

20 Ellis, *Negro Culture in West Africa*, pp. 217–18.

21 Yamba Tiendrebeogo, *Contes du Larhallé* (Ouagadougou, 1963), pp. 77–78.

in similar tales from the Dagomba of Togo and the Nkundo of Congo (Kinshasa) the dilemma is left unresolved. A version of this tale also appears in *The Palm-Wine Drinkard*.[22]

In a Pygmy tale from Gabon, a man went to bring his friend's wife back from her mother's village, as his friend had been bitten by a snake. On the way back the woman was attacked by a leopard, which the man killed with his knife. He then had her lie beneath the leopard's body, while he went to inform her husband. During the night she was terrified by the howls of the leopard's mate, but she did not budge. The man reached home and told his friend that his wife was being eaten by a leopard. He rushed there and barehanded seized the leopard's throat. Now, who was the bravest? The friend who killed the leopard with only a knife? The wife who stayed alone under the leopard in the black of night? Or the husband who threw himself barehanded on the leopard?[23] Versions of this tale have been recorded from the Fang of Gabon, the Hausa of Nigeria, and the Bambara of Mali.

In a Mano tale from Liberia, two men were executed for breaking the chief's taboo against making boasts that they could not fulfill. A third man said that if the chief gave him a wife, she would have a child by the second time he slept with her, but that same night he and the wife fled, and the chief sent pursuers to kill them. On the way, they met a woman who gave them rice on condition that she also become his wife. A third woman threw her child into the water, parting it so that they could cross, also on the condition that she become his wife. The man built a village, and each of his wives bore a child. He raised a cow, and when it was grown he killed it and took its tail. The three children fought over the cow tail, and the women went to their husband, each claiming it for her child. Which of the three wives was the chief wife?[24] Two versions of this tale have been re-

[22] Amos Tutuola, *The Palm-Wine Drinkard* (New York, 1953), pp. 113–15.

[23] H. Trilles, *Les Pygmées de la Forêt équatoriale* (Paris, 1932), pp. 268–73.

[24] Etta Becker-Donner, *Die Sprache der Mano, Österreichische*

ported for the Limba of Sierra Leone, two for the Vai of Liberia, and one each for the Bambara of Mali, the Popo of Dahomey, and the Jukun and Bura of Nigeria.

A different tale from the Hausa of Nigeria also involves an irresistible youth. He borrowed a spear from a friend, who said he could have it as a gift. He drove the spear through an enemy chief, who fled with the spear through his body. He was honored and handsomely rewarded; but his friend, becoming jealous, demanded his spear. The young man set out to retrieve it, accompanied by his fiancée, who said that if he were killed she wanted to die with him. They met the enemy chief's eldest daughter, who gave him the spear, declaring her love for the youth, and the three of them fled from their pursuers. When the ferryman refused to take them across a river, he was killed by his own daughter, who declared her love for the youth and took them across the river. On the other side the youth died, and his three wives mourned him. A fourth girl revived him magically, on condition that she could be his fourth wife. Now, which of these women should be his chief wife? They are still discussing this subject, and still have not been able to decide.[25]

In a Mano tale from Liberia a woman asked a man to set a trap for a deer that had been eating rice on her farm. When the deer was caught in the trap, she ran and told the man; and then she ran back to the deer, undressed, and lay down beside it. The man had intercourse with her, and the deer escaped. Was it the man or the woman who let the deer escape?[26]

In some dilemma tales the element of moral or ethical judgment is subordinated to contests of skill or magical power. Some of these, like some of the mother-in-law tales,

---

Akademie der Wissenschaften, Philosophisch-Historischen Klasse, Sitzungberichte 245:5 (1965), pp. 115–20.

[25] M. Landeroin and J. Tilho, *Grammaire et Contes Haoussas* (Paris, 1909), pp. 230–45.

[26] George Schwab, "Tribes of the Liberian Hinterland," *Papers of the Peabody Museum of American Archaeology and Ethnology, Harvard University,* vol. 31 (1947), pp. 447–48; retold in Jablow, *Yes and No; the Intimate Folklore of Africa,* pp. 56–58.

involve crossing a river; but both these classes are distinct from "arithmetical puzzles,"[27] such as how can a man cross a river in a small canoe with a leopard, a goat, and a yam?[28] In all three classes of tales the characters are presented with problems, but their solutions are very different. Arewa[29] refers to arithmetical puzzles as "mathematical (logical) dilemma tales" as opposed to "philosophical (moral) dilemma tales," but for the sake of simplicity and to avoid confusion, I prefer to restrict the term dilemma to the latter. It seems characteristic of the tales of contest that usually there are no answers to the dilemmas proposed.

In a Krachi tale from Togo three travelers came to a large river. One said he could walk across it on his magic sandals. Another said he could cut the waters with his magic cutlass and walk across. The third said that this was too much trouble; he had a magic thread on which all could cross the river. Which of the three had the most power has never been decided.[30] Similar tales have been reported from the Vai of Liberia, the Mosi of Upper Volta, the Hausa of Nigeria, and from the Cameroun.

In a Loma tale from Liberia one man shot through a rock and killed an elephant. Another followed the shot, butchered the elephant, and carried it back through the hole. The third picked a louse from his head, skinned it, and sewed up the elephant in the louse's skin. The tale is entitled, "Who did the biggest stunt?"[31] Similar tales have been reported for the Vai of Liberia and the Temne and Limba of Sierra Leone.

African dilemma tales are common, varied, and widespread. Most often their characters are human, but in a few cases they are animals. Dilemma tales are not unique to Africa but, judging from the Aarne-Thompson tale type index, they are characteristically African. Without having made any

[27] Archer Taylor, *English Riddles from Oral Tradition* (Berkeley and Los Angeles, 1951), p. 1.

[28] Cardinall, *Tales Told in Togoland*, p. 205.

[29] E. Ojo Arewa, "A Classification of the Folktales of the Northern East African Cattle Area by Types," doctoral dissertation in Anthropology, University of California, Berkeley, 1966.

[30] Cardinall, *Tales Told in Togoland*, p. 201.

[31] Schwab, "Tribes of the Liberian Hinterland," p. 448.

systematic search for them, and without being able to utilize the forty-five Nkundo dilemma tales in Hulstaert and de Rop's collection, I have noted over eighty different examples of this kind of African folktale, of which twenty-five have been found with two or more versions. Because they are so numerous and so diverse, I agree completely with Arewa, who, in considering only folktales from part of East Africa, concluded that they should be classified as a special subgroup of formula tales, rather than attempting to squeeze them all into Types 653 and 976 under the heading of ordinary folktales.

Dilemma tales do not constitute a fixed genre with hard and fast boundaries. The dilemma may be omitted, and conversely the widespread tale of "alternate house-building"[32] has been converted into a dilemma tale by the Swahili. Lion and bushbuck built the same house, each working on alternate days and each claiming it when it was finished. Who owned the house?[33] Another example seems to be found in a Mpongwe version of the tug of war (Type 291) which ends with a rhetorical question about Elephant, Hippopotamus, and Tortoise, who arranged it. Were they equal? Answer: Yes, they were equal.[34] Nevertheless, many of these narratives have apparently been reported only as dilemma tales.

I agree also with Archer Taylor that it is impossible to put all the varied forms of folklore into neat pigeonholes. Yet dilemma tales appear to me to have as much unity, consistency, and distinctiveness as numskull stories, tall tales, or several other recognized subtypes of the folktale. Like Taylor's "arithmetical puzzles" they share some of the features of riddle; but they differ from both these genres in the nature of their answers. They also differ from most riddles in that

[32] William Bascom, *Ifa Divination: Communication Between Gods and Men in West Africa* (Bloomington, 1969), p. 133.

[33] Gebhard Lademann, Ludwig Kausch, and Alfred Reuss, *Tierfabeln und andere Erzählungen in Suaheli, Archiv für das Studium Deutscher Kolonialsprachen* 12 (1910), p. 84.

[34] Robert H. Nassau, *Where Animals Talk. West African Folk Lore Tales* (London, 1914), pp. 37–41; retold in Jablow, *Yes and No; the Intimate Folklore of Africa*, pp. 95–98.

they are stated in the form of prose narratives. And, unlike riddles, they often have no answers; and when they do, the answers are not objects, or even abstract concepts. Rather, dilemma tales present difficult choices between alternatives, some based on judgments of relative power or skill, and others based on moral or ethical judgments. The latter, certainly, are the more interesting and the more significant in terms of cultural values. Both these kinds of dilemma tales lead to argumentation and debate, even if an "answer" is provided; whereas, to my knowledge, riddles do not. Put more concisely, riddles have answers; arithmetical puzzles have solutions; and dilemma tales involve choices.

At least as far as Africa is concerned, dilemma tales cannot be simply defined as tales ending with a question (motif Z16), since in some instances the question is answered, and in others the tale ends in an argument and no question is asked. Tales that apparently are historically related may or may not have questions, and may or may not have answers. Dilemma tales, rather, are prose narratives, presumably not accepted as fact, which present choices between alternatives and are resolved through debate.

AFRO-ARAB RELATIONS
IN THE SUDANESE FOLKTALE

Sayyid Hurreiz

This paper is concerned with the folktale of the Arabized and Islamized parts of the Sudan. It excludes those that have received little or no Islamic influences, such as certain sections of the Nuba Mountains and the southern provinces. The term folktale is used in a broad sense, to include all kinds of oral prose narrative.

Before briefly surveying the different kinds of Sudanese folktales that I will use in the discussion of Afro-Arab relations, and in order to put this study in the wider perspective of the African folktale, I should stress common influences and unifying factors that have affected African folktales. First I must question approaches that lead to false and arbitrary divisions of North Africa and tropical Africa, or Africa north of the Sahara and Africa south of the Sahara, an approach illustrated by Parrinder's study of African mythology, which excludes the whole of North Africa (including parts of the Sudan) on the premise that the Sahara stood as an impenetrable barrier to knowledge.[1]

In reality the Sahara has never been a cultural barrier in this sense. Trans-Saharan trade routes have for many centuries linked North Africa (Tunisia, Morocco, and Algeria) and the coast of the Mediterranean economically and cul-

[1] Geoffrey Parrinder, *African Mythology* (London, 1967), p. 10.

turally with West Africa.[2] In the same way, Darb al Arba'in, or the forty days' route from Assuit across the Sahara to the Nile Valley, central Sudan, and Dar Fur and Kanam, linked the Sudan with North and West Africa. Cultural links between the Sudan and Central and West Africa were strongly established through trade and pilgrimage routes across the Sudan to Mecca. Migrations from the Sudan to Central and West Africa and vice versa were also frequent. Among the most recent of these movements is the 1903 migration of Burno and their settlement in the Sudan under their leader Mohammed Bello Mai Wurno.[3] These movements have undoubtedly assisted the dissemination of tradition within the African continent and should be examined in the investigation of similarities in African folklore.

Islam has also created a network of communications within the African continent and is responsible for a certain degree of similarity and unity in the traditions of Muslim Africans. For instance, legends about a Muslim Arab ancestor, coming from outside, settling among the African natives, mixing with them, and introducing them to Islam are common among the Abdallab,[4] the Nuba,[5] and the Fur[6] of the Sudan as well as in Mali[7] and among the Hausa[8] of Nigeria.

If we try to elicit the categorization that is perceived and implicitly differentiated by the natives, we find they make a distinction between fiction and non-fiction. They refer to the

[2] For an elaborate examination of trade and culture routes across the Sahara, see E. W. Bovil, *The Golden Trade of the Moors* (London, 1968).

[3] Isam Hassoun, "Western Migration into the Sudan," *Sudan Notes and Records* 33 (1952): 62–72.

[4] Ahmed Nasr, "Writing the History of the Abdallab from their Oral Tradition" (Arabic), *Sudanese Heritage Series*, no. 7 (Khartoum, 1969), pp. 14–24.

[5] R. C. Stevenson, "Some Aspects of the Spread of Islam in the Nuba Mountains," in I. M. Lewis (ed.), *Islam in Tropical Africa* (London, 1966).

[6] Na'aum Shuqair, *The History of the Sudan* (Arabic) (Cairo, 1903), pp. 111–12.

[7] D. T. Niane, *Sundiata: an Epic of Old Mali*, translated by G. D. Pickett (London, 1969), p. 2.

[8] R. S. Rattray, *Hausa Folklore* (London, 1913), vol. 1, pp. 7–8.

fictitious tales as *hujwa* (pl. *huja*), an Arabic word meaning wisdom and used in the Sudan to denote both fictitious tale and riddle. Non-fictional tales are referred to by the words *gissa* and *hikaya*, which are used synonymously to mean story. Although there are no terms to denote minor categories, the Sudanese are implicitly aware of further distinctions within non-fictional narratives.

(1) Historical stories, which are equivalent to historical legends.
(2) Religious stories, which include Muslim saints' legends and faith-promoting episodes.
(3) Adventure and love stories, also considered to be realistic, and equivalent to the European sense of *novelle*.
(4) Humorous stories, namely jokes and anecdotes related to everyday life. Some revolve around a traditional character called Jiha.

These categories are not as sharp and as clearly defined as they appear on paper and may overlap. For instance, adventure stories are sometimes told as historical traditions.

The *hujwa* starts with a traditional formula. Its narration during daytime is tabooed.[9] Although some narrators may not abide by this taboo, they are aware of its existence and think of the *hujwa* as something set apart from real stories. The world view of the *hujwa* is dominated by magic, witchcraft, and sorcery and characterized by numerous episodes about animals and intimate relations between man and animal. It is primarily realized within the context of an African setting that has been exposed to Arabian and Islamic influences. But it is not cut off from the rest of the world, nor from the body of the folktale tradition, though similarities and influences remain to be investigated. Among thirty Sudanese tales which I have collected and which I referred to while writing this paper, I have identified such international stories as Type 551 *The Sons on a Quest for a Wonderful*

[9] Abd Allah El-Tayyib, "The Changing Customs of the Riverain Sudan," *Sudan Notes and Records* 37 (1956): 65.

Remedy for Their Father, Type 552A *Three Animals as Brothers-in-Law,* Type 511A *The Little Red Ox,* and Type 532 *The Helpful Horse.* Examples of adventure stories are found in the cycle of Abu Zeid Al Hilali, episodes of which are told in many parts of the Sudan. They function as historical legends among some tribes of Kordofan who believe themselves to be descendants of the hero Abu Zeid.

As regards the historical aspect, the cycle of Abu Zeid Al Hilali suggests that some of the Arab tribes coming to the Sudan were motivated by the search for better grazing ground for their animals, and left Arabia, among other reasons, because of the arid land and a succession of dry seasons. These stories also disclose that through wars and intermarriages with the natives, Abu Zeid's tribe Beni Hilal settled in certain parts of the Sudan either permanently or temporarily on their way to other places. Many locations at which Abu Zeid is believed to have settled, or crossed, bear names related to him or to his tribe. Among these places are Al Hilaliya, in the Blue Nile province, Tamr Abu Zeid in the northern province, and Makhadat Abu Zeid on the White Nile. Stories in the cycle also refer to similar movements of the Beni Hilal tribe to Egypt and Tunisia. Historical information supports the view that such wanderings did take place in the fourteenth and fifteenth centuries,[10] and that the movement of Beni Hilal to the Sudan was an offshoot of their migration to Egypt and Tunisia.

Some tales also stress the relationship between an Arab refugee and an African chief who offers him asylum and kind treatment. This relationship is most common in the narratives of those tribes anxious to emphasize their Arab ancestry. Many tales assign the collapse of dynasties in Arabia as the reason for Arabs seeking asylum in Africa.

Although traditions of some Sudanese tribes, such as the Ja'aliyyn, tend to ignore ethnic links with Africa, many Sudanese tribes attempt to identify their members ethnically with Africa as well as with Arabia. This identification is achieved through an African maternal ancestor and an Arab

[10] Yusuf Hasan, *The Arabs and the Sudan* (Edinburgh, 1966), p. 168.

paternal ancestor. Examples of such historical legends are common among the Masaba'at, the Humr, the Baqqara, the Fur, and the Abdallab. These legends reflect the dilemma of the Sudanese and try to resolve it by a compromise that considers the Sudanese as Afro-Arabs belonging to both races and sharing features related to both cultures.

The stories of Abu Zeid Al Hilali are also relevant to the discussion of ethnic relations, since through these traditions some Sudanese unconsciously try to identify themselves with Africa through the character of Abu Zeid, who is noted for his blackness. The blackness of Abu Zeid is not unique to the Sudanese oicotype,[11] and is a trait present in oral and literary variants told in other Arab countries, yet it has special significance for the Sudanese. Abu Zeid, unlike the rest of his people, the Arabs of Beni Hilal, was born black, and as a consequence he and his mother suffered. He was forced to grow up away from his father and the land of his paternal ancestors, and yet he came to be more valiant and worthy than others who did not have his blackness and who did not suffer because of their color.

These matters have great significance for a Sudanese, especially when he tries to see himself within the context of an Arab world. The predicament of Abu Zeid is analogous to the predicament of the black Sudanese as a whole, and they identify with him. Hence the cycle of Abu Zeid is the most popular and the most frequently narrated in many parts of the Arabized Sudan, where tales of Abu Zeid have come to exhibit many features of the folk hero, such as the motifs of abnormal birth and growth and of the hero's rejection by his father.

Tales of Abu Zeid are not unique in this sense. A number of stories that have gained popularity in some Arabized parts of the Sudan deal with Afro-Arab relations and exploit color and ethnicity. In most of these tales the hero is black and he is either born in black Africa or his mother or father is African. The romances of Antar and Seif Ibn Ziyazan are ex-

11 This is the folklorists' term for the special regional form of an international folktale.

amples.[12] So it can be suggested that the oicotypes of these stories serve as realizations of unconscious desires and tensions and have psychological significance for their narrators as well as for the audiences. Through these folktales a Sudanese who identifies with the hero tries to assert his blackness and his Africanism in the non-black Arab context in which he finds himself. It is possible that these stories perform a similar function among other dark-skinned Arabized Africans, as are some Egyptians.[13]

Many Sudanese folktales, especially the historical legends dealing with the Muslim Arab coming from outside and settling in the Sudan, portray this newcomer as a wise, knowledgeable man who brings Islam and divine knowledge with him and serves to educate the people. In contrast to the image of the suspicious native in the adventure stories, the native in the historical legends plays the role of the welcoming host, who readily accepts and embraces this newcomer. Once Islam has been spread through the work of this "wise stranger," and the basic fundamentals of the religion, such as the uniqueness and absoluteness of Allah, have been established, a certain pattern of compromise develops that is reflected both in the content and classification of folktales. For instance, the *hujwa* shows a minimum of Islamic influence, mainly because, being a fictional not a believed tale, it does not pose any threat to Islam, and also because its content of magic, sorcery, and witchcraft does not actually conflict with Islam. The Quran is teeming with mystical forces such as angels and jinn.

The main genre that was influenced and disrupted by Islam is the myth, because by its very nature the myth is expected to be a threat to Islam. So the indigenous Sudanese myth had the choice of receding into the region of *huja* and becoming fiction, or submitting to the spirit of Islam and becoming an Islamic story or Muslim saint's legend, or else falling into oblivion. An example of what has happened to a

12 Abd Al Majid Abdin, *The Folktale in the Sudan* (Arabic) (Khartoum, 1964), p. 19.
13 Abd Al Hamid Yunis, *Al Hilaliya in History and Folk Literature* (Arabic) (Cairo, 1956), p. 199.

myth is shown in the religious legend given in Part III "The Punishment of the Elephants." Although the resemblance of some variants of this narrative to an etiological myth is clear, the story has been removed from the remote past of the myth to the historical past, the time of Sheikh Mohammed Al Hamin. Whatever mythical features it still preserves, remain within a hidden stratum dominated by Islam. Another major change affected the indigenous creation myth dealing with such themes as how food came to earth, how death came to earth, and so on, which had to be altered to comply with Islamic theology and the absoluteness of Allah. Although tales of non-Islamized Sudanese such as the Azande are full of creation myths, such myths do not appear in available folktale collections of Islamized Sudanese.[14]

To sum up briefly, the Sudanese folktale reflects Afro-Arab contacts and spells out clearly the nature of the process of acculturation resulting from the interplay, compromise, and accommodation of two different cultures. This process helped in maintaining a reasonable degree of equilibrium that was disrupted only when the two cultures came into direct collision.

[14] E. E. Evans-Pritchard, *The Zande Trickster* (London, 1967), pp. 37–60.

A CHARACTERISTIC AFRICAN
FOLKTALE PATTERN

Lee Haring

Morphological study of traditional narrative patterns offers
evidence for that cryptic remark of Blake's, "Every poem
must necessarily be a perfect unity." That is true of traditional sequences of those plot elements that Propp called
functions and Dundes called motifemes. Although character
and setting vary widely, the recurrence of certain motifemes
in the same order proves that people are receiving and trans-
mitting a perfect unity. The motifemic sequence is the ir-
reducible expressive element of folk narrative. When a single
motifemic sequence appears in East Africa, Central Africa,
West Africa, Jamaica, and the U.S.A., I judge it to be a stable unity, a recurrent Gestalt that many people of African
origin have found to be meaningful. Such a pattern and its
meanings I look at here. The motifemic sequence, once embodied in an acceptable and credible texture, text, and context, constitutes that desirable and useful experience of the
hearer that keeps the tale circulating. I also suggest a way
of synthesizing two forms of structural analysis.

The following text I collected from a Kamba informant
near Machakos, Kenya, on 6 January 1968; my interpreter,
John Mwisso, translated it.

The crocodile asked the monkey to visit him. The
monkey asked the crocodile, "How shall I reach your

home when I don't know how to swim?" The crocodile told the monkey to jump on his back.

On the way, the crocodile felt hungry and asked the monkey, "Can you give me your heart? Because I am feeling hungry." The monkey told the crocodile, "This is what we are going to do: We are going to go back. Because when we become friendly to somebody we leave our hearts at home." Now the monkey told the crocodile, "You see, I am very weak. I cannot be eaten. So we have to go back and I'll get you my heart."

The crocodile agreed that they should turn back. When they reached the shore, the monkey climbed into a mango tree and picked a mango. He threw it and said to the crocodile, "There is the heart"; but the mango got into the water. He picked another one, but when the monkey threw this one the crocodile dived into the water. That is the end of our story.

The tale belongs to the familiar genre of trickster stories. I discover six morphological elements, of which the first should be thought of as Propp's *initial situation*. (1) False Friendship. In the initial situation, trickster feigns friendship with another character, here crocodile.[1] (2) Contract. The two characters make some sort of contract. Here the crocodile asks the monkey to visit him, implying he will transport him. (3) Violation. One character, usually trickster, violates friendship and contract. Here crocodile threatens to eat monkey. (4) Trickery. One character, usually trickster, tricks the other. Here monkey persuades crocodile to turn around. (5) Deception. The second character, accepting the trickery, is deceived. Here crocodile agrees to turn around. These two moves correspond to Propp's function no. VI (Dundes' "Deceit") and Propp's "Complicity" (Dundes' "Deception"). (6) Escape. Trickster escapes or is rewarded. Here monkey ends

[1] I originally called this Friendship. After hearing the paper, Daniel P. Kunene suggested that if trickster is involved, no African audience would think of that relationship as true friendship. Gratefully I adopted his suggestion, later to find that Dundes had anticipated the name False Friendship.

the tale in a mango tree, having eluded the menace of the crocodile.

A second example, from Doke's *Lamba Folk-Lore:*

> They made friends, Mr. Little-Hare and the Guinea-Fowl. Then one day Mr. Little-Hare made a crate and got in, and Mr. Little-Hare said to the Guinea-Fowl, "My friends, won't you pick me up?" Then all the Guinea-Fowl came, and couldn't pick him up. Then Little-Hare came out and said, "Now all of you get in!" Then indeed the Guinea-Fowl all got in. When they had finished getting in, the Little-Hare tied it up where they had got in and carried it.
>
> Then the Guinea-Fowl said, "Mate, put us down!" And Little-Hare answered, "No, because a certain person wants you!" Then the Guinea-Fowl, when they heard that, cried out bitterly. Then Mr. Little-Hare went in search of Mr. Leopard. When he reached the outskirts of the village, he hung up (the crate), and came to Mr. Leopard, and said, "I want to become your friend." And he agreed saying, "All right!" Then Little-Hare said, "Let us go, you shall receive some relish." Then indeed they went and found a number of guinea-fowls in the crate; and took them, and ate them as relish.[2]

Little-Hare is the traditional Lamba trickster. Relish is any meat accompanying the staple maize-meal dish.

Analysis: (1) False Friendship. Little-Hare and the Guinea-Fowl make friends. (2) Contract. Little-Hare and the Guinea-Fowl play the game of the crate. (3) Violation. Little-Hare traps all the Guinea-Fowl in the crate (trickery). (4) Deception. The Guinea-Fowl all get in. (5) Escape. Little-Hare betrays the Guinea-Fowl to Mr. Leopard (trickery again) and joins in eating them (Reward). Although the

2 Clement M. Doke, ed., *Lamba Folk-Lore* (New York, 1927), p. 75.

moves Violation and Trickery are blended in this text, the sequence of motifemes remains recognizable.

Melville and Frances Herskovits present a third text from Dahomey:

There were two animals, Lomo and Yo. These two were friends. They always went about together. When anything happened, Lomo always told Yo.

One day Yo said to Lomo, "Tomorrow we are going to have a good time." Lomo made a hole. Yo went to look for sticks. Now Yo said to Lomo, "Each of us will go into that hole. Now we will light the wood, and if one of us says, 'Zole, zole, the fire burns me, the fire burns me!' the other must put out the fire."

The first to go in was Lomo. Yo put the wood over him. Good! Yo lit the fire. Now, when the fire began to burn, Lomo called out, "Zole, zole-o!" But Yo did nothing, and the more Lomo called, the more wood Yo put on the fire. Now Lomo began to burrow underneath, and he came out through that hole. But Yo did not see him. From where he stood, he watched Yo adding and adding to the fire, believing that Lomo was already dead. When Yo finished with the fire, and there were only ashes on top, he looked inside to see whether Lomo was well cooked. But he saw nothing.

Lomo approached him, and said to him, "You are a fine friend! You wanted to kill me!"

Yo said, "I am sorry. I did not know what I was doing. I drank too much. When the fire was burning, I had dozed off and did not hear you cry out." He said, "Now we'll do something else to amuse ourselves. This game we'll play in a hole which is near a tree. This is called *atinsome*."

The two began to play this new game. This time Yo was the first to go in the hole. Lomo lit a fire.

In a few moments Yo cried, "Zole, zole!" Lomo put out the fire. Now Lomo went inside the hole. Yo made the fire.

Lomo cried out, "Zole, zole-o!"

Yo said to him, "It's your father's fire."

When Lomo cried again, "*Zole, zole-o!*" Yo said, "It's your mother's fire." And so Yo killed Lomo.

He cut up Lomo and ate him.

Now, Lomo was the hammock bearer of Dada Segbo. Yo ate Lomo, ate him all, and now he did not know what to do with Lomo's head. Then he saw Lizard. Now, Lizard is the man who whistles for Dada Segbo.

Yo said to Lizard, "Open your mouth, and let me see your tongue."

Lizard knew that Yo had already eaten Lomo. Lizard showed him his tongue, and Yo cut it out. When he cut out Lizard's tongue, he asked if he could talk now. Lizard shook his head. Yo pierced Lomo's head, put a cord through it, and hung it about Lizard's neck.

Then he said, "He who ate Lomo has Lomo's head about his neck."

Now Dada Segbo called all his people to come together. He said to them that he lost his hammock bearer. Yo went to one side, off by himself. Lizard had not yet come; he was late. When he came, Lomo's head was about his neck.

Dada Segbo asked, "Who saw my hammock bearer, Lomo?"

When none of the animals answered, Yo said, "It is better to look at people's necks than to ask them. He who killed Lomo carries his head about his neck." And he said, "If you see someone with the head of Lomo about his neck, you can be sure that it is he who ate him."

Now Lizard was there, and Lomo's head was about his neck. Dada Segbo gave forty-one sticks to flog Lizard, saying it was he who ate Lomo. In former days, Lizard knew how to talk. But as Yo had cut out his tongue, he no longer could speak. When they flogged him, he looked at Yo, and Yo got uneasy.

Yo said, "I am going away from here. Why does he look at me so?"

Now all at once Lizard escaped, and hid himself inside a hole on the king's wall. It is because of Yo that to this day lizards do not talk. If a lizard today wants to say something, he beats his head on the ground. That is how he talks. He has no tongue.[3]

Analysis: (1) False Friendship. Lomo (lizard) and Yo (glutton) are friends. (2) The two make a fire in a box and agree (Contract) to get into it in turn (*cf.* crate game in Kamba tale). When the one in the box calls out, the other will put out the fire. (3) Violation. Yo does not put out the fire as agreed. (4) Trickery. Lomo escapes. (5) Deception. Yo fails to see Lomo escape. (6) Escape. Yo gives a spurious apology.

Now the tale becomes more complex; the moves are repeated. Yo gets into the box and Lomo does put out the fire, thus reversing the Violation of the first episode. We might call that Fulfillment. Then Lomo takes his turn and (3) Violation. Yo kills and eats him. To dispose of Lomo's head and silence the sole witness, he cuts out Lizard's tongue and hangs the head around Lizard's neck. This might be classified as Propp's "Villainy." (4) Trickery. Yo gives out that Lizard has killed Lomo. (5) Deception. Dada Segbo decrees punishment for Lizard. (6) Escape. Lizard looks accusingly at Yo while being flogged. Yo goes away; Lizard goes away.

The second half of the tale increases the complexity by involving Lizard, a kind of double of Lomo, as an object of Yo's villainy (a process of splitting). Dada Segbo, the king, becomes an object of Yo's trickery. Thus the Escape motifeme is doubled in accord with the new complexity. Still the motifemic sequence remains recognizable.

The fourth text, a Jamaican Anansi tale, was collected by my student Mary Ann Goyena last year from Mrs. Frieda Brown, a Brooklyn resident of Jamaican origin.

Anansi now and Tacoomah. Anansi is always the smart man, you know. So Anansi and Tacoomah de-

---

[3] Melville J. and Frances S. Herskovits, *Dahomean Narrative* (Evanston, 1958), pp. 324–26.

cide now that they're going to steal their neighbor's chickens.

In this place, you know, the people don't keep the chickens in coops, they keep them on the trees. The chickens sleep in trees in the summer. So Anansi said to Tacoomah, "Tacoomah, you sleep at the bottom of the limb, and I'll go to sleep on the top. And when the chicken drop, you pick them up and put them in the bag." So Tacoomah said, "Oh, yes. You know, Brother Anansi, that's a good idea." But by this, Anansi mean that when Tacoomah sleep at the bottom of the tree, and the chicken make, it will cover him all over, and he wouldn't be able to see.

So Anansi go on the top and he can see what's happening. Tacoomah said, "O. K., Brother Anansi, you go on the top and I stay on the bottom." So when almost daylight, Anansi take his time, and he come down and look, and saw all that the chicken make cover Tacoomah from head to foot. He couldn't see. He couldn't move.

He took the bag from Tacoomah and put the chickens in and went away, and left Tacoomah right there. And when the owner came and saw Tacoomah there, he catch Tacoomah and cut off his head.

Analysis: (1) False Friendship. Mrs. Brown's use of *and* suffices to give us the barest statement of the initial situation. (2) Contract. Anansi suggests a method of stealing chickens to which Tacoomah agrees. (3) Violation. Through this contract Anansi means to trick Tacoomah. Trickster's hypocrisy, made clear by the narrator, constitutes the violation of the contract. (4) Trickery. Anansi's plan succeeds. (5) Deception. Tacoomah is blinded by chicken feces. (6) Escape. Anansi takes the chickens (Reward) and goes away. Escape is followed by punishment of Tacoomah for Anansi's theft of the chickens.

Finally an American text, collected in 1953 by Richard Dorson from Mrs. L. R. Toler of Pine Bluff, Arkansas.

Mr. Bear and Mr. Rabbit were good friends. Mr. Rabbit came up one day with a bucket of lard. Mr. Bear wanted to know where he got it; he wanted some.

Mr. Rabbit said, "Oh, Mr. Lion and Mr. Elephant and all of 'em down there telling big tales. Mr. Elephant laughed so long and loud, opens his mouth so wide, I jump in, go and get me a bucket of fat, jump out before he can shut it."

Mr. Bear decided he could do the same things. So both of 'em went down with their buckets, sitting by the side of Mr. Elephant, waiting for him to laugh. Soon Mr. Elephant laughed, in jumped Mr. Rabbit, in jumped Mr. Bear, began tearing out the fat. Mr. Elephant closed in on 'em before they could get out.

Mr. Rabbit said, "He never done this before."

Mr. Bear said, "What we gonna do?"

"You go in the melt, I'll go in the bladder."

Pretty soon Mr. Elephant took sick and died. Then his friends begin to wonder what killed him so quickly, better have an examination. Had a meeting, decided to cut him open and see what his trouble was. They cut him open, first thing they come across was the bladder, and they threw it down the hill. When they threw it down, it crushed.

Out jumped Mr. Rabbit, and hollered up to them, "Look out, don't throw your nasty mess down on me. What's the trouble up there?"

"Mr. Elephant's dead."

"What's the trouble?"

"Mr. Rabbit, we don't know."

Said, "Where's the melt?"

"We threw it down the hill."

Then Mr. Rabbit said, "Show it to me. All right, get you some switches every one of you. Beat on it till I tell you to stop."

Beat him into a jelly. Lifting the veil off it, found Mr. Bear in there dead.

Mr. Rabbit said, "That's what killed Mr. Elephant."[4]

[4] Richard M. Dorson, *American Negro Folktales* (New York, 1967), pp. 82–83.

Doubtless, numerous other African tales using this pattern could be found. Alan Dundes, who pointed it out to me, has found it in other East African tales.[5]

The morphological importance of False Friendship as the initial situation is its preparation for the first motifeme, Contract. Such preparation I call probability, adapting the Aristotelian concept of Paul Goodman to the study of a motifemic sequence in oral narrative. Goodman has shown that when Aristotle writes about beginnings, endings, and middles, what he is talking about is the logic of a temporal sequence. In the beginning of a literary form, "anything is possible; in the middle things become probable; in the ending everything is necessary."[6] The key to the logic of a temporal sequence is probability. I believe this concept to be cross-culturally useful. In any sequence of motifemes, each motifeme creates a probability for later ones. Köngäs and Maranda write of a "tendency" which appears to be a weaker form of the same concept.[7]

Certain motifemes, according to Dundes, create not merely a probability but a necessity for others. These are Propp's twin function pairs such as struggle/victory, pursuit/rescue, lack/lack liquidated. "If the first half of the twin function pair occurs, the second is almost inevitable. As Propp remarks, 'Interdictions are always broken, and deceitful proposals, conversely, are always accepted and fulfilled.'"[8] In my terminology, the statement of an interdiction creates a probability for a violation; a lack creates a probability for its liquidation. The second element of a twin function (or motifeme) pair is necessary from the first and is also its op-

[5] Alan Dundes, "The Making and Breaking of Friendship as a Structural Frame in African Folktales," unpublished. I thank the author for making his manuscript available to me; I did not see it until after I had written my paper.

[6] Paul Goodman, *The Structure of Literature* (Chicago, 1954), p. 14.

[7] Elli Kaija Köngäs and Pierre Maranda, "Structural Models in Folklore," *Midwest Folklore* 12 (1962): 140.

[8] Dundes, *The Morphology of North American Indian Folktales* (Helsinki, 1964), pp. 52–53.

posite, reversing its movement. Twin motifeme pairs are an extreme example; generally it will be useful to look for the probability governing any stable sequence of motifemes, for in that probability the society will be making some statement about its values or views. The temporal logic of our first move, then, is clearer: a friendship albeit false leads to a contract.

Differentiation of the main characters suggests a Lévi-Straussian opposition. The hearer differentiates the characters in physical type, intelligence, and quickness, in addition to perceiving that since one partner is the traditional trickster the contract will probably be violated. The second motifeme, Violation, dissolves the bond between the two characters. From agreement to disagreement, from trust to double-dealing, from unity to opposition, the microcosmic society is fragmented and divided against itself. Investigation of attitudes toward contracts in African customary law would help our understanding of the meaning of this point.

Contract and violation form a twin motifeme pair, especially strongly welded together since trickster is a party to the contract. No motifemes intervene between the contract and its violation. Thus the hearer experiences a movement from one state or condition to its opposite.

The violation may take place by trickery, as in the Lamba example, or it may be followed by trickery, as in the Kamba example. Whether trickery is the agency of the violation of an immediately following move, the two motifemes are closely related. Violation either requires trickery or creates a probability for trickery. Here the hearer is moved in the same direction as in the previous pair of motifemes: instability is being actualized; division is becoming more dynamic.

A familiar pair of motifemes follows, the one Dundes called Deceit/Deception.[9] Here the probability again amounts to necessity: if one deceives, another one must be deceived; if monkey persuades crocodile to turn around, crocodile indeed agrees to swim back to shore. At first this may appear to be no more than the linguistic opposition between performer

[9] Ibid., 72–75.

and receiver of an action. But consider the rhetoric: the audience for the tale is presented with an opposition, this time from a midpoint between the two extremes. Since attention is always drawn to both the trickster and the dupe, the hearer's point of view is between the two, seeing in both directions. Deception completes the incomplete half that would be represented by trickery alone. The pairing of these twin motifemes, observable in European, North American Indian, and African folktales, appears to constitute a cross-cultural constant of folk narrative with important rhetorical implications.

The final move is Escape. Anansi takes the chickens and leaves; Yo goes away; the monkey ascends the mango tree. Escape as trickster's final position functions to identify him; so we observe the interrelation of character and plot. But by what logic is escape a consequence of trickery and deception? Should we not expect trickster's complex of behavior to necessitate punishment? No, the logic of African trickster stories allows trickster to escape again and again at the ends of his tales. Escape is probable in these stories, probable from the trickery and deception, just because it is the opposite of punishment. Someone else may be punished, but trickster escapes. The Anansi story explicitly presents the opposition between punishment and escape. But if we regard this motifemic sequence as a perfect unity experienced in time, it displays its own logic. From the beginning there was a probability for escape. The making of the contract created a state of apparent equilibrium, a false zero-point that concealed its own opposite. The tale shows a movement from apparent equilibrium through real (probable) disequilibrium to equilibrium. Trickster's final escape is equivalent to equilibrium in the sense of the restoration of the world to the way the African hearer usually experiences it, with monkeys in trees rather than on the backs of crocodiles swimming rivers.

Earlier I noted the emergence of a rudimentary Lévi-Straussian opposition in the pairing of characters displayed by this tale pattern: Monkey/Crocodile and so on. The contrasts between the main characters of each tale illustrate

Olrik's Law of Contrast, correlative to his Law of Two to a Scene. More than contrast, Olrik meant opposition, antithesis (his word was *Gegensatz*): "The *Sage* is always polarized. . . . This very basic opposition is a major rule of epic composition. Other characters must display characteristics and actions antithetical to those of the protagonist."[10] The African tales well illustrate the law Olrik derived from European material. Dundes has pointed out Olrik's anticipation of "Lévi-Strauss's structural analysis of myth insofar as Lévi-Strauss sees myth as a logical model in which polarities are mediated."[11] The opposition of characters in this tale pattern is an elementary example of a Lévi-Straussian analytic schema. The dualism of character structure polarizes this tale pattern in all the occurrences I have seen. Do we not need more such testing of European-derived narrative laws on African material?

Unlike the usual oppositions studied by Lévi-Strauss, this one lies on the surface of the tale and is accessible to every hearer. By contrast, his method studies the latent content or logical rules of mythmaking, which when schematized would be incomprehensible to a folk narrator or hearer. Lévi-Strauss's abstract schemata bear little superficial resemblance to the tales forming their raw material.

The Propp-Dundes type of analysis, on the other hand, is closer to the hearer's experience, more specific. The crucial difference is the presence or absence of time. When Lévi-Strauss studies a corpus of myths in the eternal present of their artistic or logical coexistence, he has left behind the temporal level that gives life to folklore. My observations above about this African tale pattern strive to retain the actual experience of the narrator and hearer.

For the experience of the folktale for tellers and hearers is itself the solution of whatever problem is being solved. If opposites are being mediated, they are being mediated by means of the actual psychological-and-physical experience of telling and hearing the tale. For all literature, indeed, the

[10] Axel Olrik, "Epic Laws of Folk Narrative," in *The Study of Folklore,* ed. Dundes (Englewood Cliffs, N.J., 1965), p. 135.

[11] Dundes, n. 8.

actual experience of the literary piece, the person's contact with it, is the central fact for the student. The experience of oral or written literature must take place in the *now*. To the extent that folklore solves social and psychological problems for people, it must do so in their *now* rather than through an analytic schema remote from experience. (Then, the purpose of an essay such as this is to examine *how* that experience takes place.[12])

Seeking to understand the function of a piece of folklore in relation to the sequence of its elements, we must look at the impact of the sequence on the hearer in the society in which the piece is found. Because the tale pattern I study here is found in a variety of African and African-derived contexts, generalizations about those contexts would be broad and shallow. In the occurrences I have quoted, the motifemic pattern shows a typical sequence describing typical actions. The societies keeping this motifemic sequence in tradition probably do find similar values and meanings in it, though they change the identity of the characters performing the functions. If the tale pattern makes an important statement about the working of society, the making of such a statement is effected more through the motifemic sequence than through the style of the culture or of the narrator. Since it is just the sequence of motifemes that gives the meaning, it becomes possible to unite two familiar analytic tools and to talk about *the structure of the function*. The function is just the interaction of the motifemes and the hearer. Such interaction must take place in a here and now. Furthermore, these motifemes take the hearer from a zero point through a sequence of opposed moves to a final statement about things as they are. Thus is the binary opposition of Lévi-Strauss mediated. Thus can we synthesize the two prevalent sorts of structural analysis of folk narrative.

Roger D. Abrahams has shown the need for such a synthesis in different terms:

12 These uses of *now* and *how* are drawn from the Gestalt psychotherapy of Frederick S. Perls. See his *Gestalt Therapy Verbatim* (Lafayette, Calif., 1969), pp. 41–54.

Discussion of linguistic or dramatic structure does not generally explain them in dynamic terms. Structural technique does include discussion of *progression* of sounds or motives or ideas, but progression is less dynamic than *movement*. Movement is, in fact, the most important characteristic of an item of folklore as an organic object. The discernment of movement causes us not only to *see* the item as an entity but also to recognize that for it to work we must *feel* with it. This sympathetic visceral reaction is inherent in the esthetic construction of the piece, but it only takes effect as the item is voiced, enacted, performed.[13]

In this motifemic pattern, insofar as trickster embodies the antisocial tendency and the contract is a binding social relationship, the tale is a fantasied escape from social necessity, while at the same time reinforcing the unity of society by dismissing the threat posed by trickster.[14]

These African tales illustrate a process that is probably basic to humanity and probably the very thing Lévi-Strauss is studying. S. Friedländer, in his book *Creative Indifference*, called it "differential thinking." In this view,

every event is related to a zero-point from which a differentiation into opposites takes place. These *opposites* show *in their specific context* a great affinity to each other. By remaining alert in the centre, we

[13] Roger D. Abrahams, "Some Uses of Structural Analysis in a Rhetorical Theory of Folklore," privately circulated.

[14] Abrahams in discussion denied that this motifemic sequence displays any closure, citing the occurrence of long open-ended strings of such tales in West Indian traditional tale sessions. His view is that such Aristotelian analysis as mine is culture-bound and irrelevant to African-derived narrative. For me, Aristotle provides a model of how to analyze the temporal logic of narrative. When African temporal logics are more visible, no doubt Aristotle will have been left behind.

can acquire a creative ability of seeing both sides of an occurrence and completing an incomplete half.[15]

The sequence of motifemes I have been studying begins with an initial situation that seems to be just such a zero point. Friendships and contracts are part of the basis of African society. Then a differentiation into opposites takes place: the contract is violated, the friends are friends no more, one is working against the other, deceit and deception dominate the picture until trickster restores the equilibrium by escaping. The opposites friendship and enmity, contract and violation, truthfulness and trickery show in the tale a recognizable affinity to each other. As we earlier saw, the opposed characters show their affinity in each context. The rhetoric of performance invites the audience to remain alert in the center, seeing trickster and dupe just as they are. The zero point to which the whole sequence tends is the true equilibrium of the ending, in which the false zero point of the initial situation is succeeded by a restoration of things as they are and as they probably ought to be. Such a differentiation into opposites, followed in time by the completion of a Gestalt, can take place only in the chronological presentation of the actual tale to actual hearers by an actual narrator. It is just these opposed motifemes and characters that constitute the expressive elements of the tale. The persistence of a particular sequence of motifemes in tradition is prima facie evidence of its expressivity. Whatever cultural values are reflected in the style of this tale pattern in Kenya, Rhodesia, or Dahomey, whatever the relations of performer and audience, the motifemes in their actual occurrence are the successfully realized artistic experience.

[15] F. S. Perls, *Ego, Hunger, and Aggression* (London: George Allen and Unwin, 1947), p. 15.

TRADITIONAL VERBAL GENRES

THE LANGUAGE OF
THE PROVERB IN AKAN

Lawrence A. Boadi

The view is often expressed that the most important distinguishing feature of the proverb and other related spoken art forms is didacticism. Scholars say that, especially in preliterate societies, the main role of the proverb is to provide a storehouse of native wisdom and philosophy and a code of behavior for children and youth. This view seems to me too pragmatic and limiting and excludes much about certain aspects of the proverb as an art form. It ignores the importance that some societies attach to linguistic and literary features associated with the proverb, especially the sharp wit, the sarcasm, the humor, the rhetoric, and, indeed, all the aesthetic and poetic values of language use. Unless further elaborated, the didactic view would also lead one to believe that in Akan, for instance, any short utterance that expresses a moral truth is a proverb. The Akan language is spoken by between three and four million people in the West African country of Ghana and by a few thousands more in neighboring Ivory Coast.

A careful observation of language in context will reveal that in Akan society the primary function of proverbs is aesthetic or poetic and not didactic. Naturally, in most discussions and dialogues each participant is involved in putting across a point, exhorting, admonishing, or concealing a fact, and these ends could, in the majority of cases, be achieved without resort to proverbs. Yet a speaker often selects a particular proverb or striking metaphor because he wishes to embellish or elevate his message with a poetic dimension, or demonstrate to his opponent his superior sophistication, education, eloquence, or sensitivity in the use of his language. These goals need not be moral or didactic. My own experience with situations in which brilliant speakers use proverbs supports the view that they are motivated in the main by a desire to heighten their message poetically.

What I have said implies that native speakers are linguistically sensitive enough to be able to tell what constitutes a proverb in Akan and to distinguish proverbs from mere sayings intended to put across a moral point. The truth of this implication is borne out by the fact that Akan speakers do not react to translations of foreign proverbs into Akan as they do to native proverbs. For example, although most Akan Christian converts accept as incontrovertible the moral truth embodied in the sayings of the Old Testament Book of Proverbs, they intuitively exclude them from the class of native proverbs. Apparently, Old Testament verses do not capture features associated with Akan proverbs that the adult native speaker has grown to recognize. Mature native speakers of Akan deny the status of proverbs to the following biblical quotations:

". . . tie woagya nte so, na mpo wo na mmara."
(Hear the instruction of thy father, and forsake not the law of thy mother.) *Proverbs* 1, 8.

Iehowa suro ne nyansa-hu mfiasie; agyimifo bu nyansa ne net so animtia.
(The fear of the Lord is the beginning of wisdom: but the foolish despise wisdom and instruction.) *Proverbs* 1, 7.

They also deny that translations of the following English sayings are proverbs in the Akan sense of the term.

A stitch in time saves nine.
Honesty is the best policy.
A friend in need is a friend indeed.

One could give a variety of explanations for native attitudes to these proverbs. The thesis I would like to develop is that native speakers are sensitive to the poetic value of proverbs whether or not these contain a moral truth. Further, the varied emotional and intellectual reactions shown by native speakers to proverbs are conditioned more evidently by the aesthetic value of these proverbs—the quality of the imagery and of the wit—than by their moral content or truth value. Native speakers do not evaluate all proverbs equally but seem to arrange them on a hierarchical scale, with some having more rhetorical or poetic value than others. The structure of the hierarchy needs detailed study, but for my present purpose I will recognize two levels: highly valued proverbs used in serious discussions and debates, generally by adults; and little-valued ones mostly used by non-adults or by adults with children, especially during classroom instruction. (It is common for an adult to use a proverb when talking to a child, but the reverse is unusual.) Proverbs are assigned to places in the hierarchy not on the basis of their factual content and validity but on the quality of their imagery. The more concrete and unusual the image, the higher the proverb rates. Consider the following proverbs:

1. s woamma wo y nko antwa nkron a, wontwa du.
   (If you do not allow our neighbor to cut nine, you will not cut ten.)
2. Dabi y bio.
   (Some day [the future] is another, i.e., first fool is not a fool.)

The explanation for (2) is that the future will offer another, similar opportunity and a chance to retaliate. This proverb is used as a threat on occasions when a person discovers he has been cheated and regrets having helped a friend. All adult native speakers would recognize these as

Akan proverbs by their sentence structure, rhythm, and context. At a certain level of discourse and in certain social contexts, however, both these proverbs would be considered trite and uninteresting although they both convey a moral truth and may have been appropriately used. Any serious adult public speaker who hoped to drive a point home to his audience and used these proverbs to illustrate his argument would be judged an incompetent speaker. Very likely, he would receive evaluative comments such as *n' ano ntee* ("His lips have not dried up yet"). I am not saying that these are not proverbs or that they are never used, but that neither would occur in a serious debate because the imagery is too ordinary, uninteresting, and lacking in concreteness. As a step toward a taxonomy of proverbs I would rate (1) and (2) low on the scale.

In Akan society, rhetoric is a far more important part of an adult's linguistic equipment than in most other societies. A mature participant in a dialogue or public discussion always strives to use vivid language because his audience is continually making folk-literary analyses of his speech. The importance attached to brilliance and imaginativeness in public speech leads those who aspire to enter traditional public life and hope to exert influence, especially in the courts and in politics, to cultivate the use of striking images. It is not unusual for courtiers in the course of their training and education to be attached to foreign courts in order to practice the technique of public speech, in which the witty use of striking metaphor and imagery is an important ingredient.

Let us now turn to a few of the proverbs that are highly valued in the culture.

3. aserewa su agyenkuku su a ne to pae.
   (If the *aserewa* attempts to sing like the *agyenkuku*, his posterior explodes.)
4. aserewa mo danta k se a, etu no hwe h.
   (If the *aserewa* puts on a large loincloth, it is thrown off balance.)

The *aserewa* is the smallest bird recognized in the culture, and the *agyenkuku* is one of the larger ones. In order to produce the deep notes of the *agyenkuku,* the *aserewa* has to overstrain its vocal muscles and he may explode his lungs or belly thereby. The proverb is used in situations in which a person attempts to do what is far beyond his natural ability.

The *danta* is a large piece of cloth folded several times and used as a loincloth by men working in the fields or fighting on the battlefield. It can also refer to the bandages worn by women to cover their private parts. The weight of the huge *danta* throws the little bird off balance and swings him down.

What distinguishes (3) and (4) from (1) and (2) are not features such as rhythm and alliteration, but unique and concrete images. Each of these latter two proverbs is a comment on overambition, a highly abstract notion. As with most proverbs, the implied comment is very general and can apply to a wide range of situations. But the vocabulary is not general or abstract. The comment is given a poetic dimension through a series of concrete images whose semantic features are interrelated, as in (3), excepting one or two purely grammatical words which act as structural links. *Aserewa* and *agyenkuku* are exotic but also concrete. The verbs *su* and *pae* both imply activity, the latter denoting, in addition, physical violence. But the wit and humor of this proverb derive from a subtle interplay of the semantic features of the images. The two nouns are matched in semantic features but they offer a contrast in content between a small and a large bird. Both verbs denote activity, but are opposed to each other in semantic features: *su* carries with it suggestions of spontaneity and volition, whereas *pae* implies rigidity and inertia; *su* connotes joy, vitality, life; *pae* connotes pain, annihilation, and final destruction. The selection of starkly concrete images and the irony that often results from the complex relations between the semantic features of these images characterize highly valued proverbs.

The second proverb expresses basically the same idea and shares an image with the first. Here we are given a series of physical images that conjure up a picture of an insignificant, diminutive bird dressed in a huge loincloth made of bales of cloth. The irony results from the vivid contrast between two opposites, the small size of the bird and the huge *danta*. The picture is one of grotesqueness. There is, of course, an additional concealed suggestion of sexuality in the image of this insignificant bird aping humans by covering its private parts. The verb in the second part of the proverb expresses physical and highly muscular action. Clearly, the interest raised by the imagery, wit, humor, and suppressed irony is outside the practical meaning or the moral philosophy of the proverb.

Proverbs at the low end of the hierarchy lack a complexity of relationships. Compare (3) and (4) on the one hand with (5), which purports to express basically the same idea.

5. abofra te fufuo a, te nea bek n' ano.
   (The child should take a morsel small enough to fit his mouth.)

Although (5) seems to have the same meaning as (3) and (4) and lends itself to use in the same situation, an Akan adult would avoid (5) in a serious discussion or even in conversation with other adults. He might use it when talking to children and non-adults. The imagery of (5) appears too ordinary to interest mature adults. The proverb does contain concrete nouns, but their semantic features are not related to each other in any interesting or significant way. Indeed, the impression Akan people probably get on hearing this proverb is that it is not concrete at all. Proverbs such as the following share similar properties and certainly belong to a lower level of intensity.

6. wunni yaanom a, yemfr yaanom.
   (If you have no friends you do not call friends.)
7. nda nyinaa ns.
   (All days are not equal.)
8. obi nkyer abofra nyame.
   (Nobody shows the child where God is.) [The Akan believe that the heavens are inhabited by God, who

reveals himself as the gray clouds, one of the first
things seen by the child when it is born.]

9. ade nyansa w nto.
    (Wisdom is not bought.)

Each of these sayings has at least one linguistic feature associated with Akan proverbs. Example (6) is distinguished by
the rhythmic balance and the recurrence of certain phonological segments, (7) by its conciseness and generality, and
(9) possibly by the stylistic use of inversion. But there is
nothing strikingly concrete or stark about the imagery. Although (6) or (8) may occur in an adult conversation or a
serious debate, a mature speaker would, if he had other
alternatives, select those with more striking images. The
fact that (6) and (8) have a greater chance of entering a
serious debate by adults than, say (7) and (9) suggests that
the division should not be restricted to the dichotomy of
highly valued and low-valued proverbs.

It might strike people of European descent as odd that
Akan adults should prefer the concrete to the abstract proverb,
because in European culture the adult mind is expected to
express itself abstractly. The door is open for speculation
as to whether the adult Akan speaker indulges in abstract
thinking at all. But the adult Akan speaker prefers concreteness of expression in proverbs over abstractions.

In discussing the language of the proverb one should not
forget the social context with which it is closely associated.
The proverb is an important aspect in the training of courtiers, who are required to show brilliance, wit, and sophistication in debates. Concrete imagery is in keeping with the
dramatic setting and color of the court. An image must be
startling or dramatic (e.g. *etu no hwe h,* "It swings him, it
uproots him").

With the vivid concreteness of the higher-level proverbs
go directness and frankness. Imagery is drawn not only from
exotic animals but also sex, body parts, and body functions.
The free selection of sexual imagery to reinforce an argument in a public debate or discussion sometimes strikes
foreigners as an unnecessary indulgence in obscenity. Indeed,

in the past, foreign collectors of proverbs have completely ignored these proverbs, judging them to be embarrassingly crude and primitive.

Akan adults do not consider these proverbs obscene. In spite of repeated condemnations from missionaries, proverbs that allude to sex and body parts persist. Here are a few examples:

10. ayamtubin, y mb no boa mu.
    (Loose excrement, one does not pack it in a basket.)
    [A basketlike container made from palm branches is used to carry solid loads from the farm to the house. The idea being expressed here is that some situations are so delicate and complex that they can only be saved by extreme care and tact.]

11. woho b n a, yeta fra wo mu.
    (If your body stinks, people in your company take the advantage to fart.) [If you are universally known to be a thief, for example, other people will steal when you are about, hoping that you will be blamed for their thefts.]

12. wonta nsuro k tep n.
    (The twin-bearer is not frightened by the supreme penis.) [Twins in Akan culture are regarded as mystical, and the woman who bears twins is considered unusual.]

13. s wo k te awu a, no ara na wo dwons fa mu.
    (Although your penis may be dead, it still is your only means for passing water.) [You do not reject your parents or spurn your birthplace however poor or humble these may be.]

There are, of course, situations in which the use of these texts might be considered obscene, for example if a person went about saying them out of context or outside the appropriate occasions. In serious and heated debates, however, it is accepted that a speaker can freely use proverbs alluding to bodily parts and functions. The value of these proverbs lies in the starkness of the imagery, which here is much franker than what is heard in ordinary discourse.

It should be clear from the preceding paragraphs that there

exist in the language multiple proverbs which, while expressing a common central idea or philosophy, differ in the intensity and quality of their language and imagery. In attempting to characterize the imagery, I have proposed a tentative two-level hierarchy. Very likely, an extensive study would reveal that the scale is not dichotomous at all but that there are intermediate levels. Take this saying:

14. wo se akyi apor a h ara na wotafe.
(The back of your teeth may be rotten, nevertheless it is the only spot that you suck.)

This proverb occurs in serious dialogues, as we would expect from the concrete imagery derived from a body part and body function, and from its direct and frank character. Nevertheless, in a debate between adults, this proverb is likely to be less valued than its near-synonym (13). Thus, the existence of proverbs such as (14) argues strongly against a purely dichotomous scale. Furthermore, the place of a proverb on the hierarchy is not fixed. Conceivably, the value of a proverb may change if a new one expressing the same central idea is created or an old one lost through time.

These uncertainties aside, the available evidence shows that native speakers recognize a hierarchy. The question that we ask is: are reactions to conceptually related proverbs uniform, and if not, what is the motivation for the different reactions? I contend that the different reactions from a mature native speaker are determined not by the truth-value of proverbs, but by the quality of the imagination or poetry that has gone into them.

THE PROVERB IN MODERN
WRITTEN SWAHILI LITERATURE:
AN AID TO PROVERB ELICITATION

Carol M. Eastman

THE LITERATURE

The past twenty-five years have witnessed the development of a literature in Swahili written with a literate audience in mind and with a view to publication.[1] Unlike other
Bantu languages, Swahili has a long oral *and* written literary
tradition. Until recently, this body of literature (chiefly
traditional poetry and some prose of a homiletic or didactic
nature), written in Arabic script, has been thought of as
the *only* Swahili literature. Though it still may be true that
Swahili poetry is more important than prose, a considerable
body of prose and short plays are now coming to attention.

This paper ventures to show that modern Swahili drama-
tists and prose writers are blending folk art in their works
via proverbs and thereby are providing contexts for their
people's sayings. Modern folklorists who study proverbs assert that a proverb's meaning cannot be wholly understood

[1] This paper is one by-product of a study of "Swahili Oral Literature" I carried out at the University of Washington under a
Faculty Research Grant (Acct. #11-1981) from the graduate school
(spring and fall 1970).

apart from the context of its usage. Among other expressive components, the proverb often includes some value ideal.[2] Thus it should be the task of the researcher to elicit contextual information from one or more informants and thereby attempt to approach objective interpretation.

The informants for this study were all college-educated Tanzanians. Each was asked to identify proverbs in selected prose and dramatic works and to report any proverbs called to mind by certain words or contexts within these works. In what follows, suggestions are made concerning the method by which a written literature might be used in working with informants to elicit and interpret proverbs. Examples are provided of some of the proverbs found in the literature and also of some of the ones suggested, with contexts being discussed in all instances.

Five literary works are involved in the study:

Mgeni Karibu (*Welcome Stranger*) and *Afadhali Mchawi* (*Better a Witch*) are two plays by Graham Hyslop published in Nairobi, Kenya, in 1957. The author is a secondary-school teacher in Nairobi. Set on the East African coast, these plays reflect the Islamic way of life in a Swahili community, having to do with a search for identity in the first instance and with parent-child relations in a changing world in the second.

Nimelogwa! Nisiwe na Mpenzi (*I Have Been Bewitched! I Don't Have a Lover*), a play by Gerishon Ngugi published in Dar es Salaam, Tanzania, in 1961, deals with Kikuyu people living in an urban setting who use Swahili as their second or third language and who are facing the change from a traditional tribal life to decentralized modern urban life.

Alikiona (*She Saw It*), a short, two-act unpublished play written by Ebrahim N. Hussein for a class at the University of Dar es Salaam in 1968, focuses on adultery in modern-day urban Muslim East Africa. Since writing this play, the

[2] This idea is dealt with by Carolyn Duck in an unpublished paper, "Some Swahili Proverbs and Their Messages," presented at the Twenty-third Northwest Anthropological Conference, in Corvallis, Oregon (March 27, 1970).

author has also written *Kinjeketile,* the first full-length Swahili play to be published (Oxford University Press, East Africa, 1971). It has a historical theme involving the Maji Maji uprising.[3]

Plays such as these three published works and the one classroom project are quite popular in modern-day East Africa. The Swahili theater is a relatively new phenomenon, which Farouk Topan has described as follows:

> Swahili drama is midway between prose and poetry in its spontaneity of expression. Fewer people write plays than poetry, but there is a "naturalness" about drama that is very akin to poetry, and indeed the two evolved together in the traditional verse drama. The semi-spontaneous quality of Swahili drama is expressed in both writing and acting. Drama groups in Dar es Salaam, especially those belonging to factories . . . often perform unscripted pieces.[4]

Drama festivals are held and prizes are afforded the best entries. In Tanzania the Department of Theatre Arts and Department of Swahili at the University of Dar es Salaam, the Youth Drama Association of Tanzania, and the Cultural Division of the Ministry of National Education encourage playwrighting, but the most important contribution to Swahili literature on the whole appears to be in the schools.[5] The unpublished play by Ebrahim N. Hussein is a case in point, while the Hyslop and Ngugi plays were also written for performance at schools and published later.

The other literary work exhibiting contextual proverb usage to be discussed here is a biography of a famous Zanzibar singer, Siti binti Saad, written toward the end of his career by the best-known of all Swahili literary figures, Shaaban

---

[3] Farouk Topan, "Swahili Literature Plays Major Social Role," *Africa Report* (February 1971): 29.

[4] Topan, p. 30.

[5] Ibid.

Robert (1911–62). Written earlier than the other plays discussed, *Wasifu wa Siti Binti Saad* (*Biography of Siti Binti Saad*) was published in London in 1967. This work recounts significant events in the life of Siti, who rose from an inauspicious childhood to celebrity in the popular-music field in the early years of this century. Of the author, one critic has written:

> Shaaban Robert . . . is generally recognized as the greatest author who ever used the Swahili language as his medium of expression. Yet his background, his education and his inclination towards philosophy gave his works a wider basis than the majority of Swahili writers have.[6]

Although Shaaban Robert wrote many short stories and essays, he perhaps excelled as a poet. He never wrote a play, as dramatic writing only began in Swahili toward the end of his life. Ngugi, Hyslop, and Hussein are all current writers with a popular following, while Shaaban Robert is revered as "The Old Master," though his writings are becoming less popular today due to the complexities of his style.

THE PROVERBS

A popular proverb in Swahili is "Haraka, haraka, haina baraka" ("Haste, haste, has no blessing"). Graham Hyslop used this proverb in both *Mgeni Karibu* (*Welcome Stranger*) and in *Afadhali Mchawi* (*Better a Witch*). In *Mgeni Karibu*, the proverb occurs midway through the one-act play, in the following context:

[6] Review by Jan Knappert of *Utenzi wa Vita Vya Uhuru Umetungwa na Shaaban Robert* (Oxford University Press, 1967) in *Journal of African History* 10 (1969) no. 2: 341–42.

Elder: Look, Sheikh Rajabu, what are we waiting
         for? . . . Let's remove this wicked one, Saidi,
         and make Shabani the Sultan . . . it's his
         birthright.

Ali: (shaking the elder's hand) . . . In this I agree
         with you, elder.

Sheikh Rajabu: Listen.

Ali: Yes, Sheikh.

Sheikh Rajabu: *Haraka haina baraka* [Haste has no
                 blessing] . . . to go slowly is the
                 way. But, first, how do we know that
                 Shabani wants to be Sultan?

In *Afadhali Mchawi,* the proverb appears in the context
of parents talking about their son, Ali:

Mother: In my opinion, I think it is best that Ali get
         married now.

Father: What?

Mother: Get married.

Father: Get married?

Mother: Certainly.

Father: *Haraka haina* [Haste has no] . . . what?

Mother: . . . *haina baraka* [it has no blessing]. I
         know, but what kind of haste is there? Now
         Ali is already a full-grown man, isn't he?

One might be inclined to interpret the Swahili *"Haraka,
haraka, haina baraka"* ("Haste, haste, has no blessing") as
the English "Haste makes waste." The two examples of the
proverb cited show that it is not that haste makes waste but
rather that there is no advantage in haste. What is being
hastened is a desirable type of behavior: replacement of a
wicked Sultan by a good one; and marriage of a gainfully
employed mature son. The function of the proverb is to invoke caution in order to ensure that the desirable behavior

comes to pass. The proverb acts as a call to people trying to influence others to consult those others before acting.

"Haste has no blessing" in its immediate context functions to urge caution in influencing the behavior of others. In a larger context, it expresses a cultural value ideal about doing things at the right time. As the mother in *Afadhali Mchawi* says, "It [i.e., haste] has no blessing. I know, but what kind of haste is there?" After all, since the son is full-grown, it is the right time for him to marry. Nevertheless, she knows the rule that when haste is involved there is no advantage in it.

The very title of *Afadhali Mchawi* (*Better a Witch*) is part of a proverb uttered in the closing line of the play. The play ends with the father saying:

> Ali, my child, I have said many times . . . "Afadhali mchawi . . . maana fitina huua!" (Better a witch . . . because discord always kills.)

The father says this on realizing that he had almost been convinced his son was a criminal. In the context of the play the proverb seems to mean that it is better to find out that someone outside the family is an evil person. Had it been a family member causing disharmony at home, this discovery would have broken up, or "killed," the family. There is also the idea that when there is an evil person about and he has been identified, he can be coped with. Disharmony can, however, develop among people who are close, and if it does not become known until too late, it cannot but destroy the closeness.

One more proverb will be cited from *Afadhali Mchawi*. When Ali, the elder son, explains to the teacher how he told his mother that he did not want to get married, the author begins the proverb by having Ali say only, "Akamataye mbili . . ." The teacher at once understands him and completes the proverb by saying, ". . . moja humponyoka!" The proverb is:

Akamataye mbili moja humponyoka!
To the person who seizes two things, one always slips
from his grasp!

The context is:

> Ali: And I told her that I definitely want to help
> Hassani [his younger brother] with his school
> fees but if I marry hastily I will not be able to
> do that because "Akamataye mbili . . ."
> Teacher: ". . . moja humponyoka!"

Ali then perceives that the teacher understands. The proverb patently tells a person to do one thing at a time—one
cannot successfully manage two things at once.

In Gerishon Ngugi's play *Nimelogwa! Nisiwe na Mpenzi*
(*I Have Been Bewitched! I Don't Have a Lover*), use is
made of the proverb "Njia ya uwongo ina ncha saba" ("The
path of falsehood has seven endings"). The plot involves a
man, Ben, who has reached the age of thirty without a wife
and who is singularly unsuccessful in matters of love, especially in his efforts to attract Beatrice.

At the beginning of the play, Ben talks to his friend John
about his plight as if it were no fault of his own. John starts
to laugh. Ben angrily asks him to stop:

> John: I have stopped laughing but . . .
> Ben: But what?
> John: "Njia ya uwongo ina ncha saba," and why so?
> Who does Beatrice belong to?

The proverb occurs again later in the play, where Beatrice
invokes it to Ben. As the play develops, Ben resolves to try

again to woo Beatrice. Ben pretends that he is going on an important trip and needs new clothes and gifts to bring with him. He borrows these from a friend. What Ben really does is try to use the finery to impress Beatrice. She detects his ruse, calls him a liar, and says, "Uwongo una ncha saba" ("The lie has seven endings"). To reinforce her point, she continues, "*You* show that the lie has seventy times seven times seventy endings!"

John used the proverb to imply to Ben that the fact that he is thirty and not yet married through no fault of his own must be untrue because Beatrice is still available to be married. In the second usage of the proverb, Beatrice, who has known Ben to be dishonest previously, is angered by the fact that he has tried yet another bit of deceit to win her. The proverb implies that a lie can be found out in many ways and can even have consequences that the person using it cannot foresee. John hints that Ben is not telling him the real reason for his bachelorhood, that is, Beatrice's distrust for him. Beatrice tells Ben that she has detected his lying once more. Both use the proverb to admonish Ben that he will be found out somehow no matter how successful he regards his deceit.

Shaaban Robert, in his biography of Siti binti Saad, has used proverbs contextually. Stress is placed on the fact that Siti, the famous Zanzibari popular singer, used proverbs as guides for behavior in her daily life. There is the idea that others should follow Siti binti Saad's example.

A few of the proverbs follow:

Chema kilijiuza, kibaya kilijitembeza.
(Goodness sold itself, badness flaunted itself about.)

The author tells us that this proverb applies to Siti because she "made a very good appearance on stage, knew how to arrange songs well for an audience," but was not destroyed by the accompanying success. She won the heart of her audience but remained as humble as a child.

The author tells us that Siti had various mottoes to help her in life. One was "Kusema fedha, kujibu dhahabu" ("Speak silver, reply gold"). We are told that "by those four short words of much good sense she was able to distinguish good from bad and praise from slander in her journey through life." The function of the proverb was to remind her always to speak well of people.

Siti binti Saad also composed songs based on proverbs. She used the following proverb in one of her songs.

> Hasara ya mtu . . . kukosa akili.
> (The loss of a man is to lack good sense.)

People criticized her for her profession as a singer, annoyed that she had chosen not to live a life of seclusion, as befitted the position of women in her society in the first decades of the twentieth century. In self-defense and because of the need to emancipate women, Siti composed this song:

> Si hoja uzuri/na sura jamali
> kuwa mtukufu/na jadi kubali
> hasara ya mtu/kukosa akili
> One doesn't need beauty and a
> kind face or the desire to be
> agreeable in order to be exalted. . . .
> The loss of a man is to lack good sense.

The song urges people to realize that good sense will show them that women are more than just pretty faces.

Only a few of the proverbs used in modern written Swahili literature are cited above. In the works mentioned and in other modern writings, more can be found. Some Swahili speakers have pointed out to me that single words or phrases used in modern literature can evoke in the reader's mind a particular proverb.[7]

In *Afadhali Mchawi* (*Better a Witch*), the sick child asks when he will be able to go back to school and his mother replies, "Kuna haraka gani hapo?" ("What kind of haste is there?"), calling to mind again the proverb "Haraka, haraka, haina baraka" ("Haste, haste, has no blessing") already used in the play. The mother wants the ailing son to wait until he has recovered; then is time enough.

In eliciting proverbs from Swahili speakers it is useful to have them read, or read to them, literature in Swahili and ask them for proverbs that come to mind. This method is as rigorous as most elicitation techniques, enjoying the advantage of getting at each proverb in its specific sociocultural setting. It also assists the informant in interpreting the proverb, since what has called it to mind is its viable context.

My Swahili teaching assistant was reading Shaaban Robert's biography of Siti binti Saad when she came up with the following proverbs with one- or two-word clues from the text in each instance:

a. Mchimba kaburi huingia mwenyewe.
   He who digs a grave enters it himself.

The proverb reminds people who have bad intentions toward others that their intentions may turn against them: he who initiates trouble will end up in it himself. The proverb may be used of a child in the family who creates a story about his brother in order to get him into trouble with the parents. Since the story is unfounded, the one who makes it up is often found out. The mother may use this proverb to reprimand the child.

[7] I am especially indebted to Miss Salma Mbaye for suggestions at this point. Farouk Topan and John Shoka also provided helpful comments.

b. Panapo nia ipo njia.
    Where there is a will there is a way.

The proverb is used emphatically to show that if someone neglects to do what is expected of him, he has had no intention of doing it in the first place. For example, a mother asks her daughter to clean her room. The daughter replies, "Oh, yes, I meant to do it earlier." The mother says, "Why, then, isn't it clean?" With that, the daughter apologizes and the mother says to her that if she had meant to clean it, she would have done so. "Panapo nia ipo njia."

To me, the proverb implies that if a person wants to do something sincerely, then he can find a way to do it. It is used to encourage perseverance. The contextual information indicates that the proverb is used differently in Swahili. The Swahili sense is not to inspire but to reprimand. A person tells the proverb to another when he wishes to imply that the other has neglected an obligation and has pretended it was due to an oversight. The proverb indicates that when a job is not done it cannot be an oversight.

c. Mzoea punda hapandi farasi.
    A person accustomed to a donkey does not ride a horse.

This proverb is used in the following context: If a person who is not used to luxuries acquires them all of a sudden and then feels uncomfortable to the extent that he cannot enjoy the luxuries, then someone else, seeing his discomfort, would address this proverb to him. For example, if a guest comes to stay at your house, he may spend a fitful night and complain in the morning. You might then say to him, "A person accustomed to a donkey doesn't ride a horse!" Rather than condoning or disapproving a particular type of behavior, this proverb performs the function of showing sympathy to another. It does not seem to have any derogatory sense, i.e., it does not imply that your guest cannot reach your level of comfort. Rather, it is used jocularly to help a person feel more at home.

d. Mshale kwa nguruwe kwa binadamu mchungu.
An arrow to a pig, to a human is bitter.

This proverb is used of a person who is unwilling to tolerate things said or done against him or his friends but who does the same to others. When you attack someone else, it is never as bad as being attacked yourself. The same act looks different depending upon who is involved.

My informant told me that once, as a child, she took out of the icebox some candy that belonged to her brother. A few days later her brother took something of hers. On complaining to him, he replied, "An arrow to a pig, to a human is bitter." When he took her candy, she was furious because it affected her, but when she took from him, she did not stop to consider his feelings.

e. Dua la mwewe halimpati kuku.
The prayer of the chicken hawk does not get him the chicken.

This proverb's function is to tell someone prone to inactivity that when it comes to achieving an end, prayer is not enough. One must act. It is also used as a challenge to someone who threatens you to mean that his threat alone is ineffectual.

My informant offered this context: You refuse to do something that a person has asked you to do. The person tells you that he *hopes* that you will get an equal disappointment. Then you say to him, "The prayer of the chicken hawk does not get him the chicken," i.e., "Your wish that I be disappointed isn't going to make the disappointment happen." The implication is that the person who wished you ill had no right to do so. Only those to whom you are personally obligated, such as parents or family, can predict how their prayers or wishes will affect you. As the chicken hawk is unrelated to the chicken, so, too, is the outsider who tries to influence one's behavior.

Finally, an unpublished Swahili play uses a proverb in its title and interprets it within the play. The play is the short, two-act drama *Alikiona* (*She Saw It*), by Ebrahim N. Hussein.[8] The title is from the Swahili proverb

> f. Alikiona cha mtema kuni.
> She saw the challenge of the woodcutter.
> (Lit.: She saw the thing of the woodcutter. The fuller translation is that given by the author.)

The proverb is never used in its entirety within the play; the title only suggests the proverb. The play has a theme of adultery and opens with Saida in bed with her lover, Abdallah. It begins as a comedy. When the husband comes home at the wrong time, the lovers hide and then try to sneak out. To avoid such confusion a second time, Saida tells her husband that she is going away to visit her sick mother. But she goes off with Abdallah. When she returns, her husband reports to her that her mother died three days ago. Then Saida tries to provoke her husband into anger by confessing all her indiscretions. The play ends with the husband coolly recommending that Saida go to the funeral ceremony because that would please the rest of her family. We see Saida for the last time in tears because, finally, "Alikiona" ("She saw It").

[8] When he wrote this play the author was a student studying Swahili language and literature at the University of Dar es Salaam, Dar es Salaam, Tanzania. Professor Farouk Topan brought his student's play to my attention.

The proverb, "She saw the challenge of the woodcutter," implies that she got more than she deserved as punishment; she was made to recognize her wrongs, suffer for them by the loss of her mother, and then go on with her life as before. My informants were unable to explain the relevance of the woodcutter in the saying. One of them told me that this proverb resembles another one.

g. Alikiona kilichomtoa kanga manyoya.
(He saw the things that took the feathers off the guinea fowl.)

The same play, *Alikiona*, suggests this proverb just as it suggests the one with the woodcutter. The "guinea fowl" proverb occurs in a Swahili children's story called "Mamba na Kima."[9] A monkey threatens a crocodile that if he so much as sets foot near him again he will see that the humans capture him. The monkey continues:

Kama husadiki maneno yangu, basi endelea kukaa tu, nawe utakiona kilichomtoa kanga manyoya!

If you don't believe my words, well, just go on sitting, and you will see what made the guinea fowl lose his feathers!

My informants agree that the "woodcutter" proverb, like the "guinea fowl" proverb, probably originated in a tale. But no informant could cite the tale. Both proverbs are used in the sense of "You will get what you deserve."[10]

I have tried to suggest that in the absence of an ideal field-research situation, an investigator with informants avail-

[9] David E. Diva, *Mamba na Kima na Hadithi Nyingine* (London, 1951).

[10] The fact that the original context of the proverb cannot be called to mind suggests that young people, and especially the modernized generation, lack the competence of their elders in the use and understanding of proverbs.

able only in a non-African setting such as an American university, is able to use written literature to elicit oral traditions. Writings, however modern and new, may suggest to informants proverbs even when they are not necessarily explicitly mentioned in the written literature.

Only seven proverbs found in modern written Swahili literature, and seven suggested by the literature, have been discussed above. Such a small sample nevertheless illustrates how modern Swahili written literature may be used to find and interpret proverbs.

APPENDIX

1. Haraka haraka haina baraka.
   Haste / haste / it has not / a blessing
   Haste has no blessing.

2. Afadhali mchawi, maana fitina huua.
   It is better / a witch / because / discord / always kills
   Better to find a witch than discord within the family, for the latter is always more disastrous.

3. Akamataye mbili moja humponyoka.
   He who seizes / two (things) / one / always slips from his grasp
   To the person who grasps two things (at once), one always slips away from him.

4. Njia ya uwongo ina ncha saba.
   The path / of / a falsehood / it has / endings / seven
   The path of falsehood has seven endings.

5. Chema kilijiuza, kibaya kilijitembeza.
   Goodness / it sold itself / badness / it made itself walk about
   Goodness sold itself, badness flaunted itself.

6. Kusema fedha, kujibu dhahabu.
   To speak / silver / to reply / gold
   Speak in silver, answer in gold.

7. Hasara ya mtu kukosa akili.
   The loss / of / a man / to fail / understanding
   The loss of a man is to lack good sense.

8. Mchimba kaburi huingia mwenyewe.
   Digger / grave / always enters / himself
   He who digs a grave enters it himself.

9. Panapo nia ipo njia.
   Where there is / the intention / there is / a way
   Where there's a will, there's a way.

10. Mzoea punda hapandi farasi.
    An accustomed person / donkey / he does not ride / horse
    A person used to a donkey does not ride a horse.

11. Mshale kwa nguruwe kwa binadamu mchungu.
    Arrow / to / pig / to / human / bitter
    An arrow to a pig, to a human is bitter.

12. Dua la mwewe halimpati kuku.
    The prayer / of / chicken hawk / it does not get him / chicken
    The prayer of the chicken hawk does not get him the chicken.

13. Alikiona cha mtema kuni.
    She did see it / (thing) of / cutter / wood
    She saw the challenge of the woodcutter.

YORUBA TONGUE TWISTERS

Ayodele Ogundipe

In October 1966 I returned to Nigeria from Indiana University to accept a lectureship in African Studies at the University of Lagos, Nigeria, and also to do fieldwork for my doctoral dissertation on some aspect of Yoruba mythology. I could not have chosen a more inauspicious time to return home, because soon Nigeria found herself in the throes of a civil war. It became quite hazardous to roam around the countryside because of the many soldiers at the innumerable checkpoints. Early in the war the soldiers were very jittery and nervous, especially toward women drivers, whom they suspected of servicing the insurgents. Every traveler was suspect, and I was constantly asked what ethnic group I belonged to. Ordinarily, to give one's name or show an identification card of some sort was sufficient, but on one occasion, while I was on my way to Ibadan from Lagos, the soldiers would accept none of my many identification cards. Instead, they asked me to recite a Yoruba tongue twister:

Mo ra dòdò ní Ìddó;
Mo jè dòdò ní Ìddó;
Mo fi ọwọ dòdò r' ọmọ ònídòdò ní idodo ní Ìddó.

("I bought fried plantains at Iddo;
  I ate fried plantains at Iddo;

I wiped my hands on the navel of the fried-plantain seller at Iddo.")

After this scary experience, I thought it best not to venture out of Lagos until the tension at the checkpoints had relaxed a little, but the incident did give me the idea of collecting tongue twisters within Lagos, a sizable Yoruba-speaking area, now famous in the novels of Chinua Acebe and Cyprian Ekwenzi. I sent questionnaires to ten primary and six secondary schools, giving examples of tongue twisters and asking for more in return. Also, I asked questions about the informant, about his sources, and about the subsequent occasions when he had used tongue twisters. After receiving a flood of responses from the schools, I decided to collect some myself from three low-literacy areas: Ajegunle, Somolu, and Apapa.

This paper, based on these collections, examines tongue twisters as a minor but significant genre in Yoruba folklore, and attempts to define their nature, content, and function. It is also an experiment to test the possibility and value of discussing in another language a genre whose essence is its own particular linguistic features, untranslatable or muted by translation.

"Tongue twisters" are words or phrases designed to test one's ability in rapid enunciation. For example, compare the English "She sells sea shells by the seashore" with the Yoruba "Jálajàlá àjàlá fa jálajàla ba Àjàlá ("Tortoise's misbehavior brings him trouble"), or "Peter Piper picked a peck of pickled peppers" with "Ọ̀pòlopò opoló kò mo pé ọ̀pòlopó ọ̀pòló lopolo lopolopo" ("Many frogs do not know that most frogs have brains"). The list is long. Tongue twisters are a sequence of intentionally constructed words and phrases, sometimes alliterative, and difficult to enunciate quickly because of a multiplicity of similar consonantal sounds. The term "tongue twisters" is hardly precise, since these utterances do not exactly "twist" the tongue. In an article in the *Standard Dictionary of Folklore, Mythology and Legend*, Charles Potter suggests that they be called "tongue tanglers" or tongue "trippers." In the southern United States, he notes, they are called "cramp words."[1]

The Yoruba employ distinct terms for different verbal forms in folklore: folktales (*alo apagbe*), myths and legends (*itan*), proverbs (*owe*), songs (*orin*), curses (*epe*), incantations (*ọfọ̀*), but none of my informants knew a term for tongue twisters. To obtain my collection I gave and swapped examples. At "tongue twisting" sessions I happened upon, specimens were introduced by a challenge: who can say, or can you say, "Ọbọ gb'ọbọ g'ọpọ" three times without stuttering? In my own case, I had learned these twisters without a thought as to what they were called. I do not remember any name being given them.

Yoruba tongue twisters can be classified into pure and derived. Pure tongue twisters mean little or nothing and are constructed primarily for sound rather than meaning. Derived tongue twisters belong primarily to other verbal formulaic genres, such as riddle, proverb, or oral poetry, but by a happy coincidence contain word sequences adaptable to tongue twisters.

Tongue twisters exist in the collective memory of a culture and are transmitted by word of mouth. Most of my informants could not go beyond the immediate sources from which they learned or heard tongue twisters. "I just heard it from my father"; "My friends and I recite them all the time"; "I learned them at a party"; "The children in our house taught me," were the usual answers. The older people are more philosophically evasive in their answers. Usually they demand to know why I want to know. "Why do you want to find out the foundation of the ant hill?" one of them asked me. "The ant hill was always there." One of them shook his head sadly: "You modern girls must tear everything apart to get at its root; when you get there, what do you do with it?"

Most Yoruba tongue twisters, being contrivances, do not have deep meanings except when extracted from other verbal formulaic genres.

---

1 Charles Potter, "Tongue Twisters," *Funk and Wagnalls Standard Dictionary of Folklore, Mythology and Legend*, 2 vols. (New York, 1949–50), II, 1117–19.

The pure tongue twisters are easy to compose, and I have watched some of my informants singly fabricate them with remarkable facility. Here are some examples:

> Jàgùdá jẹ gbágúdá Àgùdà.
> (The thief ate Aguda's cassava.)

> Mo f'Ọlọ́runṣọ́ ṣọ́ Ọṣọ́ l'Ógbomọṣọ.
> (I pray God keep Ọsọ at Ogbomoshọ.)

These inventive individuals probably have a special ear for tricky consonantal sounds and a dexterity at stringing words together. Their compositions pass into oral tradition to remain or die. Those that meet the tests of time and popularity may engender numerous variants. For example:

> Ọbọ́ gb'ọ́bọ g'ọ̀pẹ
> (The monkey carried the monkey up the palm tree.)
> Ọbọ́ gb'ọ́bọ K'ọ̀pẹ
> (The monkey carried the monkey to collect palm nuts.)
> Ọbọ́ gb'ọ́bọ pọ̀n
> (The monkey carried the monkey on his back.)
> Ọbọ k'ọ́pẹ g'ọ̀pẹ
> (The monkey carried palm nuts up the palm tree.)

Turning to the derived tongue twisters, we see them emanating from other genres. The proverbs that abound in the Yoruba language are one source of tongue twisters. They are cryptic, epigrammatic, terse, and possess a vitality of expression that lends itself to the formation of tongue twisters. Where the proverb is also a tongue twister, it acquires a new distinction, especially among the Yoruba, who consider word play a mark of elegant expression and rhetoric. Derived tongue twisters are more interesting than pure tongue twisters because they have meaningful content, increased functions, and more complex forms.

Here are some examples of proverbial tongue twisters. The first applies to a cat and mouse situation:

Ikú ndẹ Dẹ̀dẹ̀, Dẹ̀dẹ̀ ńdẹ Ikú
(Death is watching Dẹdẹ; Dẹdẹ is watching Death)

Àgbà tí kò tiju kẹ́tẹ́kẹ́tẹ́ lati gùn
Kẹ́tẹ́kẹ́tẹ́ kí í tiju àgbà lati dá
(An elder who is not bashful about riding a donkey should not be bashful when thrown by the donkey.)

Kíelé ńjà; Apakíelé ńgbìjà
Ijà Kíelé ni Apakíelé ngbè.
(Kiele is fighting; Apakiele gives support.
It is obvious that Akapiele is involved in Kiele's fight.)

Oral verses connected with the Ifa religious system are another source of Yoruba tongue twisters. These verses contain the most colorful and poetic lines in Yoruba lore. Consider this formidable and frequently quoted verse:

Ojúmọ́ mọ́, nko gbọ́ poroporo odó
Ogànján jàn, nko gbọ́ wọ̀sọ̀-wọ̀sọ̀ kọ̀nkọ̀sọ̀
Ng ko gbọ́ sinrinkúnsinkú ká deku méiyẹ
Àfàimo, K'áwo má sùn l'ébì, Àfàimò!
(Morning comes, and I hear not the beat of pestle on mortar,
Night falls and I listen in vain for the sifting of flour,
I do not hear the sizzle of fowl and rat being fried together,
What an outlook when the Ifa priest goes to bed hungry!)[2]

[2] E. L. Lasekan, "Tone in Yoruba Poetry," *Odu, Journal of Yoruba and Related Studies,* No. 2 (1955–59): 35.

A tongue twister can also be a riddle:

> Eiye ṣínṣín, lori igi ṣínṣín
> Igi ṣínṣín ṣẹ, ẹiyẹ ṣínṣín fo lọ.
> (Wee bird on a wee tree. Wee tree breaks;
> wee bird flies away. Answer: Eyelid.)

Or a *blason populaire*, etching out derogatory characteristics of neighboring peoples, as for example:

> Èrí ará Ìlórá ni ẹran ará Ìlórá njẹ
> (Ilora people eat the dirt from their bodies.)

This *blason populaire* is about Nupe people:

> Ká ra Tápá
> Ka ta Tápá
> Ka f'owo Tápá
> Ra Tabá fun Tapa mu.
> (Buy a Nupe man, sell him;
> use the money from his sale to buy him tobacco.)

Since tongue twisters are based on phonology, and more specifically on consonantal sounds, they do not reflect traditional life, folk beliefs, and customs with the same variety and depth as other folklore genres. Poetic devices, such as alliteration and punning, are used, but not with precision. For example:

> Gbogbo igbó fi gbòngbò kọ́ gbòngbò [*alliteration*]
> (All the forest trees are linked at the roots.)

Adéwálé dé ni ijóti ti a dé wá'lé [*pun*]
(Adewale returned home on the day we returned
home.)

Adewale is a personal name, as opposed to *a de wale,* which
means "when we came home."

Dàdá da òdà sórí ada, àdá ò dá [*pun*]
(Dada poured paint on the machete, the machete did
not break.)

Dada is a personal name, while the verb *da,* with a mid-tone,
can mean to pour, and *dá,* with a high tone, means to break.

The major characteristics of Yoruba tongue twisters are to
be found in their linguistic features. The principal stylistic
distinction hinges on the consonantal sounds, especially plosive, nasal, and fricative, lateral consonantal sounds redupli-
cated with various vowel sounds:

Omo dúdú da òdà dudu sórí eedú dúdú.
(The black child pours black paint on the black
charcoal.)

Here it is the plosive "d" interchanged with u, a, vowel
sounds, to form new words.

Òmìrán tí o ti inú omírán miran wá, mo òmìrán mìran.
[*nasal consonants*]
(A giant born of a giant knows other giants.)

Aso funfun má funfun ni funfun kí funfun mó,
o le funfun, ni funfun ki funfun ju [*fricative*]
(White cloth, you are too white; don't be so white.)

Lateral l's and rolled consonants are common:

> Labalábá fò làbà làbà lọ sílé Àlàbá.
> (The butterfly flew haphazardly to Alaba's house.)

> Àràbà f'a bará dárà s'ara Mọlara.
> (Araba gave Molara many slaps.)

Wordplay is an important aspect of Yoruba poetry and is depicted to some extent in tongue twisters. A play on tone is illustrated in the following examples:

> Gbákábámi, gbàkàbànmi, akaba iya mi ki s'akabaka-
> kaba.
> (Give me a ladder; my mother's ladder is no mean
> ladder.)

Here, the tonal contrast in *gbákábámi* and *gbàkàbànmi* involves no change of meaning. *Gbakabami* is a humor-motivated word meaningless outside the context. *Àkàbà-* is an onomatopoeic reduplication meaning "no mean ladder."

Yoruba tongue twisters employ reduplications and tonal counterpoints very liberally for their descriptive and phonological needs:

> "Ore kítí kítí
> Iyekan kàtàkàtà
> Bi ọrẹ kítíkítí ba kú
> Iyekan kàtàkàtà lo ma kù"
> (A close friend versus a distant relative:
> when a close friend dies, distant relatives bury him.)

This tongue twister is an adulterated version of the proverb, in which the last *kù* has replaced the *siin* in the original. The tonal counterpoint of *kítíkítí* (HHHH) is *kàtàkàtà* (LLLL) and that of *kú* is *kù*. ("H" signifies high tone, "L" low tone.)

Other stylistic forms of the tongue twister occur in its use of simple and primitive forms of poetry. In addition to word-play, reduplication, and onomatopoeic use of verb forms to denote action and quality, Yoruba tongue twisters show considerable balance and parallelism. For example:

A pọn Mọgbẹ, Mọgbẹ npọn gbá [*balance and universality*]
(We carry Mogbe, Mogbe carries a calabash.)

Ọsa ma jẹ nku, jẹ nla
Ọsa jẹ nla, ma jẹ nkú [*parallelism by reversal of idea*]
(Deity, don't let me die, let me be rich
Deity, let me be rich, don't let me die.)

The most important aspect of tongue twisters is their function in society. They are vehicles for fun and amusement, a way to while away leisure hours. But I have read, with great exasperation, the uniform, invariably idyllic setting of African folklore described in many books: how in the evening, under the cool of a tree, before a fire under starry skies, shadowy figures sit around swapping tales. Tongue twisters, like riddles, can be swapped before a tale-telling session to warm up the audience. They are not limited to any specific time of night or day, but are used whenever any one or more persons can be "cornered" into wanting to share them. They are used for teaching elocution and for the dramatization and enhancement of verbal skill. Oratory is highly valued among the Yoruba and one of the means of learning pedagogy and rhetoric is the mastery of tongue twisters. To be a minstrel or a chronicler, the human depository of ancient myths, legends, and praise names, one must be able to rattle off complicated, jaw-breaking compound words. Yoruba tongue twisters are also employed as therapeutic aid for persons with minor speech defects. They also serve as a psychological release from the tensions of social norms. Ordinarily it is considered very cruel to laugh at someone who has a speech defect, but tongue twisters played as a game create a situation in which one can break convention without any guilt feelings or repercussions.

Tongue twisters exist in most languages, yet one can speak a foreign language for a long time before beginning to be aware of them. I do not think this situation is due entirely to the difficulty of enunciating tongue twisters. Tongue twisters are a genre that belongs to the root of a people and their culture. Knowledge of them is an indication and affirmation of one's membership in that culture. Hence the soldier at the checkpoint asked if I could say:

> Mo ra dòdò ní Ìddó;
> Mo jè dòdò ní Ìddó;
> Mo fi ọwọ dòdò r' ọmọ ònídòdò ní idodo ní Ìddó.

FOLKLORE AND LITERATURE

CRITICAL APPROACHES TO FOLKLORE IN AFRICAN LITERATURE

Bernth Lindfors

Reading criticism of contemporary African literature is rather like taking a quick sight-seeing tour over much of the continent. In several places one finds vast, uninteresting, arid stretches barren of living ideas. In others there are dense rain forests—dark, mysterious, almost impenetrable, but impressively canopied with large, umbrella-like metaphysical speculations. Then there are the oozing swamps and marshes, where slippery hypotheses and dangerous assumptions lurk. Naturally, not all the landscape is this depressing. One also notices a few well-cultivated highlands, one or two mountain peaks of truly lofty elevation, and scattered diamond fields and gold mines capable of yielding great riches if properly exploited. But most of the terrain is a bleak grassland tedious to traverse, unrewarding to excavate, and likely to infect even the thickest-skinned traveler with sleeping sickness. Literary criticism remains the most underdeveloped of African arts.

One reason it has remained so is that the majority of the practitioners of this art have not been themselves Africans. They have been foreigners—mostly Europeans and Americans —trying to cope with world views different from their own. Some have had outstanding credentials as professors of literature or anthropology, as long-term residents of Africa, or as lifetime students of African culture. And several have been very serious about their work, even to the extent of sacrificing a number of personal comforts in order to undertake difficult, painstaking research "in the field." Yet, like obstetricians or voyeurs, they have always stood outside looking in, observers rather than participants in the creative process that absorbs so much of their attention and yet is alien to their own cultural experience. They have not been unhelpful, some of these witnesses. A few have done a great deal to encourage and publicize the birth of new literatures in Africa. Others have watched these infants grow, commenting on salient trends in their development. Such discreet spectators do not offend their hosts. But there are sensitive zones—the inner sanctuaries and sacred groves—which are closed to strangers and accessible only to those within a society who have grown up learning the passwords. "No man," Chinua Achebe has said, "can understand another whose language he does not speak." And by "language" Achebe meant not simply words but a man's entire world view.[1] Foreign critics should heed this warning and not attempt to brazenly trespass on territory that belongs to others, who acquired the indigenous grammar while young and thus know how to decode and interpret the deep structures underlying their own semantic universe.

I am not arguing that there is no place for the non-African critic of African letters, only that he should know his place. Obviously, there are jobs he is competent to do and skills he brings to his work that are productive of good results. But if he tries to enter one of the sensitive zones, he should recognize his own limitations, fortify himself with every scrap of cultural information he can find, and then inch very warily but imaginatively into the arena. He may not get far—indeed, he may make no real progress at all—but at least he will have shown his respect for someone else's ancestral grounds. And he will have demonstrated by his lack of pretentiousness that he is not an ignorant interloper rushing in where even minor deities fear to tread.

One of the most sensitive areas of African literary re-

[1] "Where Angels Fear to Tread," *Nigeria Magazine* 75 (1962): 62.

search, and one of the most abused and neglected, is that in which investigators search for evidence of folklore in the literature. The evidence is not difficult to find, but the uses to which it is put vary so greatly that it may be helpful to pause here to construct a crude typology of the species and subspecies of this genus of criticism so that the distinctive features of each type may be better isolated and identified. There appear to be three basic critical approaches to folklore in African literature: the impressionistic, the anthropological, and the interpretative. These may be arranged in a hierarchy with "impressionistic" at the bottom and "interpretative" at the top, for each successive level seems to require a greater degree of critical sophistication and cultural expertise. Each category may also be subdivided by quality —i.e., from bad to good—with the best items in one category standing higher than the worst items in the next category up the ladder. There is some overlap in the hierarchy, in other words. Impressionists are not necessarily intrinsically inferior to anthropologists and interpreters. Their rank in the scale would depend to a large degree on the quality of their work. There are also some crossbreeds—impressionistic anthropologists and anthropological interpreters—who blur the diagram still further, but most critics can be pigeonholed quite neatly in one of the three major categories.

Let us begin with the impressionists. An impressionistic approach to folklore in African literature is one involving assumptions and suggestions rather than facts and proofs. The critic is content to make a few bland assertions about the presence of traditional elements in a modern literary work without bothering to ascertain whether what he says about these elements is true. This kind of critic does not like to take the trouble to do research. He prefers to merely read a work, react to it, and then record his reactions. If he happens to notice that Amos Tutuola makes use of folktales in his fiction or that Wole Soyinka's characters frequently speak in proverbs, he might draw attention to the phenomenon and offer the opinion that these tales or proverbs are undoubtedly "traditional among the Yoruba." No verification is necessary. The mere fact that the thought has crossed the critic's mind is enough justification for preserving it in print. Such criticism, needless to say, is superficial and highly unreliable.

Examples of this kind of criticism can be found in abundance in Anne Tibble's book *African/English Literature*.[2] Her discussion of Tutuola's use of oral tradition is almost as garbled as the adventures of one of Tutuola's heroes. "The quest Tutuola tells of [in *The Palm-Wine Drinkard*]," she says, "incorporates fantasies that most of us as children encountered in dream or daydream or in legends. Legends would include Biblical myth, heroic myth, Greek myth, and north-European myth. Mingled with these are myths of a lurid Africa partly of Tutuola's fervent imagination, partly of his knowledge of Yoruba folk-tales." Besides mangling the professional folklorist's nice distinctions between myth, legend, and folktale as forms of narrative, Tibble here makes immense assumptions about both Tutuola's heritage and the average reader's childhood. I want it known that I for one cannot truthfully say that I have ever met any of Tutuola's bizarre freaks and monsters in my dreams, daydreams, or readings of the Bible, Homer, Hans Christian Andersen, or the brothers Grimm. How Anne Tibble arrived at her supposed omniscience about me—much less Tutuola—is indeed bewildering!

She goes on, however, to qualify her sweeping generalizations with the following statement: "None of these types of myth can properly be called universal, as sometimes Tutuola's myths are claimed to be. Present knowledge of world myths is not sufficient to pronounce universality for any. But many undoubtedly are common to a variety of cultures." Now she is on somewhat safer ground, and she continues by drawing a number of parallels. Tutuola's "Faithful-Mother in the White Tree," for instance, is shown to have "Asian, African, and European" affinities, being comparable to "Graves's White Goddess, the earth-mother of Northern myth, the Mother Goddesses of Hindu villages, and of many another culture myth or religious myth. Her White Tree is

[2] (London: Peter Owen, 1965.) Quotations are taken from pp. 96–98.

comparable with the sacred Bo Tree, Igdrazil, The Druid's oak, the Tree of Knowledge, the Tree of Life. The swallowing of the Drinkard and his wife by the Hungry Creature, and the Drinkard's hacking his way out of Hungry Creature's stomach reminds us of Jonah and the Whale." These analogies are valid and interesting as analogies, but they are not proof that Tutuola borrowed his motifs from Scandinavian, Greek, Jewish, or Hindu mythology. Tibble unfortunately falls into the trap of actually regarding some of these fortuitous analogues as genuine sources of inspiration for Tutuola. "The last chapter of *The Palm-Wine Drinkard*," she says, "shows Tutuola using a final blend of African and European myth." And "if there is a falling-off between his first book and his later books that is solely because there isn't a sufficient number of Afro-European myths to use effectively twice." Statements like these reveal that Tibble has been hoist with her own petard.

Despite her shortcomings as a comparative mythologist, it must be conceded that Tibble at least knows something about oral tradition and tries to relate what she knows to African literature. The same cannot be said of most other impressionistic critics, whose total contribution to this branch of African literary study consists of offhand remarks unsupported by even the tiniest shred of evidence. John Povey has developed the habit of tossing off comments such as "The story of *Lion and the Jewel* is common enough, a constant theme of many folk tales,"[3] and "Soyinka's own *A Dance of the Forests* is developed from the Yoruba Egungun Festival,"[4] but these interesting tidbits of literary gossip are never authenticated, never elaborated, never even adequately thought out. Since Povey holds the view that "although [these] writers are African, it is more easily possible to seek out some link between their writing and the twentieth century western trends than the connection between their work

[3] "Wole Soyinka: Two Nigerian Comedies," *Comparative Drama* 3 (1969): 126.
[4] "Wole Soyinka and the Nigerian Drama," *Triquarterly* 5 (1966): 129.

and the traditional forms of African literature,"[5] perhaps he feels it would be unrewarding to pursue such matters further. Or perhaps he simply does not want to do the necessary homework. Of course, the real fault may lie in the very nature of impressionistic criticism itself, a kind of loose-tongued scholarship that allows the critic the luxury of making glib pronouncements about serious works of literary art.

Anthropological criticism is just the opposite. The anthropological critic who studies folklore in African literature tends to be obsessed with documentation. He wants to verify the legitimate ancestry of every item of folklore he comes across, tracing it back to published collections of oral data, to unpublished field notes, or to testimony from bearers of the culture from which it has supposedly emerged. Anthropological criticism can thus be viewed as a necessary and useful overcorrection of impressionistic criticism, but it has some limitations of its own which reduce its value as commentary on African literature. In a sense, it is an elaboration on the obvious, an illustration of an accepted truth, and as such, informative only to other outsiders. An essay that merely documents Chinua Achebe's use of traditional Ibo proverbs would tell an Ibo nothing that he did not already know. There may be a place for such criticism outside Africa, but the critics who practice it should beware of the danger of compiling data only for data's sake.

Two anthropological critics who go beyond elementary indexing of oral lore in African literature are Nancy Schmidt and Austin Shelton. Schmidt, in an essay entitled "Nigerian Fiction and the African Oral Tradition,"[6] examines the ways in which folktales, proverbs, and praise names have influenced the narrative techniques of a great number of Nigerian short-story writers and novelists. It is her contention that "even though the content of the fiction may bear little super-

[5] "Canons of Criticism for Neo-African Literature," *Proceedings of a Conference on African Languages and Literatures held at Northwestern University*, April 28–30, 1966, ed. Jack Berry et al. (Evanston: Northwestern University, n.d.), p. 73.

[6] *Journal of the New African Literature and the Arts* 5/6 (1968): 10–19.

ficial resemblance to that of oral tradition . . . the primarily narrative nature of the fiction can be traced to [it], as can the use of proverbial references and praise names for description and the use of proverbs and tales for providing commentary on the actions of the characters." The argument is well illustrated and well documented, but it seldom ventures outside narrow formal considerations to wider matters of interpretation and evaluation of the artistic uses of oral tradition in Nigerian fiction. Nevertheless, within its restricted compass, it is a job conscientiously done and a job that very much needed doing, since there were a number of impressionistic critics other than Povey who had not yet seen the light. Michael Crowder, for instance, had expressed the opinion that "there is no readily apparent continuity between the creative writing of modern Nigerian authors and the traditional literature of Nigeria. . . . Indeed one is tempted to believe that the two are of a totally different nature and that any link between them is either a fiction of the expatriate critic's imagination or merely fortuitous."[7] Schmidt's essay exposed this notion of a lack of continuity between Nigerian oral and written literatures as the real fiction of the expatriate critic's imagination.

Austin Shelton is perhaps the anthropological critic *par excellence*, for he is seldom content to simply annotate examples of oral influence on written literature. Instead he uses them to make responsible literary interpretations that are grounded on careful study of an author's culture. In this respect his work transcends that of most anthropological critics. He is an anthropological interpreter, not merely a compiler of lists or writer of footnotes. His essay on "The Articulation of Traditional and Modern in Igbo Literature"[8] surpasses Schmidt's in depth and range of insight, and his study of proverbs in Chinua Achebe's novels is a model of informed analysis.[9] Believing that "the ethnocentric application of Eur-

[7] "Tradition and Change in Nigerian Literature," *Triquarterly* 5 (1966): 117.

[8] *The Conch* I:1 (1969): 30–52.

[9] "The 'Palm-Oil' of Language: Proverbs in Chinua Achebe's Novels," *Modern Language Quarterly* 30 (1969): 86–111.

opean criteria of cultural and literary criticism to African writings" leads to false, misleading, and irrelevant evaluations of these works,[10] he strives to remain faithful to African esthetic criteria in his own critical assessments. Though one might disagree with some of his interpretations[11] and wish at times that he would display more imagination in his exegeses of folklore-ridden literary texts, one must applaud his methods and admire his assiduity. He is an outsider who tries very hard to achieve an insider's point of view.

Having examined models of bad impressionistic criticism and good anthropological criticism, let us now move a step higher and view a few representative works by the best interpretative critics. Interpretative criticism concerns itself with establishing and defending a theoretical position upon a body of literature. It avoids careless overstatements and amasses data only when the data are useful to the argument being advanced. The interpretative critic who studies traditional elements in contemporary African literature is more apt to be interested in investigating their artistic functions or their esthetic and metaphysical implications than in merely validating their existence. He seeks to go beyond the obvious into less accessible regions, sometimes even venturing to use his tools to probe the mysterious inner workings of the human mind. He is the most adventurous of all critics.

Gerald Moore is one of these. Though much of his early writing could be branded superior impressionism, he has recently published a few essays that reflect a maturity of thought unusual in African literary criticism. In "Time and Experience in African Poetry,"[12] he argues that in both traditional and modern African poetry "time seems often to be conceived simply as a projection from living experience, rather than as an abstract sequence of fixed units existing in its

[10] "Critical Criteria for the Study of African Literature," *Literature East and West* 12 (1968): 9.

[11] An Ibo critic, Donatus Nwoga, has taken strong exception to his interpretation of the Ibo concept of *chi*. See Shelton's essay "The Offended *chi* in Achebe's Novels," *Transition* 13 (1964): 36–37, and Nwoga's reply, "The *chi* Offended," *Transition* 15 (1964): 5.

[12] *Transition* 26 (1966): 18–22.

own right and imposing its pattern upon human activities.
The activity itself is paramount, the time sequence relative
and adaptable." Bolstering his case with examples from the
traditional poetry of the Acholi, Lango, and Yoruba, and
from the modern poetry of George Awoonor-Williams, Lenrie
Peters, J. P. Clark, and Tchicaya U Tam'si, Moore concludes
by briefly surveying the cosmological beliefs of the Dogon
and Dinka peoples, who also share this "dynamic conception
of time." The strength of Moore's argument (which at first
seems almost Janheinz Jahn like in its facile acceptance of
the notion of African "universals") lies in its wide range of
reference. The examples are plucked from West, East, Central, and Saharan Africa, and anthropologists of the stature of
Marcel Griaule, Godfrey Lienhardt, and John Beattie are
called upon for testimony in support of the thesis. Moore has
obviously prepared his case carefully.

In a second essay, this time on "The Imagery of Death
in African Poetry,"[13] Moore casts his net wide again to illustrate his contention that African oral poetry and contemporary African poetry written in English and French share "a
number of common themes in the imagery with which [they
handle] the fact of death." The traditional examples are
drawn primarily from the Acholi and Yoruba, but a few fleet-
ing references are made to the Ibo and Dogon. The modern
examples come from the poems of Gabriel Okara, Wole Soyinka, George Awoonor-Williams, Lenrie Peters, J. P. Clark,
Valente Malangatana, Birago Diop, and Tchicaya U Tam'si.
Moore's wide range of reference is again impressive, but one
begins to wonder if a similar kind of eclecticism could not
be used to prove an opposite point. If we were to select
different tribes or different poets or even simply different
poems from the same tribes and poets, would we necessarily
have to come to the same conclusions as Moore does about
time, experience, and death? Although Moore's aim is to
demonstrate a kind of pan-African unity of world view reflected through poetry, he might have made his case more
convincing had he commenced by showing how some of the

modern poets retain in their verse certain of the attitudes toward human experience that are traditional *among their own people* and expressed in poetry *in their own mother tongue*. The only point at which Moore comes close to this kind of tribalistic analysis is in his discussion of some of Wole Soyinka's works, which he appropriately relates to Yoruba tradition. Had he also taken pains to demonstrate that the poetry of Okara or Clark contains residual Ijaw-isms or that Awoonor-Williams is still wedded to an Ewe muse, perhaps then he would have found it easier to take the reader along with him on his great leaps across the continent in which he attempts to find correspondences between these poets and the funeral singers of Acholiland. Moore is a perceptive critic, but sometimes he asks the reader to accept too much in good faith.

Another interesting interpretative critic, who does the kind of work that Moore shirks, is Robert Plant Armstrong. In a splendid theoretical essay entitled "The Narrative and Intensive Continuity: *The Palm-Wine Drinkard*,"[14] Armstrong attempts to isolate those features of Tutuola's fiction that place it in the narrative tradition of the Yoruba. He bases his analysis on the assumption that

> one's method of telling a story is the same whether he does it in one language or in a very different one; he will assert metaphors at the same kinds of places, similarly shape events, similarly proportion them and invoke their relationships, and will even tailor the second language somewhat—if he is not a master of its own idiom—along the stylistic lines of that mother tongue he more perfectly knows, much as he will shape the sounds of a second language to conform to the phonemes of his mother tongue.

Armstrong finds that the various "media" of Tutuola's narrative—situationality, language, relationality, and experience

14 *Research in African Literatures* I (1970) 1: 9–34.

—are characterized by what he calls "intensive continuity," and that this dense, impacted, episodic mode of self-expression is itself a hallmark of the Yoruba esthetic, one that is actualized in Yoruba sculpture, painting, music, dance, and other plastic and performing arts as well as in traditional forms of oral narrative. Armstrong's strength lies in the elegance of his theoretical construct and in the remarkable support he finds for his thesis in the non-narrative arts. He is a comparative esthetician more interested in philosophy than in folklore or literature *per se*, and his obvious delight in building coherent systems of logical abstractions gives his essay a heady elevation which, though intellectually stimulating, is nonetheless a little disconcerting in its spanking neatness of architecture, its seemingly strict adherence to a prefabricated design.

For the nagging questions persist. How valid are his underlying assumptions? How responsible his use of evidence? How accurate his vision of the Yoruba arts? How wide his reading? How comprehensive his knowledge of other African esthetic systems? Can his ideas survive close scrutiny and rigorous questioning? Or is his a delicate theory that can be put to death by an uncomfortable fact? These are the kinds of questions one is tempted to ask anyone who dares to indulge in ambitious, original scholarship. But in the cases of Armstrong and Moore, the questions need answering, because there are important theoretical issues at stake.

Here is where the African critic can perform a valuable service. By exposing the faulty assumptions of his non-African colleagues, by testing their theories against his own experience of African verbal arts, by challenging or affirming their interpretations, he can help to weed out error and promote the cultivation of truth. This is not to say that he should be content with a second-class role as tenant farmer tending someone else's crops. He must also plant seeds of his own after clearing the land of worthless foreign brambles. And he must nurture his ideas carefully so that they bear mature fruit. To do his work well, he will probably need professional training in the fields of folklore, anthropology, and literature, but if he is sensitive to the needs of the soil and quick to learn new techniques, he may become a productive worker without serving a long apprenticeship. Since this fertile new land is his birthright, he should now claim it and take an interest in making it yield a rich harvest.

There is already some evidence that this is being done. The writings of Michael Echeruo,[15] Emmanuel Obiechina,[16] Sunday Anozie,[17] Ben Obumselu,[18] and Oyin Ogunba[19] are breaking fresh ground in the study of folklore in African literature. These critics usually come to their task with a distinct advantage over their European and American colleagues. Much of the cultural information that the non-African critic must labor to acquire is already in their possession, so they can proceed almost immediately to the higher levels of analysis and interpretation. They are not strangers footloose in an exotic Arcadia but natives who know their way about their own ancestral lands. If they continue to develop their powers of observation and to explore hidden regions inaccessible to others, surely those of us who wish to take future excursions into African literature will find them the most reliable and exciting guides.

[15] See, e.g., his "Traditional and Borrowed Elements in Nigerian Poetry," *Nigeria Magazine* 89 (1966): 142–55.

[16] See, e.g., his "Transition from Oral to Literary Tradition," *Présence Africaine* 63 (1967): 140–61, and "Amos Tutuola and the Oral Tradition," *Présence Africaine* 65 (1968): 85–106.

[17] See, e.g., his "Amos Tutuola: littérature et folklore ou le problème de la synthèse," *Cahiers d'Études Africaines* 38 (1970): 335–51.

[18] See, e.g., his "The Background of Modern African Literature," *Ibadan* 22 (1966): 46–59.

[19] See, e.g., his "The Traditional Content of the Plays of Wole Soyinka," *African Literature Today* 4 (1970): 2–18.

TRADITION AND HISTORY

WALA ORAL HISTORY AND
WA'S SOCIAL REALITIES

Mona Fikry-Atallah

In 1966 and 1967 I undertook fieldwork in Wa, in northern
Ghana, for purposes of studying the social structure of the
Wala townspeople through their oral traditions. Wa is midway between Tamale, the capital of the Northern Region,
and the border of Ghana and Upper Volta. It is, in fact, a dot
in the center of the northwest corner of Ghana, bordering
the Ivory Coast and Upper Volta. A town of approximately
16,000 inhabitants, Wa is the seat of chieftaincy for the Wala
people, who inhabit a district of 78,000 people, not all Wala
but most of whom pay allegiance to the Wa Na, the Chief of
Wa. It is difficult to know exactly how many Wala are in
the district, for many non-Wala, and especially Dagatis, refer to themselves as Wala and assume Muslim names because
of the prestige linked to the Wala chieftaincy and to Islam.

A town bustling with the motion of bicycles, small cars,
trucks, and one taxicab, Wa for generations has been characterized by the traditional divisiveness dominating its political, social, and economic scene. The hidden characteristic
disclosed by a study of the historical oral traditions of the
Wala in Wa is tension, felt and perpetuated chiefly by the
elder generation. This tension is virtually ignored by the
younger generation, and especially by educated youth. I
stress the oral aspect of the historical traditions, because the
Wala of Wa are not wholly non-literate. A small literate

minority learned in Arabic has always existed, and a history of the Wala has been written in Arabic, Hausa, and Walii. These histories are but the bare skeleton of events, listing arrivals and departures, names of chiefs and of Imams, the religious Muslim leaders. Study of the orally given history leads to an understanding of the reasons for the twenty-six different Wala quarters (each based on historical and religious backgrounds), for the co-existence of the local beliefs and Islam, for an awareness of the differing and often clashing versions of historical facts, and for an understanding of the complex social structure in the town.

A historian might use the oral historical data of Wa to gather factual information not otherwise obtainable. Vansina very appropriately cautions, however, that a historian should not merely function as a "detective" eager only for facts, but also should seek reasons for the distortions, which may reflect as much of the past as undistorted testimonies.[1] I would go a step further than Vansina and add that these testimonies are as revealing of the present as of the past. Historical facts, more easily manipulated than moral or social values, are vulnerable to distortion for psychological and social reasons.

The social and psychological relevance of history, therefore, is the predominant issue in my investigation.[2] To get a clear picture of the present social, religious, and political hierarchies and norms of Wa, an understanding of the various renditions of the past is essential. On the other hand, an understanding of the social stratification of the people of Wa leads to an awareness of the complexity of their historical background and an appreciation of their differing versions. To ignore the social context of Wa and its history leads the historian into error.

Several major sociohistorical stratifications exist among the

[1] Jan Vansina, *Oral Tradition* (Chicago: Aldine Publishing Co., 1965), p. 77.

[2] This paper is based on my Ph.D. dissertation (degree obtained from Indiana University in October 1969) and was researched in Wa during 1966 and 1967. I was sponsored by the Institute of African Studies at the University of Ghana, Legon, where I was a Research Fellow/Lecturer during that period.

Wala of Wa. The highest social and political group and the ruling class is the *Nabihi,* or the Princes, the children of the Na, the Chief. Following them are the *Yarehi,* or the Muslims, divided into two feuding groups: the Orthodox, or *Sunni,* and the *Ahmadiyya.* The Muslims are the religious men, the educators and counselors to the Chief and the people. The lowest group socially, politically, and economically is the *Tengdaanba,* or the Landowners, of whom many are Muslims, but most are close to the local religion and deities of *Dzandzan.* The Landowners call themselves the real Wala. Because of historical and religious differences, the conflicts and tensions are experienced on two different levels in Wa: *between* the major groups mentioned above and, in spite of the solidarity that exists in each of them in opposition to the others, *within* the groups themselves. The following discussion will present, separately, these two levels of divisiveness.

EMOTIONAL VERSUS FACTUAL HISTORY: INTERGROUP TENSION

At the end of the sixteenth century, Wa's original settlers were supplanted by conquerors who took the land, settled on it, increased upon it, and appropriated it as their own. The very name of Wa originated in the feeling of arrogance of victory, of independence from family ties, and of the superiority that emanates from power.[3] Yet affiliation to certain backgrounds and families is a basis for social differentiation and for sectional divisions and has led to an increasing amount of social tension and conflict within the Wala society, which has become inextricably linked to the historical backgrounds of the people. Immensely important in the life of Wa, history is indeed a reflection of their social life.

Lévi-Strauss' stress on the important role that history, with its own perspective, provides in the study of social life is

[3] See pp. 248–49, *supra,* for a folk explanation of the meaning of *Wa.*

relevant to the Wa scene.[4] Often an informant's historical account reflected the social tensions and rationalizations he superimposed upon facts to make them fit his conception of himself within a certain sociohistorical context. His account was thus a reflection of his social insecurity. Facts were distorted not only through reinterpretation but also through ignorance. Not all the elders whose social position permitted them to tell history were knowledgeable enough to tell it. On the other hand, an interview situation often brought into greater perspective the constant conflicts that existed because of the unwillingness of one side to believe the other. A passage from an interview with a Tuomuni elder will clarify the point brought out about tensions due to disbelief or distrust.

Elder: (as translated by interpreter): ". . . Our first great-grandfather was called Noussa Kanyanko, and when he came and settled, his first son was called Foroko. And from there, other people came and added. . . . Really, *we are the second set of people after the princes who have settled here.*"

Fikry: "It means, they came and they met the Princes."

Elder: "No! We didn't meet anybody here, we were the first settlers and *then* the Princes came and settled here."

Fikry: (to interpreter): Aah! But I thought you said that . . ."

Interpreter: It was he who misled me.

Fikry: So when they came and settled here they didn't meet anybody at all?

Elder: Later on, when we settled, there was a quarrel about the ownership of the town with the present Widana and then later on they agreed that we are the first settlers. . . ."

The assistant's first translation was colored, for he had added the last sentence, therefore prompting me to make my statement, since I was aware of his own addition. Then he de-

---

[4] Claude Lévi-Strauss, *Structural Anthropology* (New York: Anchor Books, 1967), p. xi.

fended himself by accusing the informant of misleading him. The response was immediate from the elder. Yet his own assertion that the people of his section, known as Tuomuni, were the first settlers, is undermined by the quarrel with the Widana. The people of the opposing section still uphold that they were the first settlers. The interpreter's reinterpreted version reflects the fact that he is of the Princely clan—those who glory in the conquest of the land—while also belonging, matrilineally, to the opposing clan of Landowners, who claim to be the *original* Wala. He had no interest in asserting Tuomuni's position, because the prestige of his own two heritages was threatened.

Points of view therefore differed according to historical backgrounds. Thus, when a prince was asked about Wala history, he would talk of the Dagomba Princes' migration to the Wa area from the northeast of Ghana, their meeting with the Muslim Mande mallams, and their triumphant entrance into Wa. He would describe the formation of the villages, known as the "gates," which are politically important for the chieftaincy of Wa, and then recount the succession of chiefs. When the Orthodox Muslim talked about the history of the Wala, he began with the sixteenth-century arrival of the Muslims from Mande, the meeting with the Dagomba Princes, the setting up of the Muslim leader, the Imam, and the succession of the Imams in Wa. On the other hand, an Ahmadi Muslim would add to this the advent of the Ahmadiyya movement in the 1930s and would describe the civil war that erupted because of it. The Orthodox Muslim will not talk of that war, which they lost. Meanwhile the Landowners, now on the lowest socioeconomic level, stress in their oral historical accounts the injustices inflicted upon their sections, the fact that they were the *first* settlers and owners of the land, and the importance of their position in the chieftaincy setup.

These divergent perspectives explain why the Wala have no firm historical narrative, no one way of telling their history. I was once asked, "Why don't you let them talk and narrate their history?" The Wala do not conceive of their history in so straightforward a manner, and it is wrong to assume that non-literate peoples all have a myth of origin or a historical epic. History was told conversationally, through questions and answers, a method imposing the interpretation of facts as willed by the narrator's biases. Levtzion also notes this manner of telling history in his discussion of his field methods in *Muslims and Chiefs in West Africa*. He writes that the Muslim informants, although always cordial and helpful, never provided information without being directly questioned.[5] The biases and social differences of the sections emerge in these fine interpretive distinctions.

Accuracy in telling the facts of history is a matter of great importance to the community, and the general historical lines they follow are usually very close to the facts in spite of differing interpretations on some points. The accuracy of telling history and of recording it is itself a source of tension and reveals a corresponding sense of superiority or inferiority. The sense of inferiority caused by illiteracy was most apparent in the Landowners' sections and was clearly reflected in this answer by a Landowner elder:

> We don't know (where we came from). We don't keep records at all. . . . Yes, really, the period has been so long that I can't remember. . . . Those people who have things written, they are able to give their history, but he who doesn't write, how can he know that this has happened and that happened? (Interview 39)

The informants, especially the Muslims, frequently made the point that literacy in Arabic brought to them awareness of written history and the need for accuracy. It was once said to me, ". . . now only very few people will know where they are from, otherwise they will pretend or invent," for they can't remember "something that is a hundred years old." (Interview 11) Great reservations were sometimes voiced by the informants, both Muslim and Dagaba on the

[5] Nehemia Levtzion, *Muslims and Chiefs in West Africa* (London: Clarendon Press, 1968), p. xxiv.

effects of time and memory on history. History in the form
of tales was challenged and undermined by the literate of
Wa. Thus, interviews concerned with history were held in
groups (as arranged by the informants themselves) even
though one elder may have dominated the conversation. The
presence of the older elders was essential not only to confirm
what was being said, but also to correct the main narrator.
Another matter frequently brought out in interviews was
the importance of the chiefs' establishing their claims through
historical lineages. Recently the villagers of Bresa fell into
disagreement over the credentials of a historical writing and
did not choose a chief for four years. The historical content
was not the point of issue, but the authorship. As a literate
stated: "It is important for us to know who wrote this document (of history), because now the rivals of the Busa chieftaincy each claims that he is qualified and each quotes
authorities and precedence. These things (history) have
been written by our elders and grandfathers." (Interview 83)

CONFLICTS AMONG THE GROUPS: LANDOWNERS

The oral and written traditions of the Wala agree on the
seventeenth-century invasion of the area now known as Wa
by the Dagomba Princes and the Mande learned mallams,
who begin to record their history as of that period. However,
we wish to know whom did they invade, were these people
the original settlers in the area, or had they also previously
invaded the land? These are touchy points to broach, and
here the traditions conflict with and contradict each other
in the interests of social and historical pride. It is a matter
of great prestige to be known as a descendant of the first
settlers in Wa, to be the *Tengdaana*, the owner of the land,
the *real* Wala. Yet, it is difficult to obtain a general consensus
of who these people are or were.

I had been given the distinct impression that the largest
section of Landowners, known as Sukpayiri, were considered
to be the settlers found in the area when the Princes arrived.

Yet when I went to interview the elder of a Landowners' section called Tuomuni ("under the Tuo tree"), several months after my arrival in Wa, my assistant and I were strongly reprimanded for not going to see him first, because, the elder said, the Tuomuni were the original settlers of Wa. Moreover they were already Muslims, having been Mande who had passed through northeast Ghana before finally coming to the Wa area. With the progression of my own mapping of the town and of my interviews, six sections emerged that were regarded as Landowner. Five of them emphatically claimed to be the original settlers of Wa.

Because Sukpayiri (meaning the house of Sukpa, its historical founder) had become the largest and politically one of the most important sections of the Landowners, its own sense of superiority among the other Landowners was undeniable. In fact, in my interviews the elders of Sukpayiri never made a connection with any of the other five sections, even though they are related to four of them. After several interviews in the other sections, it also became clear that the descendants of Sukpayiri originated through one of the two sons of the first remembered settler, who founded the section known as Widanayiri, the house of Widana. Dissatisfied with this connection to the first settler (and founder of Widanayiri), the elders also claim that the Princes and Muslims were each related to that settler and arrived shortly afterward. As one of the elders added, "So you would find that the people who originally came were [related]. . . . So they all came and sought for locations to settle. As a result, my grandfather gave them portions of the land, which means that they are under him. . . . The descendants of . . . the Princes we don't disregard, but sometimes when it comes to Princes, the Muslims, and the Imams, and other people, we make it clear to them that they are just strangers. And they agree." (Interview 43)

This quotation from the historical traditions of Sukpayiri reflects the psychological and social need for the Landowners to be considered the true Wala and the owners of the land usurped from them. The few educated Landowners frequently referred to themselves as "true Wala." The Landowners' historical traditions also express their need to be looked upon as socially and politically powerful members of the community. The incorrect web of relationships of the different waves of immigrants, the relatedness of all three groups—Landowners, Princes, and Muslims—may be more an expression of willful rationalization than ignorance. This self-deceptive attitude was far more apparent in this largest section of Landowners, Sukpayiri, than in any of the other five, smaller and poorer, sections. Yet all these sections expressed the need for their group to redefine itself. One section held onto its importance of being owners or "trustees" of the market, a function now totally demeaned. Another Landowner section insisted on its superiority in age to the main section of Sukpayiri, a superiority once politically significant but now forgotten. Still other sections claimed to be the earliest settlers of Wa, a claim of little significance in view of the sociopolitical order that now exists. By attaching themselves to a higher level, the members of each section, either as individuals or as part of the larger group of Landowners, temporarily solved their problem of ethnic identity by strengthening their lower ranks and by asserting themselves as being as good as the higher ones. All this is but a small reflection of the frustrations and tensions within the Landowners' group. Unable to elevate themselves, either socially or politically or economically, they rationalized their historical facts by subjectively and unconsciously redefining and manipulating them to enhance their social pride and dignity —especially *vis à vis* a total stranger.

The sections of Mande and Dagomba origins inhabited by the Muslims and the Princes all admit to being invaders, yet they do so with the nonchalance of the victorious, with no special feeling of historical injustice. Here are typical comments from both Muslims and Princes:

> Only Lobis were in Wa here. Then the Mande and the Dagomba Princes met here and they sacked the Lobis. So they—the invaders—called themselves Wala and intermarried. . . . But they didn't marry any of the Lobis. (Interview 22)

The latter statement is incorrect, for Princes are known to marry Landowners, but to be linked to Lobi and Landowners is degrading to the Princes and Muslims.

Another comment attempted to soften the impact of the invasion: "Wa was not empty; people always settled in it. Some people were called Tumbilihi [from the Genja area], others called Samuni [from the East], and then the Lobis. When the Princes came from Dagomba, they wanted to just plead with the Lobis that they go peacefully, but they didn't agree, so they had to use force. Then they [the Princes] settled in town here." (Interview 5)

In the ethnographic literature, Wala tradition considers the Landowners as being originally Lobis.[6] Yet, there is no indication anywhere that ethnographers ascertained from the Landowners themselves their traditions or, at least, their attitudes toward such traditions.

To be considered the original settlers is as much a matter of pride to the Landowners as is their tendency to link their origins with those of the Princes of Dagomba and the Muslims of Mande. Not to be considered invaders but first settlers is really a matter of social, if not mental, survival. Even though the Mande and Dagomba descendants consider the Landowners as the "oldest" Wala, the fact that they also talk of them as of Lobi descent is a point of conflict between the Landowners and the rest of the town. The Landowners violently reject any charge of being Lobi or Dagaba (who are their next-door neighbors), even if credited by the other sections as the original settlers of Wa. Being a Lobi or a Dagaba is to the Wala the lowest level of social and economic, if not also religious, degradation. Indeed, their names can be used as insults in Walii. Both Lobi and Dagaba represent different ethnic groups, yet the word Dagaba in Walii is also synonymous with the word non-believer, or "kaferi."

[6] Jack Goody, *The Social Organisation of the Lowiili*, Colonial Research Studies, No. 19 (London, 1956); R. S. Rattray, *The Tribes of the Ashanti Hinterland* (Oxford: Clarendon Press, 1932), p. 452.

Thus a non-Muslim Landowner is a *dagaba,* which does not mean that he originates from that ethnic group but that he is not a Muslim. Therefore many Landowners have become Muslims or at least assume Muslim names in order to mingle more easily in the social life of the town.

One can understand the Landowners' desires to be linked with a higher sociopolitical level by getting closer to the Mande and Dagomba descendants. Historically it may be difficult to deny their contention of being the first settlers from Mande or Dagomba areas, for there is no indication to the contrary. The only challenge to this rationalization is that the Landowners' religious rituals are similar to those of the Lobis, but they may well have adopted the religious rites of the more numerous and more populated nearby ethnic groups. Our interest here is not in the insoluble historical problem, but in the use of historical knowledge for the purpose of counteracting the social and cultural degradation inflicted upon the Landowners and relieving the tensions among them and the Muslim and Princely clans.

PRINCES

The accounts of the history of the *Nabhi,* the Princes, are as diverse as those of the Landowners, because of the political conflicts, jealousies, and favoritisms that have emanated from the divisions within the chieftaincy system of the Wala people. The social degradation of some groups is a result of the political games played against them by the other groups from the same historical background. It is not a problem of an ethnic inferiority complex, as with the Landowners, but of a political one, perpetuated through generations. As a result, these sections are incapable, economically and socially, of rising to the level they once deserved.

The seat—the *skins,* in the terminology of northern Ghana —of the chieftaincy of the Wala people is in Wa, and the chiefs traditionally succeed each other at death. Prior to being a chief in Wa, a Wa Na would have had to be a chief of one of the four villages through which the chieftaincy rotates in a defined order. Two issues in that tradition are and always have been sources of tension, divisiveness, and conflict, not because of social change but because of the manipulation of the tradition. Now it is no longer necessary to have been a chief of one of the four gate villages but it is enough to trace the incumbent chief's relationship to one of these villages: Sing, Gulle, Pirisi, and Busa. Misuse of genealogies arises, as illustrated by the recent case of the Busa chieftaincy. On the other hand, the rotation, in order, of the four gate villages presenting a political candidate to the Wala chieftaincy, each with a chance of chieftaincy, has been misused since the very earliest of the recalled Wa chiefs. The political structure in each of these villages is represented by, and is related to, a section in Wa itself (Gumbilimuni, Fongo Bemeyiri, and Yihiji), and facilitates political and historical manipulation at the centralized headquarters of the chieftaincy, which becomes more accessible to each village representative in the town.

This sectionalism, this rotation of power in Wa—which is mostly responsible for the present tensions in the town and its villages—was created by the arrival of the Princes in Wa and the quarrels of four brothers over chieftaincy. A previous quarrel between two brothers over chieftaincy was also the initial cause of the migration from Dagomba to the area that became Wa. The junior brother, Soalia, considered stubborn by many, left Dagomba with his followers and went raiding through various villages and towns until he reached Gbetore, a now-extinct village outside Wa. After the chance arrival of a Mande mallam, consultation of the Muslim oracles determined the move from Gbetore to Wa. Whether the move to Wa was due to agrarian necessities or to the need for more territories and an urge for power, the naming of Wa nonetheless expressed the sense of victory over the acquisition of a new land. Most explanations concur with the present Wa Na's own description:

> After they came, the older brother at Dagbon, his heart became cool. So he couldn't sleep because of

his brother (who had left in anger). So he sent him a message to tell him to return so that when he dies he would appoint him to be chief of either Karago or Niam (chiefdoms next to Yendi, the Dagomba capital). When the messenger came back, he said that the junior brother had told him, "Go tell my brother that I'm dancing here!" *Wa*, then, in Dagbane, is "dance": "Go tell my brother I'm happy and I'm dancing here." The name became Wala (the people of Wa). (Interview 47)

Moving into Wa for the Princes was not only the beginning of conflicts and tensions with different social and ethnic groups (the Landowners), but also the beginning of renewed conflicts within the family unit for reasons similar to those that had made the leader, Soalia, leave his land: fraternal jealousies over chieftaincy. Emotional aspects of events in Wa have dominated its history.

The tradition of the Princes explains that, after having overcome the Landowners, Soalia moved into Wa with his sons and family and the Mande mallams and declared himself chief. (The Landowners of course explain it differently, for they consider themselves the first chiefs of Wa, from whom chieftaincy was usurped through an unfair rotation of the village chiefs.) Soalia himself is the Prince who came from Dagomba and who is said to have married a Landowner's daughter. (Thus comes the Landowners' link with the Princes and their subsequent rationalization to support their chieftaincy claims.) The son from the marriage was Pelpuo, and he succeeded his father as chief of Wa. His four sons split the chieftaincy of the Wala, because each wanted to become Wa Na after their father's death. Each went to a different village and each was given a name expressing his behavior. Even today these names affect people's attitudes toward each of these gate villages as well as the members of these villages and their related sections in Wa.

Because of old-time hatreds and political manipulations, one gate has been ignored during the past four centuries, and its exclusion has become an accepted historical fact rationalized by the other three gates. Historians who do not consider

the social context of a historical tradition fall into the traps
set by the tradition's rationalized and conscious or unconscious
untruths. Thus Levtzion notes that the chiefs of Wa succeed
one another from *three* gate villages, those of Busa, Sing,
and Pirisi.[7] He ignores or does not realize that historically
a fourth gate, Nakpaha, exists, and its village, Gulle, is represented in Wa by the section known as Fongo. The exclusion
by the other gate villages demeaned Nakpaha socially, politically, and economically, just as the Landowners, with
whom, in fact, the gate is matrilineally related, are demeaned. The three other gates rationalize the exclusion of
Nakpaha by claiming the cruelty of its ancestors, a characteristic that supposedly reflects on the descendants. Yet Fongo,
the representative section of that gate in Wa, still aspires
to having one of its men succeed to chieftaincy, even though,
in actuality, there seems to be very little hope. The emotional need of attaining to the chieftaincy has led the elders
to state in their history that more than three chiefs of Wa
came from their gate, while, in truth, there were no more
than three.

This dichotomy between the traditional ideal and the actual patterns in Wa has been a primary reason for the latent
hatreds and rivalries that exist between and within groups
such as the Princes and the Landowners.

MUSLIMS

The presence of the Muslim Mande descendants does not
alleviate the Landowners' sense of cultural and ethnic inferiority. As was noted concerning the move to Wa, the oracles of the Muslim mallam determined the confrontation
with the Landowners. Only in the Tuomi section of the Landowners of Wa was any attempt made to link the Landowners'
heritage with that of the Muslims. The relationship is made
plausible because the Tuomi section is now predominantly

[7] Levtzion, op. cit., p. 142.

Muslim and, moreover, is surrounded by some of the Orthodox quarters, making their link to an Islamic heritage more convincing to themselves. The completely different ways of life between the Muslim and the Landowners are obvious. Though an increasing number of Landowners—as well as Princes—are converting to Islam, especially among the younger generation, thereby gaining prestige, in many cases the use of a Muslim name is sufficient to command that prestige.

The Muslims who came in the sixteenth and seventeenth centuries and settled in Wa and its surroundings did not arrive in large groups but in small family units belonging to different clans. They certainly did not come because of the commercial attractions of Wa (as was the case with later migrants), for no such attractions then existed. They came as adventurers, or smalltime merchants, or merely as teachers, seeking to educate and convert. They remained and developed into a prestigious socioeconomic group in the town. Their significant function in Wa is threefold. First of all, they placed Wa within the web of the commercial crossroad of northern Ghana, and they themselves became important merchants of cattle and horses. Then, having brought literacy and Islam, they also made Wa into a center of learning and of religious influence. Moreover, the Imam, always elected from a particular clan, played not only an important religious role but also a political one within the chieftaincy mechanism, often helping the Princes in strengthening their opposition to the *kaferi* Landowners.

There are three major groups of Muslims in Wa. The largest and most highly regarded originates from various Mande clans; a small group is still recognized as Hausa but is well integrated in the Wala sectors; and a third group, known as the Samuni Wala, the Wala from the East, lives in the section called Kabanya (or "Had I Known!"). The Samuni Wala's claim to have been the first Muslims in Wa is as important to them as that of having numbered the first chief of Wa among them is to the Landowners. The Mande groups, both Orthodox and *Ahmadiyya,* do not acknowledge in any way the existence of the Samuni Wala in their manuscripts. On this point the elders of Kabanya, a section within the Zongo, or strangers' area, which has its own mosque, are extremely sensitive and consider themselves not only as being the first to have arrived in Wa, but also to have their origins in one of the most venerable Muslim cities, Medina. Regardless of such claims, the most prestigious group in Wa, politically and culturally, is the Mande, known as the Limamyiri people, from whom the Imam of the Wala Muslims is always chosen.

Another complex social drama has evolved in Wa since the 1930s. Religious in nature, this drama cuts across the historical and social levels even though most of the actors involved come from the Muslims of Mande origin, those linked with Limamyiri sections. The civil war that erupted in the 1930s between the Orthodox and the *Ahmadiyya* sects led to an irreparable schism that can be resolved only through an acceptance by the Orthodox majority of the smaller sect of the Ahmadis. Since 1967, the Orthodox have taken some such steps, at a very slow pace. The changes brought about by the *Ahmadiyya* involved not only adherence to purer Islamic concepts, but also involved the family, education, and commerce in the town.

Various informants of the *Ahmadiyya* sect, in recounting this religious and social crisis, manipulated events and facts according to their sociopsychological attitudes. The irregularities committed by the Wala in following the course of tradition have been caused by the political changes emanating from social change, especially by the sectionalism and diverse allegiances and social distinctions in the town. One obvious example of this complexity involving the social and political structure in Wa is the layout of the town, with its numerous sections.

The conflicting statements as propounded by the various sections of Wa are always based on historical facts, molded to justify social behavior. The political sphere of the society is centered on the Princes, whose origin is Dagomba. Conflicting statements of the Princes do not concern their origin or their invasion of Wa but rather the rotatory system of chieftaincy, which usurps the right to rule of an entire group, the Nakpaha.

The Landowners, who are said to be the original inhabitants of the area, reject that claim and prefer being considered as first to arrive in Wa, just prior to the Princes. They also desire to relate themselves to the lineage of the Princes, therefore claiming rights to chieftaincy and ownership of the land. On the other hand, this claim of being the first to arrive in Wa is also the major bone of contention among the various Landowner sections. In the final analysis there can be justification only in words and not in actions, for the political and social hierarchy in Wa is already too settled to enable a change of position to take place. Recriminations and frictions will continue while the power in the society remains in the hands of the princely clans and the commerce of the town in the hands of the Muslims of Mande origin.

It has been my aim to show briefly the extent to which the historical and religious backgrounds of the Wala in Wa have shaped the social interactions, attitudes, and behavior of the people, and to study the reflection of their thought in their oral traditions in general and in the rendition of their history in particular. The predominant aspect in the lives of the Wala is their history. The past lives in Wa, because the descendants of those who created that past are living today and are affected by its events. The histories of Wa's different groups are alive because their truths and untruths are still relevant to its people and have affected their political and economic interactions and the social context of their lives.

TRADITIONAL POETRY

THE EPIC AS A GENRE
IN CONGO ORAL LITERATURE

Daniel Biebuyck

I address myself to the epic as a genre in the oral literature
of some populations of the Democratic Republic of the
Congo. I am concerned, in particular, with the Mwindo epic
and with other epic texts from the Nyanga in the eastern
Congo forest area.[1] Comparative data are drawn from the
Lianja epic of the Mongo in the northwestern Congo, the
Lofokefoke epic of the Mbole, the Kudukese epic of the
Hamba, and the as yet unpublished Mubela epic of the
Lega.[2]

[1] Daniel Biebuyck and Kahombo Mateene, *The Mwindo Epic
from the Banyanga* (Berkeley and Los Angeles: University of Cali-
fornia Press, 1969) [Mwindo epic]; Daniel Biebuyck and Kahombo
Mateene, *Anthologie de la littérature orale nyanga* (Brussels:
Académie Royale des Sciences d'Outre-Mer, 1970), and Daniel
Biebuyck and John Jacobs, *Littérature épique d'Afrique Noire*
(Paris, ms. prepared for Unesco) [Nyanga epic].

[2] E. Boelaert, "Nsong'a Lianja," *Congo* 1 (1934): 49–71, 197–
216; E. Boelaert, *Nsong'a Lianja, l'épopée nationale des Nkundo*
(Antwerp: De Sikkel, 1949); E. Boelaert, *Lianja-Verhalen. I,
Ekofo-versie* (Brussels: Musée Royal du Congo Belge, 1957);
E. Boelaert, *Lianja-Verhalen. II, De Voorouders van Lianja* (Brus-
sels: Musée Royal du Congo Belge, 1958); E. Boelaert, "Lianja,
het nationaal epos der Mongo," *Verhandelingen K.V.H.U.* (1960):
3–58; A. de Rop, *De gesproken woordkunst van de Nkundo*
(Tervuren: Musée Royal de l'Afrique Centrale, 1956); A. de Rop,
Lianja, l'épopée des Mongo (Brussels: Académie Royale des Sci-

All these ethnic groups are constituted by Bantu-speaking peoples who live in forest areas that are also inhabited by Pygmies or where the Pygmy influence, in general, is markedly visible. In those sections where Pygmies no longer survive, the memory of them is remarkably vivid. The texts of these epics are available in the original language in adequate transcriptions, together with precise translations and comments.

Epic texts seem to have a wide distribution in the Congo Republic. Jacobs and Vansina have provided us with the royal epic of the Kuba.[3] The *kasala* epics of the Luba are well known through Van Caeneghem's works and through many other sources that were recently synthesized by Studstill.[4] Important unpublished fragments of epics are in the possession of Professor John Jacobs (texts from the Kusu, Nkutshu, Basiamba, Tetela, Langa, and Jonga, which are similar to the Mbole and Hamba epics) and of Professor A. de Rop (various versions of the Lianja epic of the Mongo). Several students in Lovanium University (Kinshasa) are doing research on epics from the Lega, and so on. There is also a wealth of published information on epic cycles centered around animals. In general surveys of African oral literature, little attention has been given to these epics, because many of them are unknown or inaccessible and many are available only in fragments which tend to be classified together with the myths and tales.

The discussion limits itself to what is sometimes more nar-

ences d'Outre-Mer, 1964) [Mongo epic]; John Jacobs, "Le récit épique de Lofokefoke, le héros des Mbole (Bambuli)," *Aequatoria* 24 (1961) No. 3: 81–92 [Mbole epic]; John Jacobs, "Het epos van Kudukese, de culture hero van de Hamba (Kongo)," *Africa-Tervuren* 9 (1963) No. 2: 33–36 [Hamba epic]; Daniel Biebuyck, "Mubila, een epos der Balega," *Band* 12 (1953) No. 12: 68–74; Biebuyck and Jacobs, *Littérature épique d'Afrique Noire* [Lega epic].

[3] John Jacobs and Jan Vansina, "Nsong' Atoot. Het koninklijk epos der Bakuba," *Kongo Overzee* 22 (1956): 1–39.

[4] R. Van Caeneghem. "De Kasala-Zang van den Bakwangastam," *Congo* 2 (1936): 677–715; R. Van Caeneghem, "Bakwa-Tshimini (Kasai)," *Congo* 1 (1937): 103–33; John Studstill, *Trois Héros Luba; Étude d'une épopée Congolaise,* ms.

rowly referred to as the heroic epic. This can be defined as a long narrative that recounts in a coherent manner the deeds of a legendary hero with human traits and with supernatural attributes that are set against a background of extraordinary events, within the framework of a certain time span and a certain stretch of space. In such epics, the central hero has, sometimes but not necessarily, certain characteristics of a culture-bringer (Tegnaeus). The clearest examples of this kind of epic are found, at this stage, in the Lianja epic of the Mongo, the Mubila epic of the Lega, and the Mwindo epic of the Nyanga.

The heroic epic can be contrasted with what is loosely called the historical epic, which deals on a more limited scale with the genealogies, the migrations, and the chiefs of a particular people. Because of its strong cultural linkages, the heroic epic obviously recalls explicitly or implicitly certain historical events in the life of a people, but this is subordinated to the extraordinary and fictional element. The historical epic also frequently requires a verbatim recitation, which is limited to special annual or other occasions. The heroic epic leaves much room for improvisation and loose elaboration of the central themes and is not restricted to a particular circumstance. The Kuba royal epic and the Bembe and Luba recitations concerning occurrences during past migrations fall into this category.

Epic cycles centering primarily around anthropomorphized animal heroes or more-or-less theriomorphic heroes are widespread in Africa. Several of them have been recorded, to a lesser or greater extent, in the Congo area. Among the principal heroes of such cycles are the duiker, Nteta, among the Nyanga; the dwarf antelopes, Mboloko among the Tetela and Kabuluku among the Luba of the Kasai (Stappers); the gazelle, Tsese, among the Yumbe (Bittremieux); the spider, Ture, among the Zande (Evans-Pritchard); Kabundi (a mixture of squirrel and marten) among the Luba (Van Caeneghem); and Moni-Mambu among the Kongo (Van Wing and Schöller, Struyf, and others).[5]

---

[5] Biebuyck and Mateene, *Anthologie de la littérature orale nyanga*

A special case seems to be presented by Lofokefoke and Kudukese, among the Mbole and Hamba. These texts seem to fall somewhere between the heroic epics and the epic cycles. In contrast to the heroic and historical epics, the epic cycles consist of a series of separate and self-contained shorter narratives that are loosely related through the central character, an exceptionally clever, shrewd, ruthless, and powerful trickster animal. The animal is preferably small and weak in the physical realm. The different episodes in which the animal hero and his feats are celebrated do not follow a fixed sequence. For a particular circumstance, the narrator can pick any one story or series of stories that form a self-contained whole within the general framework of themes and motives. The individual storyteller is allowed much improvisation. Epic recitations and praise poems from the Congo Republic are not well known and definitely not developed as in parts of East and South Africa. Some of the recorded *kasala* songs of the Luba and the praises for chiefs and mountains of the Nyanga fit the pattern as identified by Knappert.[6]

As a distinctive category of literary composition characterized by a particular style, form, content, function, and

---

[Nyanga epic hero cycles]; John Jacobs, *Tetela-Teksten* (Tervuren: Musée Royal de l'Afrique Centrale, 1959) [Tetela epic hero cycles]; Leo Stappers, *Textes Luba. Contes d'animaux* (Tervuren: Musée Royal de l'Afrique Centrale, 1962) [Luba epic hero cycles]; Leo Bittremieux, *Mayombsche Penneschetsen* (Bruges: Sint Michiel, 1914) [Yumbe epic hero cycles]; E. E. Evans-Pritchard, *The Zande Trickster* (Oxford: The Clarendon Press, 1967) [Zande epic hero cycles]; R. Van Caeneghem, *Kabundi Sprookjes* (Brussels: Vromant, 1938) [Luba epic hero cycles]; J. Van Wing and Cl. Schöller, *Legendes des Bakongo Orientaux* (Louvain: Aucam, 1940) and I. Struyf and E. Tromont, *Les Bakongo dans leurs légendes* (Brussels, 1936) [Congo epic hero cycle].

[6] Van Caeneghem, "De Kasala-Zang der Baluba"; Van Caeneghem, "De Kasala-Zang van den Bakwangastam"; Van Caeneghem, "Bakwa-Tshimini (Kasai)" [*Kasala songs of the Luba*]; Biebuyck and Mateene, *Anthologie de la littérature orale nyanga* [Nyanga praise poems]; Jan Knappert, "The Epic in Africa," *Journal of the Folklore Institute* 4 (1967) Nos. 2–3: 189.

meaning, the Central African epic has barely received any systematic treatment. And yet it is perhaps the most fascinating and profound literary achievement of Africa, because of the wealth of cultural information it provides, the richness of the language in which it is formulated, the complexity and loftiness of its style, its synthesizing character, and the deep thought patterns it reflects.

In the Lega and Nyanga areas, where I undertook my research, the epic is classified as a separate genre in the linguistic taxonomy of the people. The Nyanga call it *kárįsį* to distinguish it from other, well-isolated categories of literature such as the tales with or without a mysterious content (*uano, mushinga*), the "true" stories (*kishambaro*), the narration of extraordinary events that happened to particular individuals (*nganuriro*), and other genres.[7] The Lega classify the epic as *lugano* and contrast it, as a distinctive category, to their other genres.

Unlike the other genres, samples of which are widely known to, and narrated by, vast numbers of individuals of different sex, age, and social status, the epics are known and recited only by very few individuals. It seems impossible to say exactly how many people narrate such texts in the traditional community. Indirectly, their scarcity can be measured from the fact that in the late fifties only rare individuals among the Nyanga, the Lega, the Mbole, the Hamba, and the Mongo knew a coherent epic text. Yet, in the Lega and Nyanga communities, no special social status relates to the position of epic bard. The individual narrators of the epics do not belong to any specific kinship groups, although among the Nyanga at least, the bard's group has a history of close association with the Pygmies. The bards do not hold any particular social, political, or ritual position, as bards; when they do hold such a position, it is purely coincidental. Among the Mongo, Hamba, Mbole, Lega, and Nyanga the bard is not a professional.

Fame and a widespread reputation as *shékárįsį* (master of the epic) among the Nyanga, and *mugani wa lugano* (teller

[7] Biebuyck and Mateene, *The Mwindo Epic from the Banyanga*.

of the epic) among the Lega, are the only immediately perceivable personal gratifications that the individuals derive from their art. The verb *kugana,* from which the deverbative *mugani* is derived, is interpreted by the Lega to apply to "a preferred son (*ngoli*) who does not go to a place of danger." From this point of view, *mugani,* which is the term for bard among the Lega, seems to place the emphasis on his role of preserver. Interestingly, the bard is sometimes referred to by the Lega as Kyanga. Kyanga is mentioned in some ethnohistorical traditions as a junior brother of Kalaga, the Messenger (a brother of Kinkung[w]a, the Creator God) who was sent by him after the initial creation of the physical world and its beings to provide the people with their customs and taboos. In other words, to provide them with culture. Under the name Yangya (?), Kyanga is known among the Bembe (the eastern neighbors of the Lega) as one of the most powerful nature spirits. Reference to the bard as Kyanga, then, seems to emphasize the fact that, in Lega thinking, the bard obtains his knowledge directly from a divine source. This idea of the quasi-divine origin of the bard's knowledge is also found among the Mongo. Some Mongo bards pretend to have been designated by the spirits and to have received the knowledge from dead grandfathers who came to fetch them during the night after a series of traumatic experiences and taught them the epic near a graveyard.[8]

The mode of presentation of the epic has special features. Invariably, the narration of oral texts draws a participating crowd in the African communities. Song, recitation, and pure narration frequently alternate as part of a single performance. Musical instruments are often played in conjunction with the narration. The narration leads to much social interaction, and sometimes to dramatic action as well. The mode of presentation of the epic, the total setting in which it takes place, although leaving room for improvisation and individualized ways of doing things, follows a formalized and prescribed

[8] E. Boelaert, "Nog over het epos van de Mongo," *Kongo Overzee* 20 (1952) Nos. 4–5: 289–92; E. Boelaert, "Lianja, het nationaal epos der Mongo," *Verhandelingen K.V.H.U.* (1960): 3–58.

method. The epic is sung, episode by episode; then the episode is narrated and dramatically acted out. The entire epic cannot, of course, be performed in a single evening or a single day. A series of consecutive evening performances may be scheduled, but a single performance may also be limited to one evening and restricted to a couple of episodes. The bard is largely free to select whichever episode he wants, depending somewhat on his mood, inspiration, and sometimes on local social circumstances. During the singing of any episode, the bard is seated and accompanies himself with a rattle. He may also hold a representation of one of the favorite symbols of the hero, such as the *conga* scepter, which, in the Mwindo epic of the Nyanga, is the major magical device the hero possesses. The singing bard is accompanied by a percussion stick, which is placed on the ground and is beaten with small drumsticks by three to four young men. Many Nyanga and Lega men know how to beat the percussion stick and many know the particular rhythms of the epic, yet the bard perfers to work with percussionists with whom he is familiar (people of his village, or individuals selected from within the bard's own field of kinship relations). These young men, together with people in the crowd, also hum while the bard sings. They sing portions of the sentences when the bard pauses for a moment at the end of a sentence or series of sentences, or when he is for a moment in "trouble" trying to recall the exact sequence of events. At all times during the singing of an episode the percussionists keep up with the rhythm and humming and singing, enhancing the sound and sometimes speeding up the rhythm when the bard pauses. As I have seen the system at work, this is a powerful method to stimulate and inspire the bard. During the singing, another man, called *mwitabizia*, is seated in front of the bard. He is an apprentice, generally a fairly close relative of the bard (a junior brother, or a son, or preferably a grandson), who maintains a constant and close relationship with the bard and accompanies him wherever he goes. The *mwitabizia* participates very actively in the performance: he sings with the choir, repeats parts of the sentences, makes exclamations and praises; he gives encouragements and most importantly, since he already knows much of the epic, he helps the bard to find the thread of the narrative whenever he is in some difficulty. This may lead to outright conversation and discussion, while the percussionists and the choir of participant spectators continue the rhythms and the humming.

When the episode is sung, the bard then proceeds to narrate it and act it out. Normally, there is no music or singing at this time, the entire focus being on the dramatic action performed by the bard. In terms of content some passages lend themselves much better for such performances than others. During the performance of the Mwindo epic, I witnessed the most beautiful pieces of dramatic action when the hero set out in quest of honey and was chased by bees or done other harm by his enemies, or when he was involved with the Herculean task of making a banana grove and growing the plants to maturity in a single day. Sometimes an episode is characterized by much dialogue or by songs in verse form. In such cases the bard, accompanied by the percussionists and the choir of spectators, may sing again. When the entire episode is finished, there may be a long break before they proceed to another episode, or no other performance may follow. During the break there is an opportunity for relaxation and further enjoyment, for the drinking of beer and general dance performances (called "evening drum" by the Nyanga) by the participants. Among the Lega and Nyanga, the bard is not specially costumed for the occasion, but among the Mongo he is dressed as an *esombi* dancer, with feathers and body painting.[9]

A large number of literary texts are linked with specific social contexts, and even specific periods of time, within which they are to be narrated. In some cases, stories can be told only in the evening after sunset; in other cases, texts are sung and narrated only during particular celebrations and rituals. The Nyanga have elaborate circumcision ceremonies (*mukumo*) and complex initiations that lead to membership in various types of voluntary associations (Mumbira,

---

[9] Boelaert, "Lianja, het nationaal epos der Mongo," p. 13.

Mpande, Mbuntsu) in which specific types of proverbs are used. The Lega also have an elaborate system of boys' circumcision ceremonies (*bwali*), post-circumcision youth education (*mutanga*), and extremely complex initiations leading to membership in the *bwami* association, for which large quantities of aphorisms are reserved. In none of these more esoteric forms of activity do epic narrations occur. The epic performance is something like a common "national" patrimony which belongs to all the members of the ethnic group. The hero is a "national" hero, and not the instrument of any specialized subgroup or subsystem in the culture. Therefore, there are no specially prescribed circumstances when the epics can be performed. Nobody in particular is excluded from attending the performances, and nobody is prohibited from narrating whatever section of the epic he may know.

In form, style, and content, the Mongo, Lega, and Nyanga epics have many distinguishing features. The language in which the epic is formulated is usually rich and subtly used by the bards, who are true masters of verbal art. The vocabulary is abundant and there are many refined variations in the use of grammar. The texts abound with complicated metaphorical expressions and subtle nuances in the choice of verbal expressions and their conjugation. The structure of the sentence is terse, succinct, precise, incisive. The style is lofty in the narrative and the speeches, and poetic in the songs. There is a true cult for stylistic effect. In the Nyanga epic, indirect discourse, unfamiliar reversal of word order in the sentence, epithets, and repetitive formulaic expressions are very numerous. All possible stylistic effects are drawn into the narration, and here the creative genius of the individual artist can manifest itself most strongly. Certain bards whom I have heard performing among the Nyanga had a special gift for the use of sonorous effects, obtained particularly through reduplication of words and a generous application of ideophones. Others were specialized in the extremely refined and nuanced metaphorical usage of verbs.

The mastery of the bard manifests itself most strongly in the completeness, the consistency, and the logical coherence

of the epic and of the constituent episodes. There are beginnings and ends to the Lega and Nyanga epics, and between these there are sequences of events that flow from
one to the other without interruption or break in the plan,
the plot, and the themes. The quality of the bard is largely
judged in terms of the control that he has over all of this.
Among the Nyanga, I was brought into contact with several
individuals who were said to know the Mwindo or Kárįsį
epic. When they were invited to perform and demonstrate
their art, they were sometimes promptly dismissed because
they were unable to keep episodes and sequences of events
clearly apart from each other. It is sometimes said that an
epic text is without end, that it can be developed and expanded *ad infinitum*, and that the number of specific episodes
is almost limitless.[10] This is theoretically possible if one were
able to get all the episodes and fragments and variations
that are known to all the narrators in the society. I conclude,
however, from my experience among the Nyanga and Lega
that, in practice, there is a complete text in the mind of
every knowledgeable individual narrator—a text that has a
beginning and an end—which follows a basic structure and
constitutes a coherent and well-rounded whole. Boelaert has
pointed out that, for the Mongo, as a minimum three key
episodes are necessary for a complete version: the fight for
the forbidden fruit, the birth of the hero Lianja and his sister
Nsongo and the vengeance over the parricide, and the trip
to the promised land.[11] Jacobs also finds an underlying pattern in the essential episodes of the epics of the Hamba,
Mbole, Langa, etc.[12]

The epic is, so to speak, a supergenre that encompasses
and harmoniously fuses together practically all genres known
in a particular culture. The Mwindo epic is typical in this
respect. There are prose and poetry in the epic, the narrative
being constantly intersected with songs in poetic form. The

[10] Boelaert, "Lianja, het nationaal epos der Mongo," p. 13;
De Rop, *Lianja, l'épopée des Mongo,* p. 17.

[11] Ibid., p. 18.

[12] Jacobs, "Het epos van Kudukese, de culture hero van de
Hamba (Kongo)," p. 36.

prose narrative to some extent, and the songs to a large extent, incorporate proverbs, riddles, praises, succinct aphoristic abstracts of tales, prayers, improvisations, and allusions and references to "true" stories and persons. Among the Lega and Tetela, where the techniques of message drumming are highly developed, drum names and drum formulae are an intrinsic part of the story. This mixture of prose and poetry, of song and narration, of aphorisms and improvisations is also present in the Mongo epics.

The content of the epic constitutes an encyclopedic inventory of the most diverse aspects of a people's culture. There are direct and indirect statements about the history, the social institutions and social relationships, the material culture, and the system of values and ideas. The Lianja epic provides considerable insights into the social, economic, and religious life of the Mongo. It gives information about customs related to birth, marriage, and death; about the various economic activities (agriculture, hunting, trapping, food gathering, fishing) and the arts and crafts; about God, the ancestors, magic, witchcraft, dreams, rituals. It is also a historical document that offers information about migrations, and interrelationships of different groups.[13] The Mwindo epic makes direct statements about such diverse features as the material culture; the economy; the technology of hunting, gathering, and cultivating; the marriage system; the kinship terminology and the code of social relationships; the political structure; the religious conceptions and the cults; and the values and sentiments. It also makes abundant reference to the physical world in which the Nyanga live. The choice of actors in the Mwindo epic provides, by itself, a wide sample of significant social personalities and beings in Nyanga social organization and thought. The hero himself has fully human, Pygmy-like characteristics, but has, in addition, supernatural gifts. He is surrounded by animals, other humans with whom he may stand in a kinship position, divinities, fabulous beings, and abstract characters (such as

[13] De Rop, *Lianja, l'épopée des Mongo,* pp. 47–50.

the Idiot and the Smart One). The Nyanga are not a history-minded people. Their ethnohistorical traditions contain only scanty information about their origins in Bunyoro and their migrations southwestward into the rain forest, where they now live, via the savanna areas west of Lake Edward and the volcanic region located east of their present habitat. It is the contact with the Pygmies that has been of particular relevance for the Nyanga, and this has been clearly suggested in the epic. Nyanga exposure to influences from their neighbors and from the West are barely perceptible in the epic. Contacts with the West are revealed only by the use of a few Nyangaized words of French or Swahili origin (such as *muramt* for *Madame*, or *karani* for *clerc*, or scribe). Some of the explicit statements about the culture are not to be taken at their face value. There are omissions and distortions, and these are deliberately made to put the hero in a certain perspective or to cause laughter and incredulity. This is brought out very clearly in the description of the courtship procedures of Mukiti and Nyangura, which become something like a parody of the normal practices.

In addition, the sentence structure, on the one hand, and the entire plan of the epic, on the other, indirectly provide deep insight into a key feature of Nyanga thinking: their preoccupation with space and place. The sentences abound with repetitive locative expressions and place indications. The plan of the epic follows all major cosmological divisions recognized by the Nyanga. The action takes place on earth (*oto*), in the underworld (*kwirunga*), in the atmosphere (*mwanya*), and in the remote sky (*butu*). Earth itself is subdivided between the inhabited world (*mbuka*, i.e., village, hamlet, and ancient village site); the forest of immediate utility (*mundura*), with fields, fallow land, and secondary forest; the virgin forest (*busara*); and the water (*rusi*). The epic is, in other words, complete, because it is comprehensive and consistent in its ground plan with the total Nyanga view of the world. The hero becomes, so to speak, a true hero only after he has successfully completed the whole cycle of events and deeds that put him through all the relevant spheres of the world. It is noteworthy in this respect that the conceptualization of the world includes, in the Nyanga view, only the territory inhabited by the Nyanga.

The Pygmies mentioned in the epic are an intrinsic part of Nyanga society and the Nyanga world. There are terms in Nyanga language to refer to strangers (*mweni*, a concept that includes the notion of guest) coming from within the society and from segments of neighboring groups that are largely adjusted and acculturated to Nyanga culture. There are no foreigners for the Nyanga (except for the few black and white foreigners who came into Nyanga society in the late nineteenth and twentieth centuries). All immediate neighboring groups, although distinctively of different ethnic origin, are named by special terms such as Bafuna (Hunde), or Bakumbure or Batiri-Baasa (Komo), and are fully involved through marriage, hunting, and friendship bonds with Nyanga society.

The life pattern of the hero follows roughly some of the criteria isolated by De Vries.[14] The principal aspects of Mwindo's life cycle can here be mentioned:

— the hero is conceived under special circumstances;
— his mother is a woman of special status (preferred wife), which she loses after the birth of her unwanted son;
— the child is born miraculously;
— the child is threatened in its early youth, in this case immediately after its birth and as a matter of fact before its birth;
— the hero is removed from his home and his social context;
— the hero goes through a series of hardships and trials during which he severely suffers to a point of almost being annihilated, but he manages to overcome the difficulties, sometimes through the performance of Herculean tasks, sometimes through his magical

[14] Jan de Vries, *Heldenlied en heldensage* (Utrecht: Het Spectrum, 1959), pp. 194–208.

powers, sometimes through the power of his word,
sometimes through his allies;
— in this series of happenings, the hero makes subter-
ranean and celestial journeys;
— the hero is involved in a dragon fight;
— the hero reaches his glory through a catharsis.

In the Lianja epic many of these patterns occur: the hero
is born through his mother's tibia; the hero leaves home in
quest of the parricide; he goes through a number of Herculean performances; he is involved in a fight with a giant snake,
etc.[15] There are significant deviations from the pattern,
however, in both the Mwindo and the Lianja epics. From
this point of view, there are striking similarities between the
epics. For example, in both epics the unborn hero speaks in
his mother's womb asking himself in what manner he should
be born. In both epics, the hero is born with certain imple-
ments which form his strength (Lianja is born with a spear,
a knife, the stick and bell of his father, a gong and his hunting
horn, his arrows and his necklace). In both texts, the hero
has a quasi invulnerability: when the hero faints because
of great hardship, he is awakened by his bell (Lianja) or
by his scepter (Mwindo).

In the Mwindo epic, the heroic stature of the child to be
born is foreshadowed by the performance of menial tasks for
his mother. The child is born through its own volition and
with several paraphernalia that have supernatural power and
are, so to speak, an intrinsic part of its personality. The hero
does not go through a process of youthful maturation. His
existence is threatened right after birth (even before his
birth, the father had said that he wanted no boys); his entire existence is taken up from birth to his glory, in a search,
first, for his paternal aunt, and second, for his father, while
fighting his enemies. In this process the hero never seems to
grow or to mature. This lack of interest in chronological
process is typical, again, of the Nyanga concern with space
and place rather than with time. Heroes frequently have a

[15] De Rop, *Lianja, l'épopée des Mongo*, pp. 31–46.

faithful friend and companion who is extremely close to them. Among the Lega this person is Mubila's wife, Kabungulu; among the Mongo it is Lianja's sister, Nsongo; among the Nyanga it is the paternal aunt, Iyangura.

The close tie between Mwindo and his paternal aunt deserves some explanation. It cannot simply be explained in terms of the special (amitate) relationship between a person and his paternal aunt which is widely found in African societies. The bond here has a deep, quasi-mystic meaning. In Nyanga custom, the chief's sister is frequently not married out, but invited to raise children as a spirit wife or lineage wife, with a "lover" of her choice on behalf of her brother's group. She continues to live in her home village and generally maintains very close ties with her brother's children. The quest of Mwindo for his paternal aunt is to be interpreted as an attempt to restore a balance that was disturbed by Mukiti's unexpected claims in Iyangura. Heroic deeds are set against a background of conflict and warfare. There is inbuilt conflict in the Mwindo and Mubila epics, and there is constant talk about fighting and feuding; there is, however, no full-scale warfare. The hero himself, moreover, is not a superior fighter. Mwindo is implicitly weak (although this is never said explicitly), since he is "The Little-One" and "A child-just-born-yesterday." His strength resides in the mind (he has some gift of premonition and he has the power of the word and of the dance) and in external objects (his *conga* scepter and objects contained in his shoulder bag). Mubila, among the Lega, is not weak, but his strength lies in external attributes (his whistle, his shoulder bag) and particularly with his wife, Kabungulu, whose apron is destructive. The Nyanga hero is vulnerable (on different occasions the heavy blows to which he is exposed put him in a deep torpor that resembles death), but there is never any reference to serious physical injury. More importantly, the hero has a quasi immortality on earth; Mwindo rules in glory at the end of the epic; Lianja, with his sister and his brother Pygmy, climbs up a giant palm tree, and his annual return is celebrated in the Lianja processions among the Mongo.[16] The theme of the quest for a *jungfrau* is completely absent in the Mwindo and Mubila epics.

The heroic stature and unlikelihood of the hero is not so much to be found in the extraordinary events in which he is involved and in the exceptional feats that he performs (the Nyanga like to narrate extraordinary events as if they had really happened). The special character of the Nyanga and Lega hero lies in the fact that, during the major part of the epic, he is in flagrant conflict with the basic value code of his people and gets away with it. Mwindo is boastful, morose, irascible, proud, intrepid, scornful, arrogant. He has his way for a long time, yet these personality traits put him in direct opposition to the values for which the Nyanga stand. During this critical period, however, Mwindo never becomes unacceptable, because he maintains certain qualities of tenderness toward his mother, respect toward his paternal aunt, generosity toward weak persons, and ultimate piety toward his father. These qualities help to maintain a certain balance, until the hero is completely purified from his excesses through suffering and impotence in the celestial realm. Mubila, among the Lega, is also a boaster, a restless traveler, aggressive, proud, and intrepid. These characteristics place him too much in opposition to the moral code of *busoga*, that search for temperance and moderation which is the key to Lega moral philosophy.

The Nyanga and Lega epics cannot simply be qualified as mythical, etiological, didactic, or moralizing. All these elements are implicit, and sometimes explicit in the narrative. The epic harmoniously blends these elements with historical fact and actual culture. The Mwindo epic, for example, partially revolves around the constant interaction between the supranatural and the human worlds, between the hero and various divinities, mythical beings, and semi-divine theriomorph personages. The origin of several customary practices, such as the worship of Lightning, is explicitly mentioned, and there is an implicit interpretation of how homogeneous king-

[16] E. Boelaert, "La procession de Lianja," *Aequatoria* 25 (1962) No. 1: 1–9.

doms came to be fragmented. The didactic nature is implicit throughout, because of the encyclopedic character of the text. The moralizing aspects are explicitly formulated at the end of the epic and here and there in dialogues or speeches; they are implicit in the direct and indirect reference to the value system. The action itself, although mostly at the heroic level, returns steadily to the familiar village context, with common people (the counselors, the princes, the commoners, the women, the little children) and Pygmies interacting with the hero. The entire epic is placed against the background of a well-known region in Nyangaland itself. In listening to the epic, the Nyanga themselves are surprised that they know and do so many things. Nowhere in their oral traditions is a more comprehensive account given of the culture in such a succinct, incisive, and poetic manner. Historically, the epic is both close and remote to them. Close because its action revolves within a cultural and environmental framework which is that of the present-day Nyanga, and remote because the Nyanga know that the tradition of the text takes them far back in time to the earliest encounters with the Pygmies, whom, they pretend, were the first narrators of these stories. In listening to the epic, the Nyanga marvel at the treasures of their culture and find pride and confidence from the epic. This is a truly "national" patrimony.

HEROIC SONGS OF
THE MANDE HUNTERS

Charles Bird

The Mande is the historic region often referred to as Old
Mali, found at the headwaters of the Niger River. The core
area extends from Ségou, Mali, in the north, down to about
Boundali in the northern Ivory Coast, and from Ségou in
the east to the river Falémé in the west. This core area has
western extensions running into eastern Senegal, Gambia,
and Guinea; northern extensions running up to Mopti, in
Mali; eastern extensions spreading into central Upper Volta
and the north of Ghana; and southern extensions descending
as far as Abidjan, in the Ivory Coast.

The people who constitute the majority of the population
in the core area are called Bambara in the northeastern section, Dyula in the southern and southeastern sections, and
Maninka, Malinke, or Mandinka in the western section of
the core. The people in the western extensions are often
referred to as Mandingo; and in northern Ghana, in the western extension, they are referred to as Wangara. In spite of
this plethora of names, it is most important to note that all
these people speak the same language, granting, of course,
considerable regional variation, and they all recognize a
largely common history. The origins of the appellations Bambara and Dyula are little understood, and most attempts to
account for their origins have been little better than spurious
folk etymologies. Mandinka is a word derived from Mande

plus the suffix *ka* meaning "people of." Maninka is, of course, a form derived from Mandinka by the very general dialect rule that converts the prenasalized stop *nd* to the nasal continuant *n*. The language has been grouped with Susu, Soninke, and Vai-Kono to form the northern set of Mande languages, which themselves are claimed by Greenberg to be included in the Niger-Congo family.[1]

As I have outlined elsewhere, there are three major types of oral art in the Mande, which may be roughly labeled as follows: folk stories, the epic songs of the griots (the casted bards of the Mande), and the songs of the hunters.[2]

The role of the hunters in providing game for the society has been of marginal economic importance for a long time. Patrick Munson, in describing the culture that was most likely the ancestor of the northern Mande peoples, states that as long ago as 2000 B.C. hunting did not play a vital role in providing food for the people. It may be that in periods of famine the hunters were the sole support of the society.

In the Mande, a man does not own land, but rather he has certain rights governing its exploitation. One man may have the rights to farm a piece of land, while another might have the rights to the fruit of the trees on the same land. Each hunter's group is also defined in this context, as having the rights to hunt on a particular piece of land. The hunters are organized in groups extending over large areas. One of the striking characteristics of these groups is that they are not defined along ethnic lines. They are in fact a mechanism for assimilating the diverse peoples of a particular region into a workable suprasocial unit. It is not at all surprising, for example, to find Bambara, Maninka, Fula, Soninke, and Senufo members of the same hunters' group. By participating in the hunters' group, the minorities not only gain access to the game available in that area, but they are more likely to cross ethnic lines through intermarriage than would other-

---

[1] Joseph Greenberg, *The Languages of Africa.*
[2] Charles S. Bird, "The Development of Mandekan (Manding): A Study of the Role of Extra-linguistic Factors in Linguistic Change," *Language and History in Africa,* ed. David Dalby (London, 1970), pp. 146–59.

wise be possible. As an institution that crosses over the traditional ethnic barriers, the hunters' group has played a vital role in the history of this area. It may well prove to be the institution that enabled the people of this area to establish bonds over extended geographic and cultural areas and to use these bonds for the formation of larger units which formed the basis of more powerful economic and military states such as the Ghana and Mali empires. It would, then, be no accident that great kings of the Mande past are portrayed as hunters first and foremost. It is also no accident that we find the names of some of these leaders to include reference to the *ton,* as in Bi-ton or Ton-tigi. *Ton* is the word meaning "group" and has an etymology deriving from the word for quiver. It was the *ton* of the hunters that formed the military arm of the extended region, and even as we see today, the military institutions used for the society's protection can become the instrument for that very society's subjugation and destruction.

In the cities, such as Bamako, the hunters' group is today largely a symbolic vestige of an impressive past. While the hunt still serves as an economic activity of minor importance in the bush, it has no major economic function in the cities and large towns. Nonetheless the societies remain strong and serve an integrating function. They also serve as extended fraternities devoted more to the reinforcement of the traditional past than to the vital functions of provider and defender. It would seem that the knowledge of one's past glories and allegiances are the stuff from which national identity and pride are made, and that these two elements are vital to the process of nation building.

Associated closely with the hunter is what in the Mande is called knowledge or science. The hunter must depend on an intimate knowledge of the bush for his survival. He must know the plants on which he can rely for food and medicine as well as for poison for either his game or his enemy. In addition, in the traditional universe of the Mande, no man had the natural power to take the life of another living thing without severe repercussions. Therefore, the hunter had to augment his natural powers in some manner to enable him to kill his prey and to protect himself from the destructive forces unleashed by the death of the animal. A large part of this protection is transferred to the hunter during the ceremonies that precede and follow the hunt. One of the principal actors in these ceremonies is the *donso-jeli* or hunters' bard.

It is most important to distinguish two types of professional bards in the Mande. One is associated uniquely with the hunters' groups and the other is associated with the major noble families of the Mande and is called simply "jeli" or "jali." The "jeli" is one of the endogamous subsets of Mande society often referred to as castes. These so-called castes do not have the usual vertical status characteristics we normally associate with castes. Some of the Malian castes seem to have more privileges than the nobles they serve. Certainly the smith and the bard are two of the most influential figures in any Mande village. The hunters' bard does not belong to any specific caste. He may be from a slave family, he may be a blacksmith, or even a noble. In Narena, it is reported that the casted bards[3] function as bards for the hunters as well, and in some areas the hunters themselves sing the praise and ritual songs.

Whereas the casted bard is born into his trade, the hunters' bard elects to serve as a singer for the hunters, or, in many cases, is apprenticed by his family at an early age. The casted bard is a formal institutional figure of the society, while the hunters' bard appears at first glance to be little more than a minstrel. This impression is soon dispelled by an in-depth study of the function of the hunters' bard. For example, although the hunters' bard usually is not a hunter himself, he serves as the seer, or reader of omens, for the hunters. Before the hunt, he sings songs that invoke the presence of the game through the singing of their praises and the endowing of the hunters with power. After the hunt, the hunters' bard will sing the praise of the kill, thereby pacifying and controlling the destructive forces unleashed by its death. The hunters' bard functions therefore as an inter-

---

[3] The term "casted bard" is equivalent to the French *griot*, signifying a member of an endogamous professional group of praise singers in the Mande.

mediary between the hunter and the supernatural forces of the bush. In this sense, he might be likened to a priest.[4]

The position of the hunters' bard is the result of a long apprenticeship spanning upward of ten to fifteen years. The principal bard with whom we worked, Seyidou Camara, has been singing for twenty years and has enjoyed the status of a master singer, or ŋara, for about the past eight or nine. His ensemble was composed of his wife and three apprentices, the youngest of whom was about twelve years old and the oldest about twenty-five. The oldest apprentice has been with the group for about six years.

The first stage in the apprenticeship is devoted principally to mastering the ŋarinya, a ridged metal pipe that is scraped with a metal bar to provide the basic rhythmic background to the hunters' songs. The next stage of his development is devoted to mastering the donso-nkoni, a six-string harp-lute with a calabash resonator. In most ceremonies, the master will be accompanied by at least one apprentice playing a harp-lute. The master himself will play a harp-lute, weaving extremely complex rhythmic patterns in between the base rhythm and the harp-lute of his apprentice. All this time the apprentices are listening to the prosodic style of their master, analyzing his techniques, and gradually perfecting their own oral art. As we will see, the complexity of this art is such that the apprenticeship is necessarily long and difficult.

The hunters' songs can be roughly divided into three interrelated sets: songs for amusement, ritual songs, and heroic works. All are presented with the basic 4:4 rhythmic background that defines the marchlike dance of the hunters. The songs for amusement are for dancing in which all can participate. Their content may be devoted to satire or to some bawdy or whimsical topic. Even the whimsy, however, is related to the hunters' philosophy. The tempo of these songs can be speeded up for the athletic dances of the younger hunters. The ritual songs, as mentioned before, are devoted

---

[4] For further information on the religious function of the hunters' bard see Youssouf Cissé, "Notes sur les sociétés de chasseurs malinké," *Journal de la Société des Africanistes* 34 (1964): 175–226.

to pre- and posthunt songs about the animals of the bush. Some of the ritual songs, such as the *Janjon,* can be danced only by men who have made a major kill, i.e., a lion, an elephant, a bush buffalo, or a man. The *Duga* is, in some areas, a ritual song for warriors as opposed to hunters and can be danced only by a recognized hero, one who has narrowly escaped death in battle or has killed a man in battle. It is through songs such as these that a sort of hierarchy of excellence is established among the hunters. At the end of the typical ceremony, the hunters gather around and listen to a heroic song sung about great hunters and warriors of the past. These heroic pieces may be of one to two hours' duration and be told in the course of one evening, or, in the case of a ceremony lasting several days, the performance may continue over several evenings, and the total recitation time may run upward of ten hours.

The piece that we will examine in some detail is entitled *Kambili.* It was presented in four performances lasting for over five hours and exceeding four thousand lines. *Kambili* is a heroic song for the hunters of the Wasulu, whose area is located at the northeastern corner of the Mali-Guinea border, centering in the town of Siguiri, on the Niger. The Wasulu extends in the east as far as Bougouni, in Mali, and the western limits seem to follow the valley of the Bakhoi to the region just south of Kita. To the south, the Wasulu, according to some, extends to Kankan. Although the Wasulu is often referred to as a state separate from the Mande, I have used the latter term to apply to the Old Mali empire, into which the Wasulu was more or less incorporated. Most of the inhabitants of the Wasulu call themselves Maninka. There are also large numbers of sedentary Fula in this region as well as small groups of other peoples. I have not found versions of this heroic song sung by non-Wasulu singers.

The story of Kambili is composed of three major sections: the events leading up to his birth, his youth up to his marriage to Kumba, and the events leading up to the death of the Jimini lion-man.

The first part opens with Kanji, Samory's field general, going to Samory and asking for his help. Kanji's problem is that he has nine wives, but no children. Samory calls all the omen readers and magicians from Kayirawane to find the answer to Kanji's sterility. If they cannot fully solve the problem, Samory threatens to take their heads. A number of magicians consult their varied arts for the truth and each in turn discovers that a great son will be born to Kanji. However, when asked which wife will have the child, the magicians cannot supply the information and they are summarily executed. Finally only two seers are left, the Marabout and Bari the Truth-Seer. Both men find out through their art that Kanji can only have a son by his rejected wife, Dugo, who has been sent out by the other wives to herd goats. It was Bari the Truth-Seer who first discovered the correct answer. The Marabout, through jealousy, tries to trick Bari, but Bari's magical ability is too great and the Marabout withdraws. This is an extremely interesting aspect of the hunters' songs. They do not necessarily denigrate Islam but they go to great effort to show that the knowledge to be gained from Islam is inferior to their own. Through a series of intrigues, Dugo is brought back to the palace and bedded with Kanji. Soon Kambili is born.

In the second section of the story, Kanji's first wife, who was to blame for all of Dugo's original hardships, tries to kill Kambili, but Kanji rescues him and kills the evil first wife. Kambili grows up to be a great hunter. Numerous episodes are told of his exploits with the animals of the bush. As a small boy, for example, he brings home a bush buffalo on a leash, explaining that he thought it to be one of his father's stray cows. He next brings home a lion on a leash, thinking it to be one of his father's stray dogs. Kambili grows up to be a leader of the hunters, and this section ends with his marriage to Kumba, a beautiful girl with considerable magical talents in her own right.

When it is announced that there is a lion-man in Jimini, Kambili is engaged to destroy him before the lion-man devours the entire village. Kumba learns the identity of the lion-man, and Bari the Truth-Seer is called to discover the source of the lion-man's secret power. Bari tells them they need some hair from the lion-man's head, from under his arm, and from his crotch; a sandal from his foot; and an old pair of his trousers. Kumba tricks the lion-man, obtains the necessary items, and returns with them. Bari tells Kambili to bury the items by an old tree near the market and to consult the idol called Nya-ji. The idol tells Kambili where he is to encounter and kill the lion-man. Kambili sets a trap, using a young boy as bait. Kumba brings the lion-man into the trap. The lion-man's magic causes Kambili to fall asleep. Just as he is about to devour the boy, the boy's pleas awaken Kambili and he shoots and kills the lion-man. The piece ends with a festive celebration in Jimini, and the Imam grants generous gifts to Kambili and Kumba.

Although the hero Kambili plays an important role, the storyteller goes to great pains to show the debt he owes to the women in his life. Through his mother's supernatural powers he becomes a great hunter, and through his wife's magical powers he is able to kill the lion-man of Jimini.

The heroic songs, as well as the epics, contain a number of sophisticated storytelling devices. Flashbacks are not uncommon and are often resorted to when there is a physical separation of two main characters in the story. Frequently, when a new character is introduced, the storyteller inserts a flashback to indicate how the new character became involved in the main story line. In Kambili, subplots such as the power contest between Bari the Truth-Seer and the Marabout are commonplace and are usually well integrated into the main plot.

In studying the poetic construction of these pieces, a good point of departure can be found in Albert Lord's brilliant book *The Singer of Tales*.[5] In this study, Lord illustrates how the epic singer masters an abstract theory of versification, enabling him spontaneously to generate highly complex poetic lines that form an epic of considerable length. Lord stresses that the epic singer does not memorize his work, and this claim is illustrated by the differences between any two performances of the same work by the same singer. The

[5] Albert Lord, *The Singer of Tales* (Cambridge, Mass., 1960).

singer has learned an additional set of rules which he adds to the normal grammar of his language and which permits him to generate an unlimited number of lines defined by a particular set of stylistic constraints and a more or less abstract thematic outline. In each performance, the singer combines the two abstract systems of style and theme to recreate the piece. That even the thematic material is highly abstract is illustrated by the performance of *Kambili* told in four sessions. At the beginnings of the last three sessions the bard would make a résumé of what had preceded. Frequently, the events would not be the same in the résumé as in the previous performance.

Lord points out that one of the keys to the epic singer's stylistic grammar is the formula. The formula may be roughly defined as a kind of abstract-pattern sentence into which the singer can substitute a great number of words, creating a line that will meet the metrical requirements of the poem.

A major difference exists between the structure of the Serbo-Croatian singer's art and that of the bard in the Mande. The nature of the line of the Serbo-Croatian singer is strictly defined by the number of syllables and the placement of stresses, whereas the nature of the line for the Mande bard is much looser, determined essentially by the rhythm of the instrumental background. The formulas of the Mande bards serve quite different functions. The singer has much more freedom than his Serbo-Croatian counterpart, and the formulas do not have to coincide with any rhythmic or accent demands. For example, in the case of the hunters' songs, the theoretical line equals the measure, and the measure equals four beats. The essential metrical requirement is that the singer keep in rhythm with his instrumental accompaniment. He may therefore form lines of one syllable or fifty syllables, depending very much on his virtuosity in rapid speech, and his subtlety in weaving the rhythms of his language around those of his instruments. The singer can play with background rhythm by forming couplets or even longer verses. In the case of the couplet, the only requirement seems to be that the singer terminate his line within eight beats without any caesura after the fourth. For example, at the beginning of *Kambili,* each of the following lines occurs in lines with four beats:

Jon b'i sumu i la	a slave spends but a late evening with you
Jon t'i to i la	a slave doesn't stay on with you

Later in the piece, the bard uses the same two lines but says both lines within one 4-beat measure.

Three very noticeable styles or genres can be detected during the performance. The first of these occurs when the singer is in what I call his proverb-praise mode. In this mode the singer illustrates his virtuosity and his claim to truth by emitting, usually at a high rate of speed, numerous proverbs, sayings, and praise lines. The singer employs the proverb mode at the beginning of the performance to tune up his vocal and mental apparatus, warm up the audience, and establish his veracity and authenticity. The singer also uses the proverb-praise mode when resting mentally, as a sort of automatic pilot, while he plans out his attack on the next part of the story. It is therefore not uncommon to find the proverb-praise mode at all major divisions in the story, or where the singer has made an error of grammar or omission and is forced to insert a flashback for the continuity of his story.

The term proverb-praise mode is perhaps deceiving, because the content of this mode is only partially accounted for by proverbs and praise lines. Frequently, formulaic expressions are used that do not have the status of proverbs, but are rather earmarks of the particular artist. It will be easier to explain the nature of this mode by example:

> derinan-fen-dun te kolo-kojuguya di
> (Eating the habitual dish is not an evil deed.)
> mògo-kalan-ci n'i se-ci ma kanya
> (A man's learning and his ability are not the same.)
> Kabaya ŋonin-fo-Sedu bara nà
> (Harp-playing Seydou of Kabaya has come.)

Ah! wuya man nyì, karamogo
(Ah! lies are evil, Master.)

Lines 41 and 42 are proverbs used commonly in the culture, whereas line 43 is one of the typical praise lines that the singer uses for himself. Line 44 is what I call a coda line, which is usually employed at the end of a set and is invariably followed by an instrumental break of a measure or two.

Frequently the proverbs and sayings are linked together in conceptual sets of suggestions and implications. The proverb in line 42 has the meaning that a man's destiny, that which has been preordained by Allah, is not the same as that which a man has learned. The singer implies therefore in line 43 that his talent is none of his doing: his excellence at his profession is the work of Allah. The relation between lines 42 and 43 becomes thereby more obvious. Apart from conceptual linking of proverbs and praise lines, there is considerable formulaic patterning in the proverb mode. Here the formula is simply defined as a sentence into which the artist can substitute in one or more slots any number of words.

In a long piece such as *Kambili*, Seyidu Camara performed more than one quarter of the time in the proverb-praise mode. He used close to one hundred and fifty different proverbs, sayings, and praise lines, many of which he repeated throughout the text. Some of the lines are repeated over thirty times within the approximately four thousand lines of the piece. In *Kambili*, the following formulaic pattern occurs over one hundred fifty times.

$$ X \left\{ \begin{array}{c} \text{nyininka} \\ \text{fo} \end{array} \right\} \text{ni Y} $$

$$ (\left\{ \begin{array}{c} \text{look to} \\ \text{salute} \end{array} \right\} \text{X as a Y)} $$

nɔ-bɔ-wulu'nyìninka ni fɛlɛ-kɛ-wulu
(look to the tracking dog for the hunting dog)

kɔgɔ. . . . . ni na-bɛɛ-diya
(. . . . . . . salt . . . . . . success of the sauce)

sìgilan-kurun . . . . ni suma-bɛɛ-lamina
(. . . . . . . stool . . . . . . seizing all the smells)

lɛmpɛn-fani . . . .
(. . . . woman's loincloth . . . .)

jakuma . . . . ko-man-di-bɛɛ-la
(. . . . . . . cat . . . . . . thing not easy for all)

nà-n-kama . . . . wolo-n-kama
(. . . . man of purpose . . . man of destiny)

Similarly the following pattern occurs close to fifty times:

sàya ' tɛ mɔgɔ ' to
(Death does not pass a man by)

sàya ' tɛ mɔgɔ ' to k'i bɔlen maka
(Death does not pass a man by if he's been to Mecca)

. . . . den-tigi-ya la
(. . . . . , with many children)

. . . . k'i kɛ sarama di
(. . . . . if he be charming)

. . . . k'i diya
(. . . . . if he be at ease)

Inserted into the proverb mode are pieces that have no direct
relevance to the story but serve to remind the audience of
other stories of great hunter heroes or to praise the game to
be hunted. Lines 270 through 284 were sung in the middle
of a string of proverbs and look suspiciously like lines from
another song.

kà n sɔn kùn nɔ
(And I was given a skull)
ko n na nya-na-ko-tinto
(as a face-washing bowl)
kà n sɔn wòlo la
(I was given a skin)
ko n na biri-fani
(as a covering cloth)
nɛn ba ' bila n da
(A great tongue has been granted me)
ko n ye kuma n'a ye
(That I may speak with it)
cɛ-ba-kɔrɔ ' bara n sɔn jeli-kɛnɛ ' la
(The brave has offered me fresh blood)
nya-na-ko-ji
(as face-washing water)
kà n sɔn gòlo la
(and offered me a skin)
iyo biri-fani
(as a covering cloth)
kà ku ba bìla n kɔrɔ
(and granted me a great tail)
iyo bon-firan-siran
(as a hut-sweeping broom)
kà n sɔn gwènɛ-kala la
(and offered me a thighbone)
da-rɔ-ko-gwɛsɛ
((for) a toothpick)

Lines 2560 through 2571 were also inserted in the midst of a
proverb set and serve to praise the bushbuck with powerful
poetic imagery.

kombo wuluga fuga rɔ
(the buck flashes across the plain)
ko i barantamu
(like barantamu)
kombo wuluga fuga rɔ
(the buck flashes across the plain)
ko i barantamu
(like barantamu)
fuga-rɔ-so-kɛ ba kirikintan

(great stallion of the plain without bridle)
à kɔnɔ-bara bon ba, haramu t'a rɔ
(his belly great, not a handout in it)
à da bara gwɛlɛn
(his mouth has whitened)
à da ma su nantanba to-mugu rɔ
(his mouth hasn't dipped into the coward's flour)
à ku ka surun dugu rɔ
(his tail is close to the ground)
nantan bolo t'à mìna
(the coward's hand won't grab it)
à tulo bon ba
(his ear is great)
nantan ba to-bɔ-yɛlɛ tɛ
(it's not a spoon for the coward's porridge)

The next distinctive style is what I will call the narrative mode, whose function is to tell the story. It is signaled stylistically by a regularization of the singer's rhythm. Here again the formulaic patterns play an important role in establishing the rhythmic regularity of the lines. Here is another example from *Kambili*

à d'i kanbɔ tìnyɛ-da-la ' mà
(he spoke out to the omen readers)
k'i kanbɔ ngòro-fili-la ' mà
(and spoke out to the cowrie throwers)
k'i kanbɔ ngòro-nin-tigi ' mà
(and spoke out to the little cowrie man)
à d'i kanbɔ mori-cɛba ù mà
(He spoke out to the great Marabouts)
à d'i kanbɔ kùrana-tigi ' ma
(He spoke out to the man of the Koran)
"à ye na n dɛmɛ den-ko ' la
("Come help me with this child matter,)
alu min ni Ala ye kumala."
(those of you who speak with Allah.")
à d'i kanbɔ jina-tigi ' ma
(He spoke out to the spirit men)

ko ngòro-tigi ' di,
(like the cowrie man,)
"à ye na n dɛmɛ den-ko ' la
("Come help me with this child matter,)
alu min ye ngòro-kisɛ ' lɔn
(those of you who know the cowries,)
yagasa Kànji ye den kelen wolo
(so that Kanji may father a child.)

In all the above lines, the accent falls naturally on the third beat. The final postpositions do not receive stress. This is a principal characteristic of the narrative mode. The background rhythm is maintained at 4:4, and the singer uses formulas that enable him to produce a line with accent falling on the third beat. The last line breaks the rhythmic pattern and signals either a changing of modes or an instrumental break.

The third and last stylistic component is the song mode. Most heroic and epic words in the Mande could be described as consisting of a series of songs tied together by narrative links. These songs seem to mark the major events of each story. The songs incorporated in the hunters' bards' heroic pieces all have a set chorus line sung by the apprentices. The lines sung by the lead singer seem to be just as free in form as those in the other two stylistic modes. This is one of the notable differences between epics such as Sunjata and the heroic songs of the hunters. In the version of *Kambili* being discussed here, there are eight songs. The first three songs form a tight set reminiscent of a scene from an opera. The first song of the set is one in which Dugo makes an appeal for help to Bari the Truth-Seer. This is followed by a song in which Bari asks Dugo why she is crying. The last song of the set is one in which Bari tells Dugo to hush and wait for a better tomorrow. The fourth song, which shows up in the marriage ceremony of Kambili and Kumba, is one commonly used for dancing at any festive occasion and has no relation per se to the story. The fifth is a haunting song sung by the woman whose child is to be used as bait in the trap for the lion-man. She pleads in vain to the Imam to release him. The next song is sung by the young boy to awaken Kambili, who has fallen asleep under the lion-man's spell. The seventh song is the celebration of the death of the lion-man and the praise of Kambili, and the last song is the praise of Kumba, Kambili's wife, for her role in the killing of the lion-man. Significantly, this song closes the piece.

As you may have noted, I have avoided calling these hunters' songs epics, even though, as I have illustrated, they meet the definition, being lengthy performances of a heroic nature with a poetic meter. As with the epics, these heroic songs require the services of a highly trained specialist and are always performed to musical accompaniment. They differ from the Mande epics in that the latter are invariably products of a long tradition of singers. No one artist can create a new epic, whereas it is not out of the ordinary to find an artist who creates new heroic songs dealing with the fairly recent deeds of a local hunter.

I would like to further define the Mande epics by the social-psychological role these epics play. In the areas in which they are performed, the epics are universally recognized as a symbol of the origin, growth, and development of the state. As such, an epic frequently includes genealogies of the ruling groups, collapsed with mythological material pertaining to the origin of the world and the like. Often events in which the gods intercede symbolize the favoritism they are claimed to demonstrate toward the culture as a whole. The epic hero is himself a superman empowered by the gods to restore the state to its deserved grandeur in the natural order of things. The strength of the culture is fully reflected in the exploits of its epic hero.

In this area of social function, the hunters' heroic songs differ greatly from the Mande epics. Whereas the hunters' songs serve to cement relations within a particular hunters' group, they do not play any role in building a national identity and their heroes do not represent anything beyond the hunters' societies themselves.

There are a number of interesting parallels between the hunters' songs, such as *Kambili,* and epics, such as *Sunjata.*

1. Stylistically and structurally there are strong parallels in the organization of the pieces in line formation and the form and function of the three modes of performance.
2. There are strong parallels in the instrumentalization and the instruments that supply it. There is, for example, little doubt that the twenty-one-string *kora* is a development of the six-string harp-lute of the hunters. In addition, it can be claimed that many of the songs incorporated into the epics have their origin as hunters' songs. This is particularly evident in the case of the *Janjon* and the *Duga,* both of which are ceremonial dances of high order in the hunters' and warriors' societies.
3. There are parallels in the training of the bards and there are parallels in some of their social roles.
4. There are, finally, strong thematic parallels in the content of these pieces, as is obvious from the outline of *Kambili* and its comparison with the *Sunjata* epic.

Such parallels inevitably lead the scholar to speculate on the development of these art forms and to form some reasonable hypothesis as to their origins.

Given the hypothesis that the societies in this area underwent a revolutionary transformation, developing from isolated ethnic groups into empires of considerable extent, it would certainly follow that the institutions of the societies were transformed accordingly. We might also reasonably posit that the military arm of the pre-empire groups was found in the hunters' societies and that these societies played an important role in the expansion of the empire. Consequently, some of the hunters' institutions would undergo considerable modification in accord with the new demands made on them by their new imperialist stance.

In Munson's archaeological study of the Tichitt area in Mauritania, he traces the development of the society from about 2000 B.C. to the birth of Christ. He shows how the society underwent two major transformations, the first, ecological, through the drying up of the large lakes in the region, and the second, political, from the intrusion of the Berber peoples into the area. He argues that the Ghana empire was most likely founded in the co-operation between the indigenous people of that area and the Berbers, a co-operation that eventually led to the dominance of the indigenous peoples.

I would like to suggest that it might have been in this synthesis of the two societies that the original hunters' societies were modified and from which the casted bard evolved from the priest-bard of the hunters. Were this the case, a number of facts would fall into place. For example, only in those areas that were closely in contact with the Ghana empire does one find the casted bards and the *kora*, the twenty-one-stringed harp-lute. The same word for the casted bard is reconstructible in all these areas. That the hunters' bard preceded the casted bard as a social institution is supported by the fact that hunters' bards or their equivalent are widespread in West Africa, whereas the casted bard is geographically quite restricted. The casted bard is not an institution directly borrowed from some other culture. In his excellent study of Shinqīṭī folklore, H. T. Norris demonstrates that the casted bard is in fact borrowed by the Mauritanian Arabic culture from the northern Mande peoples living in that area.[6] He also shows that the casted bards played a significant role in the development of the unique Hassaniya poetic style.

The evidence, thin as it may be at the present time, all seems to point to a development of the Mande epics from a base of the heroic songs of the hunters. To this was added, perhaps, the influence of Berber epic singing or, perhaps at a later stage, the influence of Moroccan Arabic oral or even written art, although here the evidence is scant indeed. What remains before us at this stage is to produce more descriptive and analytical studies on the oral art forms of this area on a par with that of Norris. From such studies will stem information of significant interest to historians and linguists, as well as to scholars and students of comparative literature.

[6] H. T. Norris, *Shinqīṭī Folk Literature and Song* (Oxford, 1968).

There is, after all, a trend toward literacy in these areas, and literacy seems to ring the death knell for the continuation of a true epic tradition. Only through the study of contemporary bards and their art can we gain insight into the nature of this type of oral art, which Western society has lost.

METAPHOR AND SYMBOLISM IN THE HEROIC POETRY OF SOUTHERN AFRICA

Daniel P. Kunene

Introduction

I use the term *heroic poetry* for what is more often referred to as *praise poetry*. The latter term owes its origin to the fact that the poem *praises* someone. The poem is a celebration: through lofty language, abounding in imagery, metaphor, simile, hyperbole, parallelism, alliteration, etc., the brave deeds of the hero of the poem are "sung."

The deeds themselves are ordinary enough: a warrior kills an opponent in battle, or he beats off the enemy, thus saving his town, or he crashes his way through the enemy defenses, or he kills a wild ferocious beast, or he fights with courage and determination against odds. These and other deeds and qualities make him worthy of the bard's oratorical attentions. Or he might compose his own poem. The point is that, unlike in classical European literature, the deeds celebrated in a southern African poem of the type discussed here do not take place in the realm of the extraordinary, the extranatural, but are historically attestable. As I have said in another context, "The heroes are not superior beings except in so far as their earthly deeds make them so; least of all are they gods or descendants of gods. They do not possess supernatural powers, nor do they pit their strength against supernatural beings, or do battle against other-worldly creatures such as monsters and demons. They do not go on adventure to worlds beyond that of man. Nor are they wont to provide lavish feasts in palatial mansions. In short, they are ordinary human beings engaged in ordinary human activities. Not seldom, however, the poet, in the vividness of his imagination, uses metaphor, imagery and symbolism which transport these ordinary activities to a level of extra-ordinariness, and the hero is often described as fighting against monsters, or as being himself a monster or other terrible creature destroying his opponent. But this is never meant to be other than figurative."[1]

The heroism in the poems here described was thrust on all men by the circumstances under which they lived: frequent wars, hunting expeditions, accidental encounters with wild predators, cattle raids, and generally the prevalence of any physical danger.[2] In the circumstances described, all able-bodied men were by definition warriors. If through sickness or age or youth they were unable to engage in combat, they were, in spirit, still warriors.

The many wars that were fought between the black people of South Africa and the northward-pushing whites in the eighteenth and nineteenth centuries were occasions for many a heroic line for the black warriors seeking to beat the intruding enemy off their land.

One of the most prominent features of the heroic poetry of southern Africa is the praise phrase coined for the hero. I employ the term eulogue, a neologism of my own, as a generic name for all praise phrases, such as names and associative references, which serve to eulogize the hero of the poem. Broadly speaking, there are two classes of eulogues: The first class commemorates the hero's acts of bravery; its structural core is a verb narrating those deeds. These are *deverbative narrative* eulogues.

---

[1] Daniel P. Kunene, *The Heroic Poetry of the Basotho* (Oxford: The Clarendon Press, 1971), Introduction, p. xvi.

[2] Ibid., 3-4.

1. *Umalamulela*
    Owalamulela abafazi namadoda,
    Walamulela izintombi namasoka[3]

                         (Zulu. Udingane. Nyembezi 50)

    Rescuer
    Who rescued the women and the men,
    Rescued the young women and the youth.[4]

The verb here is *lamulela*, intervene in a fight or quarrel to
the benefit of the weaker opponent. It is the applicative form
of *lamula*, intervene. Deverbative eulogues may, however,
also be *descriptive*, namely when they describe the hero
by reference to a unique physical or moral characteristic that
presumably distinguishes him from other men and is expected to instill fear into the hero's adversaries.

The other broad category of eulogues is made up of all the
remaining subspecies. They cover clan affiliation, descriptive
(deverbative, denominative, etc.), metaphorical, and regimen-
tal phrases, as well as praise by associative reference in genealogies and other references to blood relationship.[5] These eulogues derive their justification in the final analysis, from the
hero's praiseworthy deeds that so often lead to the coining of
deverbative narrative eulogues. The poet is saying, in effect,
that the hero's heroism should surprise no one, for, being of
clan so-and-so, or having such-and-such a frightening bodily
feature, or being as ferocious as a lion, or being sired by so-

[3] C. L. S. Nyembezi, *Izibongo Zamakhosi* (Pietermaritzburg:
Shuter and Shooter, 1958). Henceforth referred to as Nyembezi.
[4] Portions of some of the poems in Nyembezi were used by him
in an article, "The Historical Background to the Izibongo of the
Zulu Military Age," appearing in two parts in *African Studies*
7, June–September, 110 ff. and December 1948, 147 ff., respectively,
where they are accompanied by English translations. Where portions used in this chapter are found both in the article and in the
book referred to in note 3, reference is made to the book and
not to the article. I have mostly preferred my own translations, or
have sometimes taken the liberty to modify Nyembezi's. Where
Nyembezi's translations are used unmodified, this will be indicated
in footnotes.
[5] Since space does not permit, and in any case the main focus is
not on them, there is no need here to illustrate the eulogues named.

and-so, etc., he cannot but be the fine specimen he is and perform those great deeds.

We are concerned here with the metaphorical eulogue, for by its means the hero is transformed into something other than himself—something that displays to the highest degree the quality the poet is highlighting in the hero. As the hero is transformed, so also are his actions *metaphorized*, so that they are, in literal fact, the actions of the phenomenon with which the hero is being identified—i.e., the model.[6]

This paper seeks to throw light on metaphors that give us an insight into the symbolism and imagery of the people whose poetry is being described. The various symbols lend themselves to a number of possible groupings and subgroupings, as the following arrangement shows.

THE IDEA OF CONTAINING

To encompass, to encircle, to contain, to hem in, to swallow, etc., is to demonstrate power over that which is encompassed, encircled, contained, hemmed in, or swallowed, etc. The encompasser or the encircler or the container or the hemmer-in or the swallower, etc., is, naturally, larger than his victim and therefore in appearance, if not in fact, more powerful. He imprisons his victim, rendering him powerless.

(a) The mythological swallowing monster

The mythology of southern Africa provides many illustrations of such a creature in the "swallowing monster" found in various areas: the *Kgodumodumo*, or *Kammapa*, and the *Koeyoko*, among the Basotho; the *Siququmadevu* of the Zulu; the *Nabulele* of the Xhosa, and various other kinds of swallowers of human beings and other creatures.

In a poem in which the swallowing idea is used, the mythical swallower may or may not be mentioned by name. In illustrations 2 and 3 below it is actually named.

---

[6] I shall use the terms *aspirant* and *model* to designate, respectively, the hero and the phenomenon toward whose distinction the hero aspires.

2. Ngwan'a lona o jelwe ke Koeyoko,
    O jelwe ke Koeyoko ya Letsie,
    Koeyoko, Seja-bana-ba-Makgowa
                    (Sotho. Maama. Mangoaela 97)[7]

Your child has been devoured by the *Koeyoko*,
He has been devoured by the *Koeyoko* of Letsie,
The *Koeyoko*, Devourer-of-the-sons-of-the-White-man!

The *Koeyoko* in this quotation is found in a southern Sotho tale in which a little boy is daily left alone while the older people go to work in the fields. For diversion, the boy is wont to go to the river and tease the *Koeyoko*, inviting him to come and eat him up, evidently enjoying the thrill of the *Koeyoko's* pursuits and the boy's hairbreadth escapes. But one day the *Koeyoko* succeeds in catching him, and he eats him up, leaving only his head. What happens thereafter does not concern us here.

3. Kgodumodumo ya eja batho;
    Batho ba feletse mpeng ya selo
                    (Sotho. Griffith. Mangoaela 186)

The *Kgodumodumo* ate up the people;
The people are all in the stomach of the beast.

In these two lines, the hero is the all-swallower, from whom there can be no escape. In the Sotho all-swallowing-monster story, all creatures are swallowed except one expectant mother, who disguises herself so successfully that the *Kgodumodumo* takes her for a lifeless object. Shortly afterward she gives birth to a boy who, having grown in minutes to a strapping young man and been told, on inquiring, that the *Kgodumodumo* has swallowed all living things, goes and kills it, setting free all the people and their herds. His name is Senkatana in one version and Ditaolane in another.

[7] Z. D. Mangoaela, *Lithoko tsa marena a Basotho* (Morija, 1950: first published 1921). All the southern Sotho illustrations are taken from this book, which is henceforth referred to as Mangoaela. The English translations are all my own.

It is in this context alone that the idea of the hero "eating up" his opponent can be understood, and there are many poems in which this is illustrated. Hence UDingane is, *inter alia*,

4.   Owadl' uPiti kumaBhunu,
     Wamudla wamtshobotshela;
     Odl' uMzibhelibheli kumaBhunu,
     Wadl' uPhuzukuhlokoza kumaBhunu
     Wadl' uHwahwini kumaBhunu——
                         (Zulu. UDingane. Nyembezi 49)

     (One) Who, among the Boers, devoured Piet,
     Ate him up and gulped him down;
     Who, among the Boers, ate up Mzibhelibheli,
     And ate up, among the Boers, Phuzukuhlokoza,
     And ate up, among the Boers, Hwahwini——

Sometimes, however, roles are reversed, the enemy being the swallowing monster who swallows or threatens the people and property under the protection of the hero. The hero then becomes the monster-killer, the deliverer.

5.   Moqotjha-ntho, thak'a Masunya a Mmamatla,
     Ntho e tla e ahlame!
     E itse ka re e sa ahlama,
     Ra finyella ho yona ra e betsa;
     E itse ka re e sa ahlama hape,
     Ra finyella ho yona ra e betsa,
     Ya ba ya di siya di eme
     Kgomo tsa mor'a Mmamakhabane.
                    (Sotho. Mopeli Mokhachane. Mangoaela 29)

     Thing-Pursuer, peer of Masunya of Mmamatla,
     The thing is coming with open jaws!
     Vainly it opened its jaws,
     We came right close and struck it;
     Vainly it opened its jaws again,
     We came right close and struck it;
     Till it left them standing there,
     The cattle of the son of Mmamakhabane.

In "coming close and striking" we see Senkatana as he proceeds toward the *Kgodumodumo*. The monster lashes out with its enormous tongue in an attempt to lap him up, but he steps aside smartly and chops off a portion of the tongue. This is repeated several times until he comes close enough to kill the monster and hack him open.

(b)   *The lake or the deep pool: the monster of the deep*

Tales abound in which a deep pool engulfs a human being, usually a girl, either (though seldom) threatening to destroy her or (much more usual) protecting her from the cruelty of her fellow humans, often enough her own parents.[8] Some-

---

[8] The engulfing in this case achieves two purposes: it protects the maltreated child from further harm, and it punishes the culprits by depriving them of their child. Usually such stories conclude with a ransom being given to the deep pool, or a sacrificial offering being performed there, with the pool receiving the sacrifice and yielding up the child. This will probably go some way toward explaining the following lines from Cope:

IMfoloz' emnyama kaSithayi noBhiyane inketha-baweli,
Ingawelwa ngonothole,
Ongenathole angakhokh' umntwana,
Inxe engenamntwana angakhokh' igeja.

(Zulu. Shaka. Cope 115)

Black Mfolozi of Sithayi and Bhiyane who chooses those who ford it;
It can be forded by him who has a calf,
He who has no calf can pay with a child,
If he has no child he can pay with a hoe.

(Trevor Cope, editor, *Izibongo: Zulu Praise-Poems* (Oxford: The Clarendon Press, 1968), henceforth referred to as Cope. Cope's English translations are used except where otherwise stated. Cope finds the meaning of this paragraph obscure. I suggest that this refers to a tribute demanded by the serpent of the deep waters from those who would cross there. In a Xhosa story a tribute is extorted in similar circumstances from a prince about to die of thirst. Whenever he, the Prince Tfulako, who is returning from the hunt with some retainers, stoops down to drink, the river dries up, in spite of the fact that his followers have drunk their fill without any difficulty. When he realizes what this means, he promises the King of the Deep Waters his (Tfulako's) sister in marriage, whereupon the waters flow abundantly. (See A. C. Jor-

times there is a monster in the pool, often referred to in Sotho as *noha ya metsi,* snake of the waters. This monster has magnetic eyes, with which he draws into the deep people and cattle and any living thing he may wish.

(i)   The deep pool engulfs animals

6.   Ibhaka lamanzi lawoNdikidi,
Lisibekel' izinkomo zamaSwazi zanyamalala.
(Zulu. UDingane. Nyembezi 49)

The Pool-of-Water of Ndikidi and others,
He submerged the cattle of the Swazi and they were
gone

an idea expressed almost identically in the Tswana poem for Chief Pheto:

7.   Tsibogo le bophalaphala,
Bo felele bo tsaya tshopya tsa batho,
Bo tsere tshopya tsoo Ntaganyane a Mokwena
(Tswana. Pheto. Schapera 49)[9]

The Ford is a swelling flood,
In the end it takes people's hornless cattle,
It took the hornless cattle of Ntaganyane the Kwena

But perhaps even more eloquent in terms of mythological reference are the following lines:

---

dan, "Towards an African Literature," *Africa South* 1 (1957) No. 4: 90–101.
   Needless to point out, the hero of a poem never engulfs to protect, but always to destroy. It is conceivable that the hero could be described as engulfing his people to protect them, but I have not seen such a metaphor so far.
   [9] I. Schapera, *Praise Poems of Tswana Chiefs* (Oxford: The Clarendon Press, 1965), henceforth referred to as Schapera. The English translations are Schapera's except where otherwise indicated. Schapera has used the conjunctive word-division in recording the poems in his book. In my quotations from him I use the disjunctive word-division to make Tswana and Sotho uniform in this respect.

8. Ngwana wa kgosi Bodiba jwa Letamo!
   Bodiba bo letse bo digetse Moure,
   Bo digetse Moure a Masokana;
   Le jaana bo sa gomagomela mongwe,
   Bo ntse bo tlhatsa boNtebogang.

   (Tswana. Kgama Sekgoma. Schapera 203)

The chief's son is the Deep of a Dam!
Last night the Deep swallowed Moure,
It swallowed Moure Masokana;
And now it seeks another victim
As it throws up Ntebogang and company.

(ii) The deep pool engulfs men

9. Isizib' esiseMavivane, Dingane,
   Isizib' esinzonzo, sizonzobele,
   Siminz' umunt' eth' uyageza,
   Waze washona nangesicoco.

   (Zulu. UDingane. Nyembezi 46)

The Pool that is at Mavivane,
The Silent Pool is overpowering,
It gulped down a man attempting to bathe,
That even his headring was submerged.

10. Molapo waga Nkane a Masilo
    Ga o wele ditlai, o welwa gotlhe,
    Poulwe o o wetse a o lebile,
    A rototse matlho a ntse ditotwana

    (Tswana. Sechele. Schapera 132)

The River of Nkane of Masilo,
Not only the heedless fall into it, but all,
Paul fell in though looking at it,
Opening his eyes wide and staring fiercely

(iii) The monster of the deep

Since the deep pool and the monster that lurks in it be-
have identically in one respect, *viz.* their allurement of those
whom they wish to destroy by drowning, there will be found

to be quite an overlap in the decodement of the actions of the deep pool on the one hand and the monster-within-the-deep-pool on the other:

11.   Monongwaha e a dihela, Kganyapa;
       Kganyapa, Tlhware ya habo Seeiso,
       Ya kwenya Buru la fella ka mpeng.
       Mahahabo a tswatswa a mo qamaka,
       Ho lealea le mara, a mo hloka.

                              (Sotho. Lerotholi. Mangoaela 74)

       This year he draws them in, the Monster of the Deep;
       Monster of the Deep, Python of the house of Seeiso,
       He swallowed a Boer, contained him in his stomach.
       Vainly his comrades searched for him,
       Up and down among the hosts, they failed to find him.

12.   Kwena ya sheba ka har'a bodiba,
       Ya sheba ka mahlo a le mafubedu,
       Bashanyana ba makgowa ba wela.
       Bashanyana ba wetse hanong la noha!
       Noha e ntsho, Kganyapa ya Morena,
       Mmane ya o hlatsa.

                              (Sotho. Lerotholi. Mangoaela 70)

       The Crocodile stared within the pool,
       He stared with eyes that were red,
       And the little white boys fell in.
       The little boys have fallen into the mouth of a Snake!
       Black Snake, Deep-Pool-Monster of the King,
       He belched forth lightning.

Exactly the same idea—*viz.* a crocodile that is no ordinary crocodile, but a deep-pool monster, which lurks in the deep and draws in the unwary traveler—is found in one of Schapera's collections. (Tswana. Sechele. Schapera 138)

In the mythology of southern Africa, water in lakes and rivers has always been regarded as harboring some mysterious beings who are mostly helpful, life-preserving creatures. There is the well-disposed little old woman who sometimes emerges from a lake with the offer of help, like the benevolent

fairy. In the Sotho story of *Dinanabolele,* Thakane goes in
search of the mythological animals that go by that name and
eventually comes to the right lake, from which an old woman
emerges; after Thakane expresses gratitude for the old
woman's offer of help, she carries Thakane to her abode
beneath the deep, where also live the dinanabolele.[10] There
is the "crocodile," which, in the story of Mosimodi and Mosi-
motsane, re-creates Mosimodi from her powdered remains
thrown into the pool by an unnatural mother who, for an
insignificant offense, kills her daughter, Mosimodi, literally
pulverizes her, and throws the dust into a nearby pool. Very
often the heroine of a story sings a plaintive song to a lake
or pool requesting assistance when in distress. Thus at the
very beginning of her quest Thakane goes, as if through
metaphysical knowledge, to a lake and sings to it the message
of her plight. In a poem composed for Dingane, King of the
Zulus, after his assassination of his brother, Shaka, Dingane
is praised as, among other things,

13.   Obuz' amanz' eMbozamo, and' ukuwela.
      Amanz' eMbozam' osal' ebabaza!
                              (Zulu. Nyembezi 45)

(He) who appealed to the waters of the Mbozamo,
   then crossed.
The waters of the Mbozamo will marvel after he goes!

To cover in order to imprison with the intention of destroying, is an idea that overlaps to quite an appreciable extent
with that of covering to protect. And from this to the notion
of the "covering" of the female by the male as a demonstra-
tion of superior strength, and a demand for female submis-
sion, is but a short step.

[10] This is the story in which Masilo refuses to return home from
the circumcision lodge unless all his new apparel and equipment
are made from the hide of a *nanabolele.* Many are afraid to go in
search of the *nanaboleles* since these creatures have the notoriety
of being vicious, their abode being the kind of place where no one
goes and is seen again. Thakane, Masilo's sister, goes and, with
the old woman's help, brings her quest to a successful conclusion.

14. Hodiotswana la bo-Ramoretlo
    La otla Morolong, la mo apesa ka dipheo.

    (Sotho. Hlalele. Mangoaela 19)

    The Magic Lightning of the house of Ramoretlo
    Struck a Morolong and covered him with its wings.[11]

15. Lukhozi lukaNdaba
    Olumaphikw' abanzi,
    Lufulel' oSomhashi noFabase
    Lufulel' uNdengez' ezalwa uMayibuka.

    (Zulu. UMpande. Nyembezi 66)

    O, Eagle of Ndaba,
    Whose wings are wide!
    He covered Somhashi and Fabase,
    He covered Ndengezi born of Mayibuka.

(c) *The Monster of the Deep changes residence*

The Monster of the Deep can be treated both as part of the *engulfing-deep* symbolism, as in (b) above, or by itself, since some of the monster's actions are not, at the particular moment, critically associated with the deep pool, his abode. One such action, often used in poetic symbolism, is the migration of the monster from one pool, whose water level has become too low to continue to provide him with privacy from prying eyes, to another, deeper one. That is why he undertakes such moves during droughts.

Determined to ensure that he shall not be seen by human eyes, the monster raises a mighty windstorm often accompanied by rain, and he stretches himself out in the center of the dust and debris lifted up by the wind. And this is what is ordinarily referred to as a tornado or a hurricane. Despite these precautions by the monster, many people have claimed to have seen the "shape" of a snake stretched out, with head and tail clearly discernible, in the center of the tornado's funnel.

---

[11] Concerning lightning that has wings, see the description of the myth of the Bird of Thunder, below.

In order for a lake or a river or a stream to acquire the notoriety of harboring such a monster, it must look awesome. For example, it must be surrounded by a dense growth of reeds or sedges, or it must have a waterfall, or a cave in the riverbank, etc. It is quite obvious how the trail of destruction left by a tornado in its wake can capture the poet's imagination so that he transforms his hero into a monster trekking from one pool to another and destroying everything in its path.

(d) *The Sky*

To the naked eye, the sky is tangible. Also, it is dome-shaped and, wherever you are, there it is fitted snugly around your little world. Sometimes it thunders at you threateningly; sometimes, indeed, it builds up such fury that it strikes swiftly and fatally. At other times, however, it is happy, and it smiles at you with a warmth that brings with it security and peace, while it looks at you with paternal love. All these ideas can be used to predicate symbolically the actions and attitudes of the hero of a poem.

(i) The anger of the heavens expressed through thunder and lightning

16. Lehodimo, thak'a Ramahotetsa,
Thak'a bana ba Seamoha, o Leru.
Leru la duma, thak'a Lekena le Seeiso,
La kenya mmane matlung,
Thaba tsa tuka mello kaofela.
(Sotho. Joele Molapo. Mangoaela 120)

You who are the Heavens, peer of Ramahotetsa
Peer of the sons of Seamoha, you are a Cloud.
The Cloud rumbled, he, peer of Lekena and Seeiso,
And it flooded the houses with its lightning,
And the mountains all were ablaze with fire.

17. Izul' elidum' eNdulinde phezulu,
Lazithath' izihlangu zamadoda.
(Zulu. Cetshwayo. Nyembezi 87)

The Heaven that thundered high on Ndulinde,
And took away the shields of the men.

Often the thunder is unnatural; it is magic thunder made
by a man who wishes to destroy his enemy. The man hides
himself inside the thunderbolt, carrying a little ax with which
to chop up his victim. The Sotho word *tladi-mothwana*, which
is among those used to name this kind of thunderbolt, is a
compound word with the components *tladi*, lightning/
thunder, and *mothwana*, little person, he whose chariot is the
thunderbolt. In addition, the *tladi-mothwana* is said to come
out of a cloudless sky. It thus strikes its victim without
warning, its success therefore being ensured.

18. Tladi-mothwana ya Mmannehela ya bolaya Kgokong,
     Ya ratha hloho tsa baholo, Tshukudu, ya isa
     Moreneng
                    (Sotho. Peete Ramaneella. Mangoaela 140)

     The Man-Lightning of Mmannehela killed a wilde-
     beest,
     He chopped the heads of the elders, Rhinoceros, and
     carried to the Royal Place

In the following illustrations the suddenness of the thunderbolt is emphasized, in example 19 by the cloudlessness of
the sky, and in examples 20 and 21 by the flatness of the
terrain, for, since it normally strikes at conspicuous targets,
there is reason to exclaim in wonderment when it strikes "on
barren plains."

19. Tladi e ntsho ya habo Seeiso
     Ya tjhesa Maseru tsatsi le rapame
                    (Sotho. Maama. Mangoaela 96)

     The Black Thunderbolt of the house of Seeiso
     Scorched Maseru when the sun was slanting west-
     ward.

The same idea comes out in the following lines:

20. Uzulu ladum' obala,
    Lapha kungemunga, kungemtholo.

    (Zulu. UCetshwayo. Nyembezi 83)

    Heaven that rumbles in the plains
    Where there is neither thorn tree nor wattle.[12]

21. Tladi e otlang mahalaopeng,
    Eitse ba re, "Kgele!", ya be e tloha:
    Ditente e di hlothetse hodimo,
    Le dikgomo e setse e di nkile
    Le dipere e setse e di nkile,
    Le dinku e setse e di nkile!

    (Sotho. Bereng Letsie. Mangoaela 91–92)

    Lightning that strikes on barren plains,
    When they cried "What!" he already was on his way:
    And he was carrying the tents aloft,
    The cattle, too, he had already taken,
    The horses, too, he had already taken,
    The sheep, too, he had already taken!

When the Basotho first saw the gun, they had no doubt
that it was lightning: it produced fire and smoke, it boomed,
it struck with swiftness and deadly accuracy. The main difference was that it was held in the operator's hands. They
thus called it by the poetic name *tladi-ya-matsoho,* literally
"lightning of the hands." Not only is the imagery beautiful,
but the parallels are perfect. One should mention here the
fact also that death is classified in two main categories among
the Basotho: death as an act of God; and death at the hands
of Man through sorcery and witchcraft, called *lefu-la-matsoho*

---

[12] Cope has these lines for Zulu, son of Nogandaya of the Zungu
clan (Cope, 178). In his English translation Cope, in my view
mistakenly, adds "for shelter" after *thorn tree* and *wattle,* suggesting that there is no hiding place for the victim of the thunderbolt,
an idea which is not found, either expressed or implied, in the
original. To me the idea seems to be that there is no target here to
attract the lightning, therefore people would normally not expect
it to strike there; when it does strike there it takes its victims (the
adversaries) by surprise, and its success is ensured.

"death of the hands," which, as implied, excludes death by physical violence.

22.   Enoba le a bona, ba ka Thuatha,
      Hoba Tladi e teng ya matsoho, Letlama!
      Ha le ntse le kgantsha, e tla le ja;
      E tswa batla e e-ja dipere le batho!

                              (Sotho. Griffith. Mangoaela 180)

Be it that you see, you of Thuatha,
That a Lightning there is of the hands, Letlama,
If you keep on boasting, it will devour you;
Recently it almost devoured horses and men!

(ii)   The anger of the heavens expressed through storms and hurricanes

A storm, particularly a hailstorm, can also be "a thing of the hands," being magically caused with the express purpose of destroying an adversary or laying waste his crops. In example 23 below, the hero is the one threatened by the hailstorm, *viz.* his adversary. Here the hero is, by implication, a magician/doctor whose potent medicines succeed in diverting the furious storm.

23.   Seodi, Ramahwclla-sefako,
      Fako sa hoba, sa ya le maralla

                              (Sotho. Masopha. Mangoaela 42)

Seodi-warrior, Averter-of-hailstorms,
The hailstorm roared and spent itself upon the hills

(iii)   The benevolence of the sky

First there is the dome itself. It is a symbol of power. In the following illustration it protects those below it.

24.   Ngwan'a Morena, Seokamela-batho,
      Lehodimo ho batho ba ntatae!

                              (Sotho. Letsie II. Mangoaela 173)

Child of the King, Towerer-above-the-people,
Sky to the people of his father!

Then there is the rainbow, which "bestrides our narrow world
like a colossus." It is an Atlas, who, with hands and feet
firmly planted in the ground, carries the sky on his arched
back.

25. Mookodi wa naha ya Moshoeshoe
Wa tshehetsa maru le lefatshe,
Ha lefatshe le tetema
(Sotho. Lerotholi. Mangoaela 70)

Rainbow of the land of Moshoeshoe
Supported the clouds and the earth,
The day the earth trembled.

(e) *The Bird*

(i) There are birds that symbolize death, mainly
the crow, the vulture, and the eagle. These are carrion-
lovers, and they therefore fly in large swarms over the battle-
fields, to feast on the corpses of the fallen warriors. Hence
the general praise for warriors, and indeed for all men from
the day they are born to the day they die, *viz.:*

26. Ngwan'a moshemane pholo' a Letlaka
Kabelw' a manong
(No source, a popular saying)

Boy-child, one abandoned to the vultures,
One apportioned to the eagles

The idea of the bird that hovers above death is well illustrated in the following example, in which the vultures not
only thank the hero for providing so amply for them, but
are indeed moved to pity, and appeal to the hero to stay
his hand.

27. Ho bil'a tena ha tankisa dinonyana,
Nonyana tse tshweu, thabela-koduwa;

Matlaka a bua Sesotho hodimo,
A bua a tankisa Ditjotjela;
Hamorao a ba a rapella kgotso ho Tau ya Dinare,
A re, "Sewehla ba tlohele hle!"
Nonyana tsa re, "Butle!" ho mor'a kgosi,
"O re hlabetse, ho hoholo, Tall'a Mokhachane;
Oho, hloho tsa batho di setse di le fatshe!"

> (Sotho. Patso. Mangoaela 133)

Till at last the birds spoke their thanks,
Birds that are white, carrion-lovers;
The vultures spoke in Sesotho from the space of
heaven,
They spoke and thanked the Ditjotjela Regiment;
And afterward they begged for peace from the Lion
of the Dinare Regiment,
Saying, "Sewehla-warrior, let them be, we beg you!"
The birds cried "Hold!" to the son of the king,
"You have slaughtered for us amply, Ambusher (son)
of Mokhachane!
Heed us! Many are the heads of men that lie upon the
ground!"

(ii) There is the fabulous Bird of Thunder. Like the *mothwana,* or little man, the Bird of Thunder rides upon the angry cloud and streaks down toward its target. It strikes, leaving not only the usual black char marks, but also eggs, which it lays in the hole it bores through a wall or similar surface in its escape. The hero is thus sometimes simply referred to as *nonyana,* bird, with all the above associations.

Before we illustrate, we must draw attention to an interesting chain of associations resulting from this identification of bird and thunder. In this relationship, almost all the actions of a bird may be described as being those of lightning-and-thunder, and *vice versa,* plunging us into what appears to be a semantic madhouse. First we have the occurrence of the word for the idea lightning/thunder as subject with a predicate or predicates describing the actions or characteristics of a bird.

28. *Tladi* tsa benya, mello ya banana,
    Ya sala eka *di beetse* thabeng
    (Sotho. Lerotholi. Mangoaela 67)

   Lightnings flashed and fires blazed,
   That it seemed they'd *laid their eggs* on the mountain

29. *Tladi* ya duma e sa dutse fatshe,
    Ya duma *ya ikotlolla dipheo*
    (Sotho. Griffith. Mangoaela 187)

   The Thunder roared while yet upon the ground,
   He roared and *stretched out his wings*

Then there is the reverse arrangement whereby the bird is subject while the actions and characteristics in the predicate are those of lightning/thunder.

30. *Nonyana* ya heso e rata sehlaba,
    Mmane wa yona o bonahala hole
    (Sotho. Lelingoana Maketekete. Mangoaela 88)

   The Bird from my home likes the mountain peak,
   Its lightning is seen in faraway places

31. *Nonyane* la mo phuphuletsa dipheo,
    La mo tlabola dintshi, a timela
    (Sotho. Maama. Mangoaela 104)

   The Young Eagle flapped its wings vigorously at him,
   It singed his eyebrows, and he perished

Sometimes the ideas of bird and lightning/thunder both occur in the subject slot, thus leaving the poet free to predicate for either one.

32. Ngwan'a morena, *Nonyan'a* dithebe,
    Lehodimo, Tladi, mor'a Mokhachane,
    Ya duma, yaka *e behetse* ho batho
    (Sotho. Joele Molapo. Mangoaela 122)

Child of the king, *Bird* of the shields,
Sky, Lightning, son of Mokhachane,
He roared, and seemed to have *laid his eggs* among
the people.[13]

(f)   *The Bovine*[14]

Such is the importance of the bovine as a status symbol
among the black peoples of southern Africa that the Basotho
have a saying that "a man is never without a bovine while
he lives." In the Sotho group of languages it is referred to
as "the god with the wet nose."

(i)   The hero is often likened to a bull, because of
its virility, its strength and endurance. Often both the hero
and his opponent are symbolized as bulls, with the hero
being the stronger, and therefore victorious, bull, as in the
following:

33.   Tholo e fata seolo, e a tjhora,
       E tjhora lenaka Poho ya Peete.
       Ya ha Borane le yona e a fata,
       Ha e na dinaka e thula ka phatla.
       Na e re e ka betana le ya Thesele
       E hula joko ka mehla, molala o kgathetse,
       Molala o kgathetse ke diforaga?
                     (Sotho. Lerotholi. Mangoaela 67)

The Antelope gores an ant heap and his horn is
    sharpened,
The horn is sharpened of the Bull of Peete.
Borane's one is also goring,
(But) he has no horns, and he butts with his forehead.
Does he think that he can wrestle with Thesele's

---

[13] See footnote 11 above.
[14] "Bovine" is used to translate the generic term for the bovine
species in the southern African Bantu languages but which has
no modern equivalent in English. According to the Oxford English
Dictionary this word was once used in English the way I use it here.

When he carries the yoke every day and his neck is
tired,
His neck being tired from all the loads?

(ii) He is also likened to the cow, which is the symbol of life and prosperity since it yields milk, which sustains
life. The poet often, however, depicts the hero as a cow
gone mad, breaking the restraining cords around its legs,
upsetting the milk pail, kicking mud into the milk, while the
herdboys try in vain to subdue it. Here the herdboys symbolize the hero's compatriots, who try to restrain him from
taking what might turn out to be an unwise and miscalcu-
lated course of action. He is intractable, he is unreasoning,
and as he breaks free, the herdboys remain there marveling
at the wild temper of their supposedly tame cow.

34. Kgomo ya ntlo ya marumo, Seodi,
    Phatshwana e mokaka,
    E ohleleng kgwele, e kgaotse,
    Bahami ba yona ba ntse ba lla,
    Ka bo-Letlala, ka bo-Maketekete
                (Sotho. Masopha. Mangoaela 38)

Bovine of the house of spears, Seodi-warrior,
Rebellious Feminine-Black-and-White One,
Weave for her a rope, she has broken free,
Her milkers meanwhile are crying,
Such as Letlala together with Maketekete.

In the same vein we get

35. Kgomo kgwana e mo Mathubantweng,
    Tlogang, lo eme, lo e kaye, Mathubantwa;
    Kgomo e padile ka makao sakeng
                (Tswana. Sebele. Schapera 137)

There's a white-backed cow among the Mathubantwa;[15]

[15] Mathubantwa is the name of the regiment or age-set to which
the hero belongs. I have slightly altered Schapera's translation,

> Get up and tie its legs, Mathubantwa!
> The cow refused the leg-ties in the kraal

This is, of course, a behavior that could well describe the
hero versus his enemies as against the hero and his compatriots, as in the following:

36.   Kgomoatsana e thokwana, Sewehla,
     Setjhitjana sa Dinare
     Ya tlabikela mohala, ya o rola;
     Setjhitjana sa hlobola mohala.
     Bahami ba sona ba bangata-ngata:
     Ba itse ba ya hama ba ha Joele,
     Sa nna sa ba tabolela dikobo.
     Le ba ha Masopha ba itse ba ya hama,
     Yaka ba bitsa bo-tat'abo!
         (Sotho. Jonathane Molapo. Mangoaela 112)

     Fawn-colored Feminine Bovine, Sewehla-warrior,
     The Round-and-Smooth One of the Dinare Regiment,
     She trampled upon the cord and threw it aside;
     The Round-and-Smooth One doffed the cord.
     Her would-be milkers are many, many.
     They tried to milk her, the people of Joele,
     But she kept on tearing their blankets,
     Those of Masopha also tried to milk her,
     But it was like calling their fathers!

(g) *The Herdboy*

The bovine being as important as it is to the Basotho,
the herdboy, the one who watches over it and protects it
against enemy raiders, must be a very important person.
The poet takes the liberty to cast his characters in various
ways, reversing roles if and when he sees fit. Here again,
therefore, the hero may be cast as the herdboy who suc-

---

replacing his "in the Mathubantwa" with my "among the Mathubantwa." Schapera has a note to this saying that "the allusion is to
Sebele's disregard of Sechele's wishes about circumcision."

cessfully drives away the enemy. Or the enemy is the herd-boy, vanquished by the hero and deprived of his cattle.

(i) The hero and his regiment are the herdboys.

37. Rona badisa ba mor'a Mmamakhabane,
Re eme ka dithunya le ka dilepe,
Ra re, "Tsena tseso ke ditjhitjana, ha di tshwarwe,
Ke ditjhitjana, di thella diatleng."
(Sotho. Mopeli Mokhachane. Mangoaela 29)

We herdboys of the son of Mmamakhabane,
Stood armed with guns and axes,
And we said, "These of our village are round-and-smooth, they cannot be caught,
They are round-and-smooth, they slip out of one's hands."

(ii) The enemy are the herdboys.

38. Hoduotswana la Senate, Maama,
La duma la nka modisa pereng
La mo amoha marapo le ditomo,
La mo jela fatshe le dikokwana
(Sotho. Maama. Mangoaela 99)

Thunder of Senate, Maama,
It thundered and swept the herdboy from his horse
And took from him the bridle and the bit,
And devoured him on the ground, helped by the ants.

One of the most striking things about metaphor is that it can reflect for us the vividness of the imagination of him who employs it. The poet can draw pictures for us that, because of their detail, give us lively images of what that which is, seems to be. When a fast-moving train is likened to a mad-man who runs on tiptoe, swaying his head from side to side, or when the hissing steam and the puffing of the engine are likened to sneezing and coughing, or when the slow movement of the same train on entering a station is likened to an unruffled, imperturbable gait of majesty, or when a double-barreled gun is likened to two nostrils,[16] then, within the general framework of the metaphor, we have imagery, always latent, always waiting to find expression in the vividness of the mind of the author.[17]

The poet's intimate knowledge of the natural phenomena around him facilitates his use of metaphor for the hero and his qualities. The metaphor may be universally intelligible, as when the hero's bravery transforms him into a lion, or his speed and accuracy into lightning, etc. For here we have something akin to the fable, where qualities (even though not all of them illustrated from the animal world) are constant, and universally give man parallels against which he measures his own reasonably comparable characteristics.

But when our lightning develops wings and is capable of laying eggs or, conversely, when our bird thunders and is capable of scorching or singeing his adversary; when people don't simply miss their step and drown in trying to ford a river, but are "drawn in" by the pool; when the pool is given a monster whose magnetic eyes are the dread of all who wander too close to it—when these and similar characteristics manifest themselves in the metaphor used—then our definition of metaphor has become restricted as to time and place. In other words, it is culturally defined. Within this culturally defined metaphor reposes symbolism.

[16] R. C. Samuelson, *Long, Long Ago* (Durban: Knox Printing and Publishing Co., 1929), uDubulangesimakhal'amabili, Firer-with-one-that-has-two-nostrils (my translation). See Samuelson, p. 270.

[17] In fact, imagery is actually an elaboration of the details of a metaphor which is then often implied rather than expressed.

TRADITIONAL RITUAL

FOLKLORE AND YORUBA DRAMA:
ỌBÀTÁLÁ AS A CASE STUDY

Joel Adedeji

Ritual drama forms the basis of the annual Ọbàtálá festival at Èdẹ, an important Yoruba community some twenty miles northwest of Ilé Ifẹ̀, which is widely believed to be the holy city of the Yoruba peoples. The Ọbàtálá festival held in Èdẹ has been selected as a paradigm for the purpose of this study since it is believed that the first settlers were among the bands of followers of Ọbàtálá from Ilé Ifẹ̀. The scenario reveals a protagonist involved in a campaign, an ejection, and a coming back. In spite of slight variations that are the results of local interpretations of the nature of Ọbàtálá, wherever the *òrìṣà* (deity) is served and worshiped in Yoruba, the annual festival includes a dramatic enactment showing a mock fight between a protagonist and an antagonist.

This paper results from an analytical study of folkloric materials on Ọbàtálá, the arch divinity of the Yoruba pantheon. It attempts to explain the significance of the dramatic or expressive techniques of folklore used in the staging and performance of the ritual drama.[1]

[1] The folkloric materials have been drawn from the following sources:

    (a) Odù of Ifá Corpus. See Appendix.
    (b) Oral evidence.
    (c) Published materials.

For (a) and (b) I wish to acknowledge the kind assistance of

The mythical origin of the Yoruba peoples is illustrated in a dramatic conflict between two legendary heroes, Ọbàtálá[2] and Òdùduwà[3] in Ifẹ̀, the cradle of Yoruba civilization. The drama is highly romanticized, as the following myths demonstrate.

The Creation Myth.[4] Before the creation, the earth was one mass of water. Olódùmarè,[5] the Supreme Deity and Yoruba Sky God, summoned Ọbàtálá, his viceregent, to his presence. He charged him with the first act of creation: the "land mass." Accompanied by a five-toed hen and a

Ògbéni Wálé Ògúnyemí of the Institute of African Studies, University of Ibadan, and Alàgbà Agboolá Adéníji, formerly Research Assistant in the Yoruba Historical Research Scheme under Dr. S. O. Biobaku. For (c) the following books have been consulted: J. A. Ademakinwa, *Ife, Cradle of Yoruba Civilization* (Lagos, n.d.), Pts. II & III; Dr. Bolaji Idowu, *Olodumare: God in Yoruba Belief* (London: Longmans, 1966); Ulli Beier, *A Year of Sacred Festivals* (Lagos: Federal Ministry of Information, 1959); Chief M. A. Fabunmi, *Ife Shrines* (Ife: University of Ife Press, 1969).

2 "Ọbàtálá" (the great Ọbà) may be the descriptive name of the ancestor who during his apotheosis became known as "Orìsà-ńlá" (the great divinity). As the primordial "Òrìsà" (deity) of the Yoruba, this attribute may have derived from a prefix, "orí" (head or source), and a suffix, "ìsà" (pot or cooler). "Ìsà" is believed to be the "cooler" used by Ọbàtálá for his palm wine.

3 "Òdùduwà" may be the cognomen of the deified ancestor whose real name is unknown or lost. He is believed to have robbed Ọbàtálá of the "Igbá Ìwà" (the receptacle or basin containing the deed or covenant made between Olódùmarè, the Supreme God, and Ọbàtálá, his viceregent, conferring the right of creativity on the latter). "Òdùduwà," by folk etymology, is a derivation of "Eniti ó du igbá ìwà" (One who rescued the receptacle used for creativity).

4 There are several other variants of the Yoruba creation myth. The main difference, however, is Òdùduwà is credited with the creation of the "land mass." See Appendix (b). This variant is held by the Ọlọbà of Òbà.

5 "Olódùmarè," by folk etymology, is a contraction of "Olódù mọ Àrè" (the owner of the pot knows Àrè). "Àrè" is one of the names by which the leadership of the followers of Ọbàtálá came to be known. "Òdù" (pot) refers symbolically to the "pot of creation." "Olódù" therefore means the "owner of the pot of creation." This reference was attributed to the struggle between Ọbàtálá and Òdùduwà as to which of them owned Ifẹ̀.

pigeon and with a calabash containing a piece of dry soil, Ọbàtálá descended upon the watery mass to begin his job. He dropped the calabash of soil on the surface of the water and let loose the hen and the pigeon, who anchored the calabash and worked by scattering the soil about. When a portion of the surface had been covered with the soil, Ọbàtálá turned back with pleasure and reported to Olódùmarè the successful completion of the work of creating the earth. Olódùmarè thereupon dispatched the chameleon to inspect the work and report back. The chameleon returned to Olódùmarè and glowingly reported that the land "was wide!" (Ó fẹ̀!) "Ifẹ̀," by folk etymology, derives from "Ilẹ̀ tí ó fẹ̀" (the land which is wide).

Olódùmarè, having been quite satisfied with the first act of creation, again dispatched Ọbàtálá, to complete the second act: the creation of man. Ọbàtálá left the presence of Olódùmarè with the "Igbá Ìwà" (the receptacle containing the means of creation). He descended upon "Ifẹ̀" (the wide land mass) and started the creation of man out of clay. As he went about his assignment, he became exceedingly tired and thirsty. To his great relief, he came upon an "ìṣà" (a cooler filled with undiluted palm wine) and drank his fill.[6] But he became drunk and started creating "misfits." The hunchback, the albino, the cripple, and other afflicted people are regarded as victims of Ọbàtálá's inebriation. Suffering from exhaustion, Ọbàtálá fell into a deep slumber. It is believed that it was Èṣù, who tempted Ọbàtálá with the palm wine. In Appendix (a) the Eji Ogbe makes it clear that Èṣù, as a messenger of Òrúnmìlà, is not pleased at seeing Ọbàtálá successfully completing the work of creation.

When Olódùmarè realized that Ọbàtálá was no longer fulfilling his mission, he sent Òdùduwà to complete the job. When Òdùduwà descended upon Ifẹ̀, he found Ọbàtálá fast asleep. He took the "Igbá Ìwà" away from him, peopled Ifẹ̀ with his own brand of humans, and settled them under his powerful leadership. Ọbàtálá later awakened to the

---

[6] It is believed that it was Èṣù who tempted Ọbàtálá with the palm wine.

reality of the supplanter and set the stage for a long-drawn-out campaign against his adversary, Òdùduwà.

The Myth of Conquest. The creation episode left the two actors in the drama with a tantalizing experience. Òdùduwà was undeterred. He set up a civic administration at Ifè with himself at the head of a "council of elders" consisting of sixteen of his followers. After some time, he left on a pilgrimage to Òkè Òrà,[7] where he is believed to have communed with and received commandments from Olódùmarè in connection with the next phase of his work.

No sooner was Òdùduwà away than Òbàtálá, whom the former had appointed his head artist, seized the throne of Ifè as the "de jure" ruler of the autochthons of the land.[8] In spite of divisions, Òbàtálá installed himself as king "Oòyèlàgbò," which means "The King is the prime Ìgbò." Ìgbò is the name by which Òbàtálá's followers came to be popularly known. The followers of Òbàtálá still describe Ifè as "Ifè Oòyèlàgbò." Òdùduwà returned to find that Òbàtálá had usurped the throne and had sought his expulsion from Ifè.

Civil war ensued. Òbamerì, the generalissimo of the realm, intervened on the side of Òdùduwà and captured and imprisoned Òbàtálá. Furthermore, Òbamerì searched out and drove all the followers of Òbàtálá from Ifè and made it impossible for any of them, including Òbàtálá himself, to set foot within the city-state.[9]

Deprived of their privileges, the supporters of Òbàtálá became vagabonds and gangsters. They took refuge in the neighboring jungle called "Ìgbò gbò" (the grove of the Ìgbò) and later organized themselves into several secret cults. According to Idowu, the Ògbóni Society was formed to fight

[7] According to Ademakinwa, this was Oràmfè's Hill, from which Òdùduwà had originally descended. See J. A. Ademakinwa, *Ife, Cradle of the Yoruba*, Pt. II (Lagos, n.d.), p. 17.

[8] Dr. John Abiri, who is working on the reconstruction of the Ifè kings' list, said in a personal explanation that, according to official records, it was one Nímòsóyè, nicknamed Olófin Òsángangan Òbàmákin, the leader of the Òbàtálá group and worshiper of the deity, who usurped the throne—not the primordial Òbàtálá.

[9] Ademakinwa, *Ife*, pp. 28–30.

against Òdùduwà, described as the invader. Its aim was chiefly to protect the indigenous institutions of the land from annihilation under the influence of the Òdùduwà regime. They made a covenant "ìmùlè" (drinking the earth) and swore fealty to Ọbàtálá as the titulary divinity of the earth.[10] The Ògbóni Society was formed to venerate Ọbàtálá; the Ìgbò Masquerade was devised to molest the enemy.

Ọbàtálá's supporters were dispersed in several directions. Many of them went out in gangs and founded new settlements[11] and set up the worship of Ọbàtálá as the great òrìṣà (deity).[12]

The Myth of Return (the Ìgbò and Mọrèmi) The struggle for the ownership of Ifè between the autochthons and the invaders reared up again between Ọbàlùfọn Aláiyémọọrè[13]

[10] Idowu, pp. 24, 149–50. "Ògbóni," by folk etymology, has derived from "Ùgbó ni 'lè" (the Igbo own the land). This may explain why the cult venerates the earth and derives its sanctions from a mystical contact with the land. According to Idowu, the cult object of the *Ogbóni* is called "Onile" (the Landlord).

[11] Of all the settlements, those around Ilesha and Oshogbo (adjacent areas of Ede) are significant. According to Ademakinwa, an artist described as "Ògbóni" settled around the present Ilesha, where he practiced his art, which he described as "ìṣà." It was his art gallery that was called "Ilé Ìṣà." (See Ademakinwa, Pt. III, pp. 20–21.) Recent archaeological discoveries at Ilesha and the spherical or ovoid style in which the artifacts were cast may yield the clue to the work of the said "Ògbóni." (See Frank Willet, "Recent Archaeological Discoveries at Ilesha," *Odu*, No. 8 (October 1960): 5–20.

The Oshogbo settlement (which includes the present Ede) is said to have been founded by Ọbàlùfọn Aláiyémọọrè, believed to be an Igbo leader, during his period in exile. (See R. C. Abraham, *Modern Yoruba Dictionary* (London: University of London Press, 1958), pp. 278, 491.

[12] At Ìkíre, Ọbàtálá is worshiped as Òrìṣà Ìkírè, at Èjìgbò as Òrìṣà Ogiyán, at Òkò as Òrìṣà Òkò, at Ogbomosho as Òrìṣà Pópó, at Abeokuta as Òrìṣà Ọgbó, and in various other places simply as "Òrìṣà."

[13] "Aláiyémọọrè," by folk etymology, has derived from "Aláiyé mọ Ọrèlúéré" ("the Owner of the world knows Ọrèlúéré"). Ọrèlúéré, or Orè, was an aboriginal hunter who is believed to have bun a menace to Òdùduwà. See Frank Willet, *Ife in the History*

and Ọ̀rànmíyàn, two personalities described as the grand-sons of the primordial actors in the conflict. When the throne of Ifẹ̀ became vacant, Aláiyémọọrẹ̀, leading the followers of Ọbàtálá, moved in and occupied it, since Ọ̀rànmíyàn, the adventurous warrior grandson of Òdùduwà, was away from Ifẹ̀ at that time. Ọ̀rànmíyàn quickly returned at the head of his party and succeeded in asserting his authority over Ifẹ̀ by expelling Aláiyémọọrẹ̀. He considered himself the "sọ̀ókò" ("crown prince") and Aláiyémọọrẹ̀ a mere "àrẹ̀" ("stranger"). By this expulsion, Ọ̀rànmíyàn set the stage for yet another battle, which was a repetition of the first, the archetype.

Aláiyémọọrẹ̀ reorganized his followers into an underground movement to menace the invaders, and as a planned stratagem, formed the Ìgbò Masquerade. The Ìgbò gang, dressed in raffia fiber costumes, began to make periodical raids on Ifẹ̀. The successful attacks caused great commotion among the people. For a long period of time, Ifẹ̀ was plundered and the people attributed their affliction and distress to the displeasure of their gods, believing their attackers from the Ìgbò territory to be spirits of demigods.

Mọrèmi, a zealous and patriotic Ifẹ̀ market-woman, volunteered to save Ifẹ̀ by secretly ascertaining who were the Ìgbò masqueraders. She consulted "Ifá" ("the Oracle"), who confirmed for her that the Ìgbò gangs were not spirits but human beings. Ifá ordered her to sacrifice to the goddess of the Ẹ̀sìnmìrìn Stream, which lay between Ifẹ̀ and the domain of the Ìgbò. She made a solemn pledge to the goddess of the stream that should she succeed in finding out the secret of the Ìgbò strategy, she would offer a supreme sacrifice.

During another Ìgbò raid, Mọrèmi allowed herself to be captured and taken into servitude. As she was a woman of great beauty and charm, her captors thought her a significant booty, which the Ìgbò leader would treasure. Subsequently, the Ìgbò leader became enamored of Mọrèmi and admitted her to the highest rank of the Ìgbò hierarchy. Mọrèmi learned the customs of the people and was initiated into their cults.

of West African Sculpture (London: Thames and Hudson, 1967), p. 123.

When she captured the secret behind the Ìgbò Masquerade, she stole out of captivity one night and escaped to Ifè.

The Ìgbò made a great chase after Mọrèmi and attacked Ifè as usual with their masked men. But Mọrèmi, carrying two burning brands, led an army of Ifè men with lighted torches, rushed among the astonished enemy, and laid them low. The power of the Ìgbò was broken, the masks were burned to ashes, and the "face" behind them scorched to death.

Mọrèmi then repaired to the Èsìnmìrìn to offer the promised sacrifice to the goddess of the stream. To her bewilderment, she learned the sacrificial lamb was to be Èlà, her only son. Having no alternative, she fulfilled her vow with fortitude and forthrightness. The sacrificial rite was a very moving occasion for the Ifè people. In spite of her great loss, Mọrèmi ordered that the Ìgbò king and his followers be restored to Ifè to live like other inhabitants of the place.[14] Thus Mọrèmi's intervention and ransom effected the much needed rapproachement between the followers of Ọbàtálá and Òdùduwà. Her sacrifice restored peace to the realm. The Ìgbò returned to Ifè led by the Èlúyárè[15] and occupied a quarter at Ifè, where they are still represented by the Ọbàwinrin (the succeeding Ìgbò leadership) during the annual Edi festival.[16] This festival commemorates the myth of the Ìgbò and Mọrèmi.

[14] According to Dr. Abiri, the defeat of the Ìgbò took place during the reign of Ọrànmíyàn's son, Láyíamisàn. This usefully explains the reason for Aláiyémọọrè's return to the throne as one of the terms of the rapprochement.

[15] "Èlúyárè," by folk etymology, has derived from "Èlú àwọn àrè" ("the gem of the àrè"). It has been suggested that Aláiyémọọrè returned to Ifè in the Ìgbò Masquerade that was so named. Dr. Abiri, in a personal communication, said that it was "Ọbàlùfòn Aláiyémọọrè who led a group of dissidents that worried Ifè from outside."

According to Chief Fabunmi, when Aláiyémọọrè was restored to the Ifè throne in reconciliation, he inherited Mọrèmi as wife. See Chief M. A. Fabunmi, *Ife Shrines* (Ife: University of Ife Press, 1969), p. 17.

[16] Ọbàwinrin is "the priest in charge of the Groves of Iwinrin and Osongagan Obamakin." (See Willet, *op. cit.*, p. 123.)

Frank Willet has also pointed to the fact that the head of the

The annual Ọbàtálá festival at Ẹdẹ takes place in March, the Yoruba new year and the beginning of the planting season.[17] It is ushered in by the fertility ritual of the Ekurọlẹ, dedicated to the worship of the Earth, and celebrated by the Ògbóni Society, the secret cult formed by the followers of Ọbàtálá to fight political injustice perpetrated by invaders of the land. Five days later the festival commences, and on the eve of the first day of the festival, the first rain of the year falls, with such regularity that one must credit the organizers with prophetic or rain-making powers.

The two-day festival reveals two different stages of performance: the market stage and the palace stage. The dramatis personae are the Ajagẹmọ (the chief priest, who acts the protagonist), the Olúnwí (another priest, who acts the antagonist), the Tìmì (the King, who represents the mediator), and a chorus of worshipers.

On the first day of the festival, the stage is set at the marketplace and is marked by a procession. The Tìmì sits in state before the shrine of Ọbàtálá, and a circle is formed by his retinue and a crowd of spectators, to receive the Ọbàtálá worshipers, who proceed from the different shrines of the divinity in the community to the main one in the market square. The performance is brought up by the procession of the chanting chorus—female worshipers of Ọbàtálá, led by the Ajagẹmọ and other priests of the divinity. Drums summon the Ajagẹmọ, dressed up in a full robe (agbádá) and wearing a white turban. He moves to the shrine, where he

---

family who represents the Ìgbò is in charge of the two groves that have produced a large proportion of the Ifẹ̀ art in terra cotta, and suggests that the art may be that of the original indigenous population.

[17] Although there is no general agreement on March as the first month of the Yoruba calendar, because different groups of worshipers create their own, yet it is common especially among the Oyo-Yoruba, to regard March as the beginning of the new year. (See S. Johnson, *History of the Yorubas*, Lagos, 1960 edition, p. 49). The Yoruba divide their lunar month into seven weeks of four days. Each day is dedicated to the worship of the four principal divinities, namely, Ọbàtálá, Ifá, Sàngó, and Ògún. It is also known that there are variations owing to the emergence of other divinities in the Yoruba pantheon.

performs the rites of worship and offers a sacrifice. Sacrificing a goat, he presents the divinity with the first share and hands the rest to the representative of the rulers of the community. After prayers, the people resume singing and dancing and the Tìmì leads the worshipers in a dance procession to the palace, where the first day's performance is consummated.

On the second day of the festival, the stage is set at the palace and is marked by a pageant. The worshipers of Ọbàtálá gather in the open space (òde) in front of the palace. The Tìmì, dressed up for the occasion, sits in front of the porch (kòbì) surrounded by his retinue. The chorus women, wearing white blouses, white beads, and white headgear, open the performance of the ritual dance-drama with the following prologue:

Chant: "Ọbàtálá,
Ọbàtáàsà,
Ọba pátápátá
Tí nwón bí l'óde Ìgbò,
Tí ó rè é j'ọba l'óde Ìrànjé.
Òrìsà-ńlá,
Ọ̀sẹ̀rẹ̀-màgbò.
Nwọ́n fëjẹ́ tán an.
Nwọ́n d'Ọ̀sẹ̀rẹ̀ orun 'lẹ̀.
Ìgbà tí gbogbo wọn rá tán,
Nwọ́n ní'bo l'awo kù sí?"

("Obatala,
The Oba that we praise,
The truly king,
Who was born in the city of Igbo,
And went to become king in the city of Iranje.
The great Orisa,
The divinity of Igbo.
They showed him ingratitude,
They tricked him with palm wine,
They then deserted the divinity from heaven.
When they had all vanished,
They then asked where else could the secret be found?")

Song: Ta la ó má a sìn l'ọ́dún?
Òòṣà Ìgbò,
Ìwọ la ó má a sìn l'ọ́dún.
Alábàá-láṣẹ,
Ìwo la ó má a sìn l'ọ́dún."

("Whom shall we worship annually?
The Igbo divinity,
You shall we worship annually.
You, who proposes and disposes,
You shall we worship annually.")

The chanting and singing drift into a solemnity which is overtaken by the rhythms of the Ọbàtálá drums. The Ajagẹmọ steps out into the arena. He has removed his gorgeous outfit and white turban to reveal an undergarment over a white loincloth and a headpiece of plaited hair. In slow, measured, intense steps, he dances his way toward the center of the circle to meet the exuberant Olúnwí, his opponent. The Olúnwí also dances forward, wielding two whips. He attacks while the Ajagẹmọ mainly parries the strokes in self-defense. Soon the Ajagẹmọ is overwhelmed, taken prisoner, and hustled off into the interior of the palace. The Tìmì then sets out to intervene for the release of the Ajagẹmọ. He pays a ransom to the Olúnwí and, thereupon, the Ajagẹmọ is liberated.

The chorus women surge into the arena, dancing, and chant as follows:

"Ikú tí í bá ni gbé 'lé
Ikú tí í bá ni gbé 'lé
Tí í f'ọlá ran ni,
Aláṣẹ!
Ó sọ ẹnìkan-ṣo-ṣo di'gba ènìà!
Sọ mí d'irún,
Sọ mí d'igba,
Sọ mí d'ọtà-lé-l'égbèje ènìà!"

(You Death [the ancestor] that lives with a person
And imbues him with your nobility,
You are the one with authority!
You who multiplied one person into two hundred!
Multiply me into four hundred,
Multiply me into two hundred,
Multiply me into one thousand four hundred
and sixty persons!)

The Àjàgẹmọ, wearing a new costume and beaming ra-
diantly, is then carried shoulder high amid dancing and chanting in a triumphal procession back to the arena.

Òrìsà, Ẹtì!
Ẹni ọlá!
A fi ojọ́ gbogbo tóbi.
Ó tóbi, kò ṣe é gbé.
Bàntà-banta nínú àlà,
Ó sùn nínú àlà,
Ó jí nínú àlà,
Ó ti 'nú àlà dìde.
Baba ńlá, ọkọ Yemówó,
Òrìsà wu ni n'íbùdó;
Ibi 're l'Òrìsà ka 'lẹ̀."

(Orisa, the Immovable!
The noble One.
He who reveals his greatness daily.
He is mighty, he cannot be lifted.
His greatness is revealed in white robes,
He sleeps in white robes,
He wakes in white robes.
The great Father, consort of Yemowo,
I love to see Orisa at the battle front;
Orisa always settles in a fortuitous spot.)

The Tìmì and others join in the dance to mark the end
of the festival.

The source of most Yoruba myths is Ifá, the Oracle. The accounts are embodied in the *Odù*, a corpus of encyclopedic knowledge, recited and narrated by the Babaláwo (priest of the Ifá) during divination. Ọrúnmilà (the Divinity of Wisdom) is believed to have been charged by Olódùmarè to keep an account of all that happened in the Yoruba cosmos. Belief in Ọrúnmilà therefore gives the myths a religious background and reinforces them with a kind of reality. In this regard, the myths are sacred and, by nature of the operation of the Odù system, difficult to alter.

At Ifẹ̀, both the myths of conquest and of return are enacted during the Ìtàpá and Edì festivals, respectively. The Ìtàpá commemorates the defeat of Ọbàtálá by Òdùduwà and his supporters, while the Edì commemorates Mọrèmi's sacrifice and the conquest of the Ìgbò. These festivals are annual celebrations at Ifẹ̀ and involve all the inhabitants. They are not simply rituals of the particular divinities whose stories are enacted; hence the myths become social realities for the people.

The myths of creation, conquest, and return throw considerable light on the scenario of the ritual drama of the Ọbàtálá festival at Ẹdẹ. The style and form of the performance reveal an aesthetic construction as well as an ideological intent, and raise many key questions important to this study.

First, the myths that form the basis of the ritual drama are not given as part of the performance, either by recitation or narration. The myths are, in fact, separate. They seem to precede the ritual organization of the Ọbàtálá festival and yet are linked to it. To what extent, therefore, does Raglan's myth-ritual theory offer an insight into this manifestation?[18] It is likely that the Ọbàtálá ritual had its associated myth, but because such a myth was never made

[18] Lord Raglan, "Myth and Ritual," *Journal of American Folklore* 68 (1955): 454–61.

an artistic part of the dramatic performance, the story of the enactment can only now be gathered in fragments apart from the festival. The three myths of creation, conquest, and return cannot therefore be seen as existing to validate the Ọbàtálá rite. On the other hand, there may be validity in Kenneth Burke's assumption that a "combat myth" associated with a cult was used during a ritual as a mythic explanation for the cult's origin and services.[19]

Second, if the ritual performance of the festival is seen as an explanation of the life force of Ọbàtálá as a divinity, then the chronological details of the myths break down. The structure of the ritual drama has a beginning, a middle, and an end, synchronizing, as it does, with the three myths. But the detailed accounts of the myths show that only the myths of creation and conquest involve Ọbàtálá, the hero of the ritual drama. The myth of return belongs to a different historical period and is therefore outside Ọbàtálá's mythical biography.

If, on the other hand, the scenario is accepted wholly as the mythical biography of Ọbàtálá, then the performance becomes a cosmogonic act valid when the ritual drama is seen as an imitation of an archetypal model. The apotheosis of Ọbàtálá into Òrìṣà-ńlá (the great divinity), or his transformation from man into an archetype, may also have caused the transfiguration of history into myth. Assuming that the ritual drama existed since mythological times, and before the Aláiyémọọrẹ̀ episode, then its form of "denouement" could be regarded either as the product of a creative fantasy or as a sympathetic activity wherein the supporters of Ọbàtálá had seen their hero as the divine person leading them from chaos to cosmos.

According to Eliade, when a rite is reconstructed to reflect the myth of eternal return, it would then seem that the worshipers see the dramatization not merely as an imitation but as a reactualization of the cosmogony and would go through the rite every year in order to regenerate them-

[19] Kenneth Burke, "Myth, Poetry and Philosophy," *Journal of American Folklore* 73 (1960): 285.

selves.[20] An annual regeneration by the supporters of Ọbàtálá was needed to maintain their position as the *de jure* owner of the Yoruba cosmos. The ritual practice is not irrational, in spite of its manipulation; rather, it is an expression in action of the attitude of Ọbàtálá's supporters toward the transcendental aspects of reality. To this extent also, the essence of the ritual drama can be seen not only as an act to abolish history but as a strategy with an ideological intent aimed at restoring the primordial status of Ọbàtálá.

Third, ritual drama can be used as a persuasive function of religion if the aim is to promote accepted attitudes and modes of action. Kenneth Burke has been a most persistent expositor of the rhetorical method as an art of persuasion.[21] The rites of worship of Ọbàtálá are the prerogative of the cult members and would provide a valid system of governance if the hierarchy used ritual drama as a direct or indirect means of influencing its members.

In its performance, the style and form of the ritual drama of the Ọbàtálá festival reveal a rhetorical technique that seems to have been designed to produce empathy and sympathy. Roger Abrahams, who agrees basically with Burke's concept of rhetoric, explains that a performance becomes expressive folklore if by design it is used as "a way of persuading through the production of pleasure as well as the assertion of idea or a course of action."[22]

The Ọbàtálá festival seems to fit this model. Myths about Ọbàtálá certainly endow him with failings of character. Addicted to wine, he is apt to commit serious blunders. Also, in the narratives about him drawn from the Odù of Ifá, Ọbàtálá is depicted as a man of no exceptional virtues or faults but one imbued with a ruthless sincerity, pursuing his objectives with unswerving confidence in spite of his weaknesses. It is this *"hamartía,"* therefore, that contributed to

---

[20] Mircea Eliade, *Cosmos and History* (New York: Harper Torchbooks, 1955), pp. 76–77.

[21] Kenneth Burke, *The Rhetoric of Religion* (Boston: Beacon Press, 1961), p. v.

[22] Roger D. Abrahams, "Introductory Remarks to a Rhetorical Theory of Folklore," *Journal of American Folklore* 81 (1968): 145.

Ọbàtálá's downfall in the hands of his enemies. But in the ritual performance, neither the "prologus" nor the choral-chant interlude reveals Ọbàtálá's tragic flaws. On the contrary, the chants recount his attributes as Òrìṣà (divinity) and portray him as an archetype of ethical purity, an ideal apparently not developed in the myths.

As a form of folklore, Ọbàtálá's ritual drama at Ẹdẹ functions as a normative cohesive force. The original design seems to have been to use the drama as an expression against the Òdùduwà group, which threatened the existence of the Ọbàtálá group. The Ọbàtálá festival is ushered in by the Ekuròlè of the Ògbóni Society, dedicated to the security and the sanctity of the earth. The actual performance is artfully and artificially organized and seems to serve the purpose of propaganda for the attainment of both empirical and non-empirical ends. The ritual play in essence presents Ọbàtálá as a tragic hero, engulfed in, but soon relieved from, an anxiety situation. The relief re-establishes the "status quo" and produces pleasure. The performance thus affects the spectators at the festival to produce a catharsis through sympathy in the hero's travail and relief in his triumph.

The accounts of the myths examined showed that the followers of Ọbàtálá were noted for strategies and stratagems, especially in their struggle to retrieve a lost ground as exhibited by the inauguration of the Ògbóni Society and the organization of the Ìgbò Masquerade. In terms of its dramatic structure and aesthetic appeal, the ritual drama of the Ọbàtálá festival at Ẹdẹ seems to be another "strategy" activated by the followers of Ọbàtálá after their physical rejection from Ifẹ̀. The play may have been designed under this force of circumstances and introduced into the annual festival to reactualize the events that occurred at the beginning of time, to preserve and project Ọbàtálá as an archetype and to present him as the divinity through whom the Yoruba society can be periodically regenerated.

As a religious occasion, the annual festival may have served to reaffirm the common bonds of the followers and worshipers of Ọbàtálá and to reinforce their social solidarity. The conception of Ọbàtálá as given by his worshipers fits into the theory of the archetype. As a divinity, Ọbàtálá is an embodiment of the morals and ethics of the Yoruba. The Ọbàtálá ritual drama under study seems to have been designed to promote adherence to the ideals of the divinity. In this regard, it is understandable that the myths about Ọbàtálá are not fully related as a functional part of the ritual.

The dramatic performance itself is a form of folklore constructed to achieve a desirable objective. Both the dramatic structure and the rhetorical approach give the performance an aesthetic dimension which emphasizes the ingenuity of the followers of Ọbàtálá, the divinity endowed with the means of creativity at the beginning of time.

APPENDIX

The "combat myth" is contained in the following Odù and reveals Ọbàtálá as a tragic hero:

ÈJÌ OGBÈ

(a) *On Ọbàtálá:*[1]

"Gbogbo ọlá omi tí ṁbẹ ní ilé aiyé kò le è t'Ókun;
Gbogbo odò tí ó ṣẹ l'ókè, iyì wọn kò le è tó t'Ọsà.
A dá a fún Ọbàtálá Ọṣèrẹ̀-ìgbò
Ní 'jó tí yío jẹ Alábàálàṣẹ,
Tí gbogbo Irúnmọlẹ̀ ní àwọn yío gba ọkan nínú Oríkì rẹ̀.
Ọrúnmìlà yẹhùn, Ẹlẹ́gbára tẹ̀ lé e."

"All the esteem in which water is held in this world,
    cannot match that of the Sea [Atlantic Ocean];
The respect given to all the rivers that flow from above,
    cannot match that of the Lagoon [the Lagos Lagoon].
Thus the Oracle cast it for Obatala Osere-igbo [the divinity of
    the Igbo]
On the day that he was anointed Alabaalase [one who proposes
    and disposes],
When all the Irunmole [the four hundred gods of the Yoruba
    pantheon] requested to have one of his (Obatala's) *oriki*
    [praise names].
Orunmila [the divinity of wisdom] abstained, Elegbara [the
    errant divinity] followed him."

(b) *On Ọbàtálá and the Creation:*[2]

Èjì Ogbè ńsọ báyi pé:
"Igi ńlá ní í ta 'nú igbó yọ.
Àwọn ni nwọn d'ífá fún Ọbàtálá Ọṣèrẹ̀màgbò
Ní'jó tí ńti 'Kòlé Ọrun bọ̀ wá 'Kòlé Aiyé.
Igi ńlá ní í ta 'nú igbó yọ.
Àwọn ni nwọn d'ífá f'Óòduwà

[1] I am grateful to Alàgbà Agboọla Adeniji for this Odù.
[2] This Odù was obtained from Alàgbà Babalọlá Fátóògùn through the courtesy of Ọgbéni Wálé Ògúnyemí, Institute of African Studies, University of Ibadan.

Ní'jọ́ tí ńti 'Kọ̀lé ọrun bọ̀ wá Kọ̀lé Aiyé.
Nwọ́n ní kí wọn wá rúbọ;
Ọ̀ọ̀duwà nìkan ló rúbọ o.
Nígbàtí nwọ́n dé 'lé Aiyé,
Ọbàtálá mẹmu-mẹmu,
Ó gbàgé 'wà s'ójú ọ̀nà.
Ọ̀ọ̀duwà wá lọ rè é gbé 'wà náà,
Ó tún gbe padà tọ Olódùmarè lo.
Olódùmarè l'éètiri?
Léhin ìgba t'oun ti rán nyín n'ilé Aiyé tán?
Ọ̀ọ̀duwà L'Ọbàtálá mẹnu-mẹnu, Òrìṣà gbàgbé Ìwà s'ójú ọ̀nà.
Olódùmarè ní k'Ọ̀ọ̀duwà ó padà lọ s'ílé Aiyé,
Ó ní kó má a lọ rè é ṣ'ilé Aiyé.
Ó ní kó gún gégé bi igbá,
Ó ní kó tòrò bí omi àfòwúrọ̀ pọn.

Nígbà tí Ọ̀ọ̀duwà de'lé Aiyé,
Ọ̀ọ̀duà gbe'lé Aiyé ka'lẹ̀,
Ó gbé eèpẹ̀ ka'rí omi,
Ó gbé àwọn adìẹ kà á,
Ó gbé àwọn alégẹmọ kà á;
Ni'lé Aiyé bẹrẹ sí í fẹ̀ káàkiri.
Ńgbà náà ni nwọ́n wá gbà'tẹ̀ m'Ọ̀ọ̀duwà;
Ọbàtálá l'oun ó bá Ọ̀ọ̀duwà jà;
Òrìṣà l'oun ó b'Ọ̀ọ̀duwà ja'gun."

Eji Ogbe is saying as follows:
"It is the great tree that soars above the forest.
They are the ones that cast the Ifa Oracle for
Obatala Oseremagbo, on the day he was traveling
    from the expanse of Heaven to the expanse of Earth.
It is the great tree that soars above the forest.
They are the ones that cast the Ifa Oracle for Oduduwa
On the day he was traveling from the expanse of Heaven to
    the expanse of Earth.
They asked them to sacrifice;
Only Oduduwa made the sacrifice.
When they reached the Earth,
Obatala went on a drinking spree,
And forgot the pot of creation by the wayside.
Oduduwa then went and picked the pot of creation,
He then returned it to Olodumare [the Supreme Deity].

Olodumare then asked what happened
After he had sent them to the Earth?
Oduduwa said that Obatala went on a drinking spree,
And forgot the pot of creation by the wayside.
Olodumare then asked Oduduwa to return to the Earth.
He asked him to go and organize the Earth
So that the Earth could be as straight as the beaten calabash,
So that the Earth could be as settled as the water drawn in
    the early morning.

When Oduduwa reached the Earth,
Oduduwa laid the foundation of the Earth;
He deposited mud on the water,
He placed fowls on it,
He placed chameleons on it;
Then the Earth started spreading in all directions.
They then started a conspiracy against Oduduwa;
Obatala said he would fight Oduduwa;
Orisa said he would wage war against Oduduwa."

EQUATORIAL EXCURSIONS:
THE FOLKLORE OF NARCOTIC-INSPIRED VISIONS IN AN AFRICAN RELIGIOUS MOVEMENT

James W. Fernandez

A useful contribution to the enduring problem of stereotyping and creativity in folk narrative may be a consideration of traditional elements in narcotic-induced visions. Men are freer in such visions to elaborate their fantasies than when they are telling or singing tales to an audience laden with cultural expectations as to proper narrative form and content. Such expectations are a weight upon the narrator, and his spontaneity must be carefully controlled. But who is his constraining audience and what gravitational forces of social situation and cultural setting act upon him as he floats away in psychedelic reverie?

I am going to discuss what may appear to be some very bizarre narcotic visions indeed, since the African situation and setting—Fang society and culture of the equatorial rain forest—are not familiar to us. My intention is to point out that these visions undertake excursions that are well anticipated in the folklore of the Fang. The visions take place during initiation into one of the most interesting of African religious movements, the Bwiti cult. Its interest lies in a rare richness of ritual elaboration, and also in the fact that it is one of the few contemporary cults that regularly employs an alkaloid narcotic, the ground roots of the bush *Tabernan-the iboga*, for cult purposes.

Bwiti appeared among the Fang around the time of the First World War. It was adopted by the southernmost sub-tribes of the Fang from more southern and western equatorial people. The cult is a syncretism of influences from the Bwiti cult of the dead found among southern Gabonese cultures, particularly the Metsogo Massango of the upper Ngonnie, from the Bieri ancestral cult traditional to the Fang, and from Christian (primarily Catholic) evangelization. The cult has spread throughout Fang territory, though it is still much stronger in the south. It is polymorphous, there being at least six branches of the cult. As is typical of Fang anarchic egalitarianism, cult organization beyond the village level is sporadic only. Local chapels of the same branch maintain contact but usually on a casual basis.

The cult and its branches have a number of purposes, but it seems to be devoted mainly to re-creating through its microcosmogony a satisfactory relationship with the dead, who had come to be ignored by virtue of evangelical pressures. The cult also seeks to offer to its members the experience of a passage over to the afterlife (*si ayat*) and, hence, a coming to terms with death. There is heavy emphasis upon aesthetic form and the exact timing of ceremonial events in this cult, for it seeks to approximate heavenly activity.

It is hardly possible to convey to the reader the power of the Bwiti cult without playing the music. For the cult is filled with music and dance—more than a dozen different dances and several hundred different songs. The old saying well describes the feelings of the members of Bwiti: "He who knows the power of the dance dwells in God!" Well before the all-night ceremonies begin, after eight P.M., the insistent rhythms of the cult harp (*ngombi*) and the soft beat of the bamboo staves (*obaka*) build up in the membership an expectation and a spirit of engagement that is integral to the success of cult performance. Men must be powerfully attracted to engage themselves in an all-night rite. And *Tabernanthe iboga*, as we shall see, is a great aid to the success of their performance.

The most beautiful music comes in the early-morning

hours, after the spirits of men and ancestors have mingled in the cult chapel and after the membership has achieved a state of what they call "one-heartedness"—*nlem mvore*. We hear the concluding songs, which celebrate the state of grace or good luck (*okan*) that the membership has achieved and that also bid farewell to the ancestors departing again for the village of the dead. Dawn is faintly evident over the equatorial forest wall to the east. The first cock has crowed. All cult activities must be concluded before the sun rises, for Bwiti is a night cult, a cult of the female principle of the universe, Nyingwan Mebege, the Sister of God, who is the Moon. There is a deep satisfaction in the membership borne of the fact that they have danced all night, achieved "one-heartedness," and may look forward to the fellowship of the communal meal that comes immediately after the cult practices. An afterglow is brought to them by *eboka* as well, for the drug is not usually associated with undesirable after-effects.

Eboka is the Fang name for *Tabernanthe iboga*. The species name, as well as the Fang name, is taken from the Galwa-Mponqwe (Miene) term *iboga*. The bush, which is of several varieties, not always clearly distinguished botanically, is common to the equatorial underforest. But it is also grown in the open courtyards of Bwiti villages as a decorative bush. It produces yellowish or pinkish-white flowers and a small orange-type fruit whose sweet pulp is edible though not narcotic. The fruit is sometimes used as a medicine for barrenness in women in Bwiti. The capacity of the plant to suppress fatigue has constituted one of its principal attractions to the Bwitist. He must dance all night, and hence values the euphoric insomnia produced by the drug.

The *eboka* plant itself is an apocynaceous shrub growing to about four feet in height. The main alkaloid—ibogaine—is largely contained in the roots and particularly in the root bark, so the mode of consumption in Bwiti maximizes access to this alkaloid. For it is this root bark that is rasped. It is eaten directly as raspings or ground as a powder and eaten or left to soak in water to be drunk as an infusion.

Eboka is taken in two ways: (1) It is swallowed regularly in small doses of two to three teaspoonfuls for women and three to five teaspoonfuls for men before and in the early hours of the ceremonies. There may be an additional several grams eaten at mid-course, after midnight. This represents an ingestion of between four and twenty grams of powdered *eboka*. (2) Once or twice in the career of a Banzie (a cult initiate) a massive dose of *eboka* is taken for purposes of initiation and to "break open the head" in order to effect contact with the ancestors through collapse and hallucination. One to three small basketfuls may be consumed at this time over an eight to twenty-four hour period. This represents an ingestion of between three hundred and one thousand grams, some forty to sixty times the threshold dose and close to toxicity. It is not surprising that the death of initiates is commented upon in all cults, and in the past forty years a dozen cases of murder or manslaughter have been brought against Bwiti cult leaders who have lost initiates.

The massive doses taken at initiation produce a gross reduction in the initiate's ability to moderate or program motor activity. Early in the day, the initiates are allowed to arise periodically and evacuate. Several hours into their initiation they are taken down to a stream to be ritually purified in preparation for their meeting with the ancestors. Further along in the ingestion of the plant, the initiates rise no more. They sit upon their white cloth gazing expectantly toward the rear of the chapel and continuing to eat *eboka* heaped upon the civet-cat skin between their legs. They gaze with fascination upon the mirror propped before them upon the ground. In it their ancestors may appear to them. Behind them their mother or father of *eboka* (*nyuaboka* or *essaboka*) sits calming their anxieties and listening carefully to their excited mumblings as the *eboka* works upon them. They may already be experiencing a sense of departure and visionary encounter. And their mumblings may convey important information to the entire membership. Eventually the initiate will fall over and have to be carried from the chapel to a special chamber within the house or to a special arena behind it. Being initiated and eating *eboka* is often called sitting down, getting down to the earth. All members of Bwiti have to get down—*Banzie bese ba yian tobo si nge ba komo yen eboka!* Now the initiate's soul has left him and in the company of the ancestors is wending its way to a final and confirming vision in the land beyond—the land of the dead.

Here at the very heart of the initiation there is a stereotyping, for the initiate is clearly expected to go, and he desires to go, upon a journey along the "path of the dead" (*zen awu*). In fact Bwiti itself is often called a "path."

The lighter regular dosage of two to five teaspoons does not produce hallucinations, though adepts of the cult claim that once a man has "met *Eboka*" and been taken by "him" to the "other side," any subsequent amount will—like Proust's tea and madeleine—raise up in his mind many of his former experiences. The regular dosage, therefore, may have that associative power, but it is taken primarily to enable the adepts to engage in the arduous all-night ceremonies without falter or fatigue. Members often say that the *eboka* taken in this way also lightens their bodies so that they can float through their ritual dances, and enables them to mingle more effectively with the ancestors at the roof of the chapel. They do not report visions under the influence of such amounts, only modest change in body perception and some dissociation.

I spent more than a year (1959–60) studying Bwiti, during which time I conducted over sixty extended, open-ended interviews with individual members of the cult. Fifty of these interviews contain reliable information on the initiation experience. Thirty-eight vision experiences (or lacks of experiences) were reported. Twelve members of a particularly secretive cult house were reluctant to discuss the visions. Twenty-one vision experiences were noted in their entirety. Failure to see visions and refusal to tell them are frequent enough. It is not surprising that some Banzie refuse to recount visions, which are felt, after all, to be a confirming experience and to contain or impart information of great value. Some cult houses and some Bwiti leaders hold them as secret and therefore invaluable property of the individual and of his local cult group. (See Part III for field-note accounts of a vision—*ndem eboka*, portentous dream, a dream full of signs—that was refused to the ethnographer, and of a vision that failed.) Reasons given for eating *eboka*, in order of popularity, were (1) the urging of a dead relative during a dream, (2) attacks by witches, causing impotence, sterility, pain, and sleeplessness, (3) discontent with Catholicism and Protestantism, (4) the desire to know God, and (5) general malaise. It seems clear that in most cases men eat *eboka* for a variety of reasons. The reasons given to the ethnographer may or may not have been the most salient.

I also inquired about the content of what was seen in initiation visions. That is a more tricky question and is subject to much secondary elaboration after the event. It should be pointed out that in intentful "secondary elaboration" the visionary becomes a folk narrator. Would this be a restriction upon the "test of a problem" I promised at the beginning? I estimate that the Bwiti informants were as accurate in their accounts of their visions as they could be. The "secondary elaboration" was not of a calculated kind. In so far as it occurred, it was an interesting and telling kind of formulation out of the inchoate. It is my analysis and not theirs that yields the fact that these visions are narratives that exist among and owe something to other narratives in Fang folklore. There is some tendency for the visions to be more elaborately recounted the further away one is from the experience itself. No doubt men solidify and embellish their visions the more they recount them, and this is an inescapable form of secondary elaboration. But this is not always the case, and I shall make no attempt to distinguish the secondary elaboration that occurs over time.

Content:	No. = 38	Per Cent
1. Saw nothing and heard nothing.	9	24
2. Heard many voices, a great tumult, and recognized the voices of ancestors. Saw nothing.	8	21
3. Heard and saw various of my ancestors. They walked with me and instructed me on my life in Bwiti and elsewhere.	13	34
4. I walked or flew over a long multi-colored road or over many rivers, which led me to my ancestors, who then took me to the great goals.	8	21

It is not clear in my interviews, incidentally, whether the high percentage who claimed to have no significant experience (24%) are those who, not infrequently, became so nauseated as to vomit repeatedly and finally withdraw from the initiation. The last two categories of vision experience, and particularly the fourth, the most detailed, show an instructive stereotyping. In general, women's accounts of their visions are much shorter than men's accounts, although there is no belief in Bwiti that women have shorter excursions than men. But, in fact, it appears that women's primary object is to make contact with some dead relative, very often a dead child, and when this is accomplished the vision experience is fulfilled. Men are more exploratory. They also confess to being initially more skeptical, and their visions tend, as a consequence, to *be* more exploratory, as if the very richness of what they discover tends to overcome their skepticism. The two motives combine to produce longer visions.

My object in discussing these visions is to relate them to Fang folklore. The following elements can be noted in the content of twenty-one visions in which something or someone is reported as being seen. (Examples of these visions may be found in Part III.)

1. *Contact with the Dead.* All the visions involved visual contact with some dead relative or with a whole group of relatives. These could be children (7) or babies waiting to be born (2). In one vision a black baby Jesus provided passage to the great gods. Other cases involved a paternal grandmother (5), a paternal grandfather (2), a mother (4), a father (7), an elder brother (2), unspecified brothers (3), or unspecified relatives (3). Sometimes these relatives appeared in exceptional manifestations. Father or grandfather descended in the form of a bird and took the initiate flying with him (3). In one case the grandfather took the initiate upon a small airplane. On occasion the relatives changed from black to white (4). Or they might be all dressed in white. In one case the relatives wore brilliant uniforms. They might be sitting at a table, occasionally in a large house, doing paper work (3). The dead engaged in various actions

besides escorting the visionary. They gave *eboka* names to initiates (9), gave *ngombi* (harp), or the power to play *ngombi* (5), taught initiates how to cure themselves (4), passed the initiate through their legs (1), or made the initiate eat *eboka* (1). Once, the father washed the mother.

2. *Experiences of the Visionary Excursion.* Fifteen of the visions involved a prolonged excursion up a long road, usually in the company of a relative or with relatives along the way. Often the road was specified as red (8). In all cases, the mode of progress was unusual, sometimes being suggested as similar to floating or flying (6). The end of the road might offer a remarkably different landscape from that of the road itself, such as a large, grassy clearing, a grassy upland, or a grassy hill (6), or a desert (4). A house built on one post was sometimes found on this landscape (5), with entry either permitted (3) or denied (2). Descriptions of this house stated that it was built entirely out of glass (2), had one supporting pillar, one door, one window (2), or was simply a great house. In two cases *eboka* plants were seen on the grassy clearing, once a many-colored circle (full rainbow) descended from heaven on this clearing, once the *otunga* (sacred tree or post of origin) was reached. Rivers of various colors, but never more than three, were encountered as obstacles along the route (7). Twice a monster—a giant snake or a giant crocodile—who, however, enabled passage, was discovered in a river. Once a giant gold chain spanned the river, and once women were seen fishing bones in the river.

Crossroads were also encountered (11), but never more than three times. The intersecting roads were varicolored. Sometimes white men or white Africans sat at a table in the crossroads checking identity, shuffling papers, and allowing passage (4). Once a man with a spear, and another time a white man, barred passage. Visionaries commented on various features experienced on the route: passing large crowds of black people (5), or white people (2), the whites once being a crowd of Christians in animal skins; passing a village taken to be the village of the dead (5), once having only one house, the chapel of Bwiti (*aba eboka*); and once seeing

a Catholic and a Protestant church on hills on either side
of the village.

3. *Experiences with the Greater Powers.* In twelve instances the visionary encountered one of the greater supernatural powers, in particular Nyingwan Mebege, the
Sister of God and the female principle of the universe, who
is the principal object of Bwiti cult practice among the great
gods. She was seen in various manifestations (9), as a beautiful woman (4), as the moon, which is her orb (2), once
with a bayonet piercing her heart, as a *ngombi* (cult harp)
that changed into herself and back again into the harp. Once
she appeared inside the house of one post, and once she was
doubly manifested, descending on either side of the many-
colored circle.

The initiates viewed the personage of Jesus Christ (5). He
was seen three times as a person inside the one pillared
house, once as a bishop with a cap of hair and a star heart
visible in his chest, and once as a black babe that retreated
into the one-story house and locked the door against the
visionary.

4. *Physical Reaction to the Experience.* Visionaries infrequently volunteered any physical reaction to the vision. They
often described nausea, but not as a part of the visions. Three
times they mentioned a floating, flying feeling, once a feeling
that the body color was changing, and once a sensation of
the heart burning and becoming pure as flame.

The Banzie consider the many diverse elements present
in these visions as contained in the power of the root itself
to reveal realities of the land beyond. These visions have
their source in previous experiences, the first of which may
well be that experience of other Banzie who have taken the
drug in initiation doses. Though there is no formal instruction preparing the initiate for his visions, the experiences of
others are, no doubt, recounted to him. Since an occasional
overdose, moreover, may lead to the death of an initiate,
there is an air of expectancy to the whole experience, which
is heightened by the hope of seeing a dead relative. These
experiences together lead to an anxious search for pre-
information on the part of many initiates. But in my experi-

ence there is remarkably little detailed recounting or anything approaching the excited "what did you see, what did you see" atmosphere. The initiate soberly recounts his experience to the cult leaders to confirm the power of *eboka* and to see whether an inspection of the vision will reveal any secret knowledge of value to the cult. Otherwise a decorum of disinterest is shown toward the initiate, because it is recognized that the *eboka* vision is an intimate affair, which must be free from public prying.

The materials presented are sufficiently diverse to caution against an overinterpretation of the stereotypic elements in these visions. Nevertheless there is a set of motifs that are noticeably recurrent. I should like to suggest the kind of movement these stereotypic elements make in the initiate's occupancy of quality space.[1] That is to say, how do these visions situate the initiate more appropriately vis-à-vis historical and contemporary forces? There are certain obvious answers to this question: The vision experience convinces the initiate of his access to a power fully commensurate with the powers of the European civilization of science and technology, which have imposed such a sense of inferiority—powerlessness—upon the third world. The visions also definitively re-establish contact with the dead. The Fang have felt badly about abandoning their ancestors under the pressures of evangelization. The re-establishment of contact with the ancestors through *eboka* makes them feel good. And whereas the village African has felt more and more confined to the desultory inactivity of village life, which he compares to the allure and élan of life in the coastal cities and metropolitan centers, the vision experience is one of interesting, even enthusiastic, excursion.

There are two folklore sources that should be examined for their impact upon these visionary narratives: the origin legends of the Bwiti cult itself, and the origin-migration legends—which fuse with the genealogical histories—of the

[1] The notion is discussed in detail in J. W. Fernandez, *Fang Architectonics* (in press), and J. W. Fernandez, "What It Means to Be Moved: The Operation of Metaphor in Religious Behavior" (ms., 1970).

Fang themselves. There is a connection between these two sets of legends. Bwiti origin legends often adopt motifs from the more traditional Fang legends. For example, Fang migration legends feature a symbolic tree that blocks migration of the Fang ancestors into the equatorial forests. The tree is the adzap (*Mimusops djave*) and the episode in the legends is called the *Adzapmboga* (the carving of the adzap tree). In genealogical history Adzapmboga is also a landmark in the counting up of ancestry. This tree often appears in Bwiti origin legends. So also do the Pygmies, who in the traditional legends appear at Adzapmboga to aid the Fang in entering the equatorial forest and adapting to it. The Pygmies in Bwiti legends are credited with finding *eboka* and founding the cult.

Given the crucial place of the Pygmies in Bwiti origin legends, it may seem surprising that we find no references to them in our selection of visions. One reason for this is that the Pygmies are not ancestors in any genealogical sense as far as the Fang are concerned, although they were indispensable accessories in Fang history. There is, however, one reference to a motif from Bwiti origin legends: the women washing bones in the river. This is evidence enough to indicate that Bwiti origin legends, known by every Banzie and recounted at length by them, do find their way into the visions.

Bwiti origin legends are complex, rambling affairs. I spent over a week with one Banzie while he recounted in staggering detail the origin of the cult. The complexity of these legends is not surprising, for, like the cult itself, they syncretize elements from several traditions. In particular, dramatic biblical accounts of the creation of the earth, of the great flood, of the parting of the Red Sea, and of the birth and crucifixion of Christ make their appearance, although in much altered form. Christ's crucifixion is credited to white men who wished to prevent the Savior from carrying his "*bonnes nouvelles*" to the black man—always His fundamental intention. Mary was neither miraculously inseminated nor even ever pregnant in any physical sense. For Jesus is the old Adam, whom she simply carried concealed under her clothes in order the more effectively to bring about his dramatic reappearance. Amid all this syncretism, there is a core account of the discovery of *eboka* itself that abandons Christian history and goes straight to a reworking of Fang legend in which the Pygmy appears as an unlikely but palpable savior.

This legend of the origin of *eboka* is taken from the Asumege Ening (New Life) branch of Bwiti and was given to me in two villages—Sougoudzap, District of Oyem, and Ayol, District of Mitzik, both in the northern Gabonese region of Woleu Ntem. All versions, whether of this branch or any other, consider *eboka* to be a gift from the Pygmies to the Fang and the other people of Equatorial Africa. Although the Fang themselves possess an extensive knowledge of equatorial pharmacopoeia, they credit the Pygmies, who actually live within the forest without benefit of village clearings, with a greater knowledge than themselves.

> Zame ye Mebege [the last of the creator gods] gave us *eboka*. He thought how to help him. One day he looked down and saw a black man, the Pygmy Bitumu, high in an Atanga tree [*asas, Pachylobis edulis*] gathering its fruit. He made him to fall. He died and brought his spirit to him. Zame cut off the little fingers and the little toes of the cadaver of the Pygmy and planted them in the various parts of the forest. They grew into the *eboka* bush. Now the brothers of the Pygmy came to search for him but they could not find him. One day his wife, Akengue, went fishing deep in the forest. She found in a stream the bones of a man that she thought might have been her husband. She washed them and gathered them up and placed them on the bank, for she intended to return them to the camp. But while she was fishing, a wild cat [either *nsing*, the genet *Genetta servasina*, or *mve* the palm civet *Nandinia binotata*] came along and gathered these bones so that when she returned up the bank they were gone![2] In perplexity she returned

[2] The wild-cat skin is important in initiation, for the *eboka* i eaten from it. The skin is symbolically important for its mottling

through the deep forest, losing her way. Suddenly across her path a porcupine ran [*ngom, Atherurus africanus*] pursued by a dog and then by a man.[3] Peering in the direction in which they disappeared, she saw a cave [*nda akawak*], and there in the back was the pile of bones. As she entered the cave she suddenly heard a voice—like the voice of her husband —asking her who she was and where she came from and whom she wished to speak with. The voice told her to look to the left at the mouth of the cave. There was the *eboka* plant. It told her to eat of its roots. It told her to look to the right. There was the mushroom *duna*.[4] The voice told her to eat of these two things. She ate and felt herself very tired. Now the voice told her to look without the cave. Suddenly the fly that flies into men's eyes, *Olarazen* [he shows the route][5] flew into her eye and brought tears so that she could not see. Then she was told to turn around in the cave. The bones were gone and in their place stood the hus-

---

—in leopard fashion—of red and white. These are basic colors in the cult.

[3] This revelatory configuration has celestial significance: Porcupine, dog, and hunter are the three stars in Orion's belt in Fang astronomy. Tolo, Orion, and Lepus together is the most clearly marked constellation to the Fang—a constellation sometimes extended to boundaries of the stars Sirius, Aldebaran, Rigel, and Betelgeuse. Orion first appears in October and is associated with the clear skies and the planting and growing of crops during the long, cold rainy season (*sugu oyon*). It is a time when ancestral blessing is particularly important.

[4] This is a white mushroom with a very large cap often used in herbalist concoctions. In powdered form it is sometimes eaten in Bwiti but never in my experience, despite the legend. I know of no special psychedelic effect to be attributed to it. No special psychoreactive quality is mentioned by A. Raponda Walker and Roger Sillans in *Les Plantes Utiles du Gabon* (Paris, 1961), p. 457.

[5] When this small sweat fly flies into the eye, it is said to be for the purpose of warning a person that he has taken or is about to take the wrong path. The interjection of the *Olarazen* at this moment is reminiscent of the brushing of the eyeball with the latex of Ayang Beyem, to baffle the vision at the crucial moment of initiation into Bieri—the Fang ancestral cult. The purpose of Ayang Beyem, as well, was to place the initiate on the proper path to the dead.

band and other dead relatives. They talked to her and gave her a name, Disoumba,[6] and told her that she had found the plant that would enable men to see the dead. This was the first baptism into Bwiti, and that was how men got the power to know the dead and have their counsel.

The origin legends usually go on to recount the death of the woman Disoumba, who had to be sacrificed by her living husband (her husband's brother, who took her in levirate) and his fellows in payment for the gift of *eboka*. In this way she was finally able to join her first husband, for whom she had been in constant search. Following this example, all subsequent "eaters of *eboka*" undertake a symbolic death in the act of communing with their ancestors.

Several elements deserve commentary as to the movement they make. First, this legend as well as other evidence from cult life puts emphasis upon *eboka* as a plant of the deep forest—a plant *par excellence* of the Pygmies, who are the denizens of that forest. Bwiti, both in its original form among the Mitsogo and other cultures of southern Gabon and among the Fang, emphasizes by ritual sequences the integration of village and forest. In this sense *eboka* is a plant grown in the villages, yet of the deep forest, which mediates between village and forest. As an agent of transition, it enables men to pass from the familiar village to the mysterious forest, which harbors the secrets of the dead. And so the *eboka*-inspired visions of Bwiti enable men to pass—to float, really —easily into and through the forest. But the movement accomplished by these visions can be more than that. It can pass the visionary out of the forest entirely, into expanses of savannah or desert or grassy upland. So the *eboka* carries the initiate from the village clearing into the forest and through the forest to the primordial clearings of Fang culture history.

Secondly, we note that the crucial events of this legend

---

[6] The originating branch of Fang Bwiti is sometimes called Disoumba.

take place in a cave. And though it is farfetched to suggest a Platonic image of the cave here, the Bwiti cult house is treated as an arena (particularly during initiation) in which greater realities take shape and are projected from without. The membership is brought by *eboka* and the rituals to a vision of the greater realities of the realm of the dead. During initiation in Bwiti, the members involved sit in the middle of the chapel staring outward and consuming *eboka*. In time they "see" their ancestors come to them from without through a mirror placed at the entrance. As, in the origin of *eboka*, men passed from the confusions of the forest to the supernatural realities of the cave, so in initiation their visionary excursions move them from the vertiginous and often chaotic activity of the chapel to the greater realities without.

Finally we may note, despite the failure of the Pygmies to appear in the visions, the Eucharistic implication of the planting of the parts of the Pygmy to germinate the *eboka* plant. This makes the consumption of the roots an act of communion with the Pygmy originator of the cult, who had been chosen by Zame and brought to the heavenly abode. The Pygmies are in some sense saviors of the Fang, as the Adzapmboga legends imply. Hence we have in the cultic eating of *eboka* a Eucharistic experience with similarities to Christian Communion. How much of this is a syncretion with Christianity and how much original with the Fang is difficult to say. One can suspect the former. For not only do members of Bwiti practice Communion by employing *eboka* instead of bread, but they also boast of the efficacy of *eboka* over bread in its power to give visions of the dead. Some of the more Christian branches of Bwiti, not fully cognizant of the origin legend, speak of *eboka*, indeed, as the more perfect and God-given representation of the body of Christ! Be that as it may, as the Pygmies were saviors of the Fang in teaching and educating them to move about with ease in the deep forest, so the eating of the root, which is symbolically their body, gives franchise to many of those inhibitions of movement felt by the Banzie in the colonial world.

The stereotyped element of greatest interest is the passage effected by the visionary up the red road through the forest across the rivers to the grassy upland, desert, or great clearing. This interest emerges if we refer to the Fang migration legends and particularly to the literary compilation of these legends issued in 1954 by Ondoua Engutu, *Dulu Bon be Afri Kara* (*The Journey of the Children of Afri Kara*). Engutu presents a history of the Pahouin (the language group to whom the Fang belong) from the point of view of the Ntumu of the Ntem basin (among whom several of our visions were taken). The account begins with their life on the side of the great salt sea (*mañ me nku*), their traverse of the desert (*nkoto si*) and the savannah (*bilo'o si*), and their entrance into the equatorial rain forest (*beta afan* or *bile si*) through the giant barrier tree *ojambo'a* (Adzapmboga). The account continues until after the Second World War. Like the genealogies upon which it is in good part based, it begins in mythology and ends in historical actualities. *Dulu Bon* explains the origin of many of the important customs of the Pahouin but is particularly concerned with the appearance and the branching off of the many different contemporary clans. Early visions of *Dulu Bon* were widely circulated in northern Gabon, and it was something of a bible to the clan-regroupment movement *Alar Ayon* for the matrix clans, which are the basis of recruitment, are therein clearly identified at their moment of origin. So widespread was the circulation of this version of the Fang past and so well did it fill the need for a past, that it was often difficult to obtain any other version in culture-history research. *Dulu Bon* and the migration legends upon which its early parts are based are influential narratives among the Fang.

Engutu tells us of the disruption of ancestral life on the edge of the salt sea, where the ancestors are victimized by the Bivele be Bot (Red People), who take slaves from them to sell to the Whitemen across the sea. These Whitemen are given an Old Testament referent—"*mvon be Japhet.*"[7] Their manifest weakness in the face of Bivele be Bot forces the ancestors to migrate. Their life is further

[7] Ondoua Engutu, *Dulu Bon be Afri Kara* (Ebolowa, 1951) p. 7.

devastated at the moment of departure by a flooding of the salt sea, which swallows up much of their material culture and with it much of their knowledge, separating them henceforth in this respect from both the red men and the white men. But in their devastation they remember the advice of their patriarch, Afri Kara, who counseled them to follow the sun and the moon as their path (*mi ayiane kale jop ba ngon mbie bi ne mia zen*) until it took them to the sea. This counsel has been related to many early observers of the Fang as the reason for Fang migration. The missionaries seem to have been told, or interpreted this to mean, that it was the great God and the satisfaction he offered that was the object of search.

In any case, the rest of *Dulu Bon* recounts this pilgrimage, the traverse of Africa east to west, and the natural obstacles that were encountered, principally a succession of rivers of different colors. The passage of these obstacles is, in part, credited to the ingenuity of the Fang and as well to certain helpful saurian creatures. The most difficult river is passed with the aid of a giant snake (*ngan meja*), a motif directly related in one of our visions. The passage of rivers or of crossroads (a contemporary reinterpretation of the river-passage experience but also understood as the frontier between life and death) is frequently found in these visions.

The traditional legends upon which Ondoua Engutu's pamphlet is based often feature rivers that were crossed in miraculous fashion. I was given no description of the colors of these rivers, though Pierre Alexandre has collected materials from the Bulu indicating that one of these rivers was white and the other black and they were traversed in that order.[8] The symbolic significance of these colors was lost to his informants but gains importance in the study of these visions, in which colored rivers reappear, red or black at first and later white. In the original legends it appears that Fang passed from whitewash to blackwash. In these visions the process is reversed.

What we have in these visions, then, is an important re-

[8] Pierre Alexandre, "Proto-Histoire du groupe Beti-Bulu-Fang," *Cahiers d'Études Africaines* 3 (1966): 548.

versal. Whereas the migration legends detail the enforced passage for a paradisaical and highly competent existence on the margins of a great ocean through the savannah past formidable rivers into the equatorial rain forest, the *eboka* visions reverse that process and spontaneously take the visionary through the forest back out upon the illuminated plains to a grassy upland approximating paradise itself— or at least a sufficiently paradisaical arena to yield visions of the great gods. In this eternal return the initiate escapes his corporeality and becomes light as a bird; he sees his dead, and surpasses crowds of those who have not had the fortune to know *eboka*. He goes beyond the village of the dead, he passes great rivers or crossroads and sometimes changes color as he comes into contact with the great gods. His ancestors, as his legends detail, had the opposite experience and, once chased from their original home, they took up the challenge of migration and the promise of the ocean and the presumptive salvation it held out.

In the early colonial period, as Ondoua Engutu's account makes clear, this oceanic expectation was fully gratified in the material wherewithal that trade with the Europeans brought the Fang. In fact, that desire to make direct contact with the European traders and avoid the middlemen tribes was passionate enough to have even gained representation in the legends themselves. As the colonial regime was installed, however, it became repressive. The Fang saw that not only were they not going to inherit the earth but that their ancestors may have irretrievably lost it. At first they attempted to accommodate to European ways entirely; many still do. They abandoned the ancestors. But some Fang found no significant profit in that way, and revitalization cults such as Bwiti began to appear, utilizing the technical means, such as *eboka*, that lay to their hand.

I have elsewhere shown the degree to which these cult have opted out of modernization and given themselves ove to a microcosmic celebration of things past.[9] In the actua

[9] J. W. Fernandez, *Microcosmogony and Modernization* (Montreal: McGill University, Occasional Papers, Centre for Developing Area Studies, 1969), p. 36.

ritual process, there is a celebration of the primordial Fang experience.[10] One begins these ritual celebrations at the far end of the village courtyards and dances toward the chapel around a small hut that stands for the village of the dead. Then one dances into the chapel itself beside the entrance pillar, *akon aba,* in which a hole is carved and which stands among other things for the Adzapmboga, the tree that at once blocks the way and at the same time symbolizes the equatorial forest. Within the cult house the dances proceed forward to the far altar, which is known as *mang,* the sea. The ritual celebrates in this way the migration experience as the legends present it. They are a celebration of things past.

But since these past things eventuated in a present condition to which the members of Bwiti are reacting, it is not sufficient to celebrate them within the cult house as the rituals proceed. A bond must be re-established with all the formerly abandoned dead. The narrowing circularity of the succeeding dances within the cult house diminishes any sense of migratory progression. The custom of praying by reciting genealogy in which men count back up to their origins until one arrives at the founders of one's clan, fifteen or twenty names in the past, and beyond them to the great gods who created the Fang and mankind, actually begins a return. But the essential and fundamental return upon ancestral experience and the ritual expression of it is obtained in the *eboka* visions themselves. For these are much more than the celebrations of things past. They are the most powerful intimations of a vital immortality by a return to primordial origins.

The material conditions of African life in the colonial world, and the feeling of comparative deprivation and impotence derived from them, has led some Africans to treat that life as more apparent than real. They have involved themselves in certain kinds of religious movements in which all act to

10 J. W. Fernandez, "The Affirmation of Things Past: Alar Ayong and Bwiti as Movements of Protest in Central and Northern Gabon," in *Protest and Power in Black Africa,* eds. Ali Mazrui and R. Rotberg (New York, 1970), pp. 427–57.

create or exalt other realities and other potencies. In the case of Fang Bwiti there has been a celebration of things past.

I have examined a representative sample of the vision narratives produced by that plant in so far as they are available to my inquiry. Instead of being unfathomably spontaneous and bizarre, these visions make good sense if examined in terms of the attitude *set*, the social *situation*, and the cultural *setting* in which the narcotic is taken. For example, the high infant-mortality rate, the low birth rate, and the low life expectancy are all facts of the social situation that explain the appearance of the dead in these visions and particularly the number of children encountered. But all men are preoccupied with their own mortality and are likely to put psychedelic visions to use in some way relevant to that preoccupation. They may well seek to embrace the terminal fact by passing over symbolic rivers or by stepping across crossroads to obtain direct counsel from and communion with the dead. Yet with such mortality rates as the Fang have to face, and in the presence of a tradition of an ancestral cult that celebrated continuing contact with the dead, there is in the Fang a special desire to see and to know their dead. And the set of such desires is fulfilled in convincing abundance in these visions.

It is to the cultural setting of Fang folklore that I have been particularly attuned. In my view, these visions, in their narrative form, are themselves instances of folklore and must inevitably be related to the larger body of Fang folklore. In addition, an important number of these narrative visions reiterate, except in reverse, the old Fang migration legends. Here again it is no doubt true that men everywhere often put the peculiar excitations of drug states to use for purposes of regression. And surely the return, in numbers of these Bwiti visions, to a golden age, if not a golden land of origin, is a regression. Fang had reasons enough in the harsh conditions of the colonial world for regressing. But it is much more interesting to see how this visionary return reverses the essential progressions of the migration legends themselves. And how the *eboka* visions thus set the capstone upon the efforts made in Bwiti to celebrate things past by returning the initiate to the very origins of himself and his people. For in that primordial space of origin, that grassy upland or light-struck desert, the members of Bwiti have restored to them the felt qualities of effective activity and ancestral goodness that their contemporary everyday life does not yield them.

PART III

Texts of African Folklore

FOLKLORE TEXTS

TEXTS OF AFRICAN FOLKLORE

The following texts have all been tape-recorded in the field by contributors to this volume, except for the two tales from Liberia, which I obtained in typescript from the collectors. In furnishing headnotes I have referred to the following folklore indexes:

TYPE — Antti Aarne and Stith Thompson, *The Types of the Folk-tale* (Helsinki, 1961).

MOTIF — Stith Thompson, *Motif-Index of Folk Literature,* 6 vols. (Bloomington, Indiana, and Copenhagen, 1955–58).

AREWA — Erastus Ojo Arewa, "A Classification of the Folktales of the Northern East African Cattle Area by Types" (doctoral dissertation in anthropology at Universiy of California, Berkeley, 1966).

CLARKE — Kenneth W. Clarke, "A Motif-Index of the Folktales of Culture-Area V, West Africa" (doctoral dissertation in folklore at Indiana University, 1957).

KLIPPLE — May A. Klipple, "African Tales with Foreign Analogues" (doctoral dissertation in English at Indiana University, 1938).

Richard M. Dorson

THE SUDAN

Manasir and Ja'aliyyin tales collected by Sayyid Hurreiz

The Punishment of the Elephants

The reduction of this narrative from a myth to a legend is discussed by the collector, Sayyid Hurreiz, on pp. 162–63. A widely distributed motif in heroic legend is G510.4 "Hero overcomes devastating animal." The elephant appears in tradition in motifs H1154.3.4 "Capturing wild elephant," reported from the Fang in Africa, and B443.3 "Helpful elephant," known in India. Other animal motifs are B275 "Animal punished" and B315 "Animal helpful after being conquered." Also present are D1810.8.2 "Information received through dream" (in this case a vision) and P233.2 "Young hero rebuked by father."

Time of recording: August 1965.
Place of recording: Rufaa'a, a town in the Blue Nile province of the Sudan.
Informant: Ahmed Al Tayyib Khaalid. A man of about fifty whose original home is Al Gala'a Araanj. He is a strict Muslim, and works as a janitor at Rufaa'a Junior Secondary School. He is of the Rikabiya tribe.

They said that Sheikh Mohammed Al Hamim once wanted to build a mosque. Since the Butaana region was poor in big tall trees, they decided to go and bring timber for the roof from the Dinder region. The Sheikh's sons and seven of his disciples set out on their journey to the Dinder region. They had twenty-one camels for carrying the timber.

When they got to the Dinder region, they cut the timber, loaded it on their camels, and started their journey back to the Butaana. They unloaded their camels and broke their journey in order to have some food and rest. While they were resting under the shade of a tree, some elephants attacked their camels and chased them away. They (the Sheikh's party) were thus cut off from home with little food and water and no living soul to give them a helping hand. They were completely cut off in the wilderness.

Then the Sheikh's elder son gave his stick to his younger brother and ordered him to accompany some of the disciples and go to subdue and bring back those elephants which had chased away their camels so that they might use them instead of the camels. The younger brother, who could not but obey his elder brother, took the stick and accompanied his friends toward the elephants. The other men were frightened and wondered whether it would actually be possible to get those wild animals under control. But the Sheikh's son, who had his father's blessing, subdued and controlled the seven elephants, who followed him willingly to where his brother and the other disciples were camping. The timber that had been carried by twenty-one camels was loaded on these seven elephants and the home journey started again.

Every now and then the Sheikh's sons and disciples stopped for rest, and people of different tribes gathered around them to see this miracle. Those who saw this miracle told the others, who hurried to see for themselves. There was a big gathering at Al Hudayba and people from remote tribes living on the sides of the Nile came to see the elephants loaded with timber.

When the Sheikh's sons and disciples arrived at the Sheikh's dwelling at Al Mundara, the Sheikh rebuked his elder son for performing such a miracle and for drawing the attention of the people. The Sheikh's son replied to his father that when they went to subdue the elephants, they saw him (the Sheikh) standing in front of them, and they took this to be a sign of his approval and blessing for what they were about to do.

Then they unloaded the elephants and gave them some

fodder and water. One of the elephants drank more than it could hold, so it burst near a mountain in the vicinity of Al Mundara. Ever since, that mountain has been known as the Elephant's Mountain, and Sheikh Mohammed Al Hamim has been nicknamed the punisher of the elephants.

The Cycle of Abu Zeid

This string of legendary anecdotes contains many motifs familiar in heroic saga. Some pertain to the qualities of the hero himself, such as A526.7 "Culture hero performs remarkable feats of strength and skill"; F610 "Remarkably strong man," with its usual sequel F628.2.1 "Strong man kills many men at once" (as in Africa among the Upoto, told in Carl Einstein, *Afrikanische Legenden*, Berlin, 1925, p. 126, and among the Togo, told in Allan W. Cardinall, *Tales Told in Togoland*, London, 1931, p. 130 [a strong boy]); and F1088.1 "Hero spared for his beauty."

A celebrated story episode that recurs here is the "Father-son combat" (motif N731.2), which takes place before the combatants identify each other. It is known in the Persian romance of Sohrab and Rustem, in the Irish saga of Cuchulainn and Conlaech, in the Greek epic concerning Odysseus and Telegonos, as well as in Icelandic, Chinese, Philippine, and Hawaiian tradition.

Motifs reported elsewhere in Africa include D1812.3.2 "Fortune told by cutting sand," known to the Vai (George W. Ellis, *Negro Culture in West Africa*, New York, 1914, p. 214, no. 29), and K2213.4.1 "Secret of vulnerability disclosed by hero's wife," present in the Cameroons (J. Ittman, "Nyang-Märchen," *Zeitschrift für Eingeborenen-Sprachen* 17

[1926–27]: 77). Other incidents involving the wife are C932 "Loss of wife for breaking tabu" and T215.3 "Husband nourishes starving wife with his own flesh and blood."

Other motifs well known in tradition are scattered through the legends, such as F711.2 "Sea of unusual substance" (in this case blood and milk), D1030.1.1 "Food supplied by prayer," N863 "Slave as helper to Princess," D2071 "Evil eye," H92 "Identification by necklace," and Q266 "Punishment for breaking promise."

Recorded from Tam Zein in Alsalamat village of the Manasir tribe in May 1968.

Abu Zeid's mother, together with the mother of Sultan Hasan and other women of their tribe, Beni Hilal, were bathing in a stream. Over a tree nearby hovered a big white bird with a group of small birds around it. The small birds were serving the big white bird with small fish from the stream. Later a black bird came and chased away all the white birds. The bathing women admired this scene. Sultan Hasan's mother asked Allah to give her a son as impressive as the white bird and Abu Zeid's mother prayed to Allah to give her a son just like this black bird. The prayers of Abu Zeid's family never fail.

Later Abu Zeid's mother gave birth to a child who was very black, unlike members of his family or his tribe. The father denounced his child and accused his mother of having had sexual intercourse with his slave. Abu Zeid's father sent his wife to her family, but she did not want to go back because she thought the people might believe his accusation. So she sought asylum with another tribe, where her son was loved and well looked after. He grew up abnormally strong. He once beat his teacher for being unkind toward another child.

The Beni Hilal tribe happened to raid the land of the tribe among whom Abu Zeid was brought up. Abu Zeid fought courageously against his father's tribe. He was just about to kill an elderly man when his mother stopped him and told him the whole story. He then knew that the old man was his

father, and he made peace between these two tribes and
went back with his kinsmen. After that, Beni Hilal, Abu
Zeid's tribe, had a dry season and life became difficult for
them and for their animals.

The famous Hilali Sultan Hasan Abu Sarhan, the one who
feeds and brings up fatherless children, the man who is generous even in the dry years, once had some guests. He said
to them, "Welcome, come in and rest in the shade of my
tent. This season is a very dry one and I have no food to
offer you." He looked around and there was his female slave
May. Sultan Hasan said to his guests, "Take this slave. She is
yours."

They took their female slave and put her on sale in one of
the markets. The young lady Aziza, the daughter of Al
Zinati, the Sultan of Tunisia, heard about the beauty and
eloquence of this slave from her maids. She ordered her
maids to buy May and bring her to the palace. May stayed
in the service of Aziza, but she was unhappy and cried
continuously.

The young lady Aziza asked May, "Are you hiding something from us that we do not know? Do you know of a better
place, which you prefer to our place?" May, who had started
to confide in Aziza by then, answered her, "My Lady Aziza,
I left behind my sisters, my mother, and the three handsome
sons of my former lady Shiha: Yunis, Yahya, and Mar'i. I
miss them all. The beauty of Yunis has no equal either in the
Orient or in the West." May kept talking to her mistress
about Yunis until Aziza fell in love with Yunis from what she
heard of his beauty. Aziza sent for Sultan Jabur. When he
came she ordered him to go to the land of Beni Hilal, Yunis'
tribe, and tempt them to come to her father's country. She
had two mongala sets[1] made for him; one was made of gold
and the other was made of silver. She also gave him food for
the journey, and he set out.

When Sultan Jabur arrived in the land of Beni Hilal, he
came to the tent of Sultan Hasan Abu Sarhan. He greeted
the Sultan, "Peace be upon you, Sultan Hasan."

[1] Mongala is a chesslike game played in the Sudan.

"And upon you be peace, welcome, come in," replied Sultan Hasan.

After a while Sultan Jabur took out his mongala and asked one of the men to play him. Whenever he won a move, he threw the mongala piece away. Whenever he won one of the silver or golden mongala pieces he threw it away. Sultan Hasan, who noticed this, addressed him, "Sultan Jabur, look after your money and get it back before someone takes it away. We do not want you to go back and tell your people that Beni Hilal stole your money."

Jabur then said to Sultan Hasan, "Gold and silver are as abundant in our country as pebbles."

Sultan Hasan asked Sultan Jabur, "If gold and silver are the pebbles of your country, what is the fodder of your camels?"

"Different kinds of fodder grow richly in our valleys," answered Sultan Jabur.

"If gold and silver are the pebbles of your country, what is the fodder of your horses?" asked Sultan Hasan.

"Grass grows thickly in our islands," replied Sultan Jabur.

After that, Sultan Jabur returned to his country.

Sultan Hasan Abu Sarhan beat the tribal drum and all the Hilaliyya gathered and asked him what was the matter. He answered, "Sultan Jabur came here and said what he said, and now we want to go to his country, the land of Sultan Zinati." Then the wise Hilaliyya woman, Al Jaz, Mohammed's mother, whose advice was highly valued, addressed Sultan Hasan, "How do you order us to leave our present home and move to a new one which we know nothing about? I suggest that you send some people to explore that country first."

"Whom do you suggest?" asked Sultan Hasan.

She answered, "I suggest Abu Zeid, the father of Rizig and Rayya, the black, peaceful man who is remembered when he goes away and whose advice is sought when he is present."

Abu Zeid was not present at that tribal meeting. When he came, he was told that the Sultan Jabur had come to this country and that Sultan Hasan beat the tribal drum and said what he said. He said to the tribal gathering, "So you have chosen me. I will also select the best men of the tribe to accompany me."

"And whom do you choose, Abu Zeid?" they asked him.

He replied, "The three sons of Sheikha; Yunis, Yahya, and Mar'i." The three nephews of Abu Zeid said that they were ready to leave the next day.

The following morning Abu Zeid and his nephews mounted their camels at dawn. Shiha, Abu Zeid's sister and the mother of Yunis, Yahya, and Mar'i, came to bid them farewell and said these words to Abu Zeid:

"Abu Zeid, be careful about the three going with you,
    Don't make my sons cross the crowds,
    Because the evil eye never misses royal people.

"Abu Zeid, be careful about the three going with you,
    Don't make fire on the open road,
    The road brings all kinds of people and fire draws them.

"Abu Zeid, be careful about the three going with you,
    Don't make my sons sleep under walls,
    The builders build and the walls fall.

"Abu Zeid, be careful about the three going with you,
    Mar'i will look after your camels because he knows more
        about camel herding,
    Yahya will prepare your food because he cooks tasty food,
    Yunis will buy and sell because the white girls love him."

Shiha gave her golden necklace to one of her sons and said to him, "This will be of value to you. These are hard times." So they set off.

In the country of Sultan Al Zinati, Al'allam[2] was predicting the future by the aid of divining[3] sand. He was telling the

---

[2] Al'allam is an Arabic personal name, but it also means "the seer."

[3] The method of predicting the future by divining sand is called "rabul" in Sudanese Arabic.

others that Abu Zeid and his three nephews will come to explore their country. Before he finished his sentence, Abu Zeid and his nephews said to him, "Peace be upon you, 'Allam."

"And upon you be peace. Where are you coming from, Arabs?" he replied.

"We are poets and praise singers. We praise those who give to us and criticize those who stand in our way," they answered him.

He said to them, "I know this is not true. You are Abu Zeid and his nephews, coming to explore this country. Welcome, you can stay for some time, and I will not tell anybody. But when you want to leave, tell me."

They used to go on exploratory trips for a week or two, a month or two, and come back to Al'allam's place. After some time, life became difficult and they had nothing to eat. Abu Zeid gave his shirt to Yahya and told him to go and sell it and buy some bread. Yunis told them about his mother's necklace, the value of which could feed the whole tribe of Beni Hilal in the dry years.

Yunis took the necklace and went to the market ururururrrr people gathered around and kept looking at him. "Why do you look at me like this?" he asked them.

"You are very beautiful," they answered him.

"I have a necklace for sale," he said to them.

"Nobody wants necklaces in this country," they replied.

"Do not belittle its value before seeing it," he said to them while taking it out of his pocket.

"Oh, Lord," they all said, "nobody can buy this except our young Lady Aziza." Some old women went to tell Aziza about it. When they saw Aziza, they said to her, "My Lord, our Lady Aziza. You cannot imagine how handsome this young man was . . . if you only give us permission to talk." They were granted permission and one of them said to Aziza, "Today a young man came to the market. He is so beautiful, the like of his beauty can never be found in the Orient or in the West. This young man had a necklace. The necklace was as beautiful as he was, and he was as beautiful as his necklace."

"This must be Yunis," interrupted May. Aziza then sent someone to call Yunis. When Yunis came, four women slaves seized him and carried him to Aziza. When he saw May, he said to her, "How did you come here?"

She answered him, "I am a slave who is sold from one market to the other, and what are you doing here!"

After that they brought a bed with a mattress on which Yunis was laid. Under the bed they put four basins full of water to which they added some salt. Then Yunis addressed Aziza, "You see these people over there. They are hungry, and they are waiting for me to bring them some food from the market, so will you please send them some food."

Aziza ordered a lot of money and food to be sent to Abu Zeid and his two nephews, and told the woman who was going to take the food to them to put it down and rush back before they got hold of her. The slave woman took the food and went toward Abu Zeid and his nephews. When she drew near them, she put down the food she was carrying and ran off. Abu Zeid said to them, "What a shame, men, your brother has been captured."

Abu Zeid and his two remaining nephews ate the food. Later, they started exploring Tunisia, as they had used to do previously. Once Abu Zeid and Yahya left Mar'i behind, looking after their camels. One of the she-camels picked a branch from the garden of Sultan Al Zinati and ate it. The slaves of Sultan Al Zinati beat Mar'i to death. When Abu Zeid and his nephew returned, Mar'i was dead. Abu Zeid became furious and killed about a hundred of the slaves. Then Abu Zeid and his remaining nephew were imprisoned. Yunis knew about this and said to Aziza, "Either release me to free these men or tell someone to do so."

Al'allam was madly in love with Aziza and she used to pay no attention to him. When Abu Zeid was imprisoned, Aziza put on her best clothes and went to see Al'allam late at night. She knocked on the door, and one of the slaves opened it. The slave then ran to his master, saying, "My master, what shall I say, the moon has descended from the sky." Al'allam rushed to the door and found that it was Aziza.

Aziza told Al'allam to use his influence in freeing Abu

Zeid and his nephew from imprisonment. Al'allam went to Sultan Al Zinati and said to him, "Don't you know that the people whom you are holding prisoners are only minstrels and praise singers, and that they are my guests?"

Sultan Al Zinati replied to Al'allam, "These people are not minstrels or praise singers. They have come here to explore our country."

Al'allam then said to him, "If you do not release these men who are my guests, I will start trouble." The Sultan then gave his orders that Abu Zeid and his nephew should be released. After they were freed, they stayed for some time with Al'allam.

One night Abu Zeid and his nephew fled and made their way toward home without telling Al'allam.[4] Al'allam then knew that there was something serious, so he and his men started chasing Abu Zeid.

On his way home, Abu Zeid met a man who had some watermelon seeds, which he was about to plant. Abu Zeid said to this man, "If you prayed to Allah and planted the seeds and they grew up and became edible right away, what would you say if someone asks you about that?"

The man said to Abu Zeid, "I will tell him exactly what happened." So this man washed, prayed to Allah, and planted the watermelon seeds. In no time the watermelon grew and ripened, and the man gave Abu Zeid and his nephew some of it, which they ate, and they continued on their journey.

Then Abu Zeid took a container and milked his nephew's she-camel. He also wounded his camel and mixed the milk with his camel's blood. A little later the Sultan's men who were chasing Abu Zeid came to the same man and asked him, "When did the slave[5] and the boy pass by you?"

He answered, "When they passed by me, I was still taking the watermelon seed on my hand; and now as you see, I have planted the seed, the watermelon has ripened, and even ate and sold some of it, thanks to Allah." Al'allam then

[4] Abu Zeid had previously made an agreement with Al'allam not to leave without his permission.

[5] They refer thus to Abu Zeid because he was dark-skinned.

predicted the future by the aid of divining sand and said to his men, "It is hopeless, we cannot get them, they have already crossed the sea of milk and blood."[6] So they returned.

Abu Zeid said to his nephew Yahya, "Whoever gets first to the well on our way, should descend into the well to bring some water for the camels." Yahya arrived at the well before Abu Zeid and went down to draw some water. When Abu Zeid got to the well a little later, he said to his nephew, who was inside the well, "Go on, draw!"

His nephew replied:

> "I have been bitten by a poisonous snake,
>   Which made my saliva dry and black.
>   I hit him with my hand with the rings,
>   And there he was dead floating on the water."

Abu Zeid said to him, "Come out, so that I can bury you when you die."

Yahya answered him, "Let me die where I am. Give the camel water to drink and have a drink yourself and go."

"Oh! My God," said Abu Zeid, "I am in such an exposed place and these men are attacking me."

Yahya said to him, "Pull me out so that I may kill two or three of them before I die." So Abu Zeid pulled him out of the well, but there was nobody attacking him.

"Where are the men who are attacking you?" Yahya asked him.

"I only wanted to see you before you die," Abu Zeid replied.

Then Yahya said to him, "Give my love to my mother and to all my tribe and do not kill my camel, kill yours instead."

Thus died Yahya, and Abu Zeid buried him and slaughtered his camel at his grave.[7] Then Abu Zeid wanted to

---

[6] They are now out of reach in the mythical land.

[7] This is an old Arab custom from pre-Islamic times. Whenever a man died, his camel was either killed at his grave or tied there and left to die of hunger and thirst.

mount his nephew's camel and set out on his journey, but the camel refused to get up and stayed beside the grave. He left the camel where it was but refused to feed it. When it was hungry to the extent that it ate its own wool, he tried it once more. This time it was willing to move, and he mounted on its back and galloped till he came to his country.

When he got home, he hid himself in a forest near his village. There he slaughtered his camel and started eating some of its meat. A little later the Hilaliyya girls came to the forest to collect firewood. Among them was his own daughter, also the daughters of Hasan Abu Sarhan and Diyyab. He did not recognize them because they had not yet been born when he left his country. He said to them, "Come and let me give you some meat."

The girls replied, "But we do not have any carrier in which we can put it."

Then his daughter said to them, "Can't we make laces from the camel's skin, tie them together and use them for carrying the meat?" So he made some laces of the camel's skin, tied them together,[8] filled them with meat, and gave it to them.

Abu Zeid then asked one of the girls who her father was. She said to him, "I am the daughter of Hasan Abu Sarhan, the one who feeds and brings up fatherless children, the one who is generous even in the dry years."

He then asked another one, who replied, "I am the daughter of Diyyab, the warrior who fights two armies and the pious man who spends his life fasting."

Lastly, he asked his own daughter who her father was. She answered him, "I am the daughter of Abu Zeid, the father of Rizig and Rayya, the black peaceful man who is remembered when he goes away and whose advice is sought when he is present."

"So you are the daughter of the black slave!" he said to her.

"If you did not look like my father, stranger, I would have

[8] In the same way in which nets are made.

given you some words that would keep you crying for a year," she answered him.[9]

Then he asked them, "Do you know the lady whose house is situated to the west of the other houses and east of the main road?"

"Yes, we know her. She is our aunt Shiha," they replied.

"Take this meat to her and tell her that a black slave is waiting for her in the forest."

The girls went home and told Shiha what happened. She said to them, "If you tell anyone about the slave in the forest, I will kill you."

After sunset, Shiha went to meet Abu Zeid at the forest. "Peace be upon you, Abu Zeid," she said to him.

"Welcome and upon you be peace, Shiha," he answered.

"Where are the three who were traveling with you?" she asked him.

"What can I say to you? One of them was bit by a snake. The second was killed by the Sultan's slaves, and the third was captured and held prisoner by the white girls," he answered.

She then added, "So you came without them[10] and you will also soon be killed, because our tribesmen have already made a pledge that they would throw at you whatever they happen to have in their hands."

The following morning Shiha ordered her maids to cook two full sacks of boiled dura beans. A little after sunrise Shiha said to the men of her tribe that she had had an important dream the night before. She told them to put away their weapons and come to her house so that she could disclose to them her dream. When they had gathered, she ordered the boiled dura beans to be served. When everyone of them had his hands full of boiled dura beans, she told

[9] She was probably told what her father looked like, because she had not seen him before.

[10] As stated earlier, the prayers of Abu Zeid's family never fail to be answered. Before setting on his trip to Africa Abu Zeid meant to say, "May those who accompany me come back," but he said instead, "May those who accompany me never come back."

Abu Zeid to come out. When Abu Zeid appeared in front of his tribesmen without his three nephews, the men of Beni Hilal remembered the pledge they had made and threw at Abu Zeid the boiled beans they happened to have in their hands.

Then Abu Zeid told his sister to prepare some porridge and add to it some butter, sugar, and milk. When the porridge was brought, he put it on the ground and enclosed it with a hedge of thorny branches. He also brought two doves, one of which was featherless. Then he said to his tribesmen, "The country from which I have just come is a country of bliss and abundance. Life there is just like this sugar, milk, and oil. An able person should hurry (fly) to it, while an unable person should crawl to it like this featherless dove."

Sultan Hasan Abu Sarhan then beat the tribal drum, and the whole tribe gathered and set out, leaving their country behind them. Sultan Hasan said, "Only women who belong to the Hilaliyya tribe should accompany their husbands and families on that journey."

Abu Zeid confirmed that by saying, "The difficult road that I crossed cannot be tolerated by any women except those of the Hilaliyya tribe." So whoever had a wife who did not belong to the Hilaliyya tribe had to divorce her and leave her behind, except Diyyab. Diyyab disguised his wife and allowed her to accompany him.

When they were en route Diyyab's wife said to him, "I am hungry."

"But I have nothing to give you," Diyyab answered.

"I need to have something to eat, even if you give me your own flesh," she said to him. Diyyab cut some flesh from his thigh and gave it to her. She then tried it and ate it. A few days later the men of the tribe detected a bad odor which led them to know about Diyyab's leg and about his disguised wife. Diyyab was told to take his wife back. He took her back, divorced her, and followed his tribesmen.

A few days later they came to the country of Al'allam and encountered Al'allam in the same place where he had previously met Abu Zeid. They fought him. Then the wise

Hilaliyya woman, Al Jaz,[11] Mohammed's mother, said to the women of her tribe, "Put down the reins of your camels." They did as they were ordered. "Now pick up the reins of your camels." So they picked up the reins. Thus Sultan Al'allam saw their beauty and their long hair, and thought about making peace with Beni Hilal. He offered Sultan Hasan Abu Sarhan nineteen of his own women, nineteen of Al Zinati Khalifa's women, and nineteen of Sultan Jabur's women, and allowed them to stay for a short while.

They were hungry and their camels were hungry, too. They did not have much to eat at home. So they kept eating and eating and their camels kept eating and eating. They made their stay a long one. Later Al Zinati Khalifa himself came to them and asked them to marry him to the wise Hilaliyya woman, Al Jaz, Mohammed's mother. They accepted Al Zinati's proposal and married Al Jaz to him. Al Zinati took Al Jaz to his house, where she lived with him. After a few days he said to his wife, "We should invite all the men and women of your tribe for a feast."

"Why not," she answered him.

So Al Zinati ordered his slaves to slaughter many camels and cows and to cook a lot of rice. When the food was ready to be served, he poisoned the whole of it. Some of Al Jaz's maids told her about the poisoning of the food. Al Zinati then told his wife that the food was ready and asked her which one of the men of her tribe would start the feast. She sent for Abu Zeid, and when he came she said to him, "Sam[12] sam on the food and divide it among your tribesmen. Sam sam on the food and divide it among your tribesmen."

Abu Zeid understood what she meant and he replied to her, "What a shame, Mohammed's mother! Don't you know that it is one of our taboos to eat bread, rice, or even meat this month? You have wasted your husband's money."

[11] There are many references in Sudanese folklore to this Hilaliyya woman, Al Jaz, and to her wisdom. One of these examples is found in the famous oral poem *Musdar al Miterig*.

[12] Before they start eating, Muslims pray to God to bless their food. This is done by calling the name of God and saying: "We start in the name of God." There is a pun on the word *sam*; it means, "Say the prayer of starting," but it also means "poison."

They dispersed without tasting the poisoned food, which was thrown into the sea late at night. The following day Al Zinati sent for Beni Hilal and told them to move out of his country. He also divorced his Hilaliyya wife, Al Jaz, Mohammed's mother.

Soon afterward, war started between Al Zinati and Beni Hilal. The tribe of Beni Hilal killed many of Al Zinati's men, but it took their warriors a long time to get Al Zinati under control. His ex-wife Al Jaz told them his secret and they managed to wound and subdue him in the end. Sultan Hasan Abu Sarhan descended from his horse and said to Al Zinati Khalifa:

"May you recover peacefully, Zinati,

You are the repose of the destitute.

And you are the flooding sea which fills up the terraces."

Al Zinati answered him, "Your words are sweet, but they are not what I call kind words. Your victory over me is a credit to you and above all a credit to Abu Zeid, who showed you the way."

Diyyab was the one who wounded Al Zinati. A little later Al Zinati died, and Beni Hilal settled in his country. After the war was over, whoever managed to kill a man took over his property and his women. Diyyab took over Su'da, who belonged to Al Zinati, but she refused to marry Diyyab. He treated her harshly and made her do all kinds of difficult jobs. She was miserable and crying all the time. Once Sultan Hasan Abu Sarhan saw her crying and knew about her misery, so he gave her shelter and married her to another man without Diyyab's knowledge. She gave birth to a son and lived happily in Sultan Hasan's compound.

One day a few years later Sultan Hasan invited the whole tribe of Beni Hilal. Su'da's son was among the boys who were serving the guests. He was serving meat to the guests while saying, "This is your share, sir. . . . And this is yours. . . . And this is yours." Whenever he came near Diyyab he skipped him.

"Why didn't you offer me some meat? Did I kill your grandfather?" Diyyab said to the boy.

Hasan Abu Sarhan said to him, "In fact, you did."

He then asked the boy, "Whose son are you?"

"I am Su'da's son," the boy answered him.

"Isn't Al Zinati Khalifa his grandfather!" added Sultan Hasan.

Diyyab became very angry, because Sultan Hasan married his prospective wife to someone else and without his knowledge. Diyyab went to his sister, who was one of Sultan Hasan's wives, and said to her, "When Sultan Hasan comes to your house, come and tell me. I must kill him."

When Sultan Hasan came to his wife's house at night, she told Diyyab, who came sword in hand, anxious to kill him. Whenever Diyyab rushed at Sultan Hasan, he saw a flash of light, and whenever he retreated the flash of light disappeared. This was repeated many times through the night. At sunrise Diyyab tried again. The flash of light was no longer there and Sultan Hasan was slaughtered.

The tribal drum was beaten once more, and the news of Sultan Hasan's murder spread. Al Jaz, Mohammed's mother, gathered her army and her daughters. She mounted her camel and led them to Fas.[13] She stayed in Fas till her young sons became men. When they grew up strong men she told them about what Diyyab had done. At that time Abu Zeid became blind. They all gathered, armed one another, and came back beating their drum and dressed up in armor, ready to fight Diyyab. When the horses came rushing and the sound of the drums pierced the country, Abu Zeid regained his sight, mounted, and rushed toward the battlefield. They killed Diyyab and left no trace of him; nobody was spared, neither woman nor man. They rid the country of him forever. Thanks to God.

[13] Sfax, in Tunisia, on the coast of the Mediterranean. Sudanese traditions state that Sfax was thought to be the end of the inhabited world. As the Sudanese saying goes, "Beyond Fas no human beings are to be found."

LIBERIA

Vai tales collected by
Jangaba Johnson and
Bai T. Moore

Land Turtle and Leopard

Sitting in the courtyard of Bai T. Moore's home in Monrovia, Liberia, the evening of March 10, 1970, I was caught by surprise when he and his elder cousin Jangaba Johnson began telling me Vai folktales. My purpose in making this thirty-day trip to Africa had been to meet the collectors of folklore, not to collect on my own, and here tales were dropping into my lap and I did not even have pencil and notebook. Further to my consternation, the narrative Jangaba was relating, about how a small animal tricked a large animal into being his riding horse, clearly belongs to the same type I had myself recorded several times from American Negroes. I say to my consternation, for one of my pet theses is the non-African origins of the traditional stories of black Americans (see my *American Negro Folktales*, New York, Fawcett Publications, 1969, pp. 12–18).

Although I did not write down the tale at the time, I found it in a typescript of Liberian folktales, "Crime Does Not Pay," that Bai and Jangaba gave me, based on their own collecting (no. 35, pp. 53–54). Jangaba said he had heard it from a man in Freetown, Sierra Leone.

This is type 72 "Rabbit Rides Fox A-Courting" and motif K1241 "Trickster rides dupe horseback." A text I collected in Pine Bluff, Arkansas, is published in *American Negro Folktales*, pp. 87–89. May A. Klipple cites five African variants in "African Folktales with Foreign Analogues" (Indiana University doctoral dissertation, 1938). In the Uncle Remus version of Joel Chandler Harris, rabbit rides fox.

The slow, drawling manner in which Jangaba told the story whetted the relish of the audience at each new deception practiced by turtle on leopard.

One day while a group of animals were having a meeting, Land Turtle got up and told them that Leopard was his father's horse. When the meeting broke up, Gray Squirrel ran as fast as he could go to Leopard's house. He met the strong man of the forest taking siesta on his front porch. "Wake up, man!" Squirrel yelled when he got close to the house. "How was the meeting?" Leopard inquired.

"Oh, not bad," said the Squirrel. "The only thing, Turtle said that you were his father's horse and he could prove it."

"What! Turtle called me a horse? He must be losing his mind. In fact, Squirrel, I have been thinking about roasting the fool with pepper and eating him with young cassavas," Leopard growled furiously. Leopard jumped up and put on his clothes and dashed off to Turtle's house. He did not bother to knock. He pushed open the door and met Turtle resting on a bed by the fireplace. "Say, look here, Turtle, why did you tell all the animals that I was your father's horse?"

Turtle got up trembling. "Me, uncle? What fool will catch me to do such a thing? You see how mischievous some people are. Trying to break up the friendship between me and my uncle. If it weren't for the malaria I have, I would surely go and disprove this lie," Turtle said.

"I am so furious, Turtle, I don't mind taking you on my back to get this lie straightened out." Leopard lifted Turtle and put him on his back. They had not gone quite a mile when Turtle slipped and fell to the ground. "What is the matter? Why did you fall?" Leopard inquired.

"Uncle, your back is too hard and the ride is very uncomfortable. If you can let me fix a seat to sit on, I think I can make it." Turtle went and made a fine seat and put it on Leopard's back and commenced riding again. In less than a mile, again Turtle fell to the ground. This time the excuse was that he had nothing to hold on to while riding. Turtle suggested that a rope passing through Leopard's mouth would be just the ideal thing he wanted. Leopard agreed to the rope, and Turtle passed it to his mouth and held on to it. They had not gone far when Turtle fell again, for the third time. Leopard was getting annoyed, but he had to live up to his side of the bargain. This time Turtle wanted ropes tied to the seat so he could rest his legs. This was provided. As they got near their destination, Turtle again fell to the ground. This time he needed a long switch for the flies who were bothering him. Leopard said, "Oh, sure, get down and get yourself a switch." When they got to the village, Turtle began to beat Leopard on the behind as hard as he could. Leopard started galloping like a horse. All the animals came out and hollered, "Ho-o-o! Turtle was right when he said Leopard was his father's horse!" When Turtle got down this time, he ran home as fast as he could and went back into his hole.

Who Is the Greediest of the Four?

This is a characteristically African dilemma tale, of the kind discussed by William Bascom in his chapter in Part II. The theme of "Greed punished" is highly popular in West African folktales. Under motif Q2724, Kenneth W. Clarke gives references from the Ibo, the Togo, the Vai, the Yoruba, the Ashanti, the Ibibio, the Ewe, and the Kpelle ("A Motif-Index of the Folktales of Culture-Area V, West Africa," Indiana University doctoral dissertation in folklore, 1957).

From Jangaba Johnson and Bai T. Moore, "Crime Does Not Pay," no. 52, pp. 75–78.

In a certain town far in the interior of Liberia, there once lived three very prominent young men, none of whom was less greedy than any of the other two. One day, these three young men decided to make a trip to some distant place. They informed the chief of the town about their intentions and the chief gave them a cow to take on their journey.

When they were about to leave, one of them tied a rope to the cow; but the other two were not satisfied to let him lead the cow alone. So they also cut ropes and, tying them to the cow, they started off, each holding to his own rope on the cow, for fear the others might cheat him of the animal. They decided to kill this cow in an area where no fly could be found, because they did not want even a fly to have anything to do with their meat.

After the travelers had trekked through a long stretch of woods, they reached a large grassy field. Here they decided to slaughter their cow; but to be sure that there were no flies anywhere about, one of them stepped aside and eased himself. As soon as this was done, they saw a lonely fly flying to the spot. They knew then that there were flies in that area, and so they abandoned their slaughtering plan and continued their travel. After going for some distance, they halted to see whether they could kill the cow without the presence of flies. To test this, another one of them stepped aside and eased himself. Again seeing the appearance of some flies, they decided not to kill the cow, but to go on until they could find a place with no flies.

The road through the grassy field led them to a large river, which abounded in alligators. On the other side of this river stood a very thick forest. Upon reaching the edge of the river, they sat down to rest, and being now very hungry, they thought they would try once more to see whether they could kill their cow without being bothered by flies. Two of them had tested this possibility before, and now was the turn of the third man to find out about flies in the area. He therefore stepped aside and eased himself. Luckily for them no fly was seen. This was the place for the cow to be slaughtered and then cook their dinner.

As the three young men knocked the animal down to cut the throat, one of them said, "Man, I don't want the blood to waste. Let me lie down under the cow and open my mouth to catch the blood when it gushes out." Saying this, he recumbently prostrated himself by the cow. As the cow's throat was being cut, his throat was cut, too. This brought his part of greediness to an end. The meat was now the property of only two persons.

The two men cut up the meat, collected the wasted blood from the ground, and then made the fire for the cooking. After the fire was made, one of them said to the other, "Go to the river and bring some water for us to cook our soup." His companion obeyed; but in going for the water, instead of going with face forward, he went backward, keeping his eyes on his friend, for fear he might eat some of the meat behind his back. He continued going backward until he fell into the river and the alligators ate him up. His own life ended there, leaving the meat to just one man.

The happy inheritor of the meat took his bucket, went to the river, and brought the water he wanted. He then set his soup on the fire and sat down by it to watch it as it boiled. While the soup was boiling, a red deer, which was being pursued by some hunters, came and stepped in the pot of soup and passed. The man could not bear to see that deer go with all the grease from his soup on its feet. He left the soup on the fire and followed the deer until he caught it. And when he caught it, he only licked the grease of the soup from under its feet and allowed it to go at large.

During the absence of the man from his pot of soup, a pregnant woman passing by saw the soup on the fire. She was hungry and, finding no one around, she sat down and helped herself as much as she could to the broth. While she was eating she was delivered of her baby. She took the baby and put it in a bowl she was carrying, and tucked it all around with some of the meat she had been eating. This done, she took her load and moved on to her town; but before reaching home, all the meat in the bowl on her head had disappeared. Not finding any of the meat in the bowl when she reached home, she said, "Oh, what happened to all the meat I put in this bowl?" IIer baby in the bowl said, "I ate all the meat."

While the ability on the part of a baby to eat hard boiled meat and talk the same day of its birth remains a mystery, the question to be decided is, which of these four is the greediest of all: the man who had his throat cut while trying to catch the blood of the cow, the man who fell into the river and was devoured by alligators because he did not want his companion to eat any of the meat behind his back, the man who abandoned his soup pot and followed the red deer just to lick the grease on its feet from stepping in the soup, or the pregnant woman who ate the broth while she was giving birth and then tucked the newborn baby into a bowl with the leftover meat?

GHANA

Tales collected from the
Wala of Wa by Mona Fikry-Atallah

ORAL TRADITIONS
OF THE WALA OF WA

Mona Fikry-Atallah

Tales, to the Wala, are for entertainment. They are called *silima* (*silling*: singular) and are not to be taken seriously, in contrast to *lasire*, tradition or history, which is respected, serious, and mainly for elders to discuss. In fact, tales are considered to be lies. It was said about a section of Wa famous for its storytelling: "They tell tales fine! Lies sound like actual things!" Yet the entertainment aspect of the tales does not exclude their enculturative and social value. To the children, tales are one means by which they learn, indirectly, the moral codes sanctioned by the society. To the adults, the tales are sometimes used as a means of social control, as are the proverbs. To this extent, the tales are an intellectual exercise appreciated and understood by the adults far more than by the children. In situations in which antagonisms exist, a teller may well choose a tale reflecting these tensions. Tales are used to praise as well as to ridicule. It is the subtlety by which a teller recounts a tale that is most appreciated by the listeners, most of whom would be familiar with the people whom the teller depicts in his tale. The laughter and involvement in the tale, therefore, does not result from the plot, but also from its insinuations and its closeness to reality.

Children are encouraged to tell tales; yet, invariably, in a group in which many men were present, the men would enthusiastically take over the session. Thus, most of the tales collected have been told by men. The tale sessions were always held in the evening after the men had returned from the farm and had had dinner. Huddled in a group in the center of the compound, men, women, and children (the latter two mainly listening) would tell their tales, one after the other, for several hours at a stretch, with hardly any interruptions between tales. Tales would almost always begin with the simple phrase, *N sinnii be:* My story exists, or, This is my story.

Most of the tales were interspersed with songs led by the narrator himself and responded to by the group listening. Sometimes the narrator would stop the singers, criticize them for not singing well or for not knowing the words, and correct them. In a few instances, a teller had to stop his story and begin a new one because the group did not know the song well enough or did not even know it at all. Traditionally, and still in the villages, a tale session would always begin with an exchange of riddles. In Wa, except for one occasion when the researcher specifically asked for riddles, the tales were never preceded by riddles. It was explained that this was not done any more in Wa because none of the young people knew how to respond to the questions in the riddles. On this occasion everyone agreed that the way in which the riddles were told was bad, because not once did anyone get the right answer, and it proved extremely difficult to transcribe them later on. Riddles, like proverbs, are called *loge* or *loba* and are actually proverbs in question form which are answered by another proverb, such as:

Question: When a shea tree out of water dies, they say it died because of lack of water. What about the tree that has died in the water?

Response: When your child dies, they say he is killed by a witch. But how about a witch's child who dies, who kills it?

The riddle meant that the end for people of different classes is all the same. All people die and are buried in the earth.

Unless otherwise indicated, the narrators are men varying from ages twenty to fifty. It was extremely difficult in the dark to detect the narrators, and because of the manner in which the tales were told, it was deemed improper and awkward to interrupt and break through the flow of the narrations to ask for the teller's identification. All the tales have been transcribed in Walii. All the copies of literal translations and their annotations, and of general translations and transliterations of the texts, have been deposited at the Archives of Traditional Music at Indiana University.

The tales were not given titles by their narrators or the listeners, but as a means of facilitating classification and identification, a title has been given to each tale, and in most cases it has been taken from the tale itself, usually from its concluding paragraph. The following is a selection from 117 tales I collected among the Wala of Wa during 1966 and 1967.

Chief Tests His Wife's Fidelity

A popular American Negro tale plays humorously on the theme taken seriously here, of the reaction by a mortal to the literal appearance of Death. In the American form, a trickster posing as God or Death answers the prayer for death of John the Slave, either at the praying tree or by coming to his door. John decides he is not quite ready for death. Baughman suggests the motif J217.0.1.1 "Trickster overhears man praying for death to take him" and gives seven Negro and two white references. I printed versions in *Buying the Wind* (Chicago, 1964), pp. 345–46, "When Death Comes," a white text from southern Illinois, close to the Wala text below, since the wife tells Death she has decided to let her husband go first after all, and in *Negro Folktales in Michigan* (Cambridge, Mass., 1956), pp. 61–62, "Efan Prays," and note 31, page 212, where I cite thirteen more variants.

NARRATOR: Kundarbuo, man about forty years old.

My story is here. ("Let me also tell a story small," that is, a short story.) There lived a certain chief. He had several wives. The wives, he had them. One of the wives liked the chief very much and agreed that if his life were in her hands, she would take care of it. But the rest of them there were enjoying the riches of the chief. It is because they want to be chief's wives.

There lived an old woman who took notice of all their activities and finally said, "Chief, here is something. This woman that you punish so much, she is the one who loves you. She is your life." She argued with the chief and they decided to meet in three days. He went to her. The woman told him, "What you have said, I will let you know about all your wives." He said, "U huu! All right!" He said that they should test the women. "There is a war somewhere. Leave them and go. Tell all of them, 'As I am, whether I will come back or I will not come, I don't know.' When you go, leave a sun (spend a day). The third night, when all people are asleep, come back. You will know the woman whose sense is with you (who loves you). The others married you because you are a chief and they are now chief's wives. That is why they are living with you; otherwise they are telling lies." The following day, the man gave them the information. They dressed his horse. He wore his battle dress and said, all right! that he was going. They all did this. When he was out of sight, they all dispersed. He went and slept until the next day, and the sun went and entered (set). At the time he returned to the village, all people were asleep. He reached his house and went and fastened his horse outside, but he went inside. His own wife, the senior wife herself, the one he respected, he climbed a ladder to the roof of her room and stamped his foot. The woman said,

Song. "Who hit the roof?"
"I am death."
"Whom do you want?"
"I want the chief."
"The chief has gone to war.
Go down and go and kill."

He got down and went to the house of another wife and stamped on the roof. She also asked,

Song. "Who hit the roof?"
"I am death."
"Whom do you want?"
"I want the chief."
"The chief has gone to war.
Go down and go and kill."

He nodded his head. He reached another wife's house and stamped on the roof.

Song. "Who hit the roof?"
"I am death."
"Whom do you want?"
"I want the chief."
"The chief has gone to war.
Go down and go and kill."

He again nodded his head. Left was only aunt namesake (Puretogima). He hit the roof.

Song. "Who hit the roof?"
"I am death."

"Whom do you want?"
"I want the chief."
"The chief has gone to war.
Come down and kill me. . . ."

The man nodded his head. She said, "Come down and kill me, but leave the chief." He went back. He untied his horse. He went and slept. The following day he came about *walihaa* (between 9 and 11 A.M.). When they knew he had come, they were in a hurry doing everything, but he kept quiet. He went on that side.

There are two ways of caring for human beings. Either because, like this woman, their eyes are all red about you (they are very serious about you, that is, love you) or else because of something you have.

My story—this is the end.

The Filial Son

This tale is discussed in the Introduction, p. 36, where I comment on a Japanese version in my *Folk Legends of Japan* (Tokyo and Rutland, Vermont, 1962), pp. 222–24, under the title "The Mountain of Abandoned Old People," with a headnote on its entrance into literature and drama. These texts belong to type 981 *Wisdom of Hidden Old Man Saves Kingdom*, with a corresponding motif J151.1. Other applicable motifs are R154.2 "Son rescues father" and S140.1 "Abandonment of aged." This widely reported tradition is known in Europe from Ireland to Russia, as well as in India and China and among the Turks and Jews, but neither the *Type-Index* nor the *Motif-Index* cites an African source.

NARRATOR: Teacher Mumuni, man about forty
years old.

Here is my story also. ("Pay attention here.") My story
has no songs.

There lived once a wicked chief. Nobody liked him, because of his wickedness. He was wicked to old men and
women. By pretending to be kind he tried to be popular
with all the young men who lived in that country. When the
chief won over the young men, they all liked him. One day,
the chief called all the young men and told them, "My
friends, don't you see?" They asked, "What?" "Don't you see
these old men of this country?" They asked, "What?" "You
should kill all of them. Everybody should kill his father." Ai!
(That they should all kill their fathers!) As a result, everybody whose father was old brought him to be killed. This
one went and brought his father to be killed, the other went
and brought his father to be killed. They killed all the old
men, leaving only one. He was the father of a man who
said no. "Why should the chief kill all old men and why
should I send my old father to be killed?" He got down and
went and dug a large hole and concealed it nicely. He sent
his father there, where he had dug. He fetched wood and
put it across and covered it with soil, making a small hole for
air to pass through. At that time, they had finished killing
all the old men. When the chief finished executing them, he
then called all the young men. "My friends, we have now
finished killing all our old men. This is a cow I am giving
to you. I am so happy we have got rid of all these old men,
so go and kill the cow. When you have killed the cow, cut
the best part of the meat and bring it to me. If you don't
bring it, you yourselves are not safe." (That is all right!)
Eh!

The young men rushed out and slaughtered the cow.
Which is the best part of the meat of the cow? They were

worried. They went and cut the liver and sent it to him. He asked whether or not that were the best part of the meat. They answered yes. They added part of the bile. He said that wasn't the best part of the meat and that they should go and find it quickly. The people became more worried. Every night the one young man secretly took food to his father. One day he took food to his father, who asked about the news of the town. He said, "My father, now we are suffering. When we killed all the old men, the chief gave us a cow to go and kill. When we killed the cow, he said we must find both the sweetest and bitterest part of the meat and bring to him. That if we do not bring them, we are not safe ourselves. This is what is worrying us." The old man laughed, but asked him if he knew the sweet part of the meat. He said no. He again asked if he did not know the bitterest part. He said no. "The sweetest and bitterest part is the tongue. When you go, cut the tongue and send it to him and say that the sweetest part of the meat is also the bitterest." The man rushed home while all the people sat down, undecided about what to do. If something had not happened, they might have thrown the whole meat away and run away. When the boy arrived, he said, "My friends, take the tongue of the cow in." They cut the tongue for him, and he took it to the chief's palace. He went and threw it down and said, "Chief, see the sweet part of the meat and the bitterest part also." The chief sat down quietly and finally said, "You did not kill your father. Speak the truth. You have not killed your father." He said, "It is the truth, I didn't kill him. When all the other young men were killing their fathers, I went and hid mine." He said, "You are the son of a wise old man. The sweetest and bitterest part of man is the tongue. As for that, all these young men are big fools. Why should somebody send his father to be killed? But if you want the sweetest part of the meat, find the tongue. Were it not for your tongue, you would not have an enemy; and it is also because of your tongue that you will not have a friend."

That is the end of my story.

Men Deceive Women

"Marriage to python in human form" (motif B656.1) is reported only from Africa, among the Kaffir, in D. Kidd, *Savage Childhood: a Study of Kaffir Children* (London, 1906), p. 249. A tale of a king who marries a snake-woman and suffers is known in India (type 411, episode I, "The Snake-Wife"). Of special interest here is the audience's interpretation of the tale.

NARRATOR: Awusara, young woman about twenty-five
years old.

Once there was a grown woman, but she refused to marry. She was offered many men, but she refused ("Then she was a prostitute!"), and roamed about. A python ("Woo!") went and bathed himself and was sparkling like that. He became a black young man and went to her. The young woman said that she had seen her dear husband, yoo! He, too, said that he had also found his dear wife, yoo! They decided to give him water so that he could wash, but he refused and said that he had already washed before coming. They gave him a house to stay in. They went into that house. Soon after, he turned into a python and stretched all around the house. Then he took his mouth and put it at the doorway. Then he went and held the woman's legs. And the woman said,

Song.   My mother, my mother! The man said lies.
                     (Repeated several times.)

The man swallowed the woman. My mother-in-law! The
child is telling a lie. The child is lying, how can a man
swallow a woman? And yet, he was swallowing her. He
swallowed her up to her thighs, and she said again.

Song.   (Repeated)

He kept on swallowing until he reached the stomach. She
cried again,

Song.   (Repeated)

He continued to swallow, and it was not long before he
reached the chest.

Song.   (Repeated)

He got to the woman's head, broke it off and threw it
in the house. Then he came out into the yard and kept on
crawling, *kpari, kpari,*[1] here and there.

The following day broke and the sun was high up, and
it became hot, very hot. They called and called and called,
but it was for nothing. They opened the door and found
only the woman's head there.

And that one ends like that, too.

*   *   *

A conversation followed this tale, concerning its meaning:

A man: What is the meaning of the song?
A woman: As the man wants to marry a woman, he will
     keep on deceiving her until she's convinced, and as
     soon as they marry, the man will show his true character.
The man: So sweet that his tongue is able to talk!
Another woman: You keep on giving her promises but as
     soon as you marry her, you fail to keep them.

[1] This expresses the slithering manner in which a python crawls.

The man: Is the woman then foolish (for marrying that man, the python)?

The other woman: Not at all! When a man woos a girl, he tells her sweet words. After marrying her, the man changes.

A Beautiful Girl Turns into a Leper

Motif K522.0.1 "Death feigned to escape unwelcome marriage" occurs in Eastern European folktales and English traditional ballads. The ensuing motif H521 "Test: guessing unknown propounder's name" (in this case the hopeful bride trying to guess the hidden man's name) turns up in an Angola tale collected by Heli Chatelain (*Folk-Tales of Angola*, Boston and New York, 1894, No. 14, p. 141). Other motifs present are Q281 "Ingratitude punished," Q551.6.0.1 "Punishment: men stricken with leprosy," and D265 "Transformation: man [in this case woman] to grass mat," reported only from Africa (William H. Barker and Cecilia Sinclair, *West African Folk-Tales*, London, 1917, p. 127; Kenneth W. Clarke adds a Tshi tale in I. Bellon, "Märchen des Tsai-Volkes auf der Goldküste," *Mitteilungen des Seminars für Orientalische-Sprachen* 18, pp. 1 ff.).

NARRATOR: Nmiiri, man about twenty-five years old.

Another story is coming. (Stop talking and listen.) There was a very handsome young man. He was really very handsome and was called Dzerikpana. There were so many girls who wanted him and fell in love with him, but he was fed up with them. Every young lady liked Dzerikpana. They did not know that Dzerikpana was called Dzeripoli and that his home was about eight miles from Wa, at Busa. Then, one day, he told his father, Na, that there were so many girls who loved him and he did not know which one of them to marry. So he said that he would lie down and Father Na should cover him with a white cloth (a funerary cloth), and tell all the girls that if any of them knew his name, he would marry her. Then Dze was covered with a white cloth and all the girls and good-time girls in this district were told that their future husband was dead, and if any of them could weep and call Dze's real name, then he would wake up from death and marry that girl. Girls from Zongo came, but could not say the right name. Girls from Saa also came to try, but all failed. Girls from Kpagru also came to try, but failed. Women from Tshere also came but did not know Dze's name. Good-time girls from Wa came but failed. Then one woman traveling from Kpongu to Busa said she would go and say Dze's name and marry him because of his handsome features.

From Kpongo, she passed by Sukpayiri and walked toward Nayiri. On the way, she saw an old woman taking her bath. Then the old woman said, "My granddaughter," and the woman greeted her. And the old woman said, "Come and wash my back for me and go." The young woman agreed and went to wash her back, and when she finished, she said that she had finished. The old woman said, "Granddaughter, it is all right! But at Busa, there is a young man whose name is Dzerikpana." The young woman thanked her for helping her to know the name of the handsome young man. From there, she started for Busa and took the road that passes by the old police station and the chief's farms. On the way to Busa, she started her mourning song,

Song A.   Oh! Dzerikpana, (Repeated)
          I will marry Dzerikpana, oh! (Repeated)
          Oh, Dzerikpana, I will marry Dzerikpana.

Dzerikpana's father and mother had built a long compound with seven rooms, and kept Dze's corpse in the last, the

seventh room, well barred with large doors. He could hear
this girl's song when she was at the chief's farm, so he also
started his song,

Song B.   Oh, oh, oh, my mother (Repeated)
           Open the doors for me,
           Wo, wo, wo, my mother,
           Open the doors and let me out.

On nearing Kampaha, she sang again.

Song A.   (Repeated)

The young man heard her and also repeated.

Song B.   (Repeated)

After the woman had sung twice, two doors were opened,
leaving five. At Kampaha, she sang again, and the young
man also sang, and another door was opened, leaving four
more doors. The girl passed Kampaha and started climbing
Tokoro hill and again began her song.

Song A.   (Repeated)

On hearing it the young man also sang.

Song B.   (Repeated)

And another door was opened, leaving three. From Tokoro
hill, she went some few yards and started her song again.
The man heard her once and also sang his song. After this,
another door was opened and he went into the second room,
leaving two more doors. At this time, the young woman could
see the walls of Vaara and started singing again. The good-
time girls, on hearing this woman sing and mention Dze's
name, were all surprised and stood watching her call the
name while she approached. Then they stood up and started
weeping. "Wolu, wolu, wolu, wolu. . . . Who is this strange
woman from another place who has been able to know this
man's name and we *Gentras* (good-time girls) and *Tutuhi*

(prostitutes) have not been able to know it?" On seeing them, one would hate them there and then. While they were saying all this, the girl sang again, this time louder.

Song A. (Repeated)

The young man, now left with two doors to pass through, also sang his song.

Song B. (Repeated)

Then another door was opened and he was left with one door to pass through. Then the Zongo women, the Nantiri women, and the Wa prostitutes stood wondering how this woman, who was a stranger, got to know of Dze's name, and thus would now have the chance of marrying Dze.

When she was a few steps away from where Dze was, she started her song again.

Song A. (Repeated)

After this, the last door was opened and Dze came out and said, "This woman, who has been able to know my name, shall be my wife." Dze then went and embraced the woman and they started, kiri, kiri, kiri . . . fast toward Wa. On the way, as they were nearing Kampaha village, they saw the old woman bathing again. The old woman said that the young woman should come and wash her back, but the young woman, hearing this, turned sharply and said, "Stop that nonsense! How can I marry such a nice young man and come and wash the back of an old woman?" She refused. Have you heard? The young woman even said she was nearly a leper by washing her back the first time and that because of that she had large fingers and toes but went and married Dze anyway.

After saying this, they passed by Kampaha and there she turned into a leper. At this time, the young man turned and said, "Why should there be so many beautiful girls and I marry you, a leper?" And he said that he would no longer marry her and then ran as fast as he could. The leper also started, kpidu, kpidu, kpidu . . . running after him. They chased each other until they were in the middle of a thick bush. She ran after the man and later he turned into a reed (the type used for making mats). This mat is used by women who have just given birth. The leper also went and turned into a *daangu* (fiber used to weave the reeds together to make a mat).

A weaver then went to cut the reed and the fiber to weave a mat. After the mat was woven, a woman who had just given birth bought it, and while she lay on it, it made some noise, miu, miu, miu. . . . This shows that the leper has not yet stopped running after the young man and the young man has also not stopped running. So the mat continues to make noise, miu, miu, miu, miu. . . .

Penis Accepts to Bury Mouth

This and other penis-vagina stories in the Wala repertoire, which do not ordinarily get printed in African folktale collections, show the tradition behind the chants and songs of the Vandals in modern college folklore, discussed in Part I, p. 66.

Type 293 and motif J461.1 "Debate of the belly and the members as to their usefulness; all are mutually useful" is known in *Aesop's Fables*, in Jewish tradition, in India and Indonesia, and has been collected among the Ekoi in Africa by P. A. Talbot, *In the Shadow of the Bush* (New York and London, 1912), p. 393.

Mouth once died. It was last year, Djanbeu, that Mouth died.

Do you understand it? The one who never says a bad thing, do you understand it?

They called the Eye. "Eye, Mouth has died. You will bury him." The Eye said, "No!" He would not bury Mouth. "I see, but when I go to see anything the Mouth will say that he has seen something. 'But you, Mouth, you cannot see!' And so I cannot bury my father's Mouth. I will not bury my father's Mouth." They went and called the Ear. "My father Ear. Mouth is dead and we want somebody to bury him." The Ear said he couldn't bury the Mouth. "When I, Ear, hear something, even far away, Mouth cannot hear it and yet it says it has heard." They called the Hand and the Hand said, "I cannot bury him. I take hot things. When I cut hot food and it burns me, the Mouth says that the food has burnt its hand, but Mouth doesn't go into the dish." They called the Head. "My father Head, come and bury Mouth." And he said, "No!" He couldn't do it. "When I carry things and am in pain, Mouth says that his head is paining." And so he will not bury Mouth. They went and called Back and he said he couldn't bury him. "He lies on the floor and when he is bitten by an ant the Mouth says an ant has bitten him." They went and called Testicles, and he said he could not because Mouth talks, but he doesn't. "But he says I talk!" They called Penis. He said he would bury the Mouth. "I am always in my pants, but Mouth goes and finds a way to deceive a woman and bring her into the house for me. Then he keeps quiet and I do my work. So I will bury Mouth."

How Penis and Vagina Got Together

The theme of "Origin of sexual intercourse" (motif A1352) enters into traditional narrative in India, Japan, Lithuania, and among the Mkulwe and Loango in Africa (C. Einstein, *Afrikanische Legenden*, Berlin, 1925, pp. 18 f., and E. Pechuël-Loesche, *Volkskunde von Loango*, Stuttgart, 1907, p. 26). Clarke adds further West African references to collections from the Gold Coast and Dahomey and among the Temne. Two variants are given below.

Tshu is a sound signifying no. *Longon* and *bintiri* are two types of talking drums.

1.

My story is this: Penis and Vagina had an argument. Penis said, "You, Vagina, if I go to any village with you, I will get water for you to drink." Vagina said that she didn't agree and that Penis's offer would be a lie, until they go and find out one day in a village. One day, they started off from Bulenga. They were going to go from Bulenga to Wa. Penis took his *longo* and hung it on his shoulder, and Vagina herself took her *bintiri* and carried it around her neck. They walked until they reached Goripie, then Penis beat his *longo*, selen, selen! People said, "A madman is coming!" and that they should run. They all ran away. Penis came and sat with a long mouth, annoyed. Vagina then beat her *bintiri*.

Song.   Banban tin, an ban, banban yee yoobayi . . .
          (Repeat several times)

The people said, "Woe!" that the Chief of Bulenga was
coming and that they should arrange the place. They made
the place look fine and they put out the chairs. Then Vagina
came and sat down. They fetched water and gave her to
drink. She went closer to Penis. He refused, stood up and
took his *longo* and walked away. He walked very fast until
he reached Mangwe and again he beat his drum, selen,
selen! They said, "Woe!" The children ran and said that a
madman was coming. Everybody ran away. Vagina also
reached Mangwe and beat her drum.

Song.   (Repeated)

The people at Mangwe also arranged the place for her.
("My father Seidu isn't able to tell this woman everything,
because he has become shy. . . . They are all tired.") Because of that, Vagina won the argument. ("I want to tell a
sweet story.") They reached the place they were heading
for. She took the water and went to give some to Penis. He
then made tshu, and refused. He said, "No!" She left the
water, but he rushed and entered her. All right! They
rushed into each other. They are still doing this till today.

2.

Here is my story: Penis and Vagina had an argument.
Penis said he was lord of Vagina, and Vagina said it was a
lie and asked why he said so. Penis said that if they should
travel to any place he could get water for Vagina to drink.
Then Vagina said that they should argue no further, that
they should try it.

They set out from Mangwe toward Wa when Penis
fetched some water for Vagina to drink and she refused.
Penis therefore made a drum and Vagina also made a drum
with a calabash and put pieces of iron around it and said

they should start their journey. On the way, Penis took his
drum and began to play.

When he reached a town called Goripie the people took
him to be a madman and they all ran into their houses. Penis
grew very annoyed. A little later Vagina also came, playing
her drum.

Song. Ban bay tigi lee yee, ban bay tigi lee yee a tigi li
ban bay. (Repeated several times)

When the people of the town heard the song, they said
that a chief is coming, so they got brooms and swept the front
of their houses very clean and got a big pot and filled it with
water and made food, "tuon zaafi," inside their houses.
When Vagina came, she, instead of Penis, was given the
water to drink. When Vagina sipped the water and gave it
to Penis to drink, he refused and got up and began to play
his drum, geloe, geloe, geloe. He was very annoyed and set
out for Mangwe. Vagina again followed and began to drum
and sing.

Song. (Repeated)

The inhabitants of Mangwe also said that a chief and his
followers are coming. They also swept outside their houses,
and when Vagina came, she was given water. After she had
drunk, she gave some to Penis to drink, but he refused and
got up and started walking to Kampaha. When he reached
there, the people began shouting that a madman was coming and that they should all run into their houses. He went
and sat under a tree alone, his face very grave. When Vagina came, she sang again and the people gave her water to
drink. When the water was given to Penis, he became annoyed, got up and started walking to the chief's palace.
When he came to the palace the people there started saying
that a madman had come to the palace. Penis sat down and
was very, very annoyed. Again, Vagina came drumming and
singing.

Song.   (Repeated)

When she got to the palace, it was swept very nicely and water was fetched for her to drink. After she had drunk, she gave some to Penis for him to drink also. Penis just got up and ran inside Vagina. It is still there to this day! That is the end of my story.

It Is the Hunter That Brought
Men and Women Together

The stock hunter-hero is here made into a trickster-lover. All the main motifs are sexual: F112 "Journey to land of women," popular in Irish, ancient Greek, Chinese, Hawaiian, and West Indian tradition; K1384 "Female overpowered when caught in tree cleft (hole in hedge)," which is the basis for type 36 *The Fox in Disguise Violates the She-Bear;* and K1363 "Seduction of person ignorant of sexual intercourse," for which Frank A. Hoffman cites ten examples ("An Analytical Survey of Anglo-American Traditional Erotica," Indiana University doctoral dissertation in Folklore, 1968, vol. 2, p. 167). He has also many instances of X724.1 "Seduction by deception or trick."

Sau is a porridge made of millet.

"Another story?" "Tell your story, but let me tell mine next. . . ."

*   *   *

There was a hunter who was roaming in the bush. He roamed for some time until he came to a closed-in compound

But he didn't even know that this compound existed! He heard busy noises from inside the house, not knowing that there were women inside. At that time women didn't live with men. They lived alone. They also had a woman chief but the hunter didn't know this. He saw the women come out. He walked around the whole house, went about examining it, and hit upon a small opening, which he made still wider. He opened exactly where the women were sitting cooking. Now, the women had a woman chief, and she never cooked. It means, then, that each woman cooked for her ("for another?"). None had husbands. The hunter said, "Yaa! These women! This is what I will do." He then took his penis—yaa!—and inserted it into that opening. A woman was sitting with her vagina against the opening and was cooking her soup. She took her vagina and put it there—yaa! There were some named Habiba, others Minata, others Zeinabu, many named Kutuma and Fatima—each of them had a name.

Then one day, one of the women, Mama Hawwa (note reference to Hawwa—*Eve*), who was first to stir the soup, was first to start the world. She sang,

Song.   My mother's namesake, put in the flour for me. . . .
         Habiba, woi! put in the flour for me. . . .
         Minata, woi! put in the flour for me. . . .
         Fatima, woi! put in the flour for me. . . .
         Sanpagaa, woi! put in the flour for me. . . .

The women said, "Ai!" They took the food and first gave it to the senior woman. The food could not be eaten, because the body of Mama Hawwa had such great pleasure! The one who stirred the food could not stir it well, my friend! The woman chief said, "Ai! Why did you cook it like this? You're useless! Why did you stir it like this?" Not knowing that by putting the hunter's penis in just once, it had given seed to Mama Hawwa, who got up and sat down there. The following day came (to be). "I say! Today, as for this food, this sister of yours who cooked so badly . . . she will cook again and if she cooks it badly again, I will beat her up!" Again at the same time that the food was being prepared, the hunter came and went to the same small opening and took his penis and put it in.

Song. (Repeated)

They said, "Um hum! Again this food that she is cooking is thick and bad." It could not be eaten. The woman chief then became annoyed. All the women—and they were all in all thirty—cooked, but it also was no good . . . not even good enough to be sold. The woman chief then came and said, "You are very useless, hopeless, and can't do anything well. Today, I myself will cook this sau." ("That is the truth!")

The buttocks of the woman were that large and the penis was exactly like this. She took her buttocks and sat in front of the hole and placed there her vagina. Mmapp!! So he stuffed in his thing like this. She said,

Song. (Repeated)

She kept on swaying back and forth and then shouted to the women, "Go, run and see what is behind the house and come back!" They ran out to the back of the house and the cause of the disturbance was discovered, and they caught him.

Men, this is why we bring women home. The hunter brought them. If it were not for him, women would still be living alone and men would be staying by themselves. Like this my story comes to an end.

Wiser than the Chief

There are many references to motif T585.2 "Child speaks at birth" from Europe, Asia, South America, and Africa where it is reported among the Benga, Bahonga, Fang, and Mkulwe. The theme of "Tasks imposed" (H900) generates several specific motifs: H915 "Tasks assigned because of boy's own foolish boast," H1024.1.1 "Task: making a bull bear a calf. Reductio ad absurdum: have a man prepare for childbirth" (known in India), and H960 "Tasks performed through cleverness or intelligence." Also present are A728 "Sun caught in snare" (found in Leo Frobenius' collections of African tales), N338.3 "Son killed because mistaken for someone else," and R211.3 "Escape through underground passage."

NARRATOR: Woman about twenty-five years old.

There was a chief of a town who said that anyone who gave birth should bring the baby to him to be named. So everybody did as the chief said. One man had a baby, but the day on which the baby was born, he had gone to the farm. The baby said, "Who will tell my father so that he can bring along a log for firewood?" The father had the log and they all went home. On the seventh day, the day he was to be named, the parent decided to take him to the chief for the ceremony. The baby said no, that he already had a name and was called Yenga Naa (Wiser-than-the-Chief). The father was afraid and said, "Did you say, 'Wiser than the chief'?" The father was afraid because the chief said anyone who refused to bring his baby to be named would suffer for it. The baby still insisted on being called Yenga Naa. The boy grew up with the name Yenga Naa.

One day Yenga Naa and his friends went to the chief's palace. At that time, the chief was sitting outside, conversing with his elders, when all of a sudden they heard small boys shouting, "Yenga naa, go this way. . . . Yenga naa, guard this place." The chief sat up and asked, "Who is called Yenga Naa?" and ordered that he be brought to him. Yenga Naa was called and he came. The chief asked him who his father was. He mentioned his father's name and the chief sent for him to be brought to him. The chief asked the boy who named him Yenga Naa, and he replied saying that no one gave him the name, but that when he was born he chose that name. The chief then said, "If you say you are wiser than the chief, we shall see." He said he was going to put difficult tasks before him to test his wit, to know whether he was really wiser than the chief.

The first task was giving him a bull to raise. Yenga Naa raised the bull until it was quite grown, then the chief seized all Yenga Naa's father's cattle, saying that it was his bull that had given birth to them all. The boy said nothing but went behind the chief's palace and started cutting a tree, kok, kok, kok! The chief, hearing this, ordered that he should be brought to him. When the boy came, the chief asked him what he was cutting the tree for, and he replied that his father had just given birth and he was instructed to bring some sticks for firewood. The chief asked how a man could give birth. The boy then replied that although males do not give birth, "You said your ox gave birth to all of my father's cattle and therefore seized them all." The chief returned all Yenga Naa's father's cattle and called him again after three days.

When he came, he smeared a cow with sheanut butter and gave it to Yenga Naa to rear and said that he should not let the butter melt. The boy went and had some *nirii* (soup made of small white seeds) and kept the seeds in his bag. His mother fried the *nirii* and said he should go with the cow to the Valley of Shade to avoid sunlight. Father Sun then asked him what he was doing and he said he should also look to see. Father Sun then asked Yenga Naa to give him some *nirii* from his bag, but Yenga Naa said he should come inside the bag and take some. When the Sun came inside the bag, Yenga Naa closed the bag and for a week there was no sunlight. They started investigating and later found out that it was Yenga Naa who was keeping the Sun. The chief then took his cow back and made Yenga Naa let the Sun shine.

After this, the chief plotted to kill Yenga Naa, so he told the killers that when they saw two people coming down the road, they should kill the one that was riding the horse and leave the one riding the donkey. The chief was planning to send Yenga Naa and his son somewhere. The chief told Yenga Naa to ride the horse, while his son would ride the donkey, before they set off. On the way, Yenga Naa told the prince, "How can I, a poor man's son, ride the horse while you, a prince, ride a donkey?" He therefore decided they should exchange animals, and they did so. Some few yards ahead, some men emerged from the bush and killed the prince, who was sitting on the horse. Yenga Naa came back and told the prince's father, the chief, "On the way, some men attacked and killed the prince." The chief said, "Oh! Since you are so clever, I am inviting you to a feast."

He made his men dig a hole and also had rice cooked, pito brewed, and *Tuon Zafi* made. After the hole was dug, it was covered with hides and pillows, and Yenga Naa was to sit there. It is really true that he was wiser than the chief, for he got to know of this plan. From his mother's house, Yenga Naa started digging a trench to the chief's compound. When he came, he went to take the lowest seat, but the chief said he should sit on the pillows, but he said, "No." The chief still insisted, and finally he agreed. When he sat down, he went directly into the hole. When he landed at the bottom of the hole, he took the path he had dug and went to his mother's house, where she gave him some beans and he began to eat. Meanwhile, the chief ordered all the hot pito and the food to be poured into the hole. The chief then sent for Yenga Naa's father. When the messengers arrived, they saw the boy eating beans. The chief was told this, and he repeatedly asked if it was really true that he was at his mother's house, and each time they replied "Yes." The chief sent for him, and when he came the boy said, "I was just eating beans when these people said you wanted me." The chief replied, "You are really wiser than the chief."

This is the end of my story.

Know Your Relatives or Else You'll Be Mistaken for a Slave

Deception-by-disguise motifs recognizable here are K1317.1 "Serving-man in his master's place," K1810.1 "Disguise by putting on clothes (carrying accouterments) of certain person," and K1934 "Impostor forces hero (heroine) to change places with him (her)." This last motif occurs in several tale types, among them type 533 *The Speaking Horsehead*, reported three times in Africa. Other motifs are J1114.0.1 "Clever slave," J1766 "One person mistaken for another," and H12 "Recognition by song."

It is true! A man and his wife went and settled at a place like Kampaha. They had a child and a slave child. The man died but his senior brother was living in Wa. The man always used to say, "Hai! Always try to know the difference between your child and the slave boy." Yaa! After his death, his wife sent word to his senior brother in Wa saying that her son and the slave boy were coming. The mother bathed the child. She dressed him in shorts, a smock, and a hat. Then she gave the slave boy water in a gourd to carry. While they were walking, the boy sighed. "Uuhu!" The slave asked, "What?" The boy said he was thirsty. The slave boy said, "Uhuu! If you give me your smock, I will give you water to drink. If you don't, then you won't have the water." The boy took off his smock and gave it to him, and the slave boy, who put it on, gave him the water. They walked until they reached Nodzeli-boo, the valley. The boy said, "Ah! I am thirsty." The slave said, "Aah! Give me your shorts and I will also give you water." When he got the shorts and put them on, the slave boy gave the boy water to drink. They continued walking until they reached Dr. Faar's house, in Wa. The boy again said, "Ehu!" The slave asked, "What?" The boy said, "I am thirsty." The slave said "Uuh! Take off your hat for me to wear or else I won't give you water to drink." The boy gave him the hat and got the water. As soon as the boy finished with the water, the slave told him, "Umm! Hold this gourd." Yaa! When they entered the house of the father's relatives, the child's uncle was sitting down. He told the slave to come and sit by his side, but he pushed away his own brother's son. Hai!

They farmed maize, and partridges would come and peck at the seeds. The following morning, the son was given cold food and a piece of firewood. He put them on his shoulder and went to the farm. As soon as he entered the farm he said, "Haa!" to scare the birds away.

Song. Haa! Haa! Don't eat these things, don't eat!
The day my mother died, yaa!
They turned their real son into a slave, yaa!
But they made the slave their child, yaa!
They turned him into their son!
My father, wo! The day he died, woo! the elephant died.

He made a fire and then climbed up to the top of the shed. Then he took this thing and knocked on it.

Song. (Repeated)

He prepared his food and sat down until evening and then he returned home. The following day he was beaten to get up and he went again to the farm. He was again given cold food, firewood, and told to go. When he got to the farm, he opened his mouth.

Song. (Repeated)

After making his fire, he opened his mouth,

Song.   (Repeated)

Hai! An old woman had gone to pick *saalung* (vegetables) and sheanut seeds. When she stopped, she heard the boy. Then she went and told the uncle and his senior brother. She said, "To prove that what I have told you is true, you should wake him up early tomorrow morning, and then one of you should follow him and hide." The next day, yaa! they woke up the boy but only after his uncle had already gone to the farm. As soon as the boy got to the farm, he started his song.

Song.   (Repeated)

He went and made his fire.

Song.   (Repeated)

Ei! The senior brother carried him and rushed home. He brought out the slave and beat him up here and there, threw him on the ground and told him to go to the farm. They took off all his clothes.

Because of this, if you have any relatives somewhere, try to know them; otherwise, one day you will be taken for a slave. ("You are telling lies!"—"It is true!") I have finished; my story is finished.

Brain Wins over Strength

This is basically a variation of type 1074 and motif K11.1 "Race Won by Deception: Relative Helpers," for which May A. Klipple cites thirty-eight African examples distributed in East Africa, the Congo, and the Guinea coast ("African Tales with Foreign Analogues," Indiana University dissertation, 1938). Also present are motifs A282.0.1 "Wind goddess" and B491.5 "Helpful tortoise." This type is popular among American Negroes; see R. M. Dorson, *Negro Folktales in Michigan* (Cambridge, Mass., 1956), pp. 37–38 and note 4, p. 205.

NARRATOR: Nmiiri, man about twenty-five years old.

Once there was a famine and the chief had his millet still on the stalk in the house. There was no wind, and they could not sort the grain out of the husk. He therefore brought out a young woman and a cow, promising to give them to anyone who could go to the home of Wind and bring it. Then all creatures that could fly tried to call Wind, but failed. Tortoise got up and said he could bring Wind, so he should be given the chance to try. The chief then said, "How can people with wings who can fly be unable to bring Wind, and you, a four-footed creature, expect to bring it?" Tortoise still insisted on trying. He then set off for Wind's home. There he met the wife of Wind, who was preparing food, and he said,

"The chief says I should come to greet you and ask you to come to help separate some grain for him." She then said, "Very well. Take the lead, but if I should catch up with you on the way, I will return."

Tortoise went out and collected about four thousand of his children and buried them from there to the chief's door, one by one, and returned. When Tortoise left Wind's house, Wind followed directly, fufuu-fuuu. . . . And after traveling for some time without seeing Tortoise, it started singing,

Song A.   Where will tortoise go,
        Tortoise is lying. . . .
        (Repeated six times)

On hearing this, Tortoise responded from a distance, singing,

Song B.   You can run the Wangara way,
        Wangara, Wangara, Wangara running.
        You can run the fairy way,
        Wangara, Wangara, Wangara running.

Then Wind said, "Impossible."

Song A.   (Repeated)

By this time, they had gone midway. The Tortoise said,

Song B.   (Repeated)

The Tortoise then buried himself. Wind then rushed, fuu-fuu, fuu-fuu . . . and passed over Tortoise, who was already well hidden, and Wind chased Tortoise until he was tired, then started,

Song A.   (Repeated)

By this time Tortoise was at the chief's palace and sang confidently.

Song B.   (Repeated)

All this while he was hiding in his shell. When Wind reached the chief's palace it sorted out the grain and blew away the chaff. Tortoise was given the cow and the wife. This shows that it is the brain that works, and not strength. That is the end of my tale.

A False Accusation Is
More Painful than Fire

"Speaking excrements" (motif D1610.6.4) is reported, among other places, from Nigeria by Clarke and Klipple. The general motifs K2100 "False accusation" and K2150 "Innocent made to appear guilty" belong here. The spider appears in a familiar West African role as culture hero (A522.3.1).

NARRATOR: Nmiiri, man about twenty-five years old.

This is one of them. The chief and the spider. The spider went to say hello to the chief every day, and after that they would converse. God did not forbid the spider to go and greet the chief. He would sit and converse with the chief. It was then that the spider said that to be accused falsely is more painful than physical injury. The chief said that the spider should go away with its lies. The spider said, "This is true." After a long argument, the chief called his wife. He said that the wife should take fire and burn the foot of his friend. The spider's foot got burnt. For about three days, the spider was not able to go to the chief's house because of the sore. The chief asked why the spider was not coming to him, and the elders said that the spider's child had burnt him, and that was why he was unable to come. He said, "You dog! But he said false accusations were more painful than fire. As they burnt him, has that place not become a sore, and has he not stayed in bed? But if it were a false accusation, would he still not have been well enough and continued to walk about? He is stupid."

When the spider was well, he came and greeted the chief. In about seven days, the chief had forgotten. The spider went to the chief's kraal to take cow dung; it was almost about to rain. He and his son took the cow dung in a calabash and started going to the chief's palace. When they entered the entrance, the spider made Darikamanbiri, his son, lie down. He then poured the cow dung over him. The cow dung covered him and the spider turned and went away. The following day the cow dung began smelling everywhere. He also told his son, Darikamanbiri, that when he heard them talking the following day, he should say that the chief did it. (Laughter.) He stayed under the cow dung as his father had told him. Immediately the following morning, when people were going to greet the chief, all of the chief's palace smelled. "See, when it was raining and somebody felt like going, he could not go out but relieved himself in the chief's entrance." The chief said that they should find the one who had relieved himself there. Soon the spider came along. The chief said that somebody came and relieved himself in his palace and so he should help him find the one. The spider said, "All right! Since you cannot find the one, let us find the fellow through witchcraft. The excrement is too much to be dropped here without our finding the fellow." The chief called all the people of the town. Together with all his wives and children, they came to look for the one. It was late at night, and no one would come out and say he had done it. When they all assembled, the chief's elder said he must first prove his innocence. "When anybody comes to say that he or

she is not the one, but when the chief comes, say he did it."
The elder said he must first prove his innocence. Then he
said he was innocent. He said,

Song.   Excrement, yes, excrement (repeat)
        They say I did it (repeat)
        The chief's elder,
        They say I did it.

The excrement said "No!" They said it was not the elder who
had relieved himself. The excrement said it was not the
elder who had done it, and because of that, he could go back.
My father! My father, Jakalia, drew close.

Song.   Repeat and add at end, "It is me, Jakalia."

The excrement said,

Song.   Lai, lai, lai, lai
        You are the chief's Jakalia,
        But you are not the one who did it.

Everyone said the chief's wife should draw closer. The chief's
senior wife drew close.

Song.   First song repeated and add at end,
        "It is me, the chief's wife."

The excrement said,

Song.   Lai, lai, lai,
        You are the chief's wife,
        But you are not the one who did it.

She was told that she should also go. She was not the one
who had done it. She turned and went away. The spider said
he would also prove his innocence before them, because he
also has been coming to the palace every day. He also had
to come and prove himself.

Song.   First song repeated and add at end,
         "It is me, Spider."

Everyone said it was not the spider who had done it. He also
went away. The chief said he also would prove himself. The
spider said the chief should not try to prove himself, but the
chief insisted and spider finally allowed him to do it and said,
"All your people have proved their innocence." The chief
drew closer and said,

Song.   First song repeated and add at the end,
         "I am the chief."

The excrement said,

Song.   Tshong, tshong, tshong,
         You are the chief, really,
         But you did it.

The chief became hot. It was said that the chief, of all
these people, had done it. The chief just went back inside the
house and the spider secretly followed him. When the chief
entered, he took out a sword. The spider got hold of him
and yelled an alarm that everyone should come, for the chief
wanted to kill himself. He took the sword and threw it on the
roof. They all came to see the chief. The spider said that the
chief should be patient and he would tell him something.
The chief sat down sweating.

On the second day, Spider went and put forward his case.
"My father chief, the day we sat together and I said a false
accusation was more painful than fire, didn't you say it wasn't
true? You burnt my foot with fire and that became a sore.
Has it not healed? It was my son who came and said that
you relieved yourself there. If I did not come to hold you,
wouldn't you have killed yourself with the sword you took?
Is that not a false accusation?" The chief said that the spider
is right.

That is the end of my story. A false accusation is more
painful than fire.

Father, Son, and Donkey

No African version of this internationally popular numskull tale is cited in the *Motif-Index* for J1041.2 "Miller, his son, and the ass: trying to please everyone," but references are given for England, Spain, Italy, the Balkans, the Middle East, and India. American examples from Missouri and New Jersey are cited in Ernest W. Baughman, *Type and Motif-Index of the Folktales of England and North America* (The Hague, 1966).

A man who had a son farmed his guinea corn. They sold the guinea corn for much money and saved part of it and bought a donkey. After they bought the donkey, the hot season came, and they were preparing to store away yams. The man said, "I will teach my son the world today. You say you are foolish. I will show you how the world is." He got up, harnessed the donkey, and put his things on it securely. They began walking. They walked a little, the man riding the donkey (noise of the footsteps . . .), when they saw people. When they went a short distance, as from here to that tree, the people said, "Ei! See a foolish man, sitting on that donkey while his son is walking on this hot ground. My father, you are too foolish, you are hopeless!" And they continued to insult him. He was quiet and said, "Did you hear what they said?" The son said he had heard. After a short while he got down and told his son to come and ride. His son sat on the donkey. When they walked, they met some

Dagatis coming the other way. The woman said, "Ei! See a useless boy. You, like this, all strong yet will not walk and let your father ride the donkey, but make him walk on the hot ground?" They swore at him. My father! He said, "Have you heard?" The son said he had heard. They walked a little more. They both came down from the donkey. They were both walking and pulling the donkey. Soon they met some women. They said, "See a useless man and his son? Neither of them has sense. Why should you have such a donkey and yet walk without riding?" He said, "All right! Have you heard it? Haven't you heard what they said? That is the world."

Because of this, you human beings in this world, when you do something and someone else comes to see what you are doing, continue doing what you like, continue doing just that. ("That is the meaning.") (That is, do what you think is right.)

How Friendship Between Hawk and Fowl Ended

Two tales that Ruth Finnegan contrasts, of how enmity developed between a large predatory bird (vulture, eagle) and the hen, are discussed in Part I, pp. 14–15. Although the causes for the quarrel differ, these various tales are united by motif A2494.13.10.3 "Enmity between hawk and hen," reported only from Africa, for the Cameroons, in P. Simon Rosenhuber, *Märchen, Fabeln, Rätsel, und Sprichwörter der Kamerun-Neber* (Limburg, 1926), pp. 69 f. In his index Arewa gives a close Kamba variant of the Kikuyu text of the hen borrowing and losing the vulture's razor cited by Finnegan (*Oral Literature in Africa*, Oxford, 1970, pp. 338–

40; E. Ojo Arewa, "A Classification of the Folktales of the Northern East African Cattle Area by Types," University of California, Berkeley, dissertation, 1966, No. 762 [hawk and chicken]).

NARRATOR: Nmiiri, man about twenty-five years old.

One story is coming!

The guinea fowl's best friend was the hawk. The fowl's best friend was the hawk. I say! A dispute broke out between them. The hawk went up and made talking drums for them to dance the *dogho* (a dance). The fowl said, "All right!" They got to the bush and cut a big oak tree. They came and made the talking drums. After carving the talking drums, the hawk became very hungry. The hawk took the talking drums and they put them in the sun. The fowl asked the hawk to take care of them. But he got up and went away, a distance as far as from here to Danko, to go and eat and return. Otherwise it would have still been hungry. Then he told the fowl, "When the drums are dried, don't beat them until I have returned. If you beat the drums before I return, there will be trouble between us." The fowl said, "All right!" The hawk went to Danko and found food to eat. The talking drums were dried. When the drums were dry, the fowl went to inspect them and see whether they were dry. He went and took the talking drums. He stroked the drums. He beat them "gben-gben-gben." He liked the sound of the drums. The hawk's name was Setu. (Laughter) The fowl was called Nmengu. At that time, all these animals were known by these names, like ours. It was then that the fowl beat the talking drums. The sound was very nice. He beat the drum and it made the sound.

Song.   Setu, Setu, Setu, Setu,
             Setu yee Setu (Repeat three times),
             Dzaan, dzaan, dzaan (Repeat).

The hawk was in Danko, but he heard the sound of the drums. He was also known as Sitituo. The hawk became annoyed and started returning. He flew up very high. The fowl also stood like that, not knowing that as he beat more, the hawk grew angrier. He beat again.

Song.   (Repeated three times)

The hawk flew very fast past the fowl. The fowl thought that the hawk was happy so he beat them again.

Song.   (Repeated)

The hawk flew over the fowl. It passed. The fowl beat the talking drums again.

Song.   (Repeated)

The hawk came again to cut the fowl's head. As the hawk was coming, the fowl began to run, pi, pi, pi. . . . This is how the friendship between the hawk and the fowl got spoiled. Neither the fowl nor the hawk took the talking drums. But the people of the village took them and used them in dancing *dogho.* This is why the hawk and the fowl are enemies till this day.

My story is finished.

Black Man Is Ungrateful

The present tale is close to type 155 "The Ungrateful Serpent Returned to Captivity," except that the treacherous animal (in this case the frog) is killed rather than returned to captivity. For the specific motif, W154.2.1 "Rescued animal threatens rescuer," Kenneth W. Clarke cites examples from the Togo, Yoruba, and Ibo, and for W154.2.2 "Man ungrateful for rescue by animal," he has instances from the Tshi and Temne.

NARRATOR: Moghona, man about fifty years old.

There lived a hunter who was very good at shooting. He used to kill to feed the animals in the bush. One day when he was hunting, he reached the banks of the river, where he saw some ants that were carrying a frog, which they left by the river. The frog was struggling but it could not free itself. Then the hunter, after watching it for a while, said, "What a pity!" He drew closer but said, "Man is ungrateful." The frog said, "I beg you, free me. Save me from these ants." He said, "No." The frog pleaded to be saved. The hunter picked up the frog and after throwing away all the ants, threw it into the water. After falling into the water, it went down for a moment and then appeared on the surface and said, "My father Hunter!" He replied, "Yes!" The frog said that he should open his eyes and look at him. When the hunter opened his eyes, the frog threw sand into them. The hunter became blind.

For seven days, the hunter stayed there suffering. All the things that used to eat the animals he killed were going about to find him. When the vulture flew over, he saw the hunter crying. He went and said, "Ai! My father Hunter, what happened?" He said it was because of the frog. While he was lying there, the hunter would call to the river frog. It would answer "Yes?" He would say, "Frog is ungrateful." The frog would say that any black man who would do him any good, he would pay you back with wickedness."[1] "River Frog,

[1] It is of note that the reference to black man here does not refer to the racial distinction. It is the expression of the being of a

I showed you kindness and you paid me back with cruelty."
Then the frog would say, "Wickedness, wickedness, wickedness!" and then go back into the water. But the hunter lay
there for seven days. He became hungry and thirsty, but he
could not find his way home. The animals were looking for
him.

When the vulture passed, it saw the hunter lying down.
The vulture said, "You are the one who feeds us. What made
you lie here?" The hunter said it is something. The vulture
asked whether that thing were near there. He said "Yes!"
"Call it to come out so that I may see it." The hunter called,
"River Frog!" It came up to the surface and said, "Wur-r-r.
Do me good and I will spoil you." It said, "Wickedness,
wickedness, wickedness!" and went down again. The vulture
said, "All right! I have seen it. I will go and find the other
birds and we will come."

It went and called birds such as the eagle and the hawk
and they came and sat on a tree. Vulture then came and
told the hunter, "I have returned. Call your thing again to
come out and I will see." When the hunter called, "River Frog!"
like that, as soon as it came to the surface, Katshiu, the eagle,
picked it up. The birds said, "If you don't open his eyes,
we shall eat you up." The frog said, "Man, open your eyes
and look at me." He blew into them. He asked him whether
he could see yet. The man said that he could see. He repeated
this three times and his eyes opened clearly. The vulture
came down and said, "Hunter, see your enemy. What shall
we do with him?" The hunter said, "You should eat him, for
today is the seventh day without your getting meat from
me to eat. This is what you will eat first." They shared the
frog.

But black man is ungrateful. If you are kind to man he
will kill you. ("When you finish with your kindness!")—
Laughter—I have finished. ("Black man is ungrateful. So
you didn't know?")

---

people who are black and who refer to themselves as black men.
Blackness is therefore an identification of self.

Which of the Three Men Was
the Most Powerful?

This is a dilemma tale of the kind discussed by William Bascom in Part II. Dilemma themes occur in type 945 II "The Wooden Doll" (to which of three rescuers shall the mute princess belong?) and type 976 "Which was the noblest act?" Motifs F1023 "Creation of person by co-operation of skillful men" and 216.1 "Tales ending with a question" belong here.

This is my riddle. My story! This one does not have a song. There were three young men. They roamed together and were friends. They each had lovers who lived about as far away as Accra. They had to cross water to go and visit them. One of them took a mirror and looked into it. He combed his hair and exclaimed, "Eh! You, my friends, I see our lovers lying there dead." The second one said, "Eh! See? I have this medicine which will be able to take us to our lovers." The third one said that he had medicine, a wisp, that could wake up their lovers. With the aid of the medicine they were able to reach Accra within minutes.[1] Yaa! They had reached it. They pointed the wisp at their lovers and one of them asked them, "What were you doing? Come out and get dressed. Come out! What allowed you to do such mean things to us?"

[1] The word used in Walii is *minti,* from the English word "minutes."

Which of the three men was the most powerful? The one with the mirror looked into it and saw the girls dead, but could not go to them. The other one had medicine that could wake them up, but he himself couldn't get there. Which of the three was the greatest one? You show the one who was the most powerful. ("But it is the one who owned the medicine." "Ai! The owner of the mirror is powerful because he could see them, but he could not get to them. The owner of the wisp is the one.") Responsibility, Yaa! God says a person is responsible for himself. The Partridge says that it blames its killer more than the one who scared it. The one who saw their lovers was the most powerful. Because of that, the owner of the mirror is the one. Had he not seen them, would they have known that their lovers had died?[2]

Muhammed Escapes to Medina

Here is a legend known to American families in connection with Robert Bruce of Scotland. It is type 967 *The Man Saved by a Spider Web* and motif B523.1 "Spider web over hole saves fugitive," traditional among the Swedes, Lapps, Dutch, Jews, Japanese, and known in India. In Yorkshire it is told of the Christ child in the manger, in biblical lore of King David escaping from Saul, and on the frontier of colonial New York about the Indian fighter Tim Quick, who crawled into a log to escape Indians (Emelyn E. Gardner,

---

[2] My assistants agreed that this tale, which was particularly difficult to translate, was very badly constructed and badly told. It is, however, a rare example of a story in riddle form, for such stories are hardly ever heard in Wa nowadays.

Folklore from the Schoharie Hills, New York, Ann Arbor,
Mich., 1937, p. 27 and note 74). For an African instance
told by the Fang, see R. P. H. Trilles, *Le Totémisme chez
les Fân* (Münster i. W., 1912), p. 139.

NARRATOR: Usmanu of Pontomporeyiri, about fifty
years old.

Tale was simultaneously translated by Mr. Seidu Kpongu
during the interview.

*   *   *

When Mohammed was first born, the people of Mecca
were worshiping stones and other objects, and so the elderly
people rose against Mohammed and said that he was a small
boy and wanted to change their way of living and that they
should get together and kill him. These pagans in Mecca
had a certain form of worshiping, and their God was Sheytan
(Satan), so when Mohammed said that they should stop
this type of worship, Satan told them that they shouldn't
pay attention to what Mohammed was saying. All the pagans
of Mecca organized to kill Mohammed. God sent *malaika*
(angels) to come down and warn Mohammed to leave Mecca
and go to Medina. When he left for Medina the pagans
wanted to catch him and kill him. And so, on the way to
Medina, they were trying to catch him and they saw a certain hole. God had told Mohammed to go into that hole.
After Mohammed had gone into the hole, a big spider came
and spun a big web across the hole. And so, when the pagans
saw the spider web covering that hole, they didn't think
that Mohammed could have gone in it. They didn't know
where he had gone, so they said that they should go back.
They said, "We don't see him." And then Satan said, "No,
Mohammed is in the hole." And they said that this was not
true because, if he were in the hole, he would have broken
the spider's web on entering. But Satan told them that Mohammed was inside the hole. Satan kept on insisting, and

wanted to go into the hole, but the spider was in the way.
And as Satan was challenging the pagans like that, God had
Gabriel come down to challenge Satan. Gabriel was an
angel, and he said to Satan, "Do you have any doubt that
I was sent by God?"

MALI

Bambara oral prose and verse narratives collected by Charles Bird

The following song and prose texts are from a large corpus of traditional texts recorded in the field by Charles Bird in Mali from professional bards between 1965 and 1968. They have been translated from Bambara-Maninka by Charles Bird with the assistance of Massa Maghan Diabaté (Institut des Sciences Humaines, Mali), and Mamadou Konaré and Mamadou Koita. The original tapes are on deposit in the Archives of Traditional Music of the Folklore Institute, Indiana University.

The Coming of Sunjata's Ancestors

This is a short excerpt from the Sunjata epic. Sunjata was the great king in a part of West Africa called the Mande, which is now primarily incorporated in the countries of Mali, Senegal, Guinea, and the Ivory Coast. Sunjata achieved his greatness in the middle of the thirteenth century by unifying his people and casting out the Soso, the invaders. This part of the epic relates how Sunjata's ancestors came to the Mande, the kinds of problems that they faced in the division of power and responsibility, and how their conflicts were resolved.

This episode does not appear in the prose text of D. T. Niane, *The Sundiata Epic* (London, 1965), originally published in French as *Soundjata ou l'Epopée Mandingue* (Paris, 1960). This version of the epic was sung by the great bard from Kita, in Mali, Kelemonson Diabaté, in March 1968. The epic is sung in metrical lines with accompaniment on the *nkoni* (a kind of guitar). The translation that follows is an effort to represent the lines as sung by the bard.

This section of the epic follows the tasks and quests theme common in Märchen and romances. Key motifs are H912 "Tasks assigned at suggestion of jealous brothers," H1233 "Helpers on quest," and H1393 "Quest to distant sage for advice." Dramatis personae known in tradition are "Three brothers" (P251.6.1); "Personifications" (Z110), here the old man called Mystery; and "Person unusual as to his head" (F511)—one side of a boy's head is white, the other side is black. For "Avarice punished" (Q272), Clarke cites twenty-nine instances from West Africa, one of his longest lists for any motif. Other noticeable motifs are D2063.3 "Magic insatiable thirst" (the man immersed in water up to his neck and dying of thirst recalls Tantalus in Greek myth, Q501.2, except that Tantalus is being punished); F718 "Extraordinary well"; and A614 "Explanation of enigmatic phenomenon," with which the section concludes.

The three brothers,
Kanu Sinbon
Kanu-nyogon Sinbon
and Lawali Sinbon:

For three years they stayed.
No fruit trees produced.
No trees produced there in the Mande.
At the end of the three years
they looked into
the three great cases that
they brought from Mecca.
The one for the eldest held gold.
He who followed him
his held the *bark* of trees,
and the youngest,
his held the soil of the earth.
And they began to fight over the gold,
saying "Let us divide the gold."
And the older brother said,
"Division is not good."
And they said,
"You should divide the gold, brother.
You should divide the gold
and give us our share.
To remain in poverty is not good."
He said to his younger brothers,
"Division is not good."
Their dispute did not end

and they had to seek out Mystery.
They came upon a man.
He had filled his gourd with water,
and the water was up to his neck,
and yet he was crying from thirst.
They said, "Here's a mystery!"
But he said, "I am not Mystery
I am but his water carrier,
continue on!"
They crossed the river.
There were three wells.
Two of them were full and flowing into each other.
The one in between was dry as a bone.
They said, "Here's a mystery!"
The well spoke saying to them:
"I am but his well.
Continue on!"
The Mandemen, at the edge of their land,
came upon a young boy.
One side of his head was black;
the other side, white.
They sat down beside him
and they said, "Here's a mystery!"
He said, "I am not Mystery,
I'm but his younger brother.
He's up ahead."
They kept on,
and they came upon
a little old man lying on a chair.
He couldn't tell day from night;
They said, "We have finally found Mystery."
He said, "I am but his younger brother
Whatever person you see,
don't be disrespectful,
he will be Mystery."
They came upon a little man
overseeing the workers in the field.
He was standing at the edge of the land.
A cap was on his head.

He laid down his cane,
"The Mandemen have come
The Mandemen have come
The Mandemen have come
How was your trip?
So you're looking for Mystery?"
He said he was Mystery.
They remained silent.
"Don't you believe me?"
"We don't believe you."
"Don't you believe me?"
"We don't believe you."
"Isn't your father Bilali, who came from Mecca?"
They answered: "Yes."
"Isn't he the one who sent
Kanu Sinbon, Kanu-nyogon Sinbon
and Lawali Sinbon,
to found a village
and call that village Farmtown,
saying that the world started with farming
and it will end with farming?"
They answered, "Yes,
Now we believe you.
It's you who are Mystery!
Here are the three cases.
The messenger of Allah and Bilali spoke together,
and gave these three cases to us,
and told us to found the village, Kiri-Korondi,
called Farmtown,
saying all the people will come there.
My younger brothers,
They demand of me
that I divide the gold.
And I, I've told them
division is not good.
Won't you settle the dispute
between me and my brothers?"
And Mystery said
"The matter is not difficult.

Kanu Sinbon,
Your father, Jon Bilali, said
that you should hold onto the gold.
Your destiny is tied to gold.
Kanu-nyogon Sinbon,
Your father, Jon Bilali, said
that you should hold onto the plants.
Your destiny is tied to plants.
Lawali Sinbon,
Your father, Jon Bilali, said
that you should hold onto the land.
Your destiny is tied to land.
Return to your home, Men of the Mande.
Be on your way!
What sitting won't solve,
travel will."
The Mandemen had begun on their way.
When the youngest brother said,
"Why don't we ask Mystery
to explain the meaning of the four things we saw?
Mystery, wait for us!"
He stopped.
They came to him.
"Mystery, there was a man
who entered the water,
and it was up to his neck,
and yet he cried of thirst.
Won't you tell us what it means?"

"Don't you know what it means, Mandemen?
That is the man
who has gathered a fortune
and cannot spend it."

They said, "Mystery,
we found three wells side by side.
The ones on the sides flowed into each other
while the one in the middle was dry as a bone."

"Don't you know what that means?
Two rich men exchange gifts of friendship
and refuse charity to the poor man,
saying he doesn't know how to get a fortune.
Some must depend on others."

They said, "Mystery,
We found a child.
One side of his head was very black
and the other very white."

"Don't you know what that means?
That's the person
who as a child
gained knowledge before his time."

They said, "Mystery,
we found a little old man lying in a chair
who couldn't tell day from night any more
because of his great old age,
and he said you are older than he,
and yet you look robust.
Won't you tell us its meaning?"

"Don't you know what that means?
A man should do
what he is able to do.
If you try to do
that which you are not able to do,
you grow old before your time."

And the men of the Mande returned to their home.

The Little Bird

This *cantefable* was chanted and sung by Mamari Diabaté, a seventeen-year-old apprentice bard, in quasi-epic style with guitar accompaniment, in Keyla, Mali, in March 1968. In a situation familiar in European Märchen and English ballads, a rejected suitor wins his coveted bride by taking animal shape and thus gaining access to her favors. In type 440 *The Frog King*, which follows the outline of the first tale in the Grimms' collection, the animal lover is a frog. Prominent motifs are T75 "Man scorned by his beloved," known in Africa to the Ekoi (P. A. Talbot, *In the Shadow of the Bush*, New York and London, 1912, p. 357); D150 "Transformation: man to bird," for which Clarke gives seven instances in West Africa; D683 "Transformation by magician"; and D734 "Disenchantment of animal by admission to woman's bed," known in Africa among the Zulu (H. Callaway, *Nursery Tales, Traditions, and Histories of the Zulus*, vol. I, Natal and London, 1868), pp. 63, 321, 327.

Tiyoro, I'll go with you, Tiyoro.
Tiyoro, I'll dance with you, Tiyoro.
Tiyoro, I'll lie down with you, Tiyoro.

Mother, didn't you hear the bird?
The baby bird, didn't you hear what he said?
He said: Tiyoro, he'll go with me, Tiyoro.
Tiyoro, he said, he'll dance with me, Tiyoro.
He said: Tiyoro, he'll lie down with me, Tiyoro.

Let's begin with this young girl, Tiyoro. The young girl would pay no heed to any man, from the time she was born, to the time she was a young girl, right up to her womanhood. A certain young man was stricken with her charms and went to court her. He said he would never be separated from her. Whether she were to accept him or refuse him, he would never leave. One day, he took her to one side and declared himself.

"Little one, I love you. I've heard that you will accept no man." And he asked the girl, and she said simply that she had no love for him. "You won't accept me?" "No," she answered, "I don't like you." "Well," he said, "that's no matter. Let's leave it there for now." The young man went to see Tiyoro's mother. "I love your daughter," he said. "That's fine," she answered. "There's nothing wrong with that. Here she is herself. Talk to each other about it. If she says she loves you, what do I have to do with it?" "But she says that she won't accept me, that she doesn't love me." "Well," the mother replied, "I have nothing to do with that."

That evening the young man came up to Tiyoro again, saying, "Whether you accept me or refuse me, I love you." "Look," she replied, "I don't like you. What are you trying to do? If you say to someone, 'I love you,' and she says she doesn't love you, what else are you looking for? You have to leave it like that." "I can't leave you like that," he replied. This situation lasted for a long time, until the young man in desperation sought the advice of a magician to turn himself into a magnificent little bird.

As it turned out, Tiyoro had gone to the riverside to wash clothes with her younger sister. The magnificent little bird flew down and lighted on the clothes that Tiyoro had washed. "Oh!" she cried, "that little bird is beautiful. I love that little bird." The girl picked up the bird, left all the laundry, and put the little bird in her mother's safekeeping. "Mother," she said, "watch the little bird until I come back from the river. Don't give him to my sister. Don't give him to anyone. The little bird belongs to me!"

After dinner that evening, Tiyoro said that she wanted to go to the village and dance. When she was about to leave, the bird spoke to her: "You can't go and leave me here!" "And why should you be going out with me?" she asked. "If you don't want me, take me back where you found me." Then the bird began to sing:

> Tiyoro, I'll go with you, Tiyoro.
> Tiyoro, I'll go with you, Tiyoro.
> Little Tiyoro, I'll go with you, Tiyoro.
>
> Mother, can't you hear the little bird?
> Mother, can't you hear the little bird in the basket?
> Can't you hear the little bird?
> The bird said, Tiyoro, he'll go with me.
> Tiyoro, Tiyoro, he'll go with me.
> Tiyoro, Tiyoro, saying he'll go with me.

She said, "Mother, didn't you listen to the bird? He said he'll go with me." "Oh, let him go with you," replied the mother. "Mother, how am I going to do that?" "That's all the same to me. I have nothing to do with that." She picked the bird up and carried him to the village square. When they had arrived at the square, Tiyoro wanted to put the little bird down so that she could dance. The little bird did not agree. He said to the girl, "Pick me up and we'll dance together." "I won't agree to that," replied the girl. And again the little bird sang to Tiyoro.

> Tiyoro, I'll dance with you, Tiyoro.
> Tiyoro, I'll dance with you, Tiyoro.
> Little Tiyoro, I'll dance with you, Tiyoro.
>
> Sister, can't you hear the little bird?
> My sister, can't you hear the bird in the basket?
> Can't you hear the little bird?
> He said he'll dance with me, Tiyoro.

Tiyoro, he said he'll dance with me, Tiyoro.
Tiyoro, Tiyoro, he'll dance with me, Tiyoro.

She turned to her sister, asking, "Now, how am I going to
do that?" "Well," her sister replied, "if he wants to dance
with you, pick him up, hold him in your hand, and dance
with him!"

And so they danced and danced. The night grew late and
the dance ended. Tiyoro returned home with her sister and
the little bird. Getting ready for bed, she threw the little
bird outside, saying that she no longer cared for him since
he had ruined her evening of dancing. When she was in bed,
the little bird flew up and sat on the doorsill and he sang:

Tiyoro, I'll lie down with you, Tiyoro.
Ah! Tiyoro, I'll lie down with you, Tiyoro.
Little Tiyoro, I'll lie with you, Tiyoro.

Mother, didn't you hear the little bird?
Mother, didn't you hear what he said?
Didn't you hear the little bird by the door?
He said he'll lie down with me, Tiyoro.
Ah! He'll lie down with me, Tiyoro.
Mother, he'll lie down with me, Tiyoro.

"Ah!" her mother replied, "what do I have to do with that?
It's not my affair. It's all your business. Why don't you leave
me alone and let him lie down with you. A bird and his
beak, what harm can that do?"

So Tiyoro put the bird at the foot of her bed while she
got under the cover. And again the bird began to sing:

Tiyoro, put your cover over me, Tiyoro.
Ah, put your cover over me, Tiyoro.
Little Tiyoro, put your cover over me, Tiyoro.

Mother, didn't you hear the little bird?
The little bird, didn't you hear what he said?
He said, Put your cover over me, Tiyoro.
Tiyoro, put your cover over me, Tiyoro.
Tiyoro, Tiyoro, put your cover over me, Tiyoro.

"Mother," the girl said, "didn't you hear that little bird? He said I should put my cover over him! I certainly won't agree this time!" "As I said before," replied the mother, "this is entirely your affair. What do I have to do with it?"

So the girl picked up the little bird and brought him under her cover. "Mother, can a little bird under a blanket become a handsome young man?" "It's your affair. . . ."

Tiyoro, I'll go with you, Tiyoro.
Tiyoro, I'll lie with you, Tiyoro.
Tiyoro, cover me, Tiyoro.

Ncaaro

This version of Ncaaro, originally a Fula praise song, was sung in Maninlea and collected and translated into French by Massa Maghan Diabaté of the Institut des Sciences Humaines in Mali. It represents an interesting fusion of the Bambara and Fula.

The strength of the hero and the faithfulness of his wife generate such familiar motifs as T210.1 "Faithful wife," T211.2 "Wife's suicide at husband's death," and F628.2.1 "Strong man kills many men at once." A blood pact between husband and wife is cited by Clarke for the Ekoi in West

Africa (P. Amaury Talbot, *In the Shadow of the Bush*, New York, 1912, p. 269). Other motifs to appear are F402.1.11 "Spirit causes death," Q241 "Adultery punished," and D1232 "Magic lute." Clarke cites a number of magical musical instruments in West African tradition under D1210: flute, harp, fiddle, and especially the magic drum (D1211), known to the Ikom, Ashanti, Togo, Ekoi, and Ibo. For East Africa, Arewa reports the magic drum among the Satwa.

Ncaaro calls.
Let no man refuse
Ncaaro calls three things fresh
Wherever men come together
You will find fresh milk
and fresh blood
and fresh excrement.

It is Ardo Gallo
that Ncaaro calls,
Ardo Gallo of Nene
and his beautiful Fula wife.
The day when the bullets struck Ardo Gallo
She took her pestle
and stood in place of her man
head to head
with three hundred Hamdalaye braves
All of them named Amadou
and all of them first sons.

It is Ardo Gallo in readiness
that Ncaaro calls.
It speaks to him
and tells him that the horses have come
with three hundred Hamdalaye braves
all of them named Amadou
and all of them first sons.

Ncaaro calls.
It tells of the day
Ardo Gallo converted.
Ncaaro tells you
that Ardo Gallo, leaving Hamdalaye mosque,
saw a man and a woman tied together
who cried out from their torture.
And Ardo Gallo asked:
"And they, what have they done?"
And he was told adultery.
And Ardo Gallo shouted out:
"If such is the religion of men
I reject it!"
The warrior on guard returned
to Nene.
At the time of his return, many cows and calves lay in the
     grass.
The time was bountiful.

Ncaaro calls.
It calls the fresh milk
But says the three hundred and three Hamdalaye braves,
all of them named Amadou,
all of them first sons,
all of them mounted on horseback,
were riding on Nene.

Ncaaro calls the horses
and fresh blood.
Listen to Ncaaro.
It tells a great tale.
Ardo Gallo took the lives
of three hundred Hamdalaye braves,
but he left three braves living
to return with these words:
"It is Ardo Gallo who I am.
Should I deny heaven;
Should I deny the earth
I will remain Ardo Gallo,

denying heaven
and denying the earth."
Then three hundred three more Hamdalaye braves
rode upon Nene.

Ncaaro speaks again,
Listen to it.
It says that
in the mosque at Hamdalaye
the Marabouts met together.
They called to Allah
and their Master told them
that a secret force was in the lute of Ardo Gallo's bard,
And it was stronger than the force of all Hamdalaye.
Should Ardo Gallo hear it,
he could not be defeated.

Ncaaro cries out,
Saying that on the field of battle
spirits attacked the bard of Ardo Gallo;
it says that Ardo Gallo was killed
by three hundred three Hamdalaye braves,
all of them named Amadou,
all of them first sons.

Ncaaro cries.
Listen to it;
Keep this tale in your minds
so that you know
that the beautiful Fula woman
threw herself in a well.

This night, Ncaaro speaks to you.
It brings back to life the noble Ardo Gallo,
buried by his beautiful Fula wife
in Nene.

Da Monson and Samanyana Basi

The following episode is part of the extended epic cycle of Da Monson, the renowned king of the Segou empire, in central Mali on the Niger river in the eighteenth century. This version was recited in prose style by the bard Moulaye Kida of Segou, in Bamako in January 1967.

Narrative incidents involving kings, lovers, deceivers, magicians, and soothsayers that recur in romance, epic, and folktale can be identified. Familiar characters are "Remarkable beautiful woman" (F575.1), "Treacherous lover" (K2232), "Proud ruler humbled" (L410.2), and "Soothsayer" (D1712). Magical mechanisms appear in the beard that predicts the future (D991.1 "Magic beard") and the king's sorcerers and wise men who advise him on war strategy (D1814.1 "Advice from magician"). Plot contrivances with a familiar ring are "Capture through wiles of a woman" (K778), "Owner put to sleep and goods stolen" (K331.2) through sleeping potions (D1364.7), and "Tests in guessing" (H510). The old seer in the epic (D1712) has his African counterparts in Angola (Heli Chatelain, *Folk-Tales of Angola*, Boston and New York, 1894, p. 57, No. 2, and p. 139, No. 13) and the Congo (John H. Weeks, *Among Congo Cannibals*, London, 1913, p. 202, No. 1).

We have long been told that women have played important roles in establishing the power of many kings. We have also been told that women have played important roles in bringing about their downfall. In this story, told to us by the wise old men of our village, we will find out how the war came about between Da Monson and Samanyana Basi, two powerful kings of small states along the Niger River in what is today Mali. We will find out how Da Monson rose to fame and how Samanyana Basi fell to ruin through the wiles of a woman.

Everyone in those times had heard of Da Monson. His power was well established over the great kingdom of Segou, and his reign had lasted for many years. Not only was he a powerful man, but he knew the secrets of plants, animals, and men as well as many of the best-known wise men. Such was his fame that one could not find a man, woman, or child anywhere who had not heard of him.

Samanyana Basi was a king who reigned over the kingdom of Samanyana, to the south of Segou. He was a well-known king, but he was not as great as Da Monson. Samanyana Basi was a man of average stature, not too tall and not too short. He was, however, perfectly built. The people who had seen him called him an Apollo. In addition to his handsome features, he had a small, attractive beard on his chin.

The Bambara people, over whom both Da Monson and Samanyana Basi reigned, used to invite each other to drink millet beer and honey wine. On this particular occasion Samanyana Basi went to the gathering place in Segou to sample the local brew. He had dressed himself up in his most resplendent robes, of the finest material and the richest colors. He looked so outstanding in his great boubou that Da Monson, when he saw him, found that he surpassed all that people had been saying about him. Da Monson kept looking until he found himself staring at him. Suddenly he got up, strode toward Samanyana Basi, and grabbed hold of his beard, saying:

"Samanyana Basi, that's a cute little beard you have!"

Samanyana Basi looked at him coolly and with a small smile replied:

"Well, my friend, don't you know what this beard is for? It allows me to predict the future."

These words were like a knife in Da Monson's heart. H

felt that Basi was challenging his power. Basi's answer was an insult, a degradation before all the people who had gathered to drink and talk in Segou that day. Da Monson did not show his feelings. He held them inside himself, but he knew that he could never forgive Samanyana Basi. He wanted to kill him right there, but the laws of hospitality forbade his harming a guest. The desire for war came upon him. He wanted to besiege Samanyana and capture Samanyana Basi.

As soon as Samanyana Basi had returned to his kingdom, Da Monson started making preparations. He called up two of his best battalions and sent them to attack Samanyana. Although they were known as great soldiers and although they fought with their usual courage, they failed miserably. When they came to tell the bad news to Da Monson, he grew furious. He was also filled with shame. If you thought about it, you could understand how he felt. He was indeed so much older than Samanyana Basi; his kingdom was so much greater than Samanyana Basi's, and his praises were sung throughout the land in such a way that he would have preferred death to having the news of his defeat spread throughout the country.

What could Da Monson do now? He called all his wise men, seers, and sorcerers. In every part of the land, wherever his power reached, he sent out the call for all the wise men, seers, and sorcerers. He called them all—those who could see ten years back into the past, those who could see ten years into the future, whoever might be able to tell him how the matter could be straightened out, what sacrifices had to be made and what medicines and potions had to be prepared. Whatever person one could point to and say that he might have that ability, Da Monson's call came to him. They all came to gather in the center of Segou.

Remember that Da Monson was not only a king, but a man with a great knowledge of such secrets that only a few men ever get to know. In addition, he was crafty and very wise. There were few if any men who could set a trap for him and come back to tell about it. Before the wise men came, he spent a long time working in the place where he kept all his secrets, his potions, and other magical objects.

After much consideration, it was finally the tortoise and the white rooster that he chose.

Just before the assembled seers were to come to him so that he could explain their task and confide it to them, he got a great, black wooden bowl. He put the white rooster under the bowl and covered it with a black cloth. He then took the tortoise and put it under a white calabash. Da Monson began to get nervous, but he had created a good trap. Whatever person, if he wasn't an evil eye, if he wasn't a sorcerer, and this did not happen before his very eyes, if he didn't hold the truth in his hands, if his secrets and his acts did not lead to the truth, he couldn't possibly know what Da Monson had put under the bowl and the calabash.

In this way Da Monson sprang his puzzle on the wise men. When they all came, before putting them to work he said: "You all know me. I want the pure truth. Those of you who are not lost in obscurity, those of you who have not fallen into incomprehensibility, those of you who believe in yourselves and in your own powers, tell me what is under this black cloth and this white cloth. Those of you who find out what it is should come and tell me. If I believe that what you have said is the truth, you will become my workers."

Going from the cowrie-shell tossers to the sand drawers and on to the pebble tossers, and on to the fetishers and the owners of talking icons, each and every one of them consulted their own particular magic. Many tried, but both the honest and the dishonest ones came to Da Monson and said that they could not tell him what he wanted to know. Finally an old seer came to him and said: "The thing that is under the black cloth is covered by night. It is like white cloth and you might say that the white cloth had blood spilled on it."

The old seer really spoke the truth, because the wooden bowl was black like the night and the rooster was white but his crest was red like blood. Da Monson seized him by the arm and nodded his head in assent.

The man now studied the second part of the puzzle, the white cloth under which was the turtle. After studying it for a while and consulting his secrets, he said: "The thing that is under this white cloth is covered by day. It is like a small stick and resembles a lizard's head. It keeps still and then moves."

Again he spoke the truth. The white calabash was like the day. A turtle is hard like a stick and its head is like a lizard's, and if you have ever seen a turtle, you know that it moves a bit then keeps still.

Da Monson took the man into his house and said: "I want you to tell me the secret that will let me raise an army, attack Samanyana, besiege it, destroy it, and capture Samanyana Basi."

The old seer who had told the truth about the rooster and the tortoise said simply: "Samanyana Basi will never be taken unless you can get his first handful of food from his evening meal, the hat on his head, and the old sandals on his feet. If you can't get these things so that I can work on them, we'll never arrive in Samanyana, much less capture Samanyana Basi. It just can't be done!"

Da Monson then called all the men in his kingdom whom he could trust, who would not betray him. He explained the matter to them and asked them to find someone who could get Samanyana Basi's first handful of food from his evening meal, the sandals from his feet, and the hat from his head, and bring them to Da Monson.

Da Monson's advisers searched the country for someone who could do the job, but they had no success. Finally a woman appeared in Segou. She was without doubt the most beautiful woman ever to be seen in the land. To look at her was more than a pleasure. Her figure alone would make men leave their families. Her smile was hypnotizing. If a man only set his eyes on her once, the second time he would have to lower his head to save himself. If a man didn't love her as a relative, he would have to adore her as a lover or even as a wife. This woman declared herself willing to help her king, Da Monson. One of the king's counselors came to him and said:

"There is a woman here in Segou called Ten. She is the daughter of a praise singer. She is without a doubt the most beautiful woman in your kingdom. In addition, she is very crafty and knows every secret for entering men's hearts and destroying their minds."

Da Monson called Ten to his court so that she could explain her plan. Ten arrived and kneeled before the king, surrounded by his counselors, saying:

"This whole country, its trees, its animals, and its people, from the little river far to the south to the great river far to the north, belongs to you. If something is bothering you, it is we who must correct it. If you will allow me, I think that I will be able to solve your problem."

Da Monson listened to her words, nodding his head with approval. When she had finished, he said:

"What do you want me to give you?"

Ten said, "Before I go, I want the best jewelry brought to me, gold, silver, precious stones, cowrie shells, the most beautiful and elegant cloth, and the finest blankets made in Masina. In addition, I want you to call your master brewers to prepare their best beer and wine. When they have finished, I will treat it with spices. Once a man has drunk the beer that I shall prepare, he will no longer be a man. He will lose his reason and I will be able to do what I want to with him. I will go to Samanyana and Samanyana Basi will drink his own downfall."

The brewers brought Ten their finest wine and beer. After putting many secret herbs and spices in it, she sweetened the beer with honey and added both red and black pepper. The brew was so strong and fiery that the average man, such as you or me, could not even smell it without losing his senses.

Now Ten was ready. Da Monson gave her his fastest canoe. It was well over thirty feet long, sleek and shiny, and it cut through the water like a great boa. Da Monson sent her his four best Somono fishermen, the champion canoe men of the Niger River. These four young giants, arms like the trunks of trees, necks and shoulders like bulls, seized their great bamboo poles and sent the canoe laden with the beautiful Ten and her many riches shooting upstream. When the river deepened, without losing a stroke they took their paddles, making the canoe fly against the current. It seemed as if the great river held its strength back in awe, overwhelmed by the beauty and perfection of the canoe, its crew, and its cargo.

Ten was stretched out under the open cabin, which she had covered with a royal tapestry woven by the masters from Mopti, to the north. When they reached the open river, the crocodiles, the hippos, the great Niger perch and fierce dogfish, even the river terns sang their praises to the beautiful Ten. She saw every bird, beast, and fish that she had ever seen and many that she, or any man, had never seen before. Ten did not lose herself to these wonders, however. She was deep in thought, working out her plan of attack against Samanyana Basi.

The canoemen poled and paddled, paddled and poled, until finally, their whiplike bodies glistening in the orange light of the setting sun, they guided the bow of the canoe to touch gently on the sandy beach of Samanyana.

The women who had come down to the river to get water, those who were there to bathe, those who had been washing clothes, every one of them stood transfixed. They could not move their eyes from Ten. Some said that she was the daughter of some great king, who was just passing by. Some said that she was on her way to marry a powerful prince. Others said that it was Samanyana Basi himself who had called her to him. Rumors flew. Speculation grew. But Ten never set foot on the beach. She spent three days in the canoe on the beach, never even mentioning that she wanted to greet Samanyana Basi.

The news finally reached Samanyana Basi that a woman had arrived who was so magnificent that she surpassed the limits of men's most imaginative desires.

Samanyana Basi was very suspicious, but he was also too curious. He said to his counselors, "Whoever this woman is, I think she has come here to do someone's dirty work. However, we do know that, from what people say about her, she is not a woman to be neglected. In any case, if she comes before me, we'll soon find out what she is up to. Go and bring her here."

The messengers went up to Ten's canoe and told her that Samanyana Basi wanted her to be in his reception hall in the wink of an eye. Ten was radiant with jewelry and the finest cloth. She walked up the bank and through the village with such assurance and majesty that the people fell away before her as they would before a great queen. She swept into the reception hall, knelt before Samanyana Basi and greeted him before his courtiers.

It was the custom of the country to offer visitors, whether men or women, a large gourdful of millet beer so that they might first cut their thirst before explaining the purpose of their visit. They filled up a gourd and gave it to Ten. She drank it down as if it were water. They filled up another gourd and she drank that one down even quicker than the first.

"By Allah," they exclaimed, "woman, you must have been about ready to die of thirst to drink our beer like that. It's lucky you came up from the beach when you did, but you'd better not drink any more of our beer like that, if you want to stay on your feet."

"What!" Ten replied. "Was that your beer? Why, in Segou that's what we give to our children when they come in hot and sweaty from an afternoon's play. I surely didn't think that this was the beer that you drank together with your great king here. That's why I drank it the way I did. You certainly must know that it's not very strong and surely you wouldn't call it a man's drink!"

"Well," said some, "the conversation is getting interesting. As our ancestors have said, if a woman goes ahead and swallows a turtle, a man must then swallow a lizard."

Everyone fell quiet, waiting for Samanyana Basi to speak.

"Do you think, woman, that Segou Da Monson's beer is better than this?"

"Why, this doesn't even come near it!" replied Ten. "You just can't even compare them. If you call this stuff beer, just a little sip of Da Monson's would make you dizzy."

"And who," asked Basi, "knows how to make this famous beer?"

"I do," Ten replied quickly.

"All right, then. You're going to stay right here. I need you in my court. You aren't going to make beer for anyone but me."

"I agree," replied Ten. "I came here looking for the man that I have heard people praising throughout the country. I have heard that Samanyana Basi is greater than any man alive. However, from what I've seen here, I don't think you're the man I was looking for. Nonetheless, if you say I should stay here, I'm like the fruit that has fallen into the basket. I happen to have a sample of Da Monson's beer and some aged honey wine down in the canoe. I'll bring them up and you can try them. If they please you, I'll stay here and make more for you."

Ten had sprung her trap well. Basi's youthful pride was cut by her quick tongue. Not only did he want to show himself better than Da Monson, but already half crazed by the beauty of her face and body, which would quicken the blood of the oldest of men, he wanted to show her that he was the man she had been looking for, who could satisfy her and make her love him.

The servants brought up two great jugs. Samanyana Basi filled his gourd with Ten's beer and drank it down. Although he tried to remain impassive, his eyes could not help but show his pleasure at its sweetness and spicy flavor. He filled his calabash with the honey wine and drank that down. When he emptied the cup, Ten knew that he was now defenseless. Samanyana Basi could now no longer keep his eyes off her.

Like many rulers, young or old, who do not have the confidence of the people, Samanyana Basi distrusted everyone, even his closest advisers. He never ate a meal with anyone in fear of being poisoned. This evening, however, when the servants brought his meal, Basi, drunk with Ten's charms as well as her beer, ordered his counselors away as usual, but held Ten by the hand, saying,

"Woman, tonight you are going to eat with me. Before the night is over, you will not regret having come to seek Samanyana Basi."

Ten laughed, overwhelming Basi with her dazzling teeth and eyes sparkling with a fire that promised more than a man would let himself imagine. She slipped from his grasp and filled his gourd again.

"I'm also a very good cook," she said. "Why don't you let me fix a meal that you will never forget?"

Samanyana Basi, in his present state, could only agree, but bade her be quick since his desire for her left him nearly breathless. Ten prepared a heaping bowl of rice and covered it with a rich meat sauce in which the spices and pepper alone were enough to make a man lose his senses. All the while, she kept her eye on Basi's gourd. As soon as he emptied it, she filled it again for him. The meal prepared, Ten set it down before Samanyana and sat down close to him, brushing temptingly against him and letting his head fill with the aroma of the scented oils she had rubbed into her body. Samanyana Basi reached into the bowl, bringing out a handful of rice and meat. As he was bringing his hand up to his mouth, Ten reached out as if to dip her hand into the bowl and knocked the food from Basi's hand.

"Oh!" she cried. "Look how terrible I am!"

"What's the matter?" asked Samanyana Basi. "What are you crying about?"

"I am so clumsy. I've knocked the food right out of your hand onto the floor."

"So, what's the matter with that?" Basi replied. "Look at all that we have left in the bowl. We have more to do than to eat all that. There's no reason to cry about the little bit that's on the floor."

Basi took another handful and began to eat with great pleasure. Ten reached down, picked up the spilled food, wrapped it in her handkerchief and hid it to one side. The peppery sauce increased Basi's thirst and Ten was quick to fill his gourd. They ate and drank until the food was finished. In the last drink she poured for Basi, Ten slipped a strong sleeping potion. Basi, thinking of the night of adventure, drank down the potion. Moments later, he fell into a deep sleep. Ten quickly wrapped her robes around her, walked over to the helpless Basi and yanked off his sandals and pulled off his hat, as well as the amulets hanging from his neck. She snatched up her handkerchief containing Basi's first handful of food from his evening meal, and, carefully checking to see that no one was about, ran down to the beach, where the canoe and her men were waiting. The canoe flew downstream like a sliver of moonlight on the black water. The waves of its wake washing on Samanyana's shore were Ten's last caress to the young man who was brash enough to confront Da Monson.

As dawn was breaking over Segou, the canoe pulled into the port. Ten leaped out with her prizes and ran to give them directly to Da Monson. Da called the wise man and gave him the objects he had requested. After working a night and a day on them, the wise man discovered the sacrifices and potions that would allow Da Monson's army to break Samanyana Basi's magic charms and defeat him.

Da Monson sent two battalions to attack Samanyana. After one day of siege, they broke through the defenses, scattered Basi's soldiers, and razed the town. Basi, stripped of his magical protection, was just another man, helpless before Da Monson's power. He was captured and summarily beheaded.

There you see the deeds of Ten. By her beauty and her wiles, she helped build the empire of one king and destroy that of another.

A woman can be a beautiful thing, but she can also be evil. What is honey to one man may be poison to another.

May Allah protect us from them and send us only the good ones.

The Vulture

"The Vulture" ("Duga" in Bambara) is the oldest and most widespread song known in West Africa, recorded in early Arabic texts. It is a praise song for warriors and hunters celebrating heroism. This story begins with the song being sung for the King of Koré, but since Da Monson defeats him, the song becomes a tribute to the victor and was incorporated in the epic cycle for Da Monson, as was the preceding story about Samanyana Basi. It was customarily sung for the warriors who killed a lion, an elephant, or another warrior.

It was sung by Bakoroba Koné, an elderly bard, in Segou, April 1968, accompanied by two female singers, Penta Donté and Hawa Koné, who sang the songs inserted at intervals in the epic recitation (indicated by indentation).

In this part of the epic the crocodile plays a significant role. "Helpful crocodile or alligator" (B491.3) is known among the Temne (Christian F. Schlenker, *A Collection of Temne Traditions, Fables, and Proverbs, with an English Translation,* London, 1861, p. 93) and in Madagascar. "Animals hide boy [here a king] in their belly to protect him" (B529.1) has been reported for India. Other stock characters are "Treacherous wife" (K2213) who is punished (Q261.2); "Faithful servant" (P361); and the king who commits suicide (P163.0.1), also known in Yoruba tradition (M. I. Ogumefu, *Yoruba Legends,* London, 1929, p. 36). The task of bailing out a pond (H1113) has an African instance among the Benga (R. H. Nassau, *Where Animals*

Talk: West African Folklore Tales, London, 1914, p. 216,
No. 33). Clarke gives seven West African examples of
"Transformation: man to bird" (D150). Deception motifs
are K778 "Capture through the wiles of a woman" and
K818.3 "Victim's arrows [here gunpowder] made harmless."

Mawula! Mawula! Karadige,
no man speaks against the vulture
when the eagle is not on wing.
The beer drinkers behind the river
and bitterness never meet.
Ah! Karadige,
the brave is a man of the moment
but where are the braves of yesteryear?
No matter how good a man may be,
words will be said behind his back.
Ah! Karadige, I call to you,
little man, great man.
In the name of Allah,
whose prophet is Muhammed,
the matter turned badly for the cursed child.

It is the truth she sings.
This was sung for the Old Vulture of Koré,
the king seated in Koré.
This was sung for him by his bards.
No matter how good a man may be,
words will be said behind his back.
One time having drunk too much
and lying about in his palace,
he told one of his slaves
to tell Da Monson of Segou
that Da should know there was thread
to weave in Koré.
"I've yet to find a weaver for it.

Tell him to come weave my thread.
Go quickly, come back quickly!"

> Ah! Karadige.
> The day that Baguinda Mari fell,
> the eagle was flying;
> and that day of battle in Nyamina . . .
> No matter how good a man may be,
> words will be said behind his back.

The servant came and delivered the message to Da.
Da spoke to his bard:
"Dante, great master of truth," he said,
"Didn't you hear the words of the messenger?
He said we should go.
He said he had some thread.
He said that Segou should come weave his thread.
He said he knows not of Segou,
but our weaving."
And he said, "Master of truth,
send him on his way."
He spoke to the messenger, saying:
"When you arrive, tell him
that Segou will come and weave his thread
so that it will be beautiful.

> O Vulture of majestic flight!
> Vulture of beautiful flight!
> One bird, four wings.
> O bird who floats in the skies
> and yet can scratch the ground.
> When the bird lands,
> he gouges a well,
> a well of God,
> like a well in the Mande mountains.

Da Monson spoke: "Master of Truth,"
he said, "what is your thought on these words?"
"Because of these words," he replied,
"I think of one thing,
a measure of gold.
If you take one and
give it to a man
to give to the Old Vulture's first wife,
so that she will help us in this matter,
then, the way to the Vulture of Koré,
she will tell it to us."

O Eagle, only treachery can destroy familial love.
Descendance from the woman,
descendance from the woman has ended.
But descendance from the woman is better than ste-
    rility,
    and sterility is better than an evil child.

They took out a measure of gold
and placed it in the hand of a man
who gave it to the first wife of Vulture,
telling her that this was the cost of kola,
saying that Segou spoke thus,
that this was her gift,
and as such, the rest remains in Segou.
She must, he said, apply herself
and tell us the way to capture the Old Vulture.
That is the work you must do for us.

Oh! In the name of Allah!
The bird suffered much.
He slung the quiver on his shoulder.
He grabbed the bow in hand

to go seize Jakuruna Toto,
right up to Jakuruna;
and he cut off his great head
at the wide opening of his throat;
and his head rolled on the ground
like a sacrificial bull of a Mande brave;
and he, he got off with great effort
to seize Samanyana Basi,
right up to Samanyana.

The woman sent a man
to tell them that her husband
was a man who already knew his destiny.
He spoke with a crocodile.
She said that
if they did not move to the west of the village,
they would spend a year without defeating the Old Vulture.
As soon as the messenger came to say this to Da Monson,
and as soon as they understood these words,
they took the camp baggage,
and moved between the village
and the setting sun.
The first wife ran out to them
throwing herself on her knees before them:
"Dante, Master of Truth, tell the king I have come."
"Did you receive the message," he replied.
"Yes, I received the message."
"Wonderful," he answered. "This is but a gift for you.
The rest awaits you in Segou,
so that you will help us in our task."

In the name of God,
whose prophet is Muhammed,
a man is not God.
Koliko Duga Sirima became angry
and angrier and angrier.
He jammed his quiver on his head,

seized his bow in one hand,
and went to capture Sobe Masa
alive!
Come quiet, Bajubanen.
Leave loud!

When they finished talking,
she returned to the village
and assembled her servants.
They carried water and
brought it to the powder room,
where they wet all the powder.
When the powder was all wet down,
she sent a man to tell Da Monson:
"Surround the village.
I have done my work!"
The battle raged for three days.
Segou could not break through.
As soon as the original rifle charges were exhausted,
those who went to get fresh powder
found the powder wet.
They went to Vulture saying: "King!"
"Yes."
"And the powder, wasn't it made ready?"
"It was made ready," he replied.
"Well, it has all become water!"
"Then," he asked, "who will go to Segou?
Is it we who will be captured by Segou?
Now, that's an incredible thing!"
He left to go look,
and found all the powder wet.
Three days passed.
They were finally able to crack through to the
    Old Vulture's wells.
They destroyed everything without value
and carried off the rest.
The Old Vulture ran off to the men's house,
where the great crocodile awaited him.

It swallowed him and went to lie in the pond.
Da Monson's warriors looked everywhere for him,
but they didn't see him.
They began an investigation.
"A man's secret is always held by his woman.
A man's secret is always held by his woman.
Ask the woman!"
They called the woman and came with her.
The woman said her words were true.
"The great pond to the east,
That is where he and the crocodile speak.
That's who is his total master.
If, therefore, you empty the pond completely,
and you find the crocodile,
You will see him."
They all worked together,
completely emptying the pond.
The crocodile tried to flee,
but they grabbed it and cut open its stomach,
pulling the Old Vulture from inside.
"Old Vulture of Koré!"
"Yes?"
"You said Segou should come weave your thread,
and thus, we have come.
Give us some thread to weave for you."
They brought the Old Vulture of Koré out,
and sat him down in the village square.
They called the Vulture's bards.
The bards having been called, Da Monson said:
"That which you have sung for the Old Vulture of Koré,
You will sing before us now for all to hear,
because today you will go to Segou."
When this was said,
the Old Vulture, seated among his bards,
grew angrier and angrier.
In his great anger, he transformed himself
and flew off into the sky.
He circled about in the heavens
and then floated back down.

"Da," he said, "you alone are not able to defeat me.
It's my wife who betrayed me.
If she hadn't betrayed me,
you never would have defeated me."
He sat back down among his bards.
Again he grew angry
and again he transformed himself
and again he flew off into the sky
until he could calm himself.
He returned once more and said:
"Da, you still can't defeat me,
but I will not leave my bards in your hands.
Do with me what you will."
"What would please us," Da replied,
"is to bring you back to Segou."
And the Old Vulture responded: "That cannot be me,
Segou will never lay its eyes on me.
You'd better put that idea aside."
"Well, your bards," Da suggested,
"we will take them to Segou."
But the bards were quick to reply,
"Segou will never lay eyes on us.
We have drunk honey wine together.
Should it be a question of a more bitter drink,
we'll drink that together, too."
On saying this, the bards all killed themselves.
The Old Vulture turned to Da
and said that Da could never kill him,
that Da could never capture him,
but if Da would permit it,
he would kill himself.
If permission were not granted,
no one would be able to defeat him.
The Vulture took all the amulets from his body,
then grabbed a rifle and shot himself.
This done, the woman ran up, saying:
"King, as you have requested, so have I done."
He answered her, saying, "Thank you for your help.
You have greatly pleased us.

That which you have done for us,
its reward is not here with us.
That which you were given,
do you still have it here?"
"Yes, it is here," she replied.
"Then bring it here to us.
Didn't we tell you
the remainder awaits you in Segou?
It is being kept there for you."
The woman returned with the gold.
"Thank you," Da said, "you made no mistake.
But, Dante, Master of Truth, tell this woman
that we are right to fear her.
We cannot take her to Segou.
If we were to take her to Segou,
once my power was established,
if anyone were to try to crush me,
she would help him find my secrets.
I cannot take her back.
Add her to her man over there."
They bashed in her head
and threw her body by her husband's.
And Da, calling out to his drummers,
his trumpeters, and his bards, said,
"Well, let's be off to Segou
and those things of which you will sing;
if you are to sing them in Segou,
you'd better prepare them well!"

Ah! The offering of white kola by evil kin
Mawula!
None of that is new to the Vulture.
Who would speak against the Vulture?
Samanyana Basi spoke against him,
and his head was cut off
at the opening of his great throat
Ah, Bajubanen!
You might say a sacrificial bull of a Mande brave.

It is said that the poor man,
if he should speak of the affairs of kings,
will be given away as a gift by the king.

They returned to Segou;
three hundred battalions in Segou.
They gathered together
and sat in the square.
There was much beer
and honey wine.
Thus they celebrated right down to the fieriest brew.

Oh! Segou! One can succeed in Segou.
Oh! Segou! There is no one who doesn't go to Segou.
E! Even if a double-barreled king,
even if he were a king with a house of bards.
You are a great warrior, Karadige,
but Da was the greatest of warriors.

CAMEROUN

Gbaya tales collected
by Philip A. Noss

Wanto's Search for Food

by Andre Yaamgbai[1]

This narrative has the qualities of an origin myth. Mythological motifs are A541.2 "Culture hero as god of agriculture," A531 "Culture hero (demigod) overcomes monsters," A2684 "Origin of cultivated plants," A801 "Earth-mother," and A810 "Primeval water." Kenneth W. Clarke cites West African tales that deal with the origin of chili pepper, yams, calabash, and tomatoes ("A Motif-Index of the Folktales of Culture-Area V, West Africa," Indiana University doctoral dissertation in Folklore, 1957, p. 100).

It was a year of hunger, and Wanto set out in search of food. He dug up some roots of trees, came home, ate them, and slept, with nothing else to eat. He went out again and dug up some wild yams; he returned, ate them, and slept on them. No sir-ee! he decided, this was not satisfactory.

One day as Wanto was out looking for food, he climbed up out of a valley to continue on his way. But as he was about to go around a deep gully where the earth had divided and where the grass leaned over into it defu defu defu, he happened to notice that there were some peanut leaves

[1] Andre Yaamgbai was the Gbaya pastor in Kalhaldi, about forty years of age. He told the tale to a group of friends around the fire under his granary on a rainy September day in 1967. Tape VIII, 9.

protruding out of the water *kengeree*. Corn leaves protruded, leaves of different things, all the little things that we plant upon this earth, all protruded from the water. From cassava leaves to peanut leaves to yam leaves, cocoa yam leaves, leaves, what else shall I name, all the fruits that we now eat protruded out of the water. Wanto gazed at it *feee* and then left, came back home, and went to bed.

Now, what had happened was that when she heard Wanto, she had dropped into the water. So Wanto waited until the next day—his liver didn't let up on it.[2] The sun came up, and when it was overhead, Wanto set off again. He went all the way, he crept up, crept up, crept up, and then he heard her. When she heard the sound of Wanto, she dropped *huvuvuvu* and hit the water *gumm*. When Wanto came to the place where she had been, he saw a little peanut that had broken off and fallen down. A little squash had fallen off, all the various things that had been on her, an ear of corn had broken off, and Wanto gathered them, brought them back, roasted them and ate them. He hey! it was really tasty, and he said, "Oh, so what's in the water—oh, so what's in the water—so it's food that's in the water!"

Wanto said to his children, "Children, cut some herbs, cut herbs.[3] I've found something for us to eat." So the children went to the herbs and cut enough to fill a big cassava pot, and then Wanto went off and from the edge of the gully cleared a wide path all the way to the top of the hill away from the valley. He went and carved a little drum, he tuned it up carefully and set it there. Then, "Children, take the herbs and line up along the path, line up along the path. And get clubs and go alongside the herbs, go alongside them. Okay, then we will just dance up there on top of the hill and see what's in the water." He took the drums, went up on top of the hill and started to beat:

[2] The seat of the emotions and will is the liver. All night long he thought about the experience of the day at the gully.

[3] The herbs here referred to are called *wo* in Gbaya. They are used in cooking and are very slimy when prepared.

Beteeteetee, ilɛng, ilɛng, ilɛng,[4]
  That's cassava leaves, ilɛng, ilɛng.
Beteeteetee, ilɛng, ilɛng, ilɛng,
  That's squash leaves, ilɛng, ilɛng.
Beteeteetee, ilɛng, ilɛng, ilɛng,
  That's peanut leaves, ilɛng, ilɛng.
Beteeteetee, ilɛng, ilɛng, ilɛng,
  That's gourd leaves, ilɛng, ilɛng.
Beteeteetee, ilɛng, ilɛng, ilɛng,
  That's cassava leaves, ilɛng, ilɛng.
Beteeteetee, ilɛng, ilɛng, ilɛng,
  That's squash leaves, ilɛng, ilɛng.
Beteeteetee, ilɛng, ilɛng, ilɛng,
  That's yam leaves, ilɛng, ilɛng.
Beteeteetee, ilɛng, ilɛng, ilɛng,
  That's cassava leaves, ilɛng, ilɛng.
Beteeteetee, ilɛng, ilɛng, ilɛng,
  That's cassava leaves, ilɛng, ilɛng.

Then the woman rose out of the water there *Bɛt*, and the huge thing came up like lightning *gɛgɛgɛgɛgɛ*; when you looked at her body, the names of the crops that covered it *wasawuzuu*, squash *Bilong Bilong Bilong*, corn, all different kinds of things, you couldn't even name them all. She came up to the place and started dancing *lip*. As she danced, the children began pulling off peanuts and eating, they began breaking off corn. The things that fell off as she leaped in dance, the children gathered and ate, and the dance was really going *lip!* Then Wanto winked to the children *Busak* and they headed for their clubs. As she ran down and slipped on the slimy herbs they laid their clubs onto her *rut*. She leaped up *Bɛt* and carried the foods down, you know how slippery those herbs are, she fell and they laid their clubs on her *rut*, and they hit the old woman *tɔwɔrɔ* all the way down until she fell *gurum* into the water. (*laughter*)

4 *Beteeteetee* is an ideophone describing the sound of the drum. The repeated *ilɛng* describes the quantity and weight of the leaves that hung from the woman's body.

Wanto clicked *gbak* with satisfaction, "Okay, children, get the baskets. She just stays down there in the water taking the food with her and we don't have any food. So okay, see, children, when I'm about to go wandering, you say that I wander too much. Laiso, do you see? When I say I'll go and look for food, you say I wander too much, I wander too much. Okay, if I didn't wander, would you have gotten food now?"

So you see, the first thing, what happened that made food crops fill the earth, was through Wanto. If it had not been for Wanto, this woman would have hoarded the food there under the water. But what caused the food to scatter so that people plant cassava, so that we have things to eat now, squash, peanuts, corn, various things that are in the fields, sugar cane, what shall I name, yams, cocoa yams, sweet potatoes, all those things are what the woman gathered under the water there—it was Wanto, it was he who caused all those things to multiply throughout the earth so that we have today food. So it was. That's why I say that in the wanderings of a person, people wander: some wander with cleverness to find something; but some people just wander aimlessly. So we see that in Wanto's wandering, he was wandering in search of something, and some people were complaining about him without cause. So it is I, Andre Yaamgbai, telling you this again.

Rabbit and the Carnivores

by Daniel Ndanga[1]

Several animal motifs are recognizable here: B211.2.6 "Speaking rabbit," B240.4 "Lion as king of animals" (in this case of the carnivores), B260 "Animal warfare," and B297.1 "Animal plays musical instrument" (here rabbit plays a bell), reported for Africa among tribes of western Sudan, and among the Luba, where a toad and chameleon play a drum and xylophone. The deception acts of the rabbit are pivotal in the story: K1892.1 "Trickster hides in bag in order to be carried" and K2368 "Enemy deceived into overestimating opponents: retreat."

It was the little animals, all the little, sharp-toothed animals, all the fierce animals—they lived in a certain valley, and their town, no one visited it. So they lived there a long time, just always killing animals and bringing them back, killing animals and bringing them back, killing animals and bringing them back.

Then one day Rabbit was out wandering and decided to go to the valley because that is a very good place for rab-

1 Daniel Ndanga was a well-known performer among his friends. Though only about thirty years old, he had few equals. He told this tale in the home of Rev. Andre Yadji to a group of family and friends in the evening of August 21, 1966, in Betare Oya. Tape II, 43.

bits to find food. But the other people told Rabbit,[2] "Rabbit, don't go there! That's the place where the clan of dangerous, sharp-toothed animals live." Rabbit thought about it, and went back. Rabbit, when he went out again, he would sneak around the valley, avoiding the valley, avoiding the valley.

Rabbit thought, "But now, what is this? This land belongs to all of us, and then they say there is a ruler, there is a chief—now, if you are a ruler, won't your subjects go to visit you? Won't strangers come to greet you?" But they said, no, he shouldn't go there, because he kills animals. "Since your fur resembles an animal, if you go there, he will kill you," they said.

Rabbit thought, Rabbit said, "Okay, now that I have heard that the powerful ones hate us, what we will do is this: we will chase each other. The enemies will chase each other out of this valley. If I try in vain, then I will know that it was something on this earth that was too powerful for me."

Rabbit waited a while, son of a bitch! Now Rabbit had a large flock of chickens and the chickens laid many eggs, so many that if you were to come to the place, wow-wee! the eggs filled all the granaries around the house! So Rabbit went back and forged a great big bell, just the opening of the bell alone was this wide! Its clapper was so big that if you struck it, wow-wee! Rabbit girded himself all up and then came to the edge of the water that belonged to Lion and his people, where the dangerous animals lived. He climbed into a stand of reeds Mɛk Mɛk Mɛk Mɛk Mɛk Mɛk and squatted down there.

He waited there and suddenly he heard, son of a bitch! the chief of the village where they lived, it was he, Lion, who sent them to come and draw water. The chief was Lion. When he sent them to do something, they would come and do it. If he didn't send them, they wouldn't come.

So Lion sent Fox, he said that Fox should come and draw water so that they could prepare food for him, Lion, to eat, so that when the sun was up *ser*, they could scatter to hunt

---

[2] The characters in the tale, though animals, are treated also as people. Technically, the hero *dɔmɔ* is a hare, but I have chosen to translate it as rabbit.

for animals. So Rabbit, Rabbit heard the feet of Fox bounding *kirik kirik*, he readied the basket of eggs that he had,
setting it beside himself, he readied the bell, untying its cover,
putting it close at hand. Then when Fox arrived like this,
just as he took his pot and began to rinse it out *hokoro hokoro*
to wash it out before filling it with water, son of a bitch!
Rabbit began with his great bell!

> Gbevevevevevevel
> My dogs don't hunt with bells, sic 'em, Big Lion![3]
> The little animals are all dead, tɛndɛɛ vɛm
>   It will get in my eyes, tɛndɛɛ
> Hyena, it will get in your eyes, tɛndɛɛ vɛm
>   It will get in your eyes, tɛndɛɛ
> Fox, it will get in your eyes, tɛndɛɛ vɛm
>   Vɛm tɛndɛɛ
> The little animals are all dead, tɛndɛɛ vɛm
>   Vɛm tɛndɛɛ
> Hyena, it will get in my eyes, tɛndɛɛ vɛm
>   It will get in my eyes, tɛndɛɛ
> The little animals are all dead, tɛndɛɛ vɛm
>   Vɛm tɛndɛɛ

Son of a bitch! Fox listened. "Now, what kind of a bell
is this that makes the earth shake all around? Since we
moved to this place with our fathers, nothing like this has
ever come to the edge of our stream. What is it?" Son of a
bitch! and Fox ran *kiliwili!* As he was going to stop a moment to listen before tearing off for town, Rabbit let loose
with a rotten egg, son of a bitch! The egg flew *tqqq*. As

[3] The hero sings his hunting song, warning the prey that his
dogs are dangerous but silent. They do not wear bells that might
be heard as they approach. The lines are all filled with meaning.
"Big Lion" is the name of one of Rabbit's dogs, which at the same
time satirizes Lion. "The little animals" that are dead may be the
game killed by Lion and the carnivores, or by the hunter who is
now singing to the sound of his bell. The rotten egg is what will get
in the eyes. The refrain is from a farming song, as the farmer presses
down the grass before beginning to hoe his field.

Fox cocked his head to listen, *lop!* the egg landed on the top of his head, and Rabbit shouted, "Touch it with your hand! Touch it! Touch it!" And when he touched it and then smelled it, by God . . .

> My head is open, to fe, fe ye[4]
> The world is ruined, to fe, fe ye
> Scatter, scatter, to fe
> > Die, it is Rabbit's water, to fe
> > See, it is Rabbit's water, to fe
> > See, it is Rabbit's water, to fe
> My head is open, to fe, Chief,
> The world is ruined, to fe
> > See, something has come to the water's edge, to fe, fe ye
> > Rabbit's water . . .

And so, *bakatak bakatak bakatak* he burst into the compound after the chief, saying, "Chief! The world is ruined! Since we built our town here nothing like this has happened before!" And the chief said, "What is this?" He asked what had happened, and he replied, "Something has arrived at the edge of the water and as for me, I am terribly afraid! Since we began living together here with you, I have heard of nothing like this." That's what Fox went back and told the chief, who responded, "No, sir! Are you such a coward? You just always eat things raw, you just eat things raw without even putting them on the fire and cooking them before you eat them. You're too much of a glutton!"

Then he sent Hyena. Hyena was a very strong animal, Hyena was a strong person, Hyena should run down and draw water quickly and come back and prepare cassava to eat so that he could leave. And so Hyena rushed down *hɔVɔVɔvɔ*. When he arrived at the stream he rinsed, rinsed,

---

[4] The refrain sung by the fleeing animal represents a play on words. "Fe ye" is the sound of the whistle of the successful hunter returning to his village. Here it is the song of the frightened carnivore, fleeing from what might be his prey, thinking that his brains are coming out.

and rinsed, and as he washed out the pot quickly, son of a
bitch! Rabbit heard and put his hand to the bell!

> Gbeveveveveveve!
> My dogs don't hunt with bells, sic 'em, Big Lion!
> The little animals are all dead, tɛndɛɛ vɛm
>   It will get in my eyes, tɛndɛɛ
> Hyena, it will get in your eyes, tɛndɛɛ vɛm
>   It will get in your eyes, tɛndɛɛ
> The little animals are all dead, tɛndɛɛ vɛm
>   All dead, tɛndɛɛ
> The little animals are all dead, tɛndɛɛ vɛm
>   Vɛm tɛndɛɛ
> The little animals are all dead, tɛndɛɛ vɛm
>   Vɛm tɛndɛɛ
> The little animals are all dead, tɛndɛɛ vɛm
>   It will get in my eyes, tɛndɛɛ
> It will get in your eyes, tɛndɛɛ vɛm
>   It will get in your eyes, tɛndɛɛ
> The little animals are all dead, tɛndɛɛ vɛm
>   Vɛm tɛndɛɛ
> The little animals are all dead, tɛndɛɛ vɛm
>   It will get in your eyes, tɛndɛɛ
> It will get in your eyes, tɛndɛɛ vɛm

   Son of a bitch! Wow! Hyena heard that, Hyena heard
that and said to himself, "No, sir! The kind of song that is
being sung here in the reeds, see, it's bad!" Then as Hyena
turned to run *zak vakdilak* to escape up to the top of the
hill to listen from there, son of a bitch! *lôp!* As he leaped to
flee, he let loose with a rotten egg, and as Hyena turned
his head like this, *lôp!* the egg hit him on the top of the
head! And then he shouted, "Touch it! Touch it!" And when
he touched it and smelled it, mm mmm!

> My head is open, to fe, fe ye
> The world is ruined, to fe, fe ye
> Scatter, scatter, to fe

Die, it is Rabbit's water, to fe
See, it is Rabbit's water, to fe
See, it is Rabbit's water, to fe, fe ye

BaDambang baDambang baDambang baDambang baDambang baDambang purup! he burst into the compound after the chief! And he said that since he had begun living in that town he had never seen anything like that! So he should send some other really strong person to draw the water. As for himself, he wouldn't go near the place!

So all the little sharp-toothed animals came and tried to draw water. There was no way. Rabbit closed off the way from them. Finally Lion said, "No, sir! Now your actions, you are all my great followers and when I look at you, I feel proud. But now I have sent you all into battle and you have all run away. Okay, who else is there that I should send? As for you all, you're just running from something that's nothing at all! I am the chief here! There is nothing that will beat me!" And so he set out, son of a bitch! he came forward, he came, and came near the water's edge, son of a bitch! he shook, son of a bitch!

Pufufuk kpinggim![5]
I take and throw the buffalo ringgim!
I take the buffalo, I throw it ringgim! throw
  ringgim! rim! rim!

He stretched his neck *ngɛ ngɛ ngɛ,* son of a bitch! he came forward:

Tukpik kpinggim!
Tiktik kpinggim!

[5] In Lion's song the thunderous roar is combined with the crashing thud of his falling prey. But Rabbit is unimpressed.

Rabbit sat over in the stand of reeds listening, "What kind of noise is that? My bell makes more noise than that! Okay, so you make such a big fuss because you don't think that I, a rabbit, am very big?" Lion moved forward and then said that his buddy, whoever it was, his friend, the man that was making noise in the reeds there should come out and take a look. Son of a bitch! at that, Rabbit set his hand to his bell!

    Gbeveveveveveve!
    My dogs don't hunt with bells, sic 'em, Big Lion!
    The little animals are all dead, tɛndɛɛ vɛm
       It will get in my eyes, tɛndɛɛ
    Lion, it will get in my eyes, tɛndɛɛ vɛm
       It will get in my eyes, tɛndɛɛ
    The little animals are all dead, tɛndɛɛ vɛm
       It will get in my eyes, tɛndɛɛ
    Hyena, it will get in my eyes, tɛndɛɛ vɛm
       Vɛm tɛndɛɛ
    The little animals are all dead, tɛndɛɛ vɛm
    It will get in my eyes, tɛndɛɛ vɛm
    Hyena, it will get in my eyes, tɛndɛɛ vɛm

Son of a bitch, when Lion heard that, he said, "No, this place, the children really did find something bad here!" And then as Lion was going to turn *ngaldak* and escape, son of a bitch! he let loose with the rotten eggs, he let loose with the rotten eggs, *lôp lôp!* they hit the big man's head twice, "Chief, touch it! Touch it!" When he touched it and smelled it, mm mmm!

    Children, my head is open, to fe, fe ye
    The world is ruined, to fe, fe
    Let's scatter, scatter, to fe
      See, it is Rabbit's water, to fe
      See, it is Rabbit's water, to fe
      See, it is Rabbit's water, to fe, fe ye

My head is open, to fe, fe ye
The world is ruined, to fe, fe ye

BaDambang baDambang baDambang baDambang baDambang baDambang purup! into the compound, and he, they —all the women had already prepared everything, son of a bish! [sic] and it was just headlong flight *pamdal!* All the domesticated animals fled, and they ran on and on and on and on and on and on and on.

As they came to the middle of the barren plain, he said, "Children, stop a bit!" And they stopped *rip,* all his sharp-toothed followers, all his young men stopped, and he asked, "Now, our big bag that we put our powders for killing animals in and our charms, where did we leave it?" And they answered, "Oh, Chief! We left it in the *kɔfia* tree in your compound, where we put it!"

"Wow-wee! What are we going to do? See, what we kill animals with to eat. . . ." See, if your town falls into ruin around you, you will take your knowledge and move on and kill other things to eat.[6] "But now that we have forgotten our most important thing, what are we, you and I, going to do? Young men, stand still a bit. The strong one who will run here *hɔVɔVɔvɔ* to go and hit that thing quickly to bring us the bag, who is he?"

One said, "No, as for me, I won't go. That place that I have heard is so dangerous, should I go for the same thing to happen to me?"

Now, as it turned out, when they ran away like that, Rabbit climbed up *harr* with his bell and got inside it and pulled the strings of the bag closing it, and then he sat still *sɛm,* and they didn't know what had happened.

So he was quiet a while *sɛmm* and then said, "No, children, let's not leave the bag like that. Let's go, you send someone to go and get the bag." (That was someone else talking to him.)[7] So he said, "Okay, now the person who is

---

[6] This sentence is editorial comment addressed directly to the audience.

[7] These lines are said by someone in the audience.

going to run there is Hyena. Hyena is a powerful person. If the same thing happens, Hyena will escape." (A powerful person never dies, does he?) [7]

Hyena ran *hɔVɔVɔvɔ*. When he came to the place, he threw something and hit the bag that he was inside *kpikirik kpikirik*, he knocked the bag down. The bell was still *sɛm*, Rabbit was inside it. And so he swung the bag over his shoulder, Rabbit and all! He didn't know that Rabbit was inside it. He went along until he came to where the chief and the others were, and he said, "Sir, I have gotten the bag, our fortunes have changed now. Even though we have deserted our town, we will take this bag and move on and eat from it." And he agreed and said, "You have acted like a man!" And then just as he said that, son of a bitch! just as he said, "You have acted like a man!" son of a bitch! he, Rabbit, started with the bell under his arm:

> Gbevevevevevevel!
> My dogs don't hunt with bells, sic 'em, Big Lion!
> Hyena, it will get in my eyes, tɛndɛɛ vɛm
>   It will get in my eyes, tɛndɛɛ
> It will get in my eyes, tɛndɛɛ vɛm
>   It will get in my eyes, tɛndɛɛ
> The little animals have all died, tɛndɛɛ vɛm

Son of a bitch! when he heard that, he said, "No sir-ee! He has arrived!" and he fell, hitting his neck on the ground, and he moaned, "Hmm'm!" thinking that his neck was broken and that he was already dead! And as he came, he fell into a great gully, son of a bitch, and as he fell . . .

> My head is open, to fe, fe ye
> The world is ruined, to fe, fe ye
> Let's scatter, scatter, to fe
>   See, it's Rabbit's town, to fe
>   See, it's Rabbit's town, to fe

[7] These lines are said by someone in the audience.

The world is ruined, to fe, fe ye
Scatter, scatter, to fe, fe ye
The world is ruined, to fe, fe ye
        Rabbit's water . . .

Son of a bitch! he ran on and on and on, and as he ran
under a thorny vine to escape, a thorn pierced the string
of the bag and *mgbot* the string broke and it fell with him
inside to the ground. He came back *horrr,* took all their
plants and brought them back to the town that they had
deserted. He gathered his family in the place that before
had been forbidden, he gathered them and came and settled there *Dɛtɛng.* And so all the strangers who came just
found him there and they settled and made a great town.
But the people who had been jealous, saying no one should
come to their place, no one should come to their place, all
of them have left that place, they no longer rule there.

My name is Daniel Ndanga taking off the rings here, the
rings come off *rɑy ras!*[8]

---

[8] The closing formula refers to brass anklets worn by women in
traditional dances. At the close of the dance performance, the
anklets are removed, and here at the end of his performance he
removes his anklets *rɑy ras* with a final rattle and snap. This was
Ndanga's personal formula, used by no one else.

The Toad and the Frog

by Kombo Banda[1]

The theme of "Marriage to Frog" is cited three times under motif B604.5, once for India and twice for Africa, for the Luba and Togo. Unlike European Märchen, in which the frog is an enchanted prince, this frog does not change shape. The rejected ugly toad suitor does suggest L160 "Success of unpromising hero."

My children, listen to the tale that I am going to tell. It's a tale of my father's. He told it to me, I heard it, and I tell it to you. The way my father told it and later died, now I'll tell it to you so that you can hear it and tell it after me. It's a parable, not a tale. It's a parable, but we pretend and call it a tale.[2]

They set aside an area of grass for burning somewhere. They made arrangements to marry my daughter. The toad wanted to marry my daughter, the frog wanted to marry my daughter. Isn't the frog a beautiful person? He has a nice clear skin, the frog. Isn't he a very beautiful person? The toad isn't beautiful. The toad isn't beautiful, the toad

[1] Kombo Banda was an elder in Bouli. He was over fifty years of age and told the tale to an audience of his family and a few friends on January 29, 1967, in his son's house in Bouli. Tape XI, 1.

[2] In Gbaya tradition, the distinction is not always clear between the tale and the parable. Normally a narration of essentially didactic character that does not include song is considered a parable.

isn't beautiful. The people said, "He! The toad is ugly!" and they told me to give my daughter to the frog. Like the Fulani and the Gbaya, isn't the Fulani more beautiful than the Gbaya? So they took the girl and gave her to the Fulani, rejecting the Gbaya saying that he was a black person like the toad. They wouldn't give their child to a Gbaya.

They burned the grass, they burned and burned, all the people, but they didn't kill any animals. Only the toad killed a bull elephant, just one in all that grass. The toad said, "Okay, I was an ugly person and they refused to give me the wife. I don't want to butcher my animal in the bush." They should pull the animal to his door and he would butcher it there, he said. All the other hunters exclaimed, "He! He! He!" at the size, but since they hadn't killed anything, wouldn't they pull a little bit for their companion so that he would give them a little bit as reward? So he cut lots of bush rope, lots of bush rope, tied it to the elephant, and told them to pull. Pull it right back to his house and butcher it there, he said!

Now, the village where the girl's parents lived was like here at Bouli, and the boy's town, the toad's town, was like at Mbɔdɔmɔ Isa.[3] They would drag the elephant through the town of the girl's parents before going and butchering it in Mbɔdɔmɔ Isa in order for her parents to see it, since they had refused to give him the wife. That was the toad's idea. They fastened the ropes around the elephant and the toad sang—it's a hunting song:

Tough Toad-ee![4]
The girl's mother will prepare spinach for the girl to eat.[5]
Oh, tough Toad-ee!
The girl's mother will prepare spinach for the girl to eat.

[3] Mbɔdɔmɔ Isa was the next village, three miles down the road from Bouli.

[4] "Tough" is the general equivalent of the ideophone naDuk, which is used in this line to describe the toad.

[5] The toad is laughing because the girl's family has no meat, and the girl will have only spinach to eat; whereas, had he married her, they would all enjoy the elephant meat.

I, Toad, it was I who killed an elephant!
  The girl's mother will prepare spinach for the girl to eat.
I, Toad, mean young one!
  The girl's mother will prepare spinach for the girl to eat.
Oh, tough Toad-ee-ee!

Oh, tough Toad-ee!
  The girl's mother will prepare spinach for the girl to eat-ee.
I, Toad, mean young one!
  The girl's mother will prepare spinach for the girl to eat.
I, Toad, it was I who killed an elephant!
  The girl's mother will prepare spinach for the girl to eat.
To be in the mouth of Naa-yi-mboi![6]
  The girl's mother will prepare spinach for the girl to eat.
Here where we went to bed hungry last night!
  The girl's mother will prepare spinach and the girl will go
    to bed hungry.
Oh, tough Toad-ee-ee!

Oh, tough Toad-ee!
  The girl's mother will prepare spinach and the girl will go
    to bed hungry.
I, Toad, tough-skinned one!
  The girl's mother will prepare spinach for the girl to dip.
I, Toad, it was I who killed an animal!
  The girl's mother will prepare spinach for the girl to scrape.
I, Toad, it was I who killed an elephant!
  The girl's mother will prepare spinach and the girl will go
    to bed hungry.
I, Toad, mean young one!
  The girl's mother will prepare spinach and the girl will go
    to bed hungry.

Hirr, hirr, hirr, they were dragging it.
  When they got to Bouli, the girl's mother fled and hid
inside, closing the door. The girl's father fled inside and
closed the door. He! they had refused to give the girl to
this ugly young man and now he had killed an animal! They

---

[6] Naa-yi-mboi was the name of the narrator's mother, and the
phrase is an allusion to the times of his childhood when he would
enjoy the sound of his name in her mouth as she called him.

were embarrassed. So the toad dragged the elephant through the town of the handsome young man to his own town, to the town of the ugly one. The skin of the one was beautiful, his was ugly, but he had killed his animal and had taken it through your town to his own home, because you had refused to give him your daughter, saying he was ugly.

But that's not the way it is. A good person has wisdom and carefulness. Goodness isn't in the skin. If you have good wisdom and carefulness, then you are good. If you are good-looking, but your conduct is bad, then you are bad. So we Gbaya have said, "If you show respect for me, I will give my daughter to you. But if you don't show respect toward me, I won't give my daughter to you. I don't care about good looks."

So, it's a tale that my father told me and I heard it and tell it so that my children can tell it after me just as I tell it after my father. My name is Kombo Banda. My father was Banda, I am of the Bongoya clan, and that's the end of my tale.

The Two Brothers

by PɛDangkao Michɛl[1]

The rivalry between brothers forms a stock theme in traditional narrative. Motif K2211.0.1 "Treacherous elder

[1] PɛDangkao Michɛl was a man of the outdoors, a hunter and farmer of about thirty-six years. He was one of three brothers in a highly respected Bouli family. He was a superb performer who told this tale to a circle of friends in the home of Andre Abari, February 1967. Several months later he was drowned in a boating accident.

brother" is cross-listed in a number of well-known tale types, none of which fit the present story. Key motifs here are S145 "Abandonment on an island," K1616 "Marooned man reaches home and outwits marooner," and R152 "Wife rescues husband." The talking root as a *deus ex machina* (motif D967 "Magic roots") is previously reported for Africa among the Baholoholo by C. Einstein, *Afrikanische Legenden* (Berlin, 1925), p. 233.

Listen to a tale! There were two sons, the only children born to their mother. The name of the first-born was Yaa WoRa; the name of the second was Ngeɛsi. Time passed, and now Ngeɛsi was wealthy. His elder brother had no wealth. Ngeɛsi sold merchandise and married wives, at least five of them. He had children, at least ten. And his brother, when Ngeɛsi saw that he didn't have any decent clothes, he would give him clothes to wear. The only thing his big brother did was go about drinking, loafing around beside people's houses. When he thought about his younger brother's wealth, he realized that it was great, so great that you couldn't describe it. The big brother asked himself what he could do to kill Ngeɛsi to take his wealth and children and all his wives, the goats that he raised and the sheep, too. Ngeɛsi had even bought a gun![2]

Time went by and then a great big rain came, and early the next morning when the sun was shining warmly, he arrived. He said that Ngeɛsi should take his gun and go hunting along the big river. And Ngeɛsi, since his big brother had come and told him to take his gun and go along hunting, couldn't refuse, so he agreed, "Yes, my big brother, I'd like to go hunting as you suggest."

The big river beside which they hunted was called Hot Water. They hunted a long long time, until the sun was hot, but they didn't find any animals. They went down by the

[2] Guns were both extremely expensive and difficult to obtain because of government restrictions on the possession of firearms. Thus, Ngeɛsi's gun is a significant status symbol.

bank of the Hot Water to follow the shore line down-river
and head for home, and when they got to the river's edge,
they noticed a great big island, and there was a great tall
tree on it. There were vines from the shore stretching way
up into the tree out in the middle of the Hot Water. There
were lots of fruits in it.[3] They were ripe, too many to describe.

And so they arrived. Yaa WoRa told Ngɛɛsi to look at the
fruits out there in the middle of the Hot Water, saying
that he was really worn out from hunger and that Ngɛɛsi
should climb and get him some to eat. This was his trick
to kill Ngɛɛsi. Ngɛɛsi heard what his elder brother said, and
since his brother was hungry, what could he do? He took
his gun and leaned it against something there. He said his
big brother should sit down while he climbed for the fruit.
He climbed way up, way up above the big island over there
in the middle of the Hot Water. When one looked at the
way the water boiled and churned, no, it wasn't something
for people to go into. So Ngɛɛsi picked the fruit and threw it
to the shore, his brother took it. He picked more and threw
to the shore, his brother took it. He ate fruit until he was
satisfied.

Then Ngɛɛsi picked some and threw down, telling his elder
brother to gather them so that when he got down he could
eat his share to get strength and go home. He picked his
and threw them to the edge of the grass and his big brother
gathered them all on the ground. Then Ngɛɛsi swung his
foot down to grasp the vine and climb down to his brother
to eat his fruit and go home, but his elder brother pulled out
a big machete, aimed at the vine and cut it *ndung*. The vine
swung out and hung over the middle of the water *ngileng*.
The vine swung out and hung over the middle of the water
ngileng, leaving the brother up in the tree in the middle of
the water *weǫ!* Ho! Here he had climbed into the tree
and picked fruit for his elder brother, and then when he

---

[3] The fruits are known in Gbaya as *dɔn* and there are two
varieties, the small and the large. They grow on vines in the valleys
and are very tasty. The motif of climbing for the fruits and ensuing
trouble is a frequent one in Gbaya tales.

was going to climb down to his brother again, his brother cut the vine—what would he do now? And besides, having climbed up into the tree and then not even eating any of the fruit, by now he was really worn out from hunger. He started singing:

Yaa WoRa, so, my brother, Yaa WoRa, tindɛɛ tindɛɛ
The sheep at home are yours, Yaa WoRa, tindɛɛ tindɛɛ
The goats in the yard are yours, Yaa WoRa, tindɛɛ tindɛɛ
So, my brother, Yaa WoRa, tindɛɛ
Yaa WoRa, help your brother, Yaa WoRa, tindɛɛ tindɛɛ
The wives at home are yours, Yaa WoRa, tindɛɛ tindɛɛ
The goats in the yard are yours, Yaa WoRa, sindɛɛ sindɛɛ
The wives at home are yours, Yaa WoRa, sindɛɛ sindɛɛ
The children at home are yours, Yaa WoRa, sindɛɛ sindɛɛ

He sang this song on and on and on. His big brother saw that, got up, put the gun on his shoulder and *hm!* headed for home. He walked a long long long way, night fell as he walked, but finally he arrived *wɔkɔkɔ* and entered his house.

The wives waited, expecting their husband to come pretty soon—*yaa!* Ngɛɛsi didn't come. They went and asked Yaa WoRa, "Yaa WoRa, this trip that you went on with your brother, now that it is late at night and he isn't back yet, what happened?" And Yaa WoRa said, "Yes, he gave me the gun saying that he would cut across a little stream there and follow the Hot Water downstream. I took the gun and went and waited a long time in vain, so I came back." He said he didn't know where his brother went, he didn't know how Ngɛɛsi might have come home either, but he thought he was already back, so he came back following him to town. His wife said, "No, he hasn't come." They waited two whole days in vain and you know how townspeople are. They started weeping over his death. They all gathered and mourned for a week and then performed the first rite of widowhood to his wives, cutting off all their hair. The wives went into their period of mourning.

But the head wife, the first one, didn't give up. The only thing she did all the time was search. She searched and searched and searched. She went there, she came back. She searched and searched and searched, night fell, she came back. She searched and searched, night fell, she came back. She searched and searched and then as she followed the edge of the Hot Water, following it up-river, when she happened to strain her ears and listen, she heard:

> Yaa WoRa, so, my brother, Yaa WoRa, sindɛɛ sindɛɛ[4]
> So, my brother, Yaa WoRa, sindɛɛ sindɛɛ
> The goats at home are yours, Yaa WoRa, sindɛɛ sindɛɛ
> The sheep at home are yours, Yaa WoRa, sindɛɛ sindɛɛ
> So, my brother, Yaa WoRa, tindɛɛ tindɛɛ
> So, my brother, Yaa WoRa, sindɛɛ sindɛɛ
> The wives at home are yours, Yaa WoRa, sindɛɛ sindɛɛ
> The goats at home are yours, Yaa WoRa, sindɛɛ sindɛɛ
> So, my brother, Yaa WoRa, sindɛɛ sindɛɛ
> So, my brother, Yaa WoRa, sindɛɛ sindɛɛ
> The sheep at home are yours, Yaa WoRa, sindɛɛ sindɛɛ
> The wives at home are yours, Yaa WoRa, sindɛɛ sindɛɛ
> The wealth at home is yours, Yaa WoRa, tindɛɛ tindɛɛ

She stopped *kpɔɔ* and looked around on all sides in vain. When she looked out into the middle of Hot Water, there was her husband. The vine had shriveled up with her husband on it and was suspended in the middle of Hot Water above the island way over there. She went back and forth, back and forth by her husband, she wept and wept until her eyes were all red from crying. One can't describe how she looked.

She followed the bank up, she followed the bank down, and was finally about to leave when *kput* she stubbed her toe on a little root. "Say, what kind of thing is this?" she

[4] The performer sings the song with little audience participation lest the effect of the tone of the song be lost. As he repeats the song, he raises his voice to a high pitch representing the character's desperation and increasing weakness.

complained. Her husband was still out there in the middle of Hot Water and she was still seeking a way to get him down, weeping over him, and then she stubbed her toe here! What kind of joke was the root playing on her, she asked. The root responded, "No! No! A person shouldn't talk like that! I would have shown you something little, but you have complained about me now—I won't show it to you." She lay down before the root, clasping her hands, begging, until the root said, "Yes, go and get some clear water, get some rust from water, get some sharp-edged reeds, and bring them. Then I'll tell you what's in my liver."[5] The woman ran right away, got everything, and brought it to the root. "Okay, now listen," it said. See, the herb *wiki*, she should cut a lot of this herb, she should fill a wide-mouthed pot with it and stir it. When it had become liquid, she should dip it onto the end of the vine, she should just dip the liquid onto the end of the vine, and as it stretched down toward the edge of the grass, it would extend like the root of the vine all the way to the bank and her husband would get it and climb down.

The woman ran quickly and cut a big plant; she put water on it and stirred it until it became gummy, and then she got ready for the job of putting it onto the end of the vine that Yaa WoRa had cut. She dipped it on, and the herb substance stretched out to the ground. She dipped it on and the herb stretched toward the ground. She dipped on more and more until after a while the herb extended down with the root of the vine. The herb stretched out longer and longer until it reached into the bank along the water. And then her husband began climbing down. "Father, just hang on tightly lest you fall!" she called. "Don't fear death any more. Just think about me now. Hang onto the tree tightly, climb down, and come to me."

Her husband climbed down slowly, slowly—he was as

[5] The root is a frequent motif playing the role of *deus ex machina*. It gives a command which is formulaic, after which it makes a suggestion that will clarify the hero's dilemma. It often explains that the clear water is oil for its skin, the stagnant water is its facial make-up, and the reeds are what it uses to trim its hair.

skinny as a chameleon *kɔnggɔDi;* it was indescribable. Her husband came all the way down, and when he was near the shore she stretched out her hand and grasped the little thing that he was *kaBak* and set him on the ground. When she saw that her husband was down, she broke into tears and wept and wept, one can't describe it. She carried her husband on her back, put him right on her back and tied him on like a child, and carried him all the way back toward town. Since she didn't want to walk into town by day, lest Ngɛɛsi's big brother should see, she came all the way to right behind town and kneeled down there. She waited until it was quite dark *ndiying,* and then the big house that her husband had built as his bedroom, she brought him inside and put him in the room where he formerly slept.

None of her four co-wives, who had remained back there, knew what was going on. She went and made a little flour-and-pepper soup and put it to her husband's mouth. He drank it, he lay down. The next day she prepared some mild herb broth and a little cassava with it. He ate it, he lay down. Soon she took a little rooster that belonged to her husband, killed it, prepared a little cassava with it, and he ate it. Then she went and got a little goat that belonged to her husband, killed it, prepared cassava with it, and her husband ate. Then she went and took a little one of her husband's cows, killed it, prepared cassava with it, and he ate it. As time went on, his stomach was growing out *Dɔlɔk* a little bit. The husband waited a while longer, his body was stretching out until *Buturuu,* he was healthy and filled out again.

She saw that he was filling out, and after a month she decided that he looked as good as he had looked to her before. Then they made plans inside the house. She asked what they should do, and her husband said that there wasn't anything to do except for her to go and buy lots of corn. The other four co-wives should each put corn in water and make lots of beer. Her co-wives didn't know anything of what she was doing, and her husband's big brother, who had cut the vine and left him in the tree, didn't know either.

In the morning, before it was light, Yaa WoRa, who had cut the vine with Ngɛɛsi in the tree, arrived. He asked why the wives didn't bathe from their mourning; what were they trying to find? They responded that there was no reason why they should cease mourning. They had neither wanted nor expected their husband to die so that he (Yaa WoRa) should marry them right away! They argued *sokolokoo* and he went home and sat down. It still wasn't light when he went out and called some important women to come and bathe his brother's wives from their mourning quickly. The wives argued with him and argued. He wanted to have them purified quickly so that he could marry all his brother's wives and take all his brother's things, but his brother's first wife wouldn't give up. She went out with her co-wives saying they should come and buy corn. She set out with all the co-wives and bought corn, lots of it. They all put the corn in water, they pounded it and prepared it; after the second day it was brewed, and then strained into big pots in all their houses.

After the right amount of time the beer became strong, and then she went and invited the chief, she invited the civil leaders and the military leaders, and they invited all the young men of the town. His wife went out early in the morning and swept in front of the door *pem pem pem,* she swept out his great storehouses, the two great storehouses that stood the one in front of the other, she swept them clean. Then they poured out the beer, they set out the beer in rows of containers filling the storehouses *rik rik* and then she went and got his big sheepskins and spread them on the ground *fik fik fik fik.* The great men gathered, the chief went and sat on the big chair, the important civil leaders and military leaders sat on the ground, the young men sat on benches in rows *rik rik rik rik,* and then the wife brought out the beer and set it down.

The wife asked, the reason for Ngeesi's absence from their midst, did they know it? "Chief, do you know about my husband's death?" The chief said no, he didn't know. Okay, now about her husband's death, she said, today she would tell how it happened. The beer that she had made was his funeral beer to provide the occasion for her to tell them how her husband died. "Chief," she said, "excuse me a minute while I go inside. I'll be right back." Then she went and took her husband, Son of a bitch! she took this great robe, Son of a bitch! this trouser and slapped it on his feet, Son of a bitch! she put on shoes, she put on socks, Son of a bitch! she slapped on this white robe, she slapped on that white robe, she took a fez and set it on *Deng*, she wrapped a turban on her husband *zekeke* like a chief. Then she came back and got a big iron chair that her husband sat on, she came and took it like this and came and set it *mgbem* alongside the gathering next to the chief.

Then she said, "Look, Yaa WoRa who is here, the two of them, Yaa WoRa is the elder, Ngɛɛsi the younger. Okay, now if you go on a trip with your brother, do you kill your brother?" Everyone said, "No." If your brother is wealthy, then aren't you, the elder brother, also wealthy?" Everyone said, "Yes." "Now, see, Ngɛɛsi has wealth. When his elder brother didn't have clothing, it was Ngɛɛsi who gave him clothes to wear. And so it was with everything that he had in his house. But Yaa WoRa was jealous, and they went hunting together. When they came to the Hot Water, his brother climbed and picked the fruits in the tree on the island for him and he ate them. Then when his brother picked some and was going to climb down and eat them and then go home together, he took a machete and cut the vine." If she hadn't hunted very carefully, she said, her husband would have died in the tree. But she went looking, and the song that her husband was singing already sounded like death. It was thanks to the root that showed her what to do that she brought her husband back two months ago; this was the third month and now her husband was back to health again. And so this was the dinner in honor of it.

"Now, husband, come out! Sit here for the people to honor you." Immediately he came out of the house and entered the gathering. Wow, all the people from everywhere began to bow in prayers of thanksgiving. He sat down and they discussed the case, Son of a bitch! and she brought out the beer and they had a great dance that continued on and on, celebrating his funeral until late at night *tirr*.

So it is that there is the custom that says if a second son

has something, it belongs to the elder. But some hard-hearted elder brothers don't know that and go off and kill the younger brother to own what the younger possesses so that his (the elder's) reputation will spread as though it was he who got it. No, sir! But that's what Yaa WoRa did with Ngeesi. And the reason why Ngeesi lived was thanks to his wife. Because, as they say, some wives look after their husbands as though they were brother and sister, and that's how he was saved. My tale is set right under the *kolo* tree *gbat!*[6] My name is PeDangkao Michel in Bouli. That's the end of the tale.

[6] This line is a closing formula alluding to the weary hunter or traveler who sits down under the shady *kolo* tree as he crosses the hot plain.

GABON

**Fang visions collected
by James W. Fernandez**

Texts of seven narcotic-induced visions collected by James W. Fernandez document his article in Part II on rituals and visionary experiences the Fang associate with the eating of the *eboka* plant. As Fernandez states, the texts of these visions constitute a seldom recorded but valid folk narrative genre.

They are filled with folkloric motifs. Certain ones occur in most of the seven texts, and others appear in several, while rarely do motifs appear only once. The most prevalent theme is the "Journey to the otherworld as dream or vision" (F1), present clearly or obliquely in each vision. Dangers along the road suggest F151.1 "Perilous path to otherworld" (texts 4, 5). Once, the road runs through a house (F771.9, text 3). A crossroads is twice mentioned, in texts 6 and 9, and suggests D1786 "Magic power at crossroads." In vision 6 a crossroads leads to a sacred tree associated with origins of life and death (A878). In the otherworld, villages are seen (F168 in texts 4 and 6). A glass house mentioned in visions 6 and 8 is a folktale motif (F771.1.6.2).

Color symbolism is pronounced, and follows Christian tradition in the stress on white. The soul as white (E722.1.2) is indicated in visions 7 and 9. White as a magic color (D1293.3) or symbolic color (Z142) is conspicuous in texts 6, 7, 8, and 9. The transformation of black men into white men in texts 7 and 8 (in 8 the man is a transformed bird), as a good, underlines the negative symbolism of black, also present in 8 in the barrier of black iron, and recalls the association of the devil with black (G303.2.2). Red symbolism (Z141) is evident in visions 6, 8, and 9.

The appearance of parents and other relatives in dreams and visions also conforms to folk narrative motifs. Examples are "Dead mother's friendly return" (E323, text 4), "Dead father's friendly return" (E327, texts 3, 5, 6, 8), "Appearance of wraith as calamity omen" (E723.8 in text 5, in this case a living brother who prophesies his own death). Transformation motifs apply to a father becoming a bird (texts 5 and 8; this could be D150 "Transformation: man into bird" and E327.5 "Dead father returns in form of bird") to a harp changing into a woman (D430, text 7) and a child changing into a harp (D254 in text 7). Harp symbolism is twice present in vision 7 and again in vision 5, where the father gives the gift of a harp, suggesting "Magic harp" (D1231), a well-known motif often reported in Europe, for which Clarke cites a Gola example from Africa in Dietrich Westemann, *A Study of the Ewe Language*, tr. A. L. Bickford-Smith (London, 1930), p. 485.

A woman too beautiful to look at (F575, text 7) and an evil witch whose curse prevents wealth (M411.12, text 5) make unique appearances, but the fear of witches kept one *eboka* eater from revealing his vision (report 1). One group of motifs falls under "Revolting murders or mutilations" (S100–99): a bayoneted woman in the moon (text 8), a slaughtered chicken alive (text 6), a heart beating in a man's chest (text 8).

It is worth noting that Clarke reports many more instances in West African tradition of journeys to the lower world (F81) than to the otherworld as dream or vision (F1), for which he cites only one example, among the Mende (Frederick W. H. Migeod, *A View of Sierra Leone*, London, 1926, p. 258). This discrepancy can be attributed to the abundance of folktale as compared to vision sources.

The particular cult house in which the following vision was refused had years before undergone severe repression from the authorities and from the Church. This house tended to be wary in imparting any information to anyone. As far as the failure is concerned, our figures show it to be frequent enough in the encounters with *eboka*. Not all initiates are as equitable as this particular informant, however, and most would try the initiation again at a later time. Many who found nothing in the plant would leave the cult, since so much of the cult's promise hinges upon "going down with *eboka*."

1. The vision (refused) of Engomo Obama (Zambievanga).
  Age 28—a young brother. One wife, no children. Has a small cocoa plantation but gets nothing from it. Clan

Essabam. District of Medouneu, Bwiti Chapel at Efu-
lan. Ate *eboka* two years before.

Reasons given: I danced and ate a bit of *eboka* when I
was in Libreville years ago. But I saw very little. But
now recently my brother became sick in the head.
He began telling me to eat the *eboka*. I ate *eboka*
because the beyim (*witches*) had put thunder (*za-
lan*) in the head of my brother and he became a fool.
He had already seen the road and was going to become a Banzie. But when the thunder came into his
head he said he could no longer see in the *eboka*.
He told me to take it because I should see what he
had been looking for. The *Nima na Kombo* (Chief)
of our chapel said not to tell what we saw in our
vision, because it belongs to us here. But I saw those
whom my brother was seeking to see.

2. The failed vision of Nyimeh Ondo (Mendombo). Age
    42. Clan Yebingwan. Five wives and four children.
    District of Mitzik. Bwiti Chapel at Ondondo. Ate *eboka*
    eight years ago.

    Reasons given: I ate *eboka* at Ondondo. My father of
    eboka was Mba Ngwe, my mother's younger brother.
    He kept after me to eat *eboka,* but I could see no
    reason to eat it. But finally he convinced me to eat
    it because I would see something in it and perhaps
    my mother. I ate only because I wanted to see what
    was in it. He told me I would have to go to the ground
    to see. But then I ate the *eboka* several times and
    saw nothing. But I have continued to be a Banzie
    because my heart tells me it has been the right thing
    even though my head has not been opened. The heart
    of the Fang is more at home in the music and
    dance of Bwiti.

The following two visions have the incomplete quality of
many that are collected in category 2 (hearing voices) and
particularly category 3 (seeing ancestors). The incomplete-
ness may be a consequence of many factors—quality of the
eboka taken, attitude set of the individual and the nature of

the guidance he received from the leaders of the chapel, and so on, but often it is a consequence of the initiate becoming so violently ill that he cannot complete the initiation, although he may still have visions. That is the case in these two accounts. The first account shows, incidentally, how similar delirium in sickness is to *eboka* hallucinations in the eyes of the Banzie. Their supernatural component is essentially the same.

3. The vision of Mebang Mbe (Ngondo Ekumu). Age 33. Last wife of a Banzie. No children. District of Oyem. Bwiti Chapel at Kwakum.

Reasons given and vision: For a long time I resisted eating *eboka* although my husband encouraged me. But when I became very sick and nearly died, my husband decided to transport me to the Chapel at Kwakum. I was in agony and saw a road going through a house. I followed this road a long way to a crossroads, where a man with a great lance stopped me and said, "Where are you going? You are not dead." And he pointed back. I found myself in bed in Kwakum. I remained sick for some weeks and my experience decided me to find the solution to this illness in *eboka*. But when I took it a year ago I saw only my father and a woman carrying a basin with various herbs. The woman was washed by my father, and my father turned to me and said, "You must return all the things that are in your stomach." I got up and with the help of my mother of *eboka* went to the river and threw up. I have not been sick since.

4. The vision of Abeso Mungeh (Nzambi Evanga). Age 54. Clan Nkojeng. Has a small coffee plantation. Has three wives and one child. District of Oyem. Chapel at Kwakum.

Reasons given: I ate *eboka* here five years ago. I had seen Bwiti in Libreville but I had not danced it. I am a *mimia* (a person without a witch) and I have nothing to protect me, so I decided to eat *eboka* to see if that way our old people and God would listen to our prayers and grant them. Nothing was coming to me as a Christian.

Vision: I didn't see much. I traveled a red route and came to a village of one house with one door and one window. Two white men were sitting at either end of a table. They were writing. That was all. I returned then. But I was dissatisfied, so I took a big dose of *eboka* again and this time I saw my mother and she was surrounded by many people. She died when I was young and I didn't recognize her. But men surrounding her said it was my mother. She came and stood at my right. Another woman came with a child and stood at my left. I reached for the child but she held it away from me. Then I became sick and had to pass out to the edge of the forest to throw up. As I came back I saw a host of small babies laughing and playing together in the air. That was all I saw.

The following five visions, arranged by increasing length and showing some diversity within type, all have those stereotyped features characteristic of category 4 (walk down the long road)—one fifth of the visions collected. These visions particularly are treated in the analysis.

5. The vision of Biyogo Ondo (Zambi Evanga). Age 45. Two wives. Clan Evon or Nkojeng. A planter of four hectares of cocoa and coffee. District of Mimvoul. Bwiti Chapel at Engoeñ.

Reasons given: I worked at Libreville in a shop many years ago and I saw much Bwiti but I never ate *eboka*. When I returned to Mimvoul seven years ago I ate *eboka*. I was a man who ought to have been rich in the preparations my father gave to me (*akomnge essa*). But I have not become rich. Witches closed the path to me. The Banzie, whom I came to consult, told me to eat *eboka*. For if I ate *eboka* I would see my father again and he would give me counsel.

Vision: When I ate *eboka* I saw my elder brother. He didn't see me or speak to me. Then I next saw another brother, who was not dead, but I saw him there in the *eboka*. I saw his body on the ground beside the road I traveled. (Two weeks later, that brother died!) This road led to a great desert that had no limit. There my father descended before me in the form of a bird. He would accompany me back. On returning, I saw Christians dressed in animal skins—belts of antelope. They carried heavy crosses around their necks. They were to the left on a path that led off the path we followed. As we returned, my father gave me a *ngombi*, the harp, and he told me that would guarantee me in my life.

6. The vision of Mve Ndong (Mvanga Abena Mokuku Kanja). Age 36. Clan Efak. Two wives, no children. Coffee planter with four and a half hectares. District of Mitzik. Chapel at Amvan.

Reasons given: I have married many women, of whom I have only two now, but I got no children from them. One day after work I was asleep resting, and suddenly in my sleep my mother came from the left of the room and my father from the right. This was when I was working in Libreville some years ago. They asked me why I didn't eat *eboka*. I responded that it was mad medicine. My mother said no, and she showed me a small leaf package from which she ate *eboka*. She bid me go to a certain friend of mine who was a Banzie and have him give me *eboka*. Then I ate *eboka* these three days and three nights. [Interviewed just after initiation.]

Vision: I started up a red road and passed through a village full of people whom I heard in their huts crying and wailing. On each side was a hill with a fine house on each. Beyond the village I came to a river, and three women were there fishing bones out of that river and placing them on the bank. I floated across the river, at the other side of which was a crossroads with three roads: silver, gold, and red. Standing in the center there was my father. He said, "See where you have arrived with the power of *eboka*." I passed through his legs and started up the gold route, which became brighter and brighter. I came to another crossroads, where I found the *otunga* planted.[1] There, under the *otunga*, the chicken that had been killed for me when I started eating *eboka* was alive and scratching. Beyond the *otunga* a man was shining on a cross. I knew him from his pictures. It was Jesus. I passed beneath the cross to a house of glass on a hill. It was the house of Nyingwan Mebege. Within was my brother. He was secretary and writing for two men all in white, who sat at either end of a long table. He was writing my history and my name as a Banzie. Then my father of *eboka* called me back, for I should go no further.

7. The vision of Mendame Nkogo (Ngadi). Age 32. Cocoa planter. One wife, two children. District of Oyem. Bwiti Chapel at Sougoudzap.

Reasons given: I was skeptical. The Banzie challenged me, so I decided to eat *eboka*. They actually convinced me by giving me three teaspoonfuls. I felt something. That was several years ago.

Vision: I saw in the mirror that they had set in front of me, a great crowd of black men approach. They were then changed to a great crowd of white men. I found myself in a garden surrounded by a crowd of people whose color I do not know. I was surrounded by *eboka* bushes, and by two chapels of Bwiti. Then

---

[1] The *otunga* (*Polyalthia suaveolens*) is a sacred tree in Bwiti (its wood is the most commonly used in Fang construction, carpentry, and craft) and is associated with the origins of life and death. Spirits are born into the flesh at the tree, and the spirits of the dead pass there back into the land beyond. The crucifixion is often represented as taking place at the foot of the *otunga* in chapel paintings, with the sacred bird of the cult, the African gray parrot, perched on top. In initiation one speaks of "paying the *otunga*." The initiate pays a small amount, 500 francs, and sacrifices a chicken at the spot before the chapel that represents the *otunga*, so that he may pass beyond the *otunga*. Thus the appearance of this tree and the chicken in the vision.

I saw my grandfather at the other end of the garden in a hollow in the rocks. And I saw myself as a child sitting between his legs. Then that child which was me changed into a *ngombi* (the cult harp), which my grandfather was playing. And now, whenever I play the *ngombi*, I know it is my father playing through me. My grandfather arose and took me in something like a plane to the land beyond. He took me to Nyingwan Mebege. She was a beautiful woman—just a glimpse I had. She was too beautiful to look at. Then my grandfather showed me again the *ngombi* and said that I must play. It would always lead me to another land and be the route of the Banzie. My grandfather then explained to me all the parts of the *ngombi*. At midnight the *ngombi* is no longer of wood. Nyingwan Mebege comes into it and it becomes her. Grandfather told me to look at the sun. It blinded me. I saw a path to Jesus. I knocked against the door but Jesus said I could not enter. This was because I still had black skin. All the dead are white. When I die I will become white like the *ntangan*. My father of *eboka* saw that I was already gone too long with *eboka*. He brought me back. He gave me sugar cane to eat. Now whenever I eat *eboka*, I see or hear my grandfather.

8. The vision of Ndong Asseko (Onwan Misengue). Age 22. Clan Essabam. Not married, he is an "aide-chauffeur" but also plants coffee in his father's village. District of Oyem. Bwiti Chapel at Kwakum. Taken several weeks after initiation.

Reasons given: Nzambi Evanga Beyogo Ondo mwan Evon gave me the *eboka*. I was a Christian but I found no truth in it. Christianity is the religion of the whites. It is the whites who have brought us the Cross and the Book. All the things in their religion one hears by the ears. But we Fang do not learn that way. We learn by the eyes, and *eboka* is the religion that enables us to actually see!

Vision: When I ate *eboka* I found myself taken by it up a long road in a deep forest until I came to a barrier of black iron. At that barrier, unable to pass, I saw a crowd of black persons also unable to pass. In the distance beyond the barrier it was very bright. I could see many colors in the air but the crowd of black people could not pass. Suddenly my father descended from above in the form of a bird. He gave to me then my *eboka* name, Onwan Misengue, and enabled me to fly up after him over the barrier of iron. As we proceeded, the bird who was my father changed from black to white—first his tail feathers, then all his plumage. We came then to a river the color of blood, in the midst of which was a great snake of three colors—blue, black, and red. It closed its gaping mouth so that we were able to pass over it. On the other side there was a crowd of people all in white. We passed through them and they shouted at us words of recognition until we arrived at another river, all white. This we crossed by means of a giant chain of gold. On the other side there were no trees but only a grassy upland. On the top of the hill was a round house made entirely of glass and built upon one post only. Within I saw a man. The hair on his head piled up in the form of a bishop's hat! He had a star on his breast, but on coming closer I saw that it was his heart in his chest beating. We moved around him, and on the back of his neck there was a red cross tattooed. He had a long beard. Just then I looked up and saw a woman in the moon—a bayonet was piercing her heart, from which a bright white fire was pouring forth. Then I felt a pain in my shoulder. My father told me to return to earth. I had gone far enough. If I went farther I would not return.

9. The vision of Eman Ela (Misango ki Nanga). Age 30. Clan Essamenyang. One wife, who is a Banzie, and no children. He is the oldest of his brothers and a planter. District of Mitzik. Bwiti Chapel at Akuruzok.

Reasons given: A man of the Mvang Clan gave me the *eboka*. I ate the *eboka* for other black men. I am sorry for the other black men and their suffering (*Me wok minsutmibot mise olun—mi ne engongol*). I also ate the *eboka* to be able to play the *ngombi* well. I also searched in it to have many children. Years ago my father, who was a Banzie for a time, gave me some *eboka*. But I saw nothing in it.

Vision: When I ate *eboka*, very quickly my grandfather came to me. First he had black skin. Then he returned and he had white skin. My grandfather then appeared in the same way [i.e., in a white skin]. It was he that gave me my *eboka* name. Because my grandfather was dead before I was born, he asked me if I knew how I recognized him. It was through *eboka*. He then seized me by the hand and we found ourselves embarked on a grand route. I didn't have the sense of walking but just of floating along. We came to a table in that road. There we sat and my grandfather asked me all the reasons I had eaten *eboka*. A man there wrote all these down. He gave me others. Then my grandfather disappeared, and suddenly a white spirit appeared before me. He grasped me by the arm and we floated along. Then we came to a crossroads. The road on which we were traveling was red. The other two routes were black and white. We passed over. Finally we arrived at a large house on a hill. It was built on one post. Within, I found the wife of my mother's father. She gave me my *eboka* name a second time and also gave me the talent to play the *ngombi* harp. She told me to work it until eternity. We passed on and finally arrived, after passing over more crossroads, at a great desert. Nothing was there! There I saw descend from the sky—from the moon—a giant circle, which came down and encircled the earth, as a rainbow of three colors— blue, red, and white. There were two women in white at each side of that circle. I began playing the *ngombi* under the rainbow and I heard the applause of men. I returned. All the Banzie thought I had gone too far and was dead. Since then I have seen nothing in *eboka*. But each time I take it I hear the spirits who give the power to play the *ngombi*. I play what I hear from them. Only if I come into the chapel in a bad heart does *eboka* fail me.

SOUTH AFRICA

A Xhosa narrative collected
by Harold Scheub

Sikhuluma

This long, splendidly told tale clearly belongs to type 313 "The Girl as Helper in the Hero's Flight," one of the most celebrated of international folktales. It may be analyzed as follows:

I   Children go off in pursuit of birds (F989.16 "Extraordinary pursuit of birds"); the birds lead them to adventures (B151.2 "Bird determines road to be taken"); they encounter a deserted homestead (F766 "Deserted city. Inhabitants have been devoured") and travel a dangerous road in spite of Sikhuluma's warning (C14 "Forbidden road"); the children die for disregarding Sikhuluma's taboos, and finally Sikhuluma and his little brother, the only survivors, meet a woman with one arm and one leg (F516, F157.0.1). Here the little brother dies, and Sikhuluma's dog appears to lead him home (B151.1.6 "Dog indicates road to be taken"). Returned home, Sikhuluma, who had previously not spoken from birth, talks to the children's fathers (F1041.22 "Deaf and dumb people speak") and recounts his experience.

II   Sikhuluma is circumcised, and sets out after a fabulous water monster (H1220 "Quests voluntarily undertaken," H1360 "Quest for dangerous animals," F911.6 "All-swallowing monster"). A young girl, Sikhuluma's sister who had cooked for him at the circumcision lodge, accompanies the hunting party and drops loaves of bread before the monster, which it stops to eat (R231 "Obstacle flight"). She decoys the monster into the kraal, where the men kill it (F628.1.0.1) and skin it for its fur to make garments (F821 "Extraordinary dress").

III The people are ready to admit Sikhuluma to manhood, but he wishes to seek a wife (H1381.3.1.2 "Quest for bride for oneself"). He sets out with young men and meets a mouse who asks to be skinned and to have his skin put in a sack (B437.2 "Helpful mouse," D1025.3 "Magic mouse skin"). The mouse advises Sikhuluma to ask for a daughter at Mangangedolo's place, but not to stay in the beautiful house, sleep on the new mat, or eat from new dishes. By following these instructions, Sikhuluma wins the daughter of the huge Mangangedolo (G510.1 "Defeated giant gives his daughter to victor"). The mouse continues to assist Sikhuluma (B582.2 "Animals help hero win princess," B576.1 "Animal as guard of person or house"), against Mangangedolo's magic thunder and lightning (F968), but Sikhuluma finally forgets one piece of advice from the mouse and steps on soil (C520 "Tabu: touching ground"), so that Mangangedolo can work magic on his footprint (D2061.2.2 "Murder by sympathetic magic"). Sikhuluma vanishes (D2095 "Magic disappearance"), but his wife rescues him from inside an eland (F913 "Victim rescued from swallower's body," R152 "Wife rescues husband"). The wife creates a fine house (F771.3.6 "Castle rises from the ground"). Sikhuluma moves into it as the new chief.

There are various subforms of the multiple incidents in type 313, but the main characters are a hero who seeks a bride that turns out to be the daughter of an ogre (sometimes the devil), who sets tasks or traps which the hero performs or evades with the magic help of the daughter. Usually hero and bride flee from the ogre and avoid capture through the "obstacle flight" (D672), by which they delay their pursuer with magic objects thrown in his path. The basic structure of type 313 is present in "Sikhuluma," although the obstacle flight appears in episode II rather than episode III. The division of magical assistance between the mouse and the bride suggests that they might be the same figure, as in the type analysis in which the bride is a swan-maiden who loses her power of transformation when her feathers (skin) are stolen. The sister in episode II also suggests the first of two brides that appear in the type analysis.

Episode I seems separate from the rest of the tale and exhibits some curious parallels to the *eboka* visions of the Fang, in the suggestion of a dreamlike journey to the otherworld (F1).

Type 313 and its related forms are known throughout Europe and have been reported in the New World. Some individual motifs, such as the obstacle flight, the helpful mouse, and the forbidden road, are well distributed in Africa. I published a full text of type 313A *The Girl as Helper in the Hero's Flight*, in my *Negro Folktales in Michigan* (Cambridge, Mass., 1956, pp. 189–91, "The Devil's Daughter") and cited a number of New World variants in Negro and white tradition (note 153, p. 231). While popular among Negroes in the United States and the West Indies, the type was reported only three times for Africa by Klipple.

SIKHULUMA
by Nongenile Mazithathu Zenani

Taped, transcribed, and translated
by Harold Scheub

Date: September 15, 1967.

Time: About 4 P.M.

Place: On the veld in Mboxo (Nkanga) Location, Willowvale District, the Transkei, Republic of South Africa.

Performer: Mrs. Nongenile Mazithathu Zenani, a Gcaleka
diviner, about 55 years old.

The Performance: Related in Xhosa. Audience: 12 women.

Tape Data: No. 656 in the collection of Harold Scheub.
Section 5, Side 1, Tape No. 13.

Now for a *ntsomi*.

A man and his great wife. The wife gave birth, she bore
a child who could not speak. When they were older, it became clear that this child did not know how to speak, while
his playmates spoke. This child speaks with his hands. When
he speaks of something, he points to it. He speaks with his
hands, he does not hear with his ears, he does not speak
with his tongue. When it was time, he was weened.

That wife again became pregnant, and again she gave
birth to a boy. That boy grew up, and he learned to speak
in the normal time. He speaks, he is a child who speaks.
The name of this child who did not know how to speak was
Sikhuluma. The name of this child who knew how to speak
was Sitshalotshalwana. These children grew up then, until
they were big boys.

When they were big boys, they had a grandfather, the
father of their father. That old man used to like to sit outside at the cattle kraal, basking in the sun, where many
boys stayed passing the time.

One day some birds passed by. These birds suddenly ap-

peared from the left, going to the right side. They passed
by in a thick flock. Again, another flock appeared from that
same side, going to the other side. The fifth time they
passed by, the senior man spoke, "Oh! Hey, oh! Oh, in the
old days when we were boys, those birds wouldn't dare to
do a thing like this—passing above us like that, and we boys
just sitting down there and watching them go by without
beating them! What kind of boys are there these days? If
only I could be a boy again!"

When he heard that, Sitshalotshalwana turned toward the
other boys and said, "Did you hear what my grandfather
said? Don't you see that we must find some sticks and throw
them at the birds?"

The boys got up, and they spoke to the boy who didn't
know how to speak, Sikhuluma. They gestured with their
hands, they gestured as they usually did when speaking to
him, they gestured until he understood what was being said
by their motioning. He, too, got up then, and he took a stick,
this boy who could not speak, and he aimed well. And so
the boys traveled, they walked on, hurling the sticks at those
birds, the boys moving to that side to which the birds flew.
When they were left behind by one flock of birds, another
flock appeared behind them, coming toward them, and that
flock again moved toward that side. The boys went on striking those birds; from the time they started out in the morning until the sun set, they didn't turn around. When they
came to a certain place, it was said that the younger boys,
the boys who were small, should find some firewood and
kindle a fire, "so we can roast these birds and eat them,"
because there were so many of the birds that they were
weighing the boys down. They relaxed then. A fire was built,
those birds were roasted and eaten. Then the boys slept. They
awakened in the morning, they awakened in the morning,
and the birds were doing the very same thing that they
had done the day before, appearing suddenly from this side,
then going to that side.

And the boys said, "Let's get on with this again!"

Again they traveled with those birds, the boys traveled,
striking them, crossing river after river, passing place after

place, traveling through country after country, beating those birds—and yet those birds were without end! When the birds passed by, others arrived! The sun set again, the boys still beating the birds.

The boys said, "Let's sleep! We'll roast these birds. Boys, gather some firewood!"

These words were spoken to some small boys, and the little boys then gathered the firewood. That fire was kindled, those birds were roasted and eaten. Then they went to sleep. They awakened in the morning, they awakened and the birds were forming the same procession that day, too!

Again it was said, "Let's take it up again!"

Then they got some more sticks, and they traveled on, the sticks being plucked from trees and then added to their collection. New sticks were added to their arsenal at the same time that other sticks were lost as they were thrown at the birds. The boys traveled with those birds.

When they were far off, the sun set. When the sun had set, a homestead was seen shining a long distance away from them. They saw this fire, even though it was far off. "Let's go over there to that homestead!"

"We're tired of sleeping in the cold!"

"Let's just go to sleep in that homestead!"

"Let's ask for a place to stay!"

On that particular day, then, it happened that they heard this boy speak, the one who did not know how to speak! In his first speech, he said, "No, Sitshalotshalwana, my little brother! Don't lead the children into that homestead, because in that homestead nobody sleeps! There's no entering that homestead! If we go into that homestead, the children will die!"

Sitshalotshalwana got up, he stood, and when he stood, all the boys said, "Yo! At last the chief has spoken!"

"Yo! my friends, has he been able to speak this well all the time that we thought he could not speak?"

"We did well to beat those birds, so that we should finally hear him speak!"

Sitshalotshalwana said, "Get out of here! Get out of here! What's he saying? Don't you know that he's saying that we shouldn't go to sleep over there? He doesn't know anything! After all, this is the first time he's spoken! Now he's such an old man,[1] he's never spoken since the time of his birth! He doesn't know a thing, he doesn't know the proper thing to say! Go on! Let's go!"

They did go then. Sikhuluma was silent; he didn't speak again. They traveled on, they went to this homestead. They came to this homestead, and there was no one there. When they arrived, they found only dishes—and all the dishes had food in them! These boys were twelve in number, and it happened that these dishes were also twelve.

When they went in, Sitshalotshalwana said, "My! Do you realize that we almost didn't come here because of Sikhuluma? Because of Sikhuluma, who's just learning to speak? who talks of something he knows nothing about? We've been provided for! We're expected here! Look at our dishes! They're the same number as we are—twelve! Look! One, two, three, four, five, six, seven, eight, nine, ten, eleven, and twelve! Don't you see? We've been cooked for here! Let's eat, my friends!" Thus spoke Sitshalotshalwana.

Sikhuluma spoke then; he said, "No, friend, don't make the children eat that food, that food is not meant for us! It belongs to the owner of the house, and she'll arrive in her own time! I said to you, 'No one sleeps in this house!' The children will die!"

The boys stood up, they whistled *vityo vityo vityo,* calling each other.

"The chief spoke well!"

"It's good for us that the birds came along, so that we can at last hear his words!"

Then Sitshalotshalwana said, "Get out of here! Sikhuluma doesn't know what he's talking about! He's just talking nonsense again! How can he say that these dishes are not meant to be eaten, while it's clear that they're ours? Eat!" He said this, and he took his dish and ate.

The boys ate because they respected Sitshalotshalwana, and because it was only Sikhuluma who spoke against him—

[1] Spoken with sarcasm: "He's a grown-up person, and he's only now learning how to speak!"

and since this was but the first day that he had spoken, what could he know?

After they had finished eating, they slept. When they slept, while they were sleeping, during the night, Sikhuluma sat there, not sleeping. All the boys slept, along with Sitshalotshalwana, he slept too. Someone was heard entering.

When this person entered, she said, "Yo yo yo yo! Who's this? Who ate my food? All of it, all twelve! Ah! I've got a boon! I'll begin with this one, then I'll go on to this one, then this one, then this one, then this one, then this one, then this one, then this one, and I'll finish up with this fresh child!"

Sikhuluma sat there during all that time, and he listened. The boys were sleeping; Sikhuluma got up. He pinched one boy, he pulled him, he grabbed him. The boy was startled. Then that person went outside, she went outside.

He spoke here; he said, "Get up, all of you!"

All the boys got up.

Then he said, "The thing that Sitshalotshalwana wanted to happen has happened! The owner of this house has come, and she wants to know who has eaten her food, all twelve dishes! Then she said that she had got a windfall, she had got it! She said that she'll begin with this one, then this one, then this one, then this one, and she said she'll finish with me! We must sit now, we must not sleep, we must stand up! Take your sticks, and let's go!"

The boys agreed.

They said, "We're thankful that you can speak!"

His little brother, Sitshalotshalwana, got up, and he said, "Get out of here! You always do this! Do you boys like what Sikhuluma said? He knows nothing! He's just learning how to speak! He knows nothing! Who's this person who spoke? Only Sikhuluma saw her! He alone heard her when she spoke! But *we*, we didn't see her! When he talks, he knows nothing, this guy! He just babbles!"

The boys said, "No, let's go!"

"All right, if that's what you want."

These boys traveled then, and when they had been traveling for a time, they saw a big road, a big white road—and a village of many homesteads! But they saw no one! In all these homesteads, there was no one! No dog, no ox, no sheep, nothing—only these houses.

There was one homestead that appeared to have someone in it. It was the homestead in the front, and it had a white house. There was smoke in front of the house, and it seemed that it was the only homestead that had someone in it.

Sitshalotshalwana said, "Let's go on this road. We'll pass by there, by that homestead. We're thirsty now."

Sikhuluma spoke again; he said, "No, Sitshalotshalwana, don't go on that road! It's dangerous! These children will all die if they travel on that road! There's a long thing there that has destroyed people! The reason there's no one in this village is that they've been destroyed by the thing that lives over there in that house!"

"We thank you, Chief," said the boys. "You speak well! The things you say persistently turn out to be so!"

His little brother, Sitshalotshalwana, said, "Get out! Why are you thanking him? What does he know? He knows nothing! Travel on! Let's go!"

So saying, he went on to the road, and all the boys did the same. Sikhuluma also traveled on that road. When they had been traveling for a short time, it happened that one of the boys died. He lay stark dead there on the road. They traveled on; there was no one now who spoke. It seemed that these boys now understood that there was only one option now, that they would die. Again, a short time after the death of that boy, another boy died. They left him behind; he lay stark dead there. They journeyed on, they continued, and after a short time, another boy died. They traveled on, and again, a short time later, another boy died. Four of the boys were now dead. Then this Sitshalotshalwana was getting anxious. He more or less understood that, well, his turn would come, and he too would die—because it was clear that the person who stepped on this road would die, no matter who he was!

Again they journeyed on, they traveled for a short time, and another died, the fifth boy. They traveled on, they left him behind, exposed there on the road. They themselves did not know where this road led, they no longer knew if the road led to their home, because they did not know the direction from which they had come. They had left those birds that had made clear the directions from which they had come. The birds were not there now, they were gone. The boys were traveling alone. They journeyed through other places. They were traveling in darkness, not knowing the countryside, it was not very clear. Now they did not know the way to their home! Again they moved on. The sixth boy died. They walked on once more. A little farther along, the seventh boy died. They were not far from that house. It was clear that that house alone contained a person. This village was huge, but nothing came out of it! Again they traveled on, and the eighth boy died. They went on again for a short time, and the ninth boy died. They traveled on sorrowfully, the tenth boy died, and they journeyed on. They remained now, the two of them, Sikhuluma and Sitshalotshalwana. There remained Sikhuluma and his little brother.

They walked on, then, and Sitshalotshalwana said, "Sikhuluma, I'm going to that homestead! I want to see the thing that's killing the people, that puts something in the road so that people die! It makes no difference if I die now."

Sikhuluma answered, "No, son of my father, go on. Don't go over there. We're as good as dead, along with all these children. It makes no difference now. We'll return alone. Let's die here on this road. Don't go and bring that thing out of the house!"

He said, "You see, you're just speaking nonsense to me now! You speak foolishness to me, even now that you're alone! I'm going! Go on with your foolishness! I'm going, I want to see this thing!" So saying, he went there. He arrived there in the house, he arrived and the thing was sleeping in a room. He arrived, and there was a person there who had one arm and one leg. This person was a woman.

When he entered, she said, "Oh oh oh oh! What kind of person is this? Was there ever such a person in this country?"

Sitshalotshalwana said fiercely, "Go on! Get me some water! I'm thirsty!"

This person said, "O worthy child, but why? I fear to watch someone die! Well, go outside and I'll give you some water."

He said, "I won't go out! Give me some water so I can drink!"

She dipped. This woman gave him the water, and he drank it.

He said, "This thing that's sleeping here, is it the thing that destroys people? this thing that's sleeping here?"

He stabbed at it with a stick. The thing got up; it got up and broke his backbone, it broke his backbone in two. Then it put him down. He died.

Sikhuluma understood that his brother was dead, and he traveled on; he didn't go there, he traveled on. When he was in the middle of nowhere, he turned aside from this road, he took a footpath. He traveled on that footpath, and then he became thirsty. He crossed a small stream, he looked for water, not finding any. He leaned on a stick, and as he leaned on the stick in that way, he heard something below in the mud, saying, "Sikhuluma! Sikhuluma, you're stabbing us with that stick! Go up, above! There's water on the upper side."

He pulled the stick up. He carried it in his hand, he didn't lean on it. He went to the upper side; he got there, and water was there. He drank. When he had finished drinking, he stood up. He walked on his way, surprised. "What was it that was talking, down there in the mud?" He hadn't seen it. He was still traveling when his dog suddenly appeared, the dog he had left behind at home. It suddenly appeared, wet, and it was hungry. It trailed its tongue, panting. The dog came to him, wagging its tail at him. It traveled on, and he followed. He knew that "If I'm going to find the house, I'll have to follow this dog. I don't know where the house is any more." He traveled behind that dog of his, he journeyed then with that dog. The sun set. He slept, tired. The dog slept at his side. At dawn, he journeyed on with that dog of his, he walked, he walked, he walked all day. The sun set, and he slept. The dog slept at his side. He traveled again at dawn, and he saw that "My! This is my country! The only thing is that I'm still far from home." He traveled on. The dog traveled, and he journeyed in his own land now, it was clear now. This dog led him in the direction of his home.

Finally he arrived at home, and when he arrived, he did not enter any house. He cried. While he was crying, his grandfather came to him and asked, asking by speaking with his hands, knowing that Sikhuluma does not know how to talk. He gestured, he gestured with his hands, he gestured.

But he spoke, and said, "No, Grandfather, those with whom I traveled, all of them remain behind because of Sitshalotshalwana, he alone! He remained there also. He brought himself into the thick of it.[2] The others are no more. I returned alone. You should call a meeting, so that the fathers of the children might come to hear the reason for the absence of their children."

He was quiet then, he didn't speak again. As he finished speaking, the people were asked to come. The people came then, those who were the fathers of those children.

Then someone said, "Let the chief carry on!"

Sikhuluma stood up and explained, "On a certain day, we departed with flocks of birds. We were about twelve boys. Now all of those boys are not here, all of them, including my brother. He was the last one. At the beginning of the third day, we saw a homestead glowing. Sitshalotshalwana said, 'Let's go!' I began to speak on that day. I said that we should not go to that homestead. If we did, we would all die. Then Sitshalotshalwana stood up, and when he stood up, the boys were happy, they said, 'It's a good thing those birds were here,' so that they could finally hear me speak. Now, when things were like that, he said, 'Ah, get out! You're a fool who has never spoken before! who doesn't know what we're talking about! Let's go!' They went on, then, and I was quiet. We would sleep, then, in that homestead. We arrived at the homestead, and there was no one there. We arrived, and there were dishes there, just twelve of them, just matching our number. Sitshalotshalwana said that we should eat.

---

[2] *Ude wazisa entlonzeni*—lit., "therefore he even brought himself into the skin," i.e., "he brought himself into the thick of it."

Then I spoke up and said that we should not eat. 'This food belongs to a person who will come!' The boys thanked me for my speech. Then Sitshalotshalwana said that even then I was speaking of something I knew nothing about. Didn't I see that those dishes belonged to a person who expected visitors? They were the same number as we! *I* didn't sleep at all; *they* slept. The owner of the house arrived then. She said, 'Yo yo yo yo! Who has eaten the food that I prepared for myself? Who are these people? I'll start with this one, and then this one, then this one, then this one, and I'll finish with this little fresh one!' She was referring to me. I was awake then, and I made an effort to pull the boy who was next to me, to pinch him, to drag him, to rouse him. When he woke, I said that they should all get up. Then that person who had spoken went out. I reported what had happened. Then Sitshalotshalwana said there and then that I was lying, that I was speaking of things that I knew nothing about, that I was even now speaking foolishness. 'There's no one here!' How could it be that a person was heard by me alone, while the rest of them slept? I said then that we should travel. We should take our sticks. He didn't agree. 'Let's stay! No one's going to move!' *I* said that we should go. The boys said, 'Well, let's go!' We traveled then, and we were able to see this road. On this road, then, I said that we should not travel on it, that it was dangerous, that if we traveled on it, the children would die. It happened then that the boys thanked me. That brother of mine said that I was even then delirious. 'Because over there is a homestead smoking!' We journeyed then on that road, and almost immediately after we had set foot on the road, one boy lay stark dead. He died there, and we left him behind. This is the sort of thing that happened then, they formed a kind of procession until we came to this homestead. When we were near the homestead, he said that he was going over there. I said that he shouldn't go, but he was going, he wanted to see this thing in this house that destroyed people. He went; *I* didn't go. When he got there, he asked for some water. Some person said that he should go outside, I was able to hear this. He said, 'Get out! Give me some water! I'm not going out!'

He drank, and when he finished drinking, he said, 'Is this the thing that destroys people?' He attacked it with his stick. It got up then, and that thing broke his back in two, then put him down. *I* traveled on then; I traveled alone. The first thing that happened, I came upon a river. When I jabbed at it with my stick, there was something below in the mud, something that spoke, it called me by name and said, 'Sikhuluma! Sikhuluma, stop stabbing us! You're stabbing us with your stick! Go to the upper side, there's water on the upper side!' I pulled my stick up then and went to the upper side and truly found some water. I drank the water, and when I had drunk some of this water, I got up from it. As I was getting up, I saw my dog coming to me, wagging its tail at me; it was wet. It helped me to find my way home."

Then could be heard the weeping of women, the weeping of the mothers of the children. They were there, and there was profound mourning for the children.

Then the men said, "No, don't blame it on a single person, because all the boys were doing their thing together when they died. They died then, they died fulfilling their assignments of beating the birds. They did it on their own, no one pushed them into it. They pushed themselves. We're just thankful that this child of the chief has arrived, that he himself was saved, so that we might know what happened to the others, why they aren't here."

This is what they said then, and the gathering was broken up by the men. That was the end of it.

After that, the chief said, "I want to be circumcised. I want to be circumcised, I want to become a man."

"Well, all right, Chief."

Again, the men assembled.

It was said, "The child of the great one wants to be circumcised."

So it was.

"All right, then, how shall it be done? because the boys are not here now!"

The chief is never circumcised alone, according to the custom of the Xhosa. It is necessary that he have a supporter in the circumcision lodge, one on the lower side (near the door), one on the upper side, and he between the two, because he is the child of a chief.

"Well, now, the additional boys will be gathered even from among the younger boys." They will have to make do from among the smaller boys; they must find the best of the little boys. This assembly was gathered then; it was full. The people brought out their boys, so that "this child of mine might be circumcised—because when the chief is circumcised, he must not be left alone!"

"No matter how small the boy is, he'll do!"

Finally, there were as many boys as there were fingers on the hands of the chief; they were ten. And again, there were the two who were the supporters.

Then they were circumcised. When that chief had been circumcised, he was *the* circumcised lad! Oxen were slaughtered, and the dried oxskins would be used in the circumcision lodge, because a lodge of circumcised youth used to be closed by the skin of an ox at the doorway.

There were wardens there who were men. And there was one warden who was a girl, who was in charge of the chief's food, that chief who was a circumcised lad. She was staying there at the lodge.

Time passed then, time passed, time passed, he thus being a circumcised lad. Then it was said that the boys must come out from the circumcision lodge. That chief spoke, speaking again—because he no longer spoke, he spoke very rarely, not speaking at any time, speaking only when it was necessary to say something. He spoke again, and said, "I'm not coming out of this circumcision lodge! I'll come out when I can put on the kaross of a fabulous *nabulele!* Otherwise, I'm not coming out!"

Someone asked then, "What is that thing? What's a *nabulele?*"

He said, "It's a fabulous monster of the river, it's in the water. It must be drawn out from below, from the deep pool! It must be skinned for me, and then it's to be tanned so that it might become my kaross! I'll not come out under any circumstances if that kaross is not here!"

"What can we do about that, really? Who's the person

who can repeatedly enter the deep pools? How can such a thing be?"

"Well, this should be done: some loaves of corn bread should be prepared. Three baskets should be filled with loaves that have been baked, so that one can travel and go to this place, so that one can travel and look for a place that has a *nabulele*."

"Who's the person who can do this?"

"Say, when this *nabulele* comes out, doesn't it eat people? Isn't it dangerous?"

Sikhuluma said, "If it comes out, it comes to a person and chews him, and swallows him! and then he's gone! But I say just this—I want it! I want its kaross!"

"*Kwo!* This is a difficult matter!"

"Let's take it from the beginning. Let's ponder this thing!"

He said, "I don't want any pondering from any beginning! I say that the *nabulele* is wanted, that's all!"

The boys came out then on the next day.

"Well, all right, I'll remain here, even if this house burns down I'll remain! I'll never go home, not until that kaross is here!"

Someone said, "All right, then," and they departed, they went home.

When they had gone home, the corn was crushed. This corn was crushed, then, and the loaves of bread were made. The baskets were filled, three baskets with cooked corn bread. Now then, his sister took them, that girl who was the warden, who had stayed at the circumcision lodge cooking for him.

She said, "I'll go! I'll find the kaross for the son of my father, the kaross that he wants to come out with! I want this thing that eats people to eat me, it should begin with me! I'm going, I'll carry these loaves." They are provisions of people who travel. They journeyed then. They got up, and this child journeyed then. These loaves were carried, too.

It happened, then, that when they were far off, they saw a large river. They went to this river, which was huge, they arrived there and tossed a loaf of bread into the water, and said, "*Nabulele! Nabulele!* Come out and eat me!" There was silence. They passed by this river. Someone said, "It's not here in this river!"

They journeyed on for a long time, seeking another big river. And again they found a huge river, and they sought a deep pool in that big river. They went to it, and again threw a loaf of corn bread in, again they threw a loaf of corn bread in. When the loaf of corn bread was thrown, someone said, "*Nabulele! Nabulele!* Come out and eat me!" The *nabulele* was not there at all!

They passed on from that river, they traveled again for a long time. Again they sought a huge river. Little rivers were crossed, rivers that had small pools which didn't appear to contain this thing.

Finally they came to another big river, and again they stood above a deep pool. They tossed a loaf of bread into the water and said, "*Nabulele! Nabulele!* Come out and eat me!" The water stirred in that pool, the water rolled, it rolled, it rolled! it rolled! it was brown! red! green!

This girl said, "Run! all of you! And take this bread along! Make sure that you can see me at all times! Keep me in your sight!"

They traveled, then, they traveled. They ran, continually looking, continually looking. Thus it was that the *nabulele* came out. This girl ran, then, when the *nabulele* came out. A thing came out—it was huge in a way that she had never seen! It wasn't like a horse, it was huge! It wasn't like anything, this thing was massive! great! as big as this: if it entered a kraal where cattle stay, it could fill that kraal by itself! This child ran, then. It ran after her, not running with speed, but moving steadily, going well. She ran, she ran and ran. When it was far off, she sat down. Then, when it was near, she put a loaf of bread down on the ground, and she ran. It stopped and chewed it, and swallowed it. Again it picked up and pursued her—but it doesn't run, it just walks. Finally, it happened then, she was a short distance from those men who were waiting for her.

When these men saw this, they said, "Oh! Well, *we* won't stay here! This thing is getting closer!"

"*We*'re on our way, because of this thing!"

"You remain here with it by yourself—a thing which is so terrible, a thing which is so big! Yo yo yo yo!"

The men went on, they left the child behind. The child said, "Though you leave me behind, would you please do this when you're far off? Try to watch me, so that you'll know when I'm eaten by this thing, so that you'll be able to report at home that, well, I've been eaten! Never lose sight of me! Stay in a place that enables you to watch!"

The men agreed, and they departed. The child traveled on. She waited for the *nabulele*. The *nabulele* came, it came. When it was a short distance away, she put a loaf of bread on the ground. Again she went on her way. She left the *nabulele* behind, she ran. It came to the loaf, and it chewed that loaf of bread. When it had finished chewing it, it again followed her. As for her, she rested again. When it was a short distance away, she again put a loaf of bread on the ground. Then gradually, in this basket that she carried, there remained just one loaf. She ran. It came along and ate this loaf. She ran, she came to these men. Again she poured some loaves into this basket, and it was full. And so it was; the men traveled on. The thing was frightening to these men; they didn't even want to see it. This thing was dreadful! The child again, when the thing was nearby, put a loaf of bread on the ground. And again she ran, and traveled. She went and sat down, far off. It came to the loaf, and the thing ate it. The child walked on. When this child came to the men, she said, "Travel on! Go home! And say there at home that a gun should be borrowed! A gun should be sought, so that this thing might be shot! But you shouldn't come near it; shoot it from a distance! Even if there are many guns, that's fine! because we don't know if this thing can even be penetrated by a gun!" The men ran, then, they traveled and left that child behind. The child traveled on, she left a loaf of bread on the ground. The thing was a short distance away. Again she ran, she was then not far from home!

When the men got there, they reported the girl's speech. Well then, it happened then that the guns were borrowed. They were loaded, they became heavy; they were cocked *xha xha xha* there at home. All the men were carrying guns; those not carrying guns carried spears. Time passed, then, and the sun set. The girl was seen, appearing, coming a short distance from home. Then it came, that thing came! She arrived at home, she arrived and entered the kraal at home.

She said that the men should go into the house. This thing will enter the kraal because it wants this girl whom it sees. "Go into the house, so that it won't see you! Then, when it enters, when it has turned its back, entering the kraal, coming toward me, come out with your weapons and go to work! I'll come out at the other end of the kraal!"

The men heard, and then they entered the houses there, all of them. The girl arrived then, and when she stood in the courtyard above the kraal, the men saw her, they were peeping through some small holes so that they might see this thing. Then the men cried out, the women also cried out, the dogs cried out, and everything there at home ran when they suddenly saw this thing! The dogs ran and descended on the other side. Everything in this homestead ran! the cattle also ran because of the approach of this thing, because this thing resembled nothing but itself, it never having been seen! The people in the house cried out—they were inside, they had closed the doors!

Well, the *nabulele* didn't bother about them at all, crying out though they were. It was face to face with this girl! It had caught up to the girl now! She went, she entered the kraal, and the thing entered the kraal. She left a loaf of bread, then the girl came out at the other end of the kraal. The people came out, coming out to the girl in the kraal. All of them came out with these weapons of theirs. Twelve men began shooting then, they shot, they went through their ammunition. The thing stirred, still wanting to move on. Twelve other men came out, and they shot. Those men finished their ammunition. It was obvious that the *nabulele* was wounded. It stirred on the ground, not able to stand up so that it might travel. Those who were the weapon-jabbers threw their weapons, they were some distance away. It was obvious that—well, it couldn't make it, it collapsed now and the kraal was broken down, it was broken. They shot in that way repeatedly, and finally the thing was dead. It had been penetrated by the men!

When it was known that it was dead, that thing was then skinned. When it was skinned, when the skinning was completed, the karosses were divided. The *nabulele* produced three karosses, the number that was desired. The boy second in rank to this circumcised lad would put on a kaross similar to his, and the companion on the other side would also put on a kaross resembling his. Thus there were three, and these blankets were tanned then by the men. The meat of that thing was put outside, because they did not even know if it could be eaten, if it was edible or not edible. They threw that meat away, outside, and it was a windfall for the dogs and hogs—they ate that meat all month. The second month appeared, and it was still not finished, it was being eaten by all the dogs of the village, and by all the hogs of the village.

It happened, then, after a little while, when the blankets had been tanned, that they went to the circumcised lad. A song was composed, associated with boys coming out of the circumcision lodge, a song about the taking of the circumcised lad by the young men. He was taken out then, covered by that kaross. This kaross was turned inside out, because when the fur of the kaross was on the outside, nothing would approach it—everything ran, they were afraid. It was necessary then that he wear the fur next to his skin. That is how they wore their karosses then, as they came to the house. They arrived, and remained in the yard. They stayed in the yard, a mat was laid there and they sat on it. The raw young man was admitted to manhood then, with gifts, by the people. All the people presented him with gifts, admitting him to manhood. They celebrated the chief, they celebrated the warden, they celebrated the second in command, they celebrated that one on the upper side. And now that all of them had come here, the twelve of them, they were all admitted to manhood. It became necessary then that they go to the house, they would remain in the house and something would be prepared for them to eat. They would smear their bodies with red clay, as is the custom of the Xhosa.

When he appeared from the circumcision lodge, well, Sikhuluma spoke, "I am not going into the house! The others can go into the house, I'm not going into the house! I'll stay here. I'll never go into the house. I'll go only when I have a wife!"

"Oh!"

"What is it now?"

"Is there such a thing—a person who refuses to go into the house? who will go to the house only when he has a wife?"

But all that time, this person sat there, refusing to eat. He will remain there, not going to the house. He did not speak again; he speaks of just one thing and does not speak again! He'll speak again on the day that he next speaks!

"What'll we do?"

"What is this, friends? Now he won't answer us!"

"What he speaks, he speaks!"

He didn't speak again.

"*Kwok'!* This is difficult!"

But, then, it was fitting that the youth entering manhood should walk to the house, and they did so. They arrived, and were smeared with red clay. Food was dished up for them and they ate. All the things of young manhood were done for them. They were sung for, and they were also taught the songs of a men's party, dancing songs.

He sat in the kraal. Food was brought to him in the kraal, and Sikhuluma said, "I'm not eating! I told you that I'll eat when I have a wife! I want a wife! I want a daughter of Mangangedolo!"

Someone said, "Oh! At Mangangedolo's place! How can anyone go there?"

"People who want girls from there are finished!"

"The bridegroom does not return!"

Sikhuluma did not speak again; he'll speak in his own time. He slept here, not eating. It dawned, and at dawn the men were called.

It was said, "He says he wants a wife. The people, then,

must go with him, as always. They must go and ask for that daughter of Mangangedolo's place! The latest of the unusual things that we find here at home is that this child wants a daughter of Mangangedolo's place!"

The men said, "Yes, when he says something, it's all right! No one will forsake his chief! Even those boys who have died, they didn't die because of him. He was rousing them! They died because they despised his words! As for us, then, we won't despise his words! We'll bring out those young men of ours, they'll journey with him and look for that daughter wherever he sees fit!"

Some young men were brought out, then, they were five. They came, then, there were three among the five, he was the sixth one, those supporters were among them, and so they became eight people. They traveled, then, going to Mangangedolo's place.

Along the way, they met a mouse. The mouse crossed the road, and when it had crossed the road, it again returned. It stopped on the road and said, "Sikhuluma!"

He said, "Hnnn?"

"Well, child of the chief, slaughter me, and put that skin of mine here in the sack, and go on with it! As for my flesh, hide it here in this tuft of grass. I'll help you when you get to that place you're going to!"

He said, "I'll put you in my bag! How would you know where I'm going?"

"You'll ask for a daughter at Mangangedolo's place! You see, then, at Mangangedolo's place—look here, I'll point it out to you. Do you see that hill way over there? on the upper side of the homestead?"

He said, "Yes!"

"That's the heads over there! the heads of the people who continually come and ask for the daughter! Your heads will be put over there on that hill! If you put me into the sack, I'll advise you when you're over there!"

Sikhuluma was quiet. He took a knife and killed the mouse. He skinned it, he skinned it. He took its flesh and hid it. He took its skin and put it into the sack. He went on his way then, he traveled on. Then, when they were close to the homestead, the mouse said, "Sikhuluma, consider this! You'll be brought to a beautiful house over there, very beautiful! But don't you agree! You will say, 'We don't stay in a beautiful house!' Then you'll say that you want to stay in a house where the calves are tethered, where the fowl sleep. A new sleeping mat will be brought to you. You'll say that you don't use such a mat. Say that you want an old mat, a mat of a young mother, a mat which is in rags. Then food will be brought on new plates, with new utensils. You'll say that you don't eat it, say that you eat on a leaky dish, you don't want a new dish. And when you're over there, don't walk on mole hills, walk on the grass. Never ever walk in a place that has no grass! In the morning, they'll say over there, in the morning, you should meet together at the cattle kraal, the bridegroom's party. Enter the gate then, and when you're about to come out, come out on the other side. Don't come out of the gate again! When someone says 'Hello' over there, you say 'Mmhmmmm.' Don't say 'Yes,' say 'Mmhmmmm.'"

"All right."

"Put me in the sack."

Sikhuluma put that mouse into the sack then, and he traveled on. He truly traveled. When he arrived at that homestead over there, he walked on the way that had grass, he walked on the grass. He arrived, and sat in the yard, in the place in which the bridegroom's party stays. The owner of the homestead arrived, the thumping steps of this Mangangedolo could be heard. His knee was huge! He arrived, he stamped on the ground, he stamped, he stamped.

He said, "Hello, party of the bridegroom!"

They said, "Mmhmmmm!"

"I say, 'Hello, party of the bridegroom!'"

"Mmhmmmm!"

"What is this? Don't you know how to say yes?"

They said nothing, they were silent.

He said, "I greet you! Hello—especially you, bridegroom!"

He said, "Mmhmmmm!"

He said, "Ah, this is a different groom's party!" Mangangedolo was quiet then. He chatted with them, asking, "Where do you come from?"

Sikhuluma explained; he said, "Well, I come from home. I have come here to seek a wife!"

He said then, "Select for yourself from among the daughters here at home! There are many. Let them come and greet the groom's party, then!"

The daughters were called; they came to greet the groom's party. Sikhuluma selected a wife for himself.

He said, "It's that one, my wife is that one!"

Mangangedolo laughed. He said, "Ha ha! This is the first time I've heard such a forward groom! Well, then, I see the way it is with you, husband! We shall meet again! We'll see each other again! Please say, then, on what basis are you claiming her?"

He said, "I do so by means of cattle, which you want. You will declare the number you want regarding your daughter."

He said, "Do you have eighty cattle that you can bring here to pay dowry for my daughter?"

Sikhuluma said, "Even above that number! Ask whatever number of cattle you want for your daughter!"

Then he said, "All right, then, I want those eighty."

He said, "You as much as have them!"

That fellow then said, "Go, girls, and arrange for the groom's party."

They went then, the girls left the groom's party. That girl got up and grasped her groom's hand. Sikhuluma grasped her hand; he grasped it, not sure that he should grasp it; wary, not being sure if this might be the cause of his death. But he grasped her hand anyway. Then the girl left. They went then, and those girls made the house of the bridegroom ready. The house in which the girls would sleep was beautiful. They were taken there then. Someone said that the spokesman should go and take the groom's party and bring them to the house. He left with the groom's party, bringing them to the house.

When Sikhuluma appeared in the doorway, he said, "No, no! *I*'m not entering this house!"

"Why is that? Why won't you enter the house? Are you staying outside? What kind of bridegroom are you?"

He said, "No! I have never stayed in such a house! Those houses at home have pillars supporting the roof. The houses are made of mud. The houses at home have pillars, and they're thatched with grass, and so on, and so on. On the floor, we sleep with the calves and the fowl. Take me to the house in which the calves and fowl sleep!"

They said, "Yo yo yo yo yo yo yo! We've never seen such a bridegroom!"

"This is another type of groom!"

He was quiet, he did not speak again. Then he was taken to a dusty house, it had manure in it, it had fleas and bed-bugs, the calves were sleeping in it, the fowl were sleeping in it, the hogs entered.

A bed mat was brought, it was new. They said that a bed was being made up for this bridegroom.

He said, "No! I'm not sleeping in a bed like this! I want an old mat, the mat of a young mother, a ragged mat! At home, a mat like this is not laid! I'll not sleep on such a mat!"

"Here we go again!"

"Really, this groom is something else!"

"We're used to grooms' parties here at home, and never have *we* seen such a thing!"

A ragged bed mat was brought, and it was put down for him. He sat. They sat on it. They turned these blankets of theirs inside out then, they turned them inside out, they put them on with the fur on the inside, this fur of the blankets was next to their skin, they didn't turn them out.

"We've never seen such a groom's party!"

"We could see that they were strange by the fact that they wore long skin skirts!"[3]

Sikhuluma sat, and food was brought on new dishes with beautiful new spoons. The food was placed there, and he said, "No! Go on with this food of yours! We don't eat out

[3] Long skin skirts—women wear them. This is an insult, and is meant as an insult. The men are actually wearing blankets. But the groom's party will turn this insult to its own advantage later, when its members insist that they wear the girls' aprons.

of such nice dishes, we fear them! *We* eat from dirty dishes that leak, we eat with dirty spoons! We don't know these things, we won't eat with such things!"

"Heeeee! Never have we seen such a bridegroom's party!"

"This is something else!"

"What kind of groom is this?"

They went away muttering, saying, "This is really a marvel!"

"No, sir!"

"Today my father has come face to face with something different!"

"Something that's strange here at home!"

"Tsk! Take it! Here's the food! The groom's party doesn't want this food, they say they want dishes that leak in that house!"

"Kwok'!"

And it thus began to be a wonder to the people there at home. Leaky dishes were taken, and the food was dished up. Dirty spoons were brought, and he entered and ate. From the time that he came out of the circumcision lodge, this was the first time that he had eaten. He ate. Well, he ate, and when he had eaten, he finished eating and it was said that the groom's party was wanted at the cattle kraal.

He said, "All right, I have heard."

He traveled, he went to the kraal, and they entered the gate. They arrived and sat down.

Someone said, "Well, now let's get down to business. You must speak about it now to these men, because when we spoke before, we were alone, these men were not there." So said Mangangedolo, turning to him.

Now that groom, Sikhuluma, answered and said, "Yes, all right, Father. Now, I still say eighty cattle, that amount is okay. I want your daughter, so that she can come to my home and kindle a fire."

"Oh." Well, then, this was heard.

"Well, then, you may go into the house."

Here at the entrance, a trap had already been set, so that when they went out, they would die there at the gate. He got up now, and went to the other end of the kraal. He went out at that end.

Someone said, "Oh oh oh! Why don't you go out at the other end?"

He said, "This is the way we do it at home! We don't enter the gate and then come out again through the gate. We enter through the gate, then come out at the other end!"

Someone said, "*Yeha ke!* This is really a different kind of groom's party!"

"It's a wonder!"

"This thing is a wonder today!"

And so it was, then, that medicine of Mangangedolo's did not work in the gateway.

Time passed then, and at night they went to sleep.

The mouse said, "Sikhuluma! Take me out of the sack, and hang me over there, above the door, so that I can keep on the lookout for you! Now, this will be done while you sleep —the girls will come here, to sleep with you. Each man will have to sleep with a girl. Now, you must do this—all the men should take these aprons, and put them on themselves! They should say that they are borrowing them from the girls, say that it is their custom. You and your wife should just remain idle, do nothing, lest I go to sleep. If I fall asleep, you turn the blanket over. If it happens that I sleep, just turn the blanket over, this one of yours, so that the fur is on the outside."

"Oh, all right."

And so it was that, at night, the girls came in, and when they had entered, each girl went to bed with her appropriate young man. All the girls did that, and then the bride of the honored guest went to sleep with her groom, Sikhuluma.

She remained, and the groom's party over there said, "Well, girls, we have a custom. We usually have a *dindala*, a *dindala*. Do you know what a *dindala* is?"[4]

---

[4] *Idindala*—"A constable, a policeman, from Dutch dienaar." (Albert Kropf, *A Kafir-English Dictionary*, Lovedale, 1915, p. 77). "Dindala" is used in the narrative because, as is customary when

The girls said, "No, we don't know. What is a *dindala?*"

He said, "A *dindala* is a man who straightens you out, he orders you, he prepares the girls. He takes the aprons and places them on the members of the groom's party. One of us will make himself that *dindala!*"

One of them got up then, and made himself that *dindala.*

The girls agreed.

They said, "*Kho!* This is really a wonder! We've never been in such a situation!"

"We're used to having bridegroom's parties, but we've never seen a groom's party that takes aprons and wears them!"

"This is a wonder!"

"You're a different bridegroom's party!"

"Even if this groom were not handsome, he ought to be jilted by this girl! He's made up for it already because he's handsome. But his habits—no, we don't understand them!"

"Well, it's like this, Girl."

They unfastened the aprons then, and gave them to the groom's party. The groom's party remained, then. Sikhuluma and his wife did nothing. They slept then, they chatted and they slept.

When they were asleep, Mangangedolo came along with the thing with which he killed people, the thing with which he cut off the heads of the grooms' parties, a saber, a big knife! He stepped heavily, *gqi gqi gqi gqi!* He stood at the door, and while he stood at the door in this house of the groom's party, the mouse said, "Return! Return, Mangangedolo, return with that magic! Return with it!"

Oh! Mangangedolo ran! He stomped on the ground, he stomped on the ground, he stomped and stomped. He arrived at that house and said, "Mmhmmmmmm! Do you know that over there in that house they're awake? Something said, 'Return with it, Mangangedolo! Return with that magic!' Let's try another way, so that they sleep!"

They did their things, they made their magic so that they

a Xhoŝa noun appears in the context of another language, the definite article is removed from the word.

would go to sleep, so that they would sleep over there, so
that they would sleep. They made it, they made it.

"*You* should go this time, my wife!"

Well, his wife went. Having thrown her breasts behind,
she walked with a swaying gait, *ngqish' ngqish' ngqish'
ngqish'*. She arrived and stood in the doorway.

Before she could enter, the mouse said, "Return with it,
wife of Mangangedolo! Return with that magic, return with
it!"

Wo! She ran!

"Oh! oh! oh! Do you know that they're not asleep in that
house? Someone said, 'Return with the magic, wife of
Mangangedolo!'"

The man said, "I told you so! They're awake in that
house! These are different people! Do you realize that it'll
soon be dawn—and they're still awake?"

"Mm."

Well, then, it was said that a dog should go! There was a
big dog there, and hanging from this dog were concoctions
and bottles and capsules, all these things.

"Please go, my dog! Go now! If they escape from this
dog, then they're beyond us!"

Well, it went then, this shaggy dog, and it arrived and
stood in the doorway.

It barked, "*Nhu nhu!*" It jumped there at the door.

The mouse said, "Return with it, dog of Mangangedolo!
Return with that magic! Return with it!"

Then the groom turned his blanket around. He saw that
this dog would enter by force. Indeed, it's just this skin of
the mouse that's speaking, and there's nothing that skin can
do to this dog! So he turned his blanket so that the fur was
on the outside—he was sleeping lower down, at the extreme
end, and the others were on the upper side.

It barked, "*Nhu!*" It barked, "*Nhu!*" It jumped, and came
to him. Then the kaross of the *nabulele* began to maul the
dog, it mauled the dog! it mauled this dog! it reduced the
dog to shreds, to shreds, to shreds! to shreds! It chopped the
dog up, all all *all* of it! even the legs, it chopped the dog up
and tied it. Then it put the dog in front of the house, and

returned. The kaross shook itself, then came and covered its owner. They slept.

When it was morning, the girls awakened. They awoke, and took their aprons and went out. When they came out, there was now a wonder at their place! And the wonder centered about this dog.

"We don't know what chopped it up!"

"Did you see the dog in that house?"

The girls said, "It didn't go there!"—because *they* had been asleep, *they* didn't see it, it must have been there when they were asleep.

"This dog didn't go there!"

"Why was it chopped up?"

"We were just sitting then! When our father went, we were still awake, we heard our father!"

"The groom's party was asleep, and *we* were awake!"

"But this dog, it didn't go!"

"Well, this is a mystery!"

"What sort of group is this groom's party?"

"Well, we must try something else on them now! Don't bother them, let them sleep!"

In the morning, the cattle kraal was about to be opened for the cattle.

Someone said, "We've come to visit the groom's party here, to bring food so that they can eat. The groom's party here at home must go out with the cattle, they must herd the cattle! They must herd the cattle—that's the custom here at home!"

Sikhuluma said, "All right, we want to follow such customs of yours."

"Yes."

Then the food was brought, on leaky dishes. They ate, and finished.

Someone said that they should move on then, and they went to the kraal to take the cattle out. A trap was sprung! A trap was sprung, a trap was sprung on the lower side, as they entered the gate. Before, they had not agreed to come out the gate, they had come out at the lower end. So a trap was sprung there, at the lower end!

Today, it was said, "Go on in, then, and bring the cattle out!"

Then the groom's party entered the cattle kraal, and they brought the cattle out through the gate. When they had finished bringing the cattle out through the gate, *they* came out through the gate too, on the *upper* side! They did not go out on the lower side!

"Why have you come out through another place—when you said you were coming out on the lower end?"

Sikhuluma said, "We go by our customs, and you go by yours. *We* do it this way at home!"

"*Kwek!* This groom's party is something else!"

"It's a wonder!"

"Travel on, herd these cattle, then!"

There was a plateau that was very far from home. Someone said, "Go and herd on that plateau over there!"

Then they traveled with those cattle, they went to herd them on that plateau. Sikhuluma had his bag with him on that plateau, and the skin of the mouse was also with him.

The mouse said, "Sikhuluma! You're as good as dead today!"

"Yes?"

"Do you see that cow over there? The one with the big udders?"

He said, "Yes!"

"You must go over there, get under it—all of you! All of you, all eight of you must go over there beneath that cow! Grab its legs! Some of you grasp its tail! The others should seize the neck! Keep it stationary. Then a cloud is going to appear suddenly, and this cloud will thunder. That thundering will be sent by Mangangedolo, because you have triumphed over him at his home! He wants you to be beaten now by the lightning, so that you'll be killed here! Then it'll pass by, and when it passes by, you'll see some women coming with sacks. They will pick up your heads."

"Oh, all right!"

Then the cloud suddenly appeared. And so it was that, when that cloud over there suddenly appeared, they grasped the cow, they grasped that cow over there. All of them. Some grabbed it by the neck, others seized its horns, others grasped it by the legs, others clung to the tail, they went beneath it, they also clutched this cow by the udders. The cow stood, and they remained there.

It thundered, there was a mighty thundering! The sound of the thundering was unsurpassed. The other cattle were struck by the lightning, and they died there.

Then the storm passed over, then the sun came out and shone brightly. When the sun came out, some women suddenly appeared carrying sacks.

When they got there, they said, "Heeeeee!"

"Mmhmmmmmm!"

"Such a rain!"

"Eheeeee!"

"Didn't it reach you?"

"Such a great storm?"

"Ehee! You're safe!"

Sikhuluma said, "If you think that you've come here to take the heads from me, you've got another think coming! You'll have to take manure, you'll not be taking any heads from me at all!"

"Well, now, what's this groom saying now? We've just come to gather manure, that's all!"

So they said, and the women gathered manure. The groom's party went on its way, going home with those cattle.

Yeeeeeeee, when they got home, Mangangedolo said, "Well, I'm giving you your wife! Travel on out of here!"

He brought that wife out, and when he did so, he said that she should travel with her groom's party.

The chief said, "Well, all right, that's all I wanted anyway, all this time that I've been here at this homestead!"

"Mmmm!"

They traveled then, the wife with this groom and the party. The girls of the bride's home accompanied them, showing the groom's party the way.

They turned around after a time.

"Well, we're going back, In-laws."

"All right."

All those girls turned around then, and these members of the groom's party traveled on with this wife of theirs. It happened after a time that Sikhuluma forgot, and he stepped on a place that had soil, even though he had been warned by the mouse that he should never tread on the earth, that he should always walk on a place that has grass, because otherwise it will be held against him and his foot.

Mangangedolo traveled, he went after them, seeking the footprint of this groom! Finally he found it! he came upon it by surprise at that place over there where he happened to set foot.

He said, "*Kho!* Thanks a lot! I've found his footprint!"

Then he took it up, he took that footprint from the earth there, and he arrived and worked his magic, he worked at home on the groom through his magic, he spread this earth out, he spread the footprint out thus.

As he was carrying on in this way, the groom said, "Mmm! I'm hurt!"

The mouse said, "Yes, you're hurt! You stepped on the earth! You forgot what I told you, so you're hurt! If there's anything I can do nothing about, it just happened, this is it. What can I possibly do with a thing like that?"

He said, "No, it is *I* who forgot."

The mouse felt very bad about this, because it had helped him this much—and now, so close to home, he's about to die!

Then Sikhuluma went to that place where he had hidden the flesh of the mouse. He took it, and put it into the skin of the mouse.

The mouse got up, it said, "Hello, Sikhuluma. And now, you're dying!"

Sikhuluma said, "Yes."

Then the mouse traveled on its way.

As they traveled on, Sikhuluma said, "My body feels run down."

"What did you say, Chief?"

"My body is run down."

"How is it run down?" his wife asked. She asked him, "How is it run down?"

"My body is run down, I'm weighed down by the blankets." His blanket dropped to the ground. He said, "Pick it up, pick it up, old friend!"

One of them picked it up and carried it. They traveled on. He said, "My head is in pain!"

"What did you say, Chief?"

"I said, 'My head is in pain!'" His stick dropped. "Pick it up, pick it up, old friend!"

Another picked it up, and carried it. They traveled on.

Again he said, "My back is in pain, and my legs are in pain, and my feet are in pain!" His penis cover fell to the ground. "Pick it up, pick it up, old friend!"

Another picked it up and carried it.

He said, "I'm thirsty now!"

It was obvious that he was giddy, feeling faint. He walked on.

"There's a pool up ahead."

He went to that pool, he came to the pool and drank. He drank, he drank, and he disappeared! He disappeared completely, he was not seen!

They considered the possibility of going into the water and bringing him out, even if he was dead. Well, then, they did not see him. Then they saw some elands, the elands—things which have horns—came out from the pool here. The groom's party traveled on. This wife walked on, too, crying for her dead husband.

She said, "*Kwewu!* I don't want this! I don't want to go home!" She sat down; she said, "Let's just sit down, and I'll try to do some of the tricks of my father! I know them. The things he does, he does them in our presence—and we, his children, we know everything about his goings-on! Heeee!"

That bride took a bottle out of her bag and opened it. She lit a fire, she heated the concoction and then threw it into the pool, when it was hot she threw it into this pool.

The elands came out, these elands came out. She grabbed one of the elands, and she said, "Gather some firewood, and roast this eland! This eland—here's the chief, in this eland! He's here, in the stomach of this eland!"

"Oh, really?"

"Is that true?"

She said, "Yes, here's the chief! Inside this eland!"

Then they kindled a fire. All these people sorrowed here, but they wept inside because they were men. They kindled a fire, it became huge! Then they cut the eland's neck, they skinned it.

And the chief came forth! He came forth alive! He was sick, he was not well.

She said, "Roast this eland and eat it!"

It was roasted, and it was eaten here by all of them, they ate it. She and her groom did not eat it. When things were thus, she took an ember from the fire, and she opened another bottle, she blew on it, and said, "Go, Spirit! Go and scatter that earth! There it is, the earth of the footprint of the chief! It has been spread out by my father by the cattle kraal! When you get there, become a whirlwind!"

The spirit traveled then, it was not visible, there was no wind. When it arrived over there at the side of the kraal, it became a whirlwind, and then it went off with that earth that he had spread out on a patch of cloth! It flew off with it, it scattered it! and threw it out, far off, together with that patch of cloth!

Mangangedolo said, in the house, "*Kwo!* Hasn't that wind passed by yet? *Kwewu!* Hasn't it caused me some damage?"

He stepped heavily, and went to the side of the kraal. When he got there, he arrived and no longer saw the patch or the earth.

He said, "*Kwewu!* Satan is alive, he's active wherever he is!"

On the other hand, the chief was very well! He was as he had been before, and he went home with his wife. When he got home, he sat outside by the cattle kraal. He said that his wife should sit at the side of the house, and should not go into the house. As for the rest of the people, they should enter the house. His second in rank would stay with him outside at the kraal, both of the seconds.

The people went, then, and when they had entered, they said, "The chief is outside!"

They went, then, and asked, "Chief, when will you come into the house?"

He said, "I'm not entering the house until I have my own house! I'll enter my own house! I cannot enter any other house!"

"Oh, Chief!"

"That house—when will you have it?"

"The house *is* being built fast! But it takes a long time to build a house—it takes days, months to build a house!"

He said, "*My* house will not take months to build! The house will have to be built, and then I'll enter! Speak to this wife, please ask her what sort of house she wants."

They went to his wife on the side of the house. "Woman, please tell us what sort of house you want, how big you want it to be, where you want it to be!"

In answer, the bride said, "Well, Father, I want the house to be on the upper side of the sheepfold, and I want this house to be big because it is going to house a family, and because you, too, will stay in it when you wish. I'll build the house myself, the way I like it."

"Oh, all right, then. When will you build it?"

She said, "All I want is permission, and then I'll build it."

It was said, "All right, then, build!"

The bride traveled then, she arrived and opened her concoction, she took out something that was not seen by the people. She put it down.

She said, "Move over there!"

The people went over there, and she put the thing down. Then she also went over there. She said that all the people should look to one side. The people then looked to one side, in the opposite direction. When the time came for them to look back, they looked back and there was now a house that had six doors! This thing was a wonder!

Then she entered and said, "We should go into the house!"

They entered the house. They arrived, and in the house there was no kind of bedding that was lacking, everything proper for making a bed was there, and things to sit on, things for standing and things for sleeping, things for clothing, things for eating, things for washing.

"Well, then, we've seen the house!"

She said, "Tell the chief that he may come into the house, his house is ready now!"

They went and told the chief then, and he got up from the side of the kraal with those people surrounding him, and he came and went into the house.

And so it was that he sat as a chief then. And when it was dawn, he was given his mantle, the mantle of the chieftainship was transferred from his father, so that he might be pensioned and his son might rule. In the morning, a huge meeting was held, and the authority was transferred to his son. His son was then the chief, he took charge. They all lived in happiness.

The *ntsomi* is ended.

CONTRIBUTORS

Joel Adedeji is on the faculty of the School of Drama, University of Ibadan, Ibadan, Nigeria.

William Bascom is Professor of Anthropology and Director of the Robert H. Lowie Museum at the University of California, Berkeley.

Dan Ben-Amos is Associate Professor of Folklore in the Graduate Department of Folklore and Folklife at the University of Pennsylvania.

Daniel Biebuyck is Rodney Sharp Professor of Anthropology at the University of Delaware in Newark, Delaware.

Charles Bird is Chairman of the Department of Linguistics at Indiana University.

Lawrence A. Boadi is in the Department of Linguistics at the University of Ghana in Legon.

Richard M. Dorson is Distinguished Professor of History and Folklore and Director of the Folklore Institute at Indiana University.

Carol M. Eastman is in the Department of Anthropology at the University of Washington.

James W. Fernandez is Professor of Anthropology at Dartmouth College.

Mona Fikry-Atallah has taught in the Afro-American Studies Program at Howard University and presently lives in Algeria.

Lee Haring is in the Department of English at Brooklyn College of the City University of New York.

Sayyid H. Hurreiz is Lecturer in the Sudan Research Unit at the University of Khartoum, the Sudan.

Daniel P. Kunene is Professor of African Languages and Literature at the University of Wisconsin.

Bernth Lindfors is Associate Professor of English and African Literature at the University of Texas at Austin.

Philip A. Noss is in the Department of African Languages and Literature at the University of Wisconsin.

Ayodele Ogundipe is on the faculty of the Institute of African and Asian Studies at the University of Lagos, Lagos, Nigeria.

Harold A. Scheub is in the Department of African Languages and Literature at the University of Wisconsin.

INDEX